1'4   6—

AMERICAN AUTHORS SERIES

GENERAL EDITOR
STANLEY T. WILLIAMS

THE HAFNER LIBRARY OF CLASSICS

[Number Nineteen: POEMS OF FRENEAU]

POEMS OF FRENEAU

EDITED WITH A CRITICAL INTRODUCTION BY

HARRY HAYDEN CLARK

HAFNER PUBLISHING CO.
NEW YORK

CONTENTS

CONTENTS

CONTENTS

CONTENTS

INTRODUCTION

In spite of the fact that Jefferson credited Philip Freneau with having "saved our constitution which was galloping fast into monarchy,"[1] in spite of the fact that E. C. Stedman traced to Freneau "the first essential poetic spirit in America,"[2] there has been as yet no popular edition of his poetry, no collected edition of his prose, and there has been slight effort to go beyond a description of his work, to view him against his international background—political, religious, social, and literary—in search of a central principle which may have motivated both his political and his poetic interests. Such a principle is found, I think, in Freneau's naturalism, which may be likened to the hub of a wheel, from which the spokes of his varied activities radiate. His is the naturalism of the eighteenth century which involved a fresh interest in nature, the belief that nature is a revelation of God, humanitarian sympathy for the humble and oppressed, the faith that man is naturally good, that man led an idyllic and benevolent life in a primitive past before the advent of civilization, and the radical doctrine that the golden age will dawn again when man modifies the institutions which are responsible for existing evil. For the sake of convenience, Freneau may be considered, first, as the *Poet of American Independence;* second, as the *Journalist of Jeffersonian and French Democracy;* third, as an *Apostle of the Religion of Nature and Humanity;* and last, as the *Father of American Poetry.*

I

Since the details of Freneau's life have been elaborately set forth by Mary Austin and, more competently, by Professor F. L. Pattee, they need not detain us here except in brief

[1] T. Jefferson, *Writings* (ed. by Ford), Vol. I, p. 231.
[2] E. C. Stedman, *Poets of America,* Boston, 1896, p. 35.

summary, prior to more fundamental considerations. Poet, editor, sea-captain, and farmer, Philip Freneau was born of French Huguenot parentage in New York on January 2, 1752, nearly a quarter of a century before the Declaration of Independence. His grandfather, of sturdy yeoman stock, had come to New York in 1707 from the little French village of La Chapelle, following the insecurity of Protestants after the Revocation of the Edict of Nantes. He had married Mary Morin, a member of the quaint little church "du St. Esprit" on Pine Street, and bequeathed to his son Pierre, father of the poet, a lucrative shipping business and a large estate in New Jersey—later called Mount Pleasant—near what is now Matawan. To this estate, almost a plantation, with its thousand acres, its slaves, and its spacious buildings, Philip's parents moved in 1762, when he was ten years old. Here in the stately old colonial home he spent his long vacations from the New York boarding-school. Ascribe to his natural endowment and to the Celtic strain in his blood as much as one will of the poetic effects which he evokes from flower and field and sea, there will remain something which can only be set down to the environment of his childhood, to the house of many shadows in which he lived with his widowed mother, to the long winter evenings by the fireside in his father's well-selected library, to the voice and breath of the blue Atlantic visible to the eastward. Later, when the birth of a nation demanded all that was harsh and bitter in the satirist of her enemies, one likes to think that the occasional lyric glimpse of a gentle, sensitive, poetic nature may be the result of the influence of those early formative days. When he was thirteen he was sent to the Latin school at Penolopen, where he obtained a training both in the English poets and the classics which called forth a letter of congratulation from President Witherspoon when Freneau entered Princeton in his sixteenth year, following the death of his father.

At Princeton Philip developed his talent for creative work, as evidenced by such precocious poems as *The History of the Prophet Jonah*, *The Pyramids of Egypt*, and *The Power of Fancy;* but the essential influence of his college life and asso-

ciates, such personalities as James Madison, H. H. Brackenridge, William Bradford, Aaron Burr, Samuel Spring, Henry
Lee, and Henry B. Livingston, was to inspire him to become
the poet of American independence. A "hotbed of Whig-
gism," Princeton encouraged her sons to rebel against British
domination, ominous news of which came daily from Boston.
A letter written by Madison in 1770 describes a vivid night
scene in the college yard where students, dressed in black
gowns of American manufacture only, burned, amid the tolling of bells, the letters to merchants who had failed to keep
their non-importation agreements. Political feeling led Freneau, Madison, and others to found in 1769 the American
Whig Society; out of the young poet's satirical attacks on the
rival Cliosophic Society he later patched together that slash-
ing attack first called *MacSwiggen*. As undergraduates, he and
Brackenridge, who later produced *Modern Chivalry*, wrote
several chapters of an unfinished novel whose title, *Father
Bombo's Pilgrimage to Mecca in Arabia*, is suggestive of its
fantastic contents. But politics and belletristic experiments
did not prevent Freneau from acquiring that solid eighteenth
century mastery of the classics which appears on almost every
page he wrote. "In the first year," President Witherspoon
told the inhabitants of Jamaica, in 1772, "they read Latin
and Greek with the Roman and Grecian antiquities, and
Rhetoric." And he had himself "also taught the French
language last winter." At Commencement, September 25,
1771, when Freneau graduated, one of the addresses listed
reminds us of the neo-classic Dryden's *Essay on Dramatic Poesy*: "An English forensic dispute on this question,
'Does ancient poetry excel the modern?' Mr. Freneau,
the respondent, his arguments in favor of the ancients were
read. Mr. Williamson answered him and Mr. McKnight
replied."

The Commencement account, however, does not credit
Freneau with what was so far his most significant work: we
are simply told that "A Poem on 'The Rising Glory of
America' by Mr. Brackenridge, was received with great
applause." As a matter of fact, although Freneau was ab-

sent from the Commencement, he had himself written most of the poem which Brackenridge read, as the latter acknowledged. *The Rising Glory of America* is the product of that national self-consciousness which the Revolution was to strengthen and which inspired the epic flights of Dwight and Trumbull as well as the dramatic independence of Royall Tyler. Five years before the Declaration of Independence, this gray-eyed Princeton senior foretold the results of the Boston Massacre:

> And here fair freedom shall forever reign. . . .
> The sons of Boston, resolute and brave,
> The firm supporters of our injur'd rights
> Shall lose their splendours in the brighter beams
> Of patriots fam'd and heroes yet unborn.

Thus did he help to quicken the spirits of the colonists and create the public feeling which made the Declaration possible.

For a time after college Freneau's life seems to have been somewhat desultory. On November 22, 1772, he wrote Madison of his desertion from a Long Island school, after serving as master for thirteen days; he explains that he now, as "assistant to Mr. Brakenridge" [*sic*]—at what was later called Washington Academy, Maryland—is teaching "30 students who prey upon me like leeches." He has just "printed a poem in New York called the American Village, . . . damned by all good and judicious judges." In "rocking-horse" Popean couplets, this first publication synthesizes and foreshadows many of his characteristic interests such as his love for nature and for indigenous and rural themes; his eighteenth century kinship with Goldsmith, as well as " heav'nly Pope" and "godlike Addison"; his scorn for luxury and civilization, matched by a naturalistic glorification of primitive life and the noble savage. Just as the youthful Wordsworth became a "Dedicated Spirit," so Freneau here, finding himself " unfit for cities and the noisy throng," vows that his "one comfort" shall be poetry, in which "shall center every wish." The summer of 1775, however, found him in New York hurling satire after satire at the British in such pieces as *American Liberty* and *General Gage's Confession.* Then in November came *MacSwiggen,* a stinging reply to a stinging attack, and a sad and characteristic resolve to seek refuge on the sea:

> I to the sea with weary steps descend,
> Quit the mean conquest, that such swine must yield
> And leave MacSwiggen to enjoy the field.
> In distant isles some happier scene I'll choose
> And court in softer shades the unwilling muse.

The "distant isles" proved to be the West Indies—Santa Cruz—whither Freneau went at the invitation of a friend. Whether the real interest of the Poet of the Revolution at this time was in the war or in exotic beauty and poetry is rather obvious. "My agreeable residence at this place for above two years," he wrote, "off and on during the wars in America, renders the idea of it all too pleasing. . . ." Here, amid tropical luxuriance and the exotic south seas, he wrote *The Jamaica Funeral, The Beauties of Santa Cruz,* and the weird *House of Night,* the latter two of which appeared in the *United States Magazine* in 1779. After a visit of "upwards of five weeks" to the Bermuda Islands, where tradition pictures him the lover of Amanda, the governor's daughter, he started home in June, 1778, to be captured, and set free again, by the British. At home, the "young philosopher and *bel esprit,*" as editor Brackenridge introduced him, became a "valued contributor" to the unique and short-lived *United States Magazine.* His poem, *America Independent* (1778), a somewhat tardy ratification of the Declaration of Independence, is a clarion call to his besieged countrymen to avenge the "hell-born spite" of British bondage; "from Europe's realms fair freedom has retired" to "savage woods and wilds," to "uncultured nature."

When Freneau, restless as ever, attempted early in 1780 a third visit to the West Indies, having already escaped the British in a second visit, he was captured, after a bloody fight between the American ship *Aurora* and the British *Iris.* His account includes the realistic story of how a "twelve-pound shot"

struck Captain Laboyteaut in the right thigh, which it smashed to atoms, tearing part of his belly open at the same time with the splinters from the oars; he fell from the quarter-deck close by me, and for some time seemed very busily engaged in setting his legs to rights. He died about eleven the same night.

Physical horror, wrought by a warring oppressor, fired his as yet rather doctrinaire love of liberty. After considerable argument regarding his status as a passenger who had fought, Freneau was placed on the *Scorpion*, a prison ship in New York harbor. One night some of the prisoners tried to escape, and Freneau describes the conduct of the British sentries: "as there was no resistance made, they posted themselves at each hatchway, and most basely and cowardly fired fore and aft among us, pistols and musquets, for a full quarter of an hour without intermission." His ghastly experience, especially on the *Hunter*, a hospital ship lying near his peaceful ancestral home, is told in the searing lines of *The British Prison Ship*, written just after his release. He was imprisoned in the dark, filthy hold of "the slaughter house," among the dead and dying, nearly dead himself with fever and thirst, and beaten by the physician—"a dog of Hesse." Freneau describes his meals:

> Such food they sent, to make complete our woes,
> It looked like carrion torn from hungry crows,
> Such vermin vile on every joint were seen,
> So black, corrupted, mortified, and lean.

A piteous prayer for mercy brought this comforting response:

> But this, damned rebel dogs, I'd have you know,
> That better than you merit we bestow!

Finally, in July, after about two months of imprisonment, he was set free; he tells us he "came home round through the woods, for fear of terrifying the neighbors with my ghastly looks had I gone through Mount Pleasant."

These rather unpleasant passages are quoted in order that the reader may understand some of the forces which led this humanitarian, tender-hearted poet—whose daughter says he "was usually absent when poultry was wanted for dinner"— to dislike the British. The milder, but somewhat analogous Wordsworth, walking through revolutionary France in 1791, met a "hunger-bitten girl" who crept along leading a starved heifer. "'Tis against that," his friend Beaupuis had muttered, "that we are fighting," and the humanitarian Wordsworth turned to defend bloody revolt, looking forward to the "dawn" when "all institutes" would be "forever blotted out." Henceforth Freneau devoted himself to letting his "best arrows at these hell-hounds play." He will "one scene of death prolong, and hang them up to infamy, in song." War propaganda! Gone were the languorous dreams of exotic Santa Cruz: Freneau now became the poet of American independence in dead earnest. "From Concord to York-town," says Mary Austin, "during the bleak winter at Valley Forge, and round the campfires at Temple Hill, his verses encouraged the desponding soldiers. The newspapers widely published them, and they were written on slips of paper and distributed throughout the army, or posted in some con-spicuous place to be memorized." [1] Was not the Father of His Country, whose praises the poet sang in a dozen odes, a bit unmindful of this timely service in tempering the morale of his discouraged army when he pilloried him for posterity as "that rascal Freneau"? As the most important contributor, if not editor, of *The Freeman's Journal* (Philadelphia) from 1781 to 1784 he hymned *The Memorable Victory* of Paul Jones, glorified the valiant "friends of freedom" who died at Eutaw Springs, and ridiculed the British in *The Fall of General Earl Cornwallis* and *The Political Balance*. Griswold says that his rollicking patriotic ballads were sung by sailors on deck and were sold in broadsides at all our ports.

In June, 1784, being attacked by an editor Oswald, Freneau again bade a sad farewell to the muse in the *Epistle to Sylvius*

[1] Mary S. Austin, *Philip Freneau* (New York, 1901), p. 131.

on the Folly of Writing Poetry.   Told that American verse is
"merely nonsense, fringed with rhyme," Freneau is crushed:

> Then, Sylvius, come—let you and I
> On Neptune's aid, once more rely:
> Perhaps the muse may still impart
> Her balm to ease the aching heart.

For the next six years he served as master of various freight
vessels.   While thus employed, Freneau permitted his friend
Bailey to publish his poems in the edition of 1786.   According
to the introduction:

The pieces now collected and printed in the following sheets were
left in my hands, by the author, above a year ago, with permission
to publish them whenever I thought proper.   A considerable number
of the performances contained in this volume, as many will recollect,
have appeared at different times in newspapers (particularly the
Freeman's Journal) and other periodical publications in the different
States of America, during the late war, and since. . . .

The success of this first volume may be inferred by the fact
that in 1788 four hundred and sixty-three more subscribers en-
abled Bailey to publish a second (unrevised) volume, prefaced
in part as follows:

The following Essays and Poems, selected from some printed and
manuscript papers of Mr. Freneau, are now presented to the public
of the United States in hopes they will prove at least equally acceptable with his volume of poems published last year.   Some few
of the pieces in this volume have heretofore appeared in American
newspapers. . . .

All this time the poet was at sea.   By a coincidence, when on
April 24, 1789, a gorgeous naval procession escorted the President elect to New York, Freneau, with a cargo of monkeys,
brought his ship into line, and together the austere Federalist
president and his future critic approached the Capital.   The
Federalists were triumphant, but even among their welcoming
procession were those, then still obscure, who were to cause
their overthrow.

Having married Miss Eleanor Forman, of distinguished family, in April, 1790, Freneau abandoned "wintry seas and tempests"—as recorded in *Neversink*—to become editor, in name at least, of the New York-*Daily Advertiser*. In the autumn of 1791, following the birth of a daughter, he was mentioned by Aedanus Burke to Madison as "struggling under difficulties" with his family. Madison evidently reported the matter to Jefferson, for the Secretary of State on February 28, 1791, offered him "the clerkship for foreign languages" in his office, requiring only "a moderate knowledge of French."[1]

The details of the appointment are important, for they have been the subject of bitter controversy ever since Hamilton anonymously[2] charged that Freneau was "hired" to "bite the hand that puts bread in his mouth" and that Jefferson used the patronage of his Federal office to encourage an anti-Federalist newspaper. Mr. S. E. Forman and Professor Pattee are inclined to defend Freneau and Jefferson; Mr. P. E. More and Mr. V. H. Paltsits find the evidence damaging. It is true, of course, that Hamilton was himself guilty of the same offense in subsidizing the *Gazette of the United States*, with the exception that the editor, Fenno, supported rather than attacked the government which paid him; but after all, two wrongs do not make a right! The details are too complex to present here in full, but the crux of the matter is as follows. It is true, as Freneau swore, that Jefferson's offer of the clerkship had contained no word about a newspaper; he did say, however, that the office "gives so little to do as not to interfere with any other calling the person may chuse." Is there any evidence that Jefferson's real motive was the establishment of an anti-Federalist newspaper? On May 15, he sent his son-in-law, Randolph, Bache's and Fenno's papers, commenting on the latter's "pure Toryism, disseminating the doctrines of Monarchy, aristocracy, & the exclusion of the people. We have been trying," he confides, "to get another *weekly* or *half-weekly* set up, excluding adver-

[1] T. Jefferson, *Works*, Vol. III, p. 215.
[2] *Gazette of the United States*, July, 1792.

tisements, so that it might go through the States and furnish a whig vehicle of intelligence. We hoped at one time to have persuaded Freneau to set up here but failed." [1] Surely his motive stands confessed. But if the astute Secretary did not mention the matter to Freneau, how did the latter happen to promise Madison, on July 25, 1791, a "decisive answer relative to printing my paper at the Seat of Government instead of in N. York"? The answer is suggested in Madison's letter of May first to Jefferson in which he says, "I have seen Freneau." [2] But have we a right to suppose that the diplomatic Madison, in a personal interview, urged Freneau to establish an anti-Federalist newspaper while in the employ of the Federal government? He confessed later, at least, in regard to the matter, that "Our main object in encouraging it, was to provide an antidote against Fenno's paper, which was devoted to monarchy. . . . " [3]

At any rate, Jefferson succeeded in appointing Freneau "Clerk for Foreign Languages in the office of Secretary of State" on August 16, 1791; only nine days later—significantly?—there appeared in *The Daily Advertiser* "PROPOSALS for publishing . . . *The* NATIONAL GAZETTE, A periodical Miscellany of *News, Politics, History, and Polite Literature*, By PHILIP FRENEAU." [4] The first number appeared October 31, praising Paine and the French Revolutionists. The violent career of *The National Gazette*, amid the transient storm of enthusiasm for the French Revolution, will be discussed in another section. The sudden reaction against the French insurgents affected the circulation of the paper, and, since Jefferson, his patron, had resigned, Freneau resigned his clerkship October 1, 1793, and *The National Gazette* ended with the issue of October 23.

Embittered, Freneau retired from "knaves and fools," according to his affectionate farewell *To Sylvius*, to Mount

[1] Jefferson, *Writings* (ed. by Ford), Vol. V, p. 336.
[2] Madison, *Writings*, Vol. I, p. 535.
[3] *Ibid.*, Vol. I, pp. 569–570.
[4] V. H. Paltsits, *A Bibliography . . . of Philip Freneau* (New York, 1903), p. 8.

Pleasant, now reduced to "a couple of hundred acres of an old sandy patrimony." There he edited for a year, from May 2, 1795, to April 30, 1796, the weekly *Jersey Chronicle*, "a free, independent, republican paper," as he called it, devoted to "the natural and political rights of nations." Most of his contributions were in prose, written under his favorite locust tree while he neglected his farm. In June, 1795, he printed with his own hands his collected poems, the first edition to receive his personal revision. The tendency toward omission of what had been purely poetic in his earlier work and toward stress on what was politically radical indicates the progressive, if reluctant, surrender of the poet to the journalist of contemporary affairs. "The necessary number of subscribers," Freneau confessed, "having not yet appeared," he abandoned the *Jersey Chronicle* and migrated to New York, where he began editing *The Time-Piece* on March 13, 1797. After a year, financial resources becoming exhausted, he in turn gave up this paper and retired again to Mount Pleasant, where, on December 30, 1799, he issued a collection of *Letters on Various Interesting and Important Subjects*—a series of essays, representing some of his finest prose,[1] contributed from time to time to the Philadelphia *Aurora*.

His last years were somewhat melancholy. In 1801 he wrote his beloved brother Peter of South Carolina, from whom he had evidently borrowed money, of his discouraging work "repairing old fences" and of "more cares and vexations coming on." His old friend Aedanus Burke later appealed, this time in vain, to Madison to help Freneau's family, now consisting of four daughters, in their "embarrassed circumstances." Finally, driven by poverty, he resumed his old calling as master of coast-line freight vessels from 1803 to 1807. After these long dreary years we find him again at Mount Pleasant, preparing the 1809 two-volume edition of his collected poems, the most valuable of all the five editions, since it embodies his final judgment regarding the version of the great bulk of his poetry. He wrote President Madison,

[1] See *The Philosopher of the Forest* (N. Y., 1929), a selection of Freneau's prose, edited with an introduction by H. H. Clark.

somewhat airily, that "the present popular frenzy" for the work forced him to a new edition to prevent piracy. He told Jefferson that "the whole Subscription plan was Set going without my knowledge or approbation." The Advertisement records his decision "to restrict what is now printed to the date 1793." The War of 1812 revived all his slumbering hatred for the British, all his patriotic fire: again he cheered American soldiers and sailors in such spirited verse as *On the Lake Expeditions*, *The Battle of Lake Erie*, *The Volunteer's March*, and *The Battle of Stonington*. In 1815 appeared his final edition, containing only poems "composed . . . between the years 1797 and 1815." These "two duodecimo volumes," he wrote Madison, were issued, "for the benefit of and to assist Mrs. Bailey," the widow of his former Republican friend and the publisher of the volumes of 1786 and 1788. The poverty which shadowed his last years must have intensified his lifelong sympathy for the poor, the humble, and oppressed. In 1815 his old home burned, destroying much of his remaining possessions as well as the correspondence of a lifetime. The poverty-stricken family moved to a farmhouse near the town of Freehold. Mr. Forman's research indicates that "his once ample estate had nearly slipped out of his hands. The records of the county court tell of sales of portions of the land of Philip Freneau and of foreclosures of mortgages upon his property."[1] He suggests his weakness in his later years for the "tavern and the flowing bowl."

At any rate, one night just a week before the Christmas of 1832, in trying to find his way home from Freehold, about two miles distant, the gray-headed man of eighty lost his path in a blinding snowstorm, and was found the next morning dying from exposure. The nature whose benevolence he had so beautifully celebrated had betrayed him. Near the site of the ancestral home at Mount Pleasant stands a monument inscribed as follows:

[1] S. E. Forman, *Johns Hopkins University Studies in Historical and Political Science*, Series XX, Nos. 9–10, "The Political Activities of Philip Freneau," p. 95.

POET'S GRAVE.

PHILIP FRENEAU,

Died Dec. 18, 1832.

Age 80 years, 11 months, 16 days.

He was a native of New York, but for many
years a resident of Philadelphia and New Jersey.

His upright and benevolent character is the memory of many and will remain when this inscription
is no longer legible.

"Heaven lifts its everlasting portals high
And bids the pure in heart behold their God."

There is no authentic portrait of Freneau. The best
personal impression is perhaps that given by his friend Dr.
John W. Francis of New York.

He was at that time about seventy-six years old, when he first
introduced himself to me in my library. . . . He was somewhat
below the ordinary height; in person thin yet muscular, with a firm
step, though a little inclined to stoop; his countenance wore traces
of care, yet lightened with intelligence as he spoke; he was mild in
enunciation, neither rapid nor slow, but clear, distinct, and emphatic.
His forehead was rather beyond the medium elevation, his eyes a
dark grey, occupying a socket deeper than common; his hair must
have once been beautiful, it was now thinned and of an iron grey.
He was free of all ambitious displays; his habitual expression was
pensive. His dress might have passed for that of a farmer.[1] . . .
There was no difficulty in versification with him. I told him what
I had heard Jeffrey, the Scotch Reviewer, say of his writings, that
the time would arrive when his poetry, like that of Hudibras, would
command a commentator like Gray. . . .

Freneau was widely known to a large circle of our most prominent
and patriotic New Yorkers. . . . While in the employment of Jefferson, as a translator in the department of state, upon the organiza-
tion of Congress, with Washington at its head, he had the gratifica-
tion of witnessing the progress of improvement, and might have
enjoyed increased facilities had he not enlisted with an indiscreet
zeal as an advocate of the radical doctrines of the day. Freneau was,

[1] We learn elsewhere that he retained the small-clothes, long hose,
buckled shoes, and cocked hat of the colonial days until his death.

nevertheless, esteemed a true patriot; and his private worth, his courageous manner, and his general bearing won admiration with all parties. His pen was more acrimonious than his heart. He was tolerant, frank in expression, and not deficient in geniality. He was highly cultivated in classical knowledge, abounding in anecdotes of the revolutionary crisis, and extensively acquainted with prominent characters.[1]

II

Just as the differences between the English Puritans and Cavaliers, who fought side by side against the Armada of a foreign oppressor, were only manifest later in the absence of external pressure, so in America the differences between the Federalists and the Democrats, who fought side by side against British oppression, were only manifest in the days when men turned from the Revolution to organizing the government. Noble as had been Freneau's rôle in the Revolution, his rôle after 1791, when he suddenly skyrocketed into fame as the journalist of Jeffersonian and French democracy, as the anti-Federalist editor of "the leading paper in America,"[2] has been the subject of violent dispute. To understand his service at this time we must see him against the political background, his own extreme democratic defense of the rights of the common man counterbalancing the extreme Federalist tendency to neglect those rights.

If Federalist political theory, distrusting human nature and advocating a strong coercive government to protect property, is of Puritan and Whig derivation, democratic political theory may be traced to (a) the liberty and equality of the agrarian and cosmopolitan frontier and the masses; (b) the influence of radical English thinkers such as Locke, Shaftesbury, Priestley, Paine, and Godwin; and (c) the idealists who motivated the French Revolution. The "continuous recession" of the American frontier—an environment,

[1] E. A. and G. W. Duyckinck, *Cyclopædia of American Literature* (New York, 1855), Vol. I, p. 332, "written in answer to our inquiries on the subject by Dr. John W. Francis of New York."

[2] G. H. Payne, *History of Journalism in the United States* (New York, 1920), p. 163.

before which all men were equal, inculcating the lesson of self-dependence—has determined much that is distinctive in Jeffersonian and Jacksonian democracy, as Professors F. J. Turner and F. L. Paxson have demonstrated. And with this dissenting, deistic, agrarian, anti-capitalistic, anti-British, optimistic frontier, as well as with Hamilton's "people of no particular importance," Freneau was in hearty accord; he became their spokesman, and as "the leading editor in America" he aided in crystallizing the democracy of the West, whose "freedom sings from every tree":

> No realm so free, so blest as this—
> The east is half to slaves consigned,
> Where Kings and priests enchain the mind.

"Your works are in Kentucky found," he assures "The Democratic Country Editors," "And there your politics go round." He laments the "Death of a Republican Printer" who sent:

> . . . his works . . . beyond the Ohio flood—
> And, since he had no time to lose,
> Preach'd whiggish lectures with his news.

In the lines on *A Tax upon Newspapers*, he attacks the Federalist policy that

> The well-born sort alone, should read the news,
> No common-herds should get behind the scene
> To view the movements of the state machine.

In *To My Book* he says, fondly:

> . . . you've spread your wings afar,
> Hostile to garter, ribband, crown, and star;
> Still on the people's, still on Freedom's side,
> With full determin'd aim, to baffle every claim
> Of well-born wights, that aim to mount and ride.

"Soon the Jeffersonian farmers in Georgia," says a historian, "were talking what he was writing, and Jeffersonian editors were following his lead. In the barrooms of Rhode Island men of no consequence were reading the paper aloud over their mugs."[1] Like Goldsmith and Burns, like the agrarian Franklin, Freneau, himself a farmer, thought the farmer's "calling the first and the best." He attacks the Federalist speculators who had bought the frontier patriots' government bonds for an eighth of their true value before news of Hamilton's funding of the national debt could reach the back-country:

> On coaches, now, gay coats of arms are wore
> By *some* who hardly had a coat before:
> Silk gowns instead of homespun, now, are seen,
> And, Sir, 'tis true ('twixt me and you)
> That some have grown prodigious fat,
> And some prodigious lean!

Mr. Jay's Treaty and its *Parody* helped to create the storm of hatred for the ambassador who had reported to Congress that England was justified in retaining the western posts. The Federalists, who later made the Alien and Sedition Laws, feared alien immigrants, "the most God-provoking Democrats," in the pious words of a New Englander, "this side of Hell." Freneau's lines *On the Emigration to America and Peopling the Western Country* glorify those who have come "from Europe's proud, despotic shores" to the Mississippi Valley of Democracy. In *Crispin's Answer*, the Irishman who "scornful . . . . left a land of slaves" for the charms of frontier liberty proudly remarks:

> The axe has well repaid my toil:
> No king, no priest I yet espy—
> To tythe my hogs, to tax my soil,
> And suck my whiskey-bottle dry.

Freneau's contempt for Federalist ceremony is reinforced in *The Bergen Planter* by his pre-Wordsworthian sympathy for the simple life of the rustic:

> He to no pompous dome comes, cap in hand,
> Where new-made squires affect the courtly smile:
> Nor where Pomposo, 'midst his foreign band

[1] C. G. Bowers, *Jefferson and Hamilton*, Boston, 1925, p. 156.

Extols the sway of kings, in swelling style. . . .
Where wandering brooks from mountains roll,
He seeks at noon the waters of the shade, . . .
In humble hope his little fields were sown,
A trifle, in your eye—but all his own.

It must be remembered, of course, that *The National Gazette* appeared at a time when the weakness of the Articles of Confederation and the consequent national distress had led Federalists to recoil from extreme democracy, to distrust the common people. If Freneau's democracy seems extreme, we must remember that he sought to offset the contempt for democracy voiced in *The Gazette of the United States*, subsidized by the Hamiltonian party. Hamilton himself held that the masses were "turbulent and changing; they seldom judge or determine right." John Adams said "the people" are the "worst conceivable . . . keepers of their own liberties." "They can neither judge, act, think, or will as a political body." While framing the Constitution, Elbridge Gerry admitted he "had been too republican heretofore," and he charged that "the evils we experience flow from the excess of democracy." Edmund Randolph also said the national distress was caused by "the turbulence and follies of democracy." Gouverneur Morris had as soon trust the vote to children as to "the ignorant and dependent." Sage Roger Sherman wished the people directly "should have as little to do as may be about the government." When Jefferson arrived in New York in March, 1790, coming from the triumphant democracy of France, he expressed his "wonder and mortification" at the all but unanimous "preference for the kingly over the republican government." To this ardent frontiersman, this crusader for liberty in the Virginia legislature, this witness of the Parisian Assembly of Notables, this witness of the razing of the Bastille by the masses, to one who had listened, fascinated, to the audacious oratory of Mirabeau, the trend of American thought seemed reactionary and dangerous. We can understand his concealed joy at his success in getting Freneau to establish his "whig vehicle of intelligence."

Freneau's salutatory *To the Public* (October 31, 1791) in the *National Gazette* struck the keynote of what was to be for the next two years "the leading paper in America"— espousal of the democratic radicals and the French Revolution:[1]

> The King of the French and the Queen of the North
> At the head of the play, for the season, we find:
> From the spark that we kindled, a flame has gone forth
> To astonish the world and enlighten mankind:
> With a code of new doctrines the universe rings,
> And PAINE is addressing strange sermons to kings.

Although instrumental in crystallizing, by means of journalism, the democracy of the frontier and the dissatisfied masses, Freneau now did much to popularize French radicalism, which later united with Jeffersonian and frontier equalitarianism to produce Jacksonian democracy. If "French radical influence upon the Revolution was comparatively small,"[2] America was now getting her own Revolutionary doctrines—those of English Whigs such as Locke—on the rebound from France, stripped, significantly, of moral and religious restraint. Gratitude for Revolutionary aid from France fostered a receptivity to things French which was most marked about this time (1791–93[3]) in Philadelphia, where Freneau's office on High Street became a meeting-place for French sympathizers. Of French descent, trained in French at Princeton, a broadcaster of Rousseau as clerk of foreign languages for Jefferson, Freneau became the agent for "The French Society of the Patriots of America" in raising funds to send to France. When Burke, whom the humanitarian Freneau called "the drudge of Britain's dirty work,"[4] launched his hostile *Reflections on the French Revolution* (1790),

[1] For Freneau's relation to radical English thought, see Section III below.

[2] Merriam, *American Political Theories* (New York, 1903), p. 91.

[3] See H. M. Jones, *America and French Culture* (Chapel Hill, North Carolina, 1927), pp. 195, 487, 536.

[4] See p. 145 following.

Freneau championed Paine's radical reply, as he said, "to Mr. Edmund Burke's rant upon this subject," [1] in *The Rights of Man*, published in England in 1790–92. While Mackintosh was writing *Vindiciae Gallicae* (1791), while Godwin was writing *Political Justice* (1793) and Barlow his *Advice to the Privileged Orders* (1792–95), Madison lent *The Rights of Man* to Jefferson, who found it not only a refutation of Burke but also of John Adams' *Discourses of Davilla*, copied from Fenno's *Gazette* by the whole Federalist press. The people, he wrote Paine, "love what you write, and read it with delight." [2] A private note of praise, printed as signed by the Secretary of State, created a furor.

Freneau took every occasion to hamstring the pro-English Federalists; ceremony, the funding scheme, the bank, excise—all met with scathing ridicule and attack. Hamilton, wearied with his Herculean labors in establishing the credit of a nation, and exasperated at the constant heckling from a man paid by the government he attacked, rebuked Freneau, as we have seen, in an unadvisedly anonymous letter (printed in Fenno's *Gazette*, July, 1792), which led to an ugly quarrel between the Secretaries. In January, 1793, Louis Capet lost his caput, in the irreverent phrase of the democratic press. England declared war on France, who called on America for aid promised under the treaty of 1778. Citizen Genêt, diplomatic representative of the new republic, arrived in Charleston in the spring of 1793, and began, amid tumultuous acclaim by the anti-Federalists, a triumphal progress to Philadelphia. Everywhere Jacobin clubs were organized. Sedate men of affairs donned the *bonnet rouge*. Manners and customs, dress, jewelry, ornaments, perfume—all were *à la française*. Liberty poles were raised in public places. Restaurants introduced French soups, salads, ragouts, fricassées, and olive oil. Only French bread was tolerable. The stately English minuet gave way to the lively cotillon. The streets of Philadelphia, New York, and even Boston were musical at night with *La Marseillaise* and the *Carmagnole*. The ardent

---

[1] See p. 120.
[2] Jefferson, *Works* (ed. by Ford), Vol. VI, p. 87.

Freneau, regarded according to Dwight as "a mere incendiary, or rather as a despicable tool of bigger incendiaries," favored the French Revolution body and soul.

> "Plung'd in a gulf of deep distress
> France turns her back"—(so traitors say)
> Kings, priests, and nobles, round her press, . . .
> Ye sons of this degenerate clime,
> Haste, arm the barque, expand the sail;
> Assist to speed that golden time
> When Freedom rules, and monarchs fail.

Who but Citizen Freneau could be chosen to translate the French ode sung at the tumultuous banquet tendered Genêt, a correspondent of Rousseau, at Philadelphia? And who but Citizen Freneau could have penned for a later Genêt banquet the stirring ode beginning, "God save the Rights of Man"?

But all this was a demonstration hostile to Washington and the Federal government, which had declared neutrality on the very day Genêt arrived. Commended today for withholding America from that dark vortex of the Reign of Terror, Washington was for the first time openly abused: "The publications in Freneau's and Bache's papers," he wrote Lee, "are outrages to common decency." [1] Drunk with popular adulation, Genêt had appealed to the people over Washington's head. Even Jefferson recoiled,[2] and Madison called him a "madman."[3] But the rash Freneau openly addressed the President, defending Genêt, and reminding the first magistrate that he was only a "public servant" "so buoyed up by official importance as to think it beneath his dignity to mix occasionally with the people." "Why all this outcry against Mr. Genêt, for saying he would appeal to the people? . . . The minister of France, I hope, will act with firmness and with spirit. . . . The people are sovereign in the United States."[4]

[1] July 21, 1793, *Works* (ed. by Ford), Vol. XII, p. 310.
[2] Jefferson, *Works*, Vol. IX, pp. 211ff.
[3] Madison, *Works*, Vol. I, p. 601.
[4] *National Gazette*, July, 1793.

Washington sent for Jefferson, the employer of "that rascal Freneau." "By God," he burst out, "he had rather be in his grave than in his present situation."[1] "There never had been an act of government," Washington told Jefferson, "not meaning in the Executive line only, but any line, which that paper had not abused." "I took his intention," Jefferson records, "that I should interpose in some way with Freneau; perhaps withdraw his appointment of translating clerk to my office. But I will not do it. His paper has saved our constitution, which was galloping fast into monarchy, and has been checked by no other means so powerfully as by that paper."[2] However, on account of financial difficulties following the reaction against Genêt, Jefferson, his patron, having resigned as Secretary of State, Freneau discontinued the *National Gazette*, on October 26, 1793. Concluding his exhaustive study of Freneau's political activities, Mr. Forman says:[3]

Freneau's paper did much to give a French coloring to our political philosophy. The doctrines of liberty, fraternity, equality, of equal rights to all and special privilege to none, were unwelcome to many American minds in Freneau's day, yet this was the keynote of all Freneau's writings. The editor of the National Gazette was the schoolmaster who drilled Jeffersonian or French democracy into the minds—willing or unwilling—of the American people.

Yet Freneau omitted nearly all his poems on the French Revolution from the edition of 1809, after Wordsworth and Coleridge had recanted their similar enthusiasm. Why? With the death of Louis XVI, the excesses of the Reign of Terror, the tyranny of Napoleon, the distrust of French morality, and above all the friction arising from the X.Y.Z. papers, there came a strong conservative reaction against all things French. Mobs hurled stones through editor Bache's windows, and Franklin's statue was smeared with mud. But the reaction was most violent against what a New England

[1] Jefferson, *Works*, Vol. I, p. 251.
[2] *Ibid.*, Vol. I, p. 231.
[3] S. E. Forman, *op. cit.*, p. 78.

clergyman called "the atheistical, anarchical, and in other respects immoral principles of the French Revolution." Everywhere the pulpit combated insubordination by insisting that "a spirit of licence and French infidelity was abroad, which could be repressed only by a strenuous and combined effort."[1]

III

To the hostility which Freneau's political principles excited among the Federalists was added the hatred of the orthodox for the religious radicalism of the poet who praised and echoed the reputed infidel, Thomas Paine.[2] The bitter attack which Freneau answered in "MacSwiggen" was made by one "clad in the garb of sacred sanctity." The Boston *Columbian Centinel* as well as other papers asserted that "the Clergy of this country are constantly vilified, and *religion* ridiculed through the medium of the *National Gazette*."[3] Fenno accused him of trying to popularize "opposition to the great principles of order, virtue, and religion."[4] *The Connecticut Courant*, he tells us, published "serious animadversions" on his "profane parody" of Dr. Watts' famous hymn. Nor were these attacks entirely unprovoked. Priests are always linked with kings in his diatribes against despotism. "There is not a sight in all the walks of men," he remarks in one of his milder moods, "that gives me half the disgust, as that of a Christian clergyman rolling in his coach, swelling with pride and impertinence, associating only with princes, nobles, and the wealthy men of the land."[5] The democrat welcomed "bold Sammy," Bishop Samuel Seabury of Connecticut, the first Episcopal bishop in America, by saying, "If they give us their Bishops, they'll give us their law."[6] And his *Sketches of American History* pours contempt on the Puritan "oppressors," "bedevilled and blind," who regarded this "beau-

---

[1] Henry Adams, *History of the United States* (1801–1817) (New York, 1891), Vol. I, p. 79.

[2] Pp. 124 and 166.

[3] P. 119.

[4] P. 117.

[5] Edition of 1788, p. 306.

[6] P. 95.

tiful system of nature" as a "dog-house wherein they were pent," and sought to enforce universal conformity to their "narrow-souled creed" and the "nonsense from Mather" regarding the doctrine of "indwelling evil."

Rightly understood, Freneau's religion, the religion of nature and humanity, not only illustrates the neglected transition from Puritanism to deism and from deism to Unitarianism and pantheism, but motivates both his political and his poetic interests. Here we are on pioneer ground; Professor Forman scoffs at the subject,[1] and Professor Pattee deprived scholars of significant evidence by omitting from his otherwise valuable edition "most of the moralizings" of the period when the poet became "more and more philosophical."[2] Nevertheless, we recall Carlyle's dictum that a man's religion, "the thing a man does practically lay to heart and know for certain concerning his vital relations to this mysterious universe, and his duty and destiny there," is the "chief fact with regard to him," and "creatively determines all the rest."

Freneau's religion, like that of Paine, Jefferson, and Franklin, belongs to that type technically called deism. In England the way had been prepared for deism by rationalism, science, and the habit of dissent engendered by Protestant individualism. Among its heralds were Locke, Shaftesbury, Collins, Woolston, Tindal, Bolingbroke, Pope, and Priestley. Partly a reaction against the Puritan suppression of natural impulses, this old-world faith found congenial soil on the American frontier, an environment inculcating freedom, self-reliance, and optimism in place of determinism, passivity, and gloom. About deism there has always been a popular misunderstanding, illustrated within recent years by Theodore Roosevelt's reference to Tom Paine as "a dirty little atheist." Was the deist an atheist? What was his conception of the deity? Paine begins *The Age of Reason*, the later deists'

[1] S. E. Forman, *op. cit.*, p. 99. He inaccurately calls Freneau a "pantheist" whose "religion was of very little consequence."

[2] F. L. Pattee, *Poems of Philip Freneau* (Princeton, 1902–07), Vol. III, p. 199.

handbook, with the declaration, "I believe in one God, and no more." And Freneau reverently tells us that the "Great Frame" of the Universe—its "exact design," a "structure complete in itself"—teaches "the reasoning, human soul" to infer "an author of the whole." [1] Let it be noted that Freneau, a transitional figure, does not merge the creator and his creation, God and Nature, as did Emerson in *The Over-Soul* or the true romanticists such as Shelley, who, holding that "the universe is God," said that his negation in *Queen Mab*—"there is no God"—"must be understood solely to affect a creative Deity." Freneau addresses a distinct Creator who was before the creation:

> All that he did he first approved
> He all things into *being* loved;
> O'er all he made he still presides. . . . [2]

Like the "benign religion" of Jefferson, whose God "delights in the happiness of man," Freneau's religion centers about a God who is "One Power of Love," who "deals not curses on mankind" even for unbelief. In contrast we think of the *New England Primer's* Puritan summary, "In Adam's fall We sinned all"; of Increase Mather's God, whose worshipers besieged during King Philip's War, "were not yet fit for Deliverance . . . except a great deal more Blood be taken" from them; we think of Edwards' "sweet contemplations" of his "great and glorious God" who casts men "for millions and millions of ages" into "a fiery oven, all of a glowing heat, or into the midst of a glowing brick-kiln." Believing in a benevolent God, Freneau echoes the optimistic theme of his annotated copy of Pope's *Essay on Man:* [4]

> All, nature made, in reason's sight
> Is order all, and *all is right*. [5]

[1] P. 415.   [2] P. 423.
[3] I have treated Freneau's sources in *Studies in Philology*, Vol. XXII, pp. 1-33. The *Essay on Man* had been in his library since 1761.   [4] P. 424.

The Creator has wound up "the vast machine" [1]—Freneau uses the very words of Paine—and now nature "scorns to change her wonted course" "to work unusual things for man." [2] All is "fixed on general laws," beneficent but immutable, and unlike the fickle and capricious God of Increase Mather's *Illustrious Providence*, who specially answers the prayers of starving sailors adrift by inspiring huge fish to hop out of the sea into their boat, Freneau's God "impartially . . . rules mankind." Although Freneau was not a pantheist, and although "the mechanical separation between deity and humanity . . . was held almost up to Emerson's" day, [3] as the deists' God became increasingly set apart from the world and powerless to interfere with the inexorable laws He had ordained, He tended to be neglected and worship tended to be transferred from the "absentee landlord" to the universe which revealed His wisdom and benevolence. Discrediting supernatural revelation, the divinity of Christ, and the power of selfish prayer, Paine said that "The creation is the Bible of the Deist. He there reads, in the handwriting of the Creator himself, the certainty of his existence, and the immutability of his power, and all other Bibles and Testaments are to him forgeries." [4] One can understand how this sort of thing would annoy devout Presbyterians! To Freneau, nature is not God but a revelation of God. And that God is not a Trinity, for "Enlightened *Reason* proves that GOD IS ONE," according to the lines "On a Book Called Unitarian Theology." [5] "Enlightened reason" was the ideal of Freneau and his fellow deists of the rational, sceptical, hard-headed, and mechanical eighteenth century. Religion is no longer emotional or spiritual ecstasy, but merely an attitude of intellectual belief. And tolerance followed rationalism: "Unbelief not guilt attests," for

[1] P. 423.

[2] P. 423.

[3] I. W. Riley's *American Thought* (New York, 1915), p. 147.

[4] *Selections from the Writings of Thomas Paine* (ed. A. W. Peach, New York, 1928), p. 373.

[5] P. 341.

> In evidence belief is found;
> Without it, none are fairly bound
> To yield assent.[1]

Nature is herself rational. Lands, seas, flowers, trees, beasts, and man are

> But thoughts on Reason's scale combin'd,
> Ideas of the Almighty mind.[2]

Since the Creator—who is "the First spring of Reason," an "Intellectual Flame" [3] —has revealed His Reason in nature and natural laws, the study of these laws in science, which "stands firm on Reason," enables man (in Paine's words) to "see God, as it were, face to face."[4] Freneau concludes, much as did Franklin and Jefferson, that human progress is dependent upon science, which is also a power to "tame and civilize mankind," and is "favorable to virtue."

> The lovely philanthropic scheme
> (Great image of the power supreme,)
> On growth of science must depend;
> With this all human duties end.[5]

If such was Freneau's conception of the deity, what was his conception of man's duty, his ideal of conduct? We must remember that Freneau, as well as Jefferson, Paine, and Franklin, belonged to the nascent humanitarian movement which during the latter part of the eighteenth century inspired a new sympathy for the humble and oppressed, a new faith in reason as the chief agent in furthering human perfectibility, and a new sense of social responsibility. In place of the Puritans' "vertical" love of man for God, a stress on developing one's higher self, there appeared a "horizontal" love of man for man, a stress on perfecting one's neighbors. Franklin, who read Shaftesbury and Collins and confessed that he "became a thorough deist," concluded that "the most acceptable service of God was the doing good to man."

[1] P. 421.   [2] P. 208.   [3] P. 343.
[4] *Thomas Paine, op. cit.,* p. 376.   [5] P. 417.

According to Paine's "religion of humanity," "religious duties consist in doing justice, loving mercy, and endeavoring to make our fellow creatures happy." [1] We have already witnessed Freneau's boundless sympathy for "the common herd," the persecuted alien, and the poor and oppressed. Like Jefferson, who foresaw a "total emancipation" of the slaves, [2] Freneau was one of the first abolitionists, freeing his own slaves, and lamenting the lot of those in Jamaica:

> If there exists a hell—the case is clear—
> Sir Toby's slaves enjoy that portion here. [3]

He envisages the day "when man shall man no longer crush," and grieves that

> . . . still the African complains
> And mourns his yet unbroken chains.

Notwithstanding his own weakness for the tavern, he was one of the early prohibitionists. [4] And everywhere we find his sympathy for animals. His daughter tells us that when her mother wanted poultry killed for dinner, so tender-hearted was the bluff old sea-captain that "Mrs. Freneau had to give orders to the blacks to do it privately." [5] While Franklin, apostle of humanitarian service, busied himself about the paving-stones on Chestnut Street, Freneau, having "splash'd my stocking," was advocating "repairing roads" instead of "supporting a standing army and useless embassies." [6] And, notwithstanding his unrivaled hatred for kings, priests, Tories, Englishmen, and critics, he announces in his expansive way that

> . . . this heart no narrow notions bind,
> Its pure good-will extends to all mankind. [7]

[1] *Thomas Paine, op. cit.*, p. 231.
[2] From Jefferson's *Notes on Virginia*, an extract from which Freneau published in the *Time-Piece*, January 31, 1798.
[3] Pattee, *op. cit.*, Vol. II, p. 258.   [4] P. 110.
[5] *Ibid.*, Vol. I, p. lxxxvii.
[6] *Ibid.*, p. lxxvii.   [7] P. 119.

It would be interesting, indeed, to ponder upon the extent
to which each age creates a deity in its own image, the extent
to which the humanitarian movement, which may be dated
from 1711 when Shaftesbury proclaimed man naturally benevolent, compassionate, and altruistic, was the cause rather
than the result of growing faith in a deity loving and benevolent. After reading Rousseau and the English deists,
after receiving the impact of the humanitarian movement
and the back-to-nature cult, Channing returned from the
South to preach his Unitarian doctrine that God is love, that
man is perfectible, and that religion is simply "the adoration
of goodness." For, as he argued in refuting doctrines of depravity and divine wrath, "a doctrine which contradicts our
best ideas of goodness and justice cannot come from the just
and good God, or be a true representation of his character."[1]
Since man loves man, God must love man even more. As
Freneau said, religion's

> . . . early sway
> Inclines the tender mind to take
> The path of right, fair virtue's way
> Its own felicity to make.[2]

We approach now a theory which underlies, I think, most of
Freneau's political radicalism: his faith in natural goodness.

> Left to himself, wherever man is found,
> In peace he aims to walk life's little round;
> In peace to sail, in peace to till the soil,
> Nor force false grandeur from a brother's toil.[3]

Instinctively benevolent, man should have absolute freedom:

> No! leave the mind unchain'd and free,
> And what they ought, mankind will be,
> No hypocrite, no lurking fiend,
> No artist to some evil end,
> But good and great, benign and just,
> As God and nature made them first.[4]

[1] W. E. Channing, *Works*, Vol. I, pp. 160–172. King's Chapel
became in 1785 the first Unitarian church in America.   [3] P. 157.
[2] *On the Religion of Nature*, p. 424.   [4] P. 166.

He imagines in one passage that "the Goddess of Nature" "last of all, and with the utmost exertion of her skill, formed, in one heart, the seeds and principles of a just, disinterested, benevolent, upright and honest man."[1] Instead of believing, with Hobbes and the leading thinkers of the seventeenth century, that the state of nature is the state of war, "nasty, solitary, brutish, and short," instead of seeing egotism as the mainspring of human activity, Freneau sees the state of nature, in the phrase of "heav'nly Pope," as "the state of God," and benevolence as the mainspring of human activity. The "triumphant discord" in the modern world leads Freneau to a primitivism which is in general conspicuously absent in American literature; he glorifies the primitive days of idyllic innocence:

> Not so that age of innocence and ease
> When men, yet social, knew no ills like these; . . .
> The hoary sage beneath his sylvan shade
> Impos'd no laws but those which reason made;
> On peace, not war; on good, not ill, intent,
> He judg'd his brethren by their own consent;
> Untaught to spurn those brethren to the dust,
> In virtue firm, and obstinately just.[2]

His charming pictures of a terrestrial paradise foreshadow Melville's *Typee*, with "its buoyant sense of a healthful physical existence" of "which Rousseau told us," before "the worst attendances of civilization" drove "all peace and happiness from the valley."[3]

> Sweet sylvan scenes of innocence and ease,
> How calm and joyous pass the seasons here! . . .
> No lordly palaces—no tyrant kings
> Enact hard laws to crush fair freedom here. . . .[4]
> All, all are free! Here God and Nature reign. . . .

[1] Edition of 1788, pp. 293–294.
[2] Pp. 85–86.
[3] H. Melville, *Typee* (Boston, 1892), pp. 185 and 287.
[4] P. 254.

> Nor think this mighty land of old contain'd
> The plundering wretch, or man of bloody mind: . . .
> The gen'rous soul inspir'd the honest breast,
> And to be free, was doubly to be blest:
> 'Till the east winds did here Columbus blow, . . .
> And rav'nous nations with industrious toil,
> Conspir'd to rob them of their native soil.[1]

What is this but Rousseau's theme that the progress of civilization has tended to corrupt the morals of mankind?

Man, in a state of simplicity [wrote the editor of the *Time-Piece*, who published many translations of Rousseau's "judicious sentiments"], uncorrupted by the influence of bad education, bad examples, and bad government, possesses a taste for all that is good and beautiful. He is capable of a degree of moral and intellectual improvement, which advances his nature to a participation with the divine. . . . Pleased with himself and all around him, his heart dilates with benevolence as well as piety. . . . But where is man to be found thus noble, thus innocent, thus happy? Not in so many parts of the terraqueous globe as he ought to be; but still he is to be found wherever the rights of nature and the virtues of simplicity are not violated or banished by the false refinements, the base artifices of *corrupted governments*. Unhappily for man, society has been almost universally corrupted, even by the arts intended for its very improvement, and human nature is gradually depraved in its very progress to civilization.[2]

Thus does the naturalist parody Puritanism: man is fallen, not from Calvin's God, but from Rousseau's nature. The source of evil is obvious. "Whence came these ills?" he exclaims.

---

[1] P. 219. In view of the fact that social historians might say that the Revolution determined Freneau's philosophy, that I am trying to make a by-product motivate what produced it, it may be relevant to point out that Freneau's natural-goodness and primitivistic theories were expressed in *The Pictures of Columbus* (1774) and *The American Village* (1772), *before* the war.

[2] *Time-Piece*, February 5, 1798. Forman (*op. cit.*, p. 98) says Freneau was "steeped in the philosophy of Rousseau and Condorcet." Payne (*op. cit.*, p. 161) says the *National Gazette* was "filled with praise of Thomas Paine and Rousseau."

> Accuse not nature for the dreary scene. . . .
> She, equal still in all her varied ways,
> An equal blessing to the world displays.[1]

It is not nature, then, but "the crowns and sceptres," the "priests that hold the artillery of the sky," the "*corrupted governments*," that have caused evil. Instead of being innate in man, evil is simply dependent upon social institutions. On the basis of his tutor Locke's assumption that man is the product of sensation and environment, Shaftesbury had argued that man is therefore not innately evil; then the radicals such as Priestley and Godwin had argued that evil must derive from a thwarting of naturally good instincts by institutions and environment, and the path to perfection lies through a modification of environment and institutions. This doctrine in Freneau, which I think "creatively determines all the rest," is strikingly parallel to Shelley's doctrine in *Queen Mab*, produced about the same time. Shelley seeks the source of evil, the "ruin, vice, and slavery" heaped on man, and he asks whether evil is innate, whether nature is responsible:

> . . . Nature! No!
> Kings, priests, and statesmen blast the human flower
> Even in its tender bud; their influence darts
> Like subtle poison through the bloodless veins
> Of desolate society.

Freneau's attitude corresponds, also, to that of Paine, to whom "Government is the badge of our lost innocence." Clearly, the poet's natural goodness theory and his faith in the supremacy of reason motivate his extreme democracy; as Shelley thought, the golden age of his iridescent dream will dawn when man is emancipated from the restraints embodied in kings and priests:

> Peace to all feuds!—and come the happier day
> When Reason's sun shall light us on our way;
> When erring man shall all his RIGHTS retrieve,
> No despots rule him, and no kings deceive.[2]

[1] P. 155.   [2] P. 112.

Strong confirmatory evidence of the validity of my belief that the natural goodness theory is central in Freneau's political radicalism may be found in the fact that it was on this theory of the radicals generally that the Federalists centered their attacks. To doctrines such as the above, Fessenden, for example, replied:

> . . . democrats
> . . . all object to the propriety
> Of law and order in society,
> Think reason will supply restraints,
> And make mankind a set of saints. . . .
> Such principles, alas, will flood
> Columbia's "happy land" with blood.[1]

Joseph Dennie, disciple of Burke, said that "instead of viewing man as he is," the democratic "professors of the new philosophy of France" "are continually forming plans for man as he should be."[2] And the Federalists in general shared the Puritan Winthrop's fear of a "Liberty of corrupt Nature, which is affected By *Men* and *Beasts*, to do what they list," and they advocated what he called "a Federal *Liberty*, . . . maintained in a way of *Subjection* to *Authority*, . . . A *Liberty* for that only which is *just* and *good*."[3] John Adams sought in vain through the whole gallery of the past for the benevolent, rational, altruistic man proclaimed by such democrats as Freneau; Adams marshals a formidable array of philosophers and statesmen to prove that "whoever would found a state, and make proper laws for the government of it, must presume that all men are bad by nature; that they will not fail to show that natural depravity of heart whenever they have a fair opportunity."[4] Hamilton, field marshal of the Federalists, who considered the idealists of the French Revolution mere "fanatics in politics," held that in "contriving any system of government, and fixing the several

---

[1] *Democracy Unveiled*, Vol. I, pp. 84–85.

[2] From Stedman and Hutchinson, *A Library of American Literature* (New York, 1887–90), Vol. IV, p. 250.

[3] *Cotton Mather* (ed. K. B. Murdock, New York, 1926), pp. 76–77.

[4] J. Adams, *Works*, Vol. IV, p. 408.

checks and controls of the constitution, *every man* ought to be supposed a *knave;* and to have no other end, in all his actions, but *private interest.* By this we must govern him; and by means of it, make him coöperate to the public good, notwithstanding his insatiable avarice and ambition."[1] Deriving partly from Whig merchants, seeing self-interest as men's dominant motive, the Federalists naturally sought to safeguard property. "The essence, and almost the quintessence, of good government," according to Fisher Ames, "is to protect property and its rights. When these are protected, there is scarcely any booty left for oppression to seize."[2] Said Timothy Dwight, President of Yale, "Man, unrestrained by law and religion, is a mere beast of prey." He attacks the natural goodness myth in *The Triumph of Infidelity* (1795), ironically dedicated to Voltaire, who had said, "L'homme n'est point né méchant; il le devient, comme il devient malade."

> With him all *natural* desires are good;
> His thirst for stews; the Mohawk's thirst for blood.

The Federalists mainly derived from such thinkers as Hobbes, who "put forth," as he said, "for a general inclination of all mankind, a perpetual desire of power after power that ceaseth only in death." "Why," exclaimed Hamilton,[3] "has government been instituted at all? Because the passions of men will not conform to the dictates of reason and justice," as Freneau and Jefferson thought, "without restraint." That is really the essence of the matter: the Federalist sought a check on the expansion of natural impulse; Freneau and the democrats did not think such a check necessary. "There must be," said Hamilton, who often resembles Burke, "a permanent *will.*" Distrusting the untrained and unreflective multitude driven by natural impulse, he thought "there ought to be a principle in government capable of re-

---

[1] A. Hamilton, *Works,* Vol. II, p. 51.
[2] F. Ames, *Works,* "Phocion."
[3] In *The Federalist,* No. 15.

sisting the popular current."[1]   The "turbulent and un-controllable disposition" of the people "requires checks."[2]

While deism had strengthened the Puritan reliance upon Locke's theory that government is a contract between the governors and the governed which the latter may dissolve when the entrusted power is abused, deism had extended distrust for governmental authority which, as in the case of Winthrop, was held by the Puritans to safeguard their liberty.   An essential difference, then, between deism and Puritanism is a difference in the attitude toward the natural man, and consequently a difference in the attitude toward authority, toward checks upon what Winthrop called the "corrupt Nature" of the individual.   Freneau acted in part as the journalistic broadcaster of Jefferson's democracy, which was itself founded on the faith that "the good sense of the people will always be found to be the best army. . . . Were it left to me to decide whether we should have a government without newspapers, or newspapers without a government, I should prefer the latter."[3]   He was "not clear" that the liberty of the Indian, "without government," is not "the best,"[4] and he not only proclaimed human rights but also state rights, as in drafting the Kentucky Resolutions, 1799. By such typical judicial decisions as that regarding the Marbury vs. Madison case, establishing the power of the Supreme Court to nullify an act of Congress, the Federalist John Marshall, according to Joseph Quincy Adams' Diary, "cemented the Union which the crafty and quixotic democracy of Jefferson had a perpetual tendency to dissolve."

Thus the Federalists' determination to refute the theory, as well as the fact that a similar theory held by Jefferson led to the same conclusion, supports the abundant evidence given by Freneau himself that his theory of the natural goodness of humanity mainly determined his hostility toward embodiments of social restraint, his extreme democracy, which

[1] A. Hamilton, Works, Vol. II, p. 415.
[2] Ibid., Vol. I, p. 422.
[3] T. Jefferson (Monticello edition), Vol. V, p. 150.
[4] T. Jefferson, Works (Ford edition), Vol. IV, p. 362.

possibly merits praise as helping to offset the opposite and contemporary Federalist extreme.

IV

It remains to indicate briefly the relation between Freneau's naturalism and his poetry.[1] If his naturalism made him the journalist of Jeffersonian and French democracy, it is no less true that his naturalism determined his treatment of the actual life of the American forest and field, the very ground under his feet becoming, in the phrase of Burroughs, his lineal descendant, "the Divine Soil." Several years ago Professor C. A. Moore demonstrated that "deism may be said to be the starting point for our modern romantic treatment of nature."[2] This is especially true in the case of Freneau, and is but one instance of how fruitful in American literature would be a more thorough and detached study of the interrelations of poetry and religion. Confident that "GOD IS ONE,"[3] Freneau venerates all nature, from the lowest to the highest, as equally a divine revelation:

> Ah! what is all this mighty WHOLE,
> These suns and stars that round us roll!
> What are they all, where'er they shine,
> But *Fancies* of the Power Divine!
> What is this *globe*, these *lands*, and *seas*,
> And *heat*, and *cold*, and *flowers*, and *trees*,
> And *life*, and *death*, and *beast*, and *man*,
> And *time*—that with the *sun* began—
> But thoughts on reason's scale combin'd,
> Ideas of the Almighty mind![4]
>
> . . . .
>
> All that we see, about, abroad,
> What is it all, but nature's God?[5]

[1] I have treated this subject in somewhat more detail in "What Made Freneau the Father of American Poetry?" (*Studies in Philology*, January, 1929.)

[2] *Studies in Philology*, Vol. XIV, "The Return to Nature in English Poetry of the Eighteenth Century," p. 243.

[3] P. 341. [4] P. 208. [5] P. 422.

In contrast to the Puritan Edwards' faith in a "divine and supernatural light," Freneau's faith aligns itself, as we have seen, with the international deism, which was versified in *The Essay on Man* (1734), a copy of which had been in Freneau's library since 1761:

> All are but parts of one stupendous whole,
> Whose body Nature is, and God the Soul.

Later, after deism had evolved into Unitarianism, and Emerson had resigned his Unitarian pulpit, he said that to "Study nature" and to "Know thyself" were "the same thing," for both are but parts of that "Unity, that Over-Soul, within which every man's particular being is contained and made one with all other." Coleridge was a Unitarian before he became a pantheist in *The Aeolian Harp* and *Frost at Midnight*. Wordsworth did homage to a god "whose dwelling is the light of setting suns," Shelley proclaimed that "the universe is God" and "mixed awful talk" with his "Great Parent." The rebellious Byron had learned to "worship Nature with a thought profound," his "altars" being "the mountains and the ocean, earth, air, stars,—all that springs from the great Whole." When men became conscious of the identity of God and nature, they rushed out of doors, ceased to feel that "Nature and Homer were . . . the same," and they began to write, as Wordsworth said, "with the eye on the object." In place of abstractions, men like Emerson came to see that "the veritable mark of wisdom is finding the miraculous in the common"; ideas were transmuted into images as men turned to the concrete, physical, sensuous world—the true world of poetry.

In connection with Freneau, however, we must remember that his work marks the starting-point in America of this fruitful trend toward the concrete in poetry. And it was naturalism which explains why, concurrent with our political independence, he heralded our literary independence, so far as themes are concerned, by bringing into poetry for the first time truly American nature. He introduces the indigenous elm, pumpkin, blackbird, whippoorwill, wild honey suckle, and squirrel. In his work even a casual reader will find roses, daisies, daffodils, the honey suckle, pumpkins, cedars, "the apple, apricot, and plum," "the tall chestnut," corn, "wheaten sheeves,"·the oak, "shrubby hazels," "dry alders," the aspen, the "sad pine," buckwheat, oats, the "weeping willow," ivy, mint, the beech and the cypress-tree, as well as the lynx, the panther, "howling wolves," the "fearless doe," the pheasant, the blackbird, the lark, the "timorous deer," the buffalo, the beaver, the hare, leverets, dogs, the caty-did, the honey-bees, the "angry tiger," the "staring owl," the squirrel, the parrot, and the goldfinch.

The aesthetic significance of his frank love of what Wordsworth called "the mighty world of ear and eye" is apparent only when one recalls that up to this time, with a minor exception here and there, American poetry had been mainly versified homiletics, such as Wigglesworth's *Day of Doom*. In an age of generality and abstraction Freneau was a pioneer—inspired by his naturalistic faith—in turning, as a poet, to the concrete and the particular, around which true emotion hovers, and from the fertile soil of which authentic poetry draws its abiding strength. Naturalism, then, bred in Freneau that "requickening of the artistic senses" which Professor Elton finds to be one of the significant marks of nascent romanticism. "The history of our imaginative writing," he remarks, "is at bottom very much the history of the artistic senses and their growth."[1] At times Freneau's all-embracing sensuousness is almost Keatsian; unusual indeed in the year 1776 in American verse are the multitude of "sense-appeals" which throng *The Beauties of Santa Cruz*, especially the appeal to the senses of touch, taste, and smell with their consequent impression of immediacy and warmth. In the "soft shade" of a "sweet orange grove" "luxuriously reclined" in his fragrant bed, by "cool woodland streams" amid "soft breezes" he watches in Lotus-eater mood the fishes, colorful as the Ancient Mariner's water-snakes:

[1] *A Survey of English Literature 1780-1880* (New York, 1920), Vol. I, p. 11.

> Some streaked with burnished gold, resplendent glare,
> Some cleave the limpid deep, all silver'd o'er,
> Some, clad in living green, delight the eye,
> Some red, some blue; of mingled colours more.

His mouth waters at the thought of "this luscious food,"
"delicious to the taste," and the chance to "cool thy thirst"
with the "sweetest syrups of this liquorish clime." The
"fragrant" fruit of the tropics is "alluring to the smell":

> Sweet orange groves in lonely vallies rise
> And drop their fruits, unnoticed and unknown,
> And cooling acid limes in hedges grow,
> The juicy lemons swell in shades their own.

Correlated with this refreshed and sharpened attention to
the physical world there appears in Freneau a natural, simple,
concrete diction very different from the tasteless and abstract
periphrasis, "the gaudiness and inane phraseology" of Pope.
Read such genuine and simple poems as *The Wild Honey
Suckle*, *The Indian Burying Ground*, *The Dying Indian*, or
To a Caty-Did, and you will seek in vain for the false Ar-
cadianism of Thomson, for landscapes peopled with Damons,
Palaemons, and Musidoras in the sentimental array of the
sham idyl. Imagine the shudder which would run through
the fastidious author of *The Rape of the Lock* at an illustration
of disillusionment such as Freneau used at the end of *The
Vanity of Existence*:

> So nightly on some shallow tide,
>   Oft have I seen a splendid show;
> Reflected stars on either side,
>   And glittering moons were seen below.

> But when the tide had ebb'd away,
>   The scene fantastic with it fled,
> A bank of mud around me lay,
>   And sea-weed on the river's bed.

It seems to me that it is just such simple, concrete, genuine,
and beautiful diction as the above—in this instance springing
from Freneau's own observation as a sailor—which makes him

merit the title, "father of American poetry."   And the superior aesthetic quality is due in no small measure to naturalism, which led him to observe directly, thus enabling him
to solve what Pater regarded as the greatest technical problem
of the artist, "the transmutation of ideas into images." Naturalism peopled his mind with images, and the faith that God
is revealed in nature's meanest forms did not make it necessary for him "to go too far below that outside of things in
which art really begins and ends."[1] "All art," Conrad asserted categorically, "appeals primarily to the senses, and the
artistic aim, when expressing itself in written words, must
also make its appeal through the senses, if its high desire is to
reach the secret spring of responsive emotions."[2] However
much one may disparage naturalism on philosophical or
ethical grounds, it is difficult to escape the fact that his-
torically the return to nature, to sensuous life, resulted in
poetry of immensely increased aesthetic value.

If naturalism determined Freneau's treatment of indigenous
American nature, if the consequent sensuousness accounts for
the aesthetic quality of his poetry, it must be pointed out that
his naturalism is distinctively of the eighteenth century
transitional sort. His work falls between two eras, the neo-
classic and the romantic, the age of Pope and the age of
Wordsworth, and it partakes of the character of each. His
genius and individuality were not so great as to prevent him,
chameleon-like, from taking protective coloring against his
changing age; this fact, however, renders his work valuable
as a cross-section of the complex age of transition in American
letters. This transitional position helps to account for the
absence in Freneau of what Emerson called "a foolish con-
sistency." He is unconsciously a bundle of apparent con-
tradictions. He is both a bitter satirist, in his own description,

> So full of invective and loaded with spleen,
> So sneeringly smart, and so hellishly keen,[3]

[1] *Renaissance* (Modern Library Edition), p. 93.
[2] Preface to *The Nigger of the Narcissus*.
[3] Pattee, *op. cit.*, Vol. II, p. 205.

and a sentimentalist who laments popular indifference toward the "plaintive elegy" and "lyric ode."[1] Idolizing "thrice happy Dryden," "godlike Addison," and "heav'nly Pope,"[2] he leads the revolt against their themes and diction. An ardent student of the classics, he rebukes "the Student of the Dead Languages" for wasting time on the "antique gibberish" of "Latin lore and heathen Greek."[3] Glorifier of the "gen'rous soul" of the benevolent and noble red man, he attacks his vices. His ferocious hatreds are equaled only by his humanitarian sympathies, his humor only by his pensive melancholy. The poet of Reason, he grieves that he dwells

> Where rigid *Reason* reigns alone,
> Where lovely *Fancy* has no sway.[4]

An ardent apostle, as we have seen, of natural goodness and human perfectibility, he is the author of the apparently contradictory poems on *The Projectors*[5] and *The Millennium*.[6] And finally, he is the poet of deistic optimism—"all, all is right"—as well as the poet of transience and death. His eighteenth century tastes are more striking when one recalls that he outlived but never referred to Byron, Shelley, Keats, and Hazlitt, and that Hawthorne, Whittier, Poe, as well as Tennyson and Carlyle, were all writing at his death. The parallels to his nascent romanticism appear in precursors such as Parnell, Shenstone, Thomson, Blair, Young, Collins, Gray, the Wartons, Beattie, Cowper, Crabbe, Goldsmith, Beckford, Blake, and Burns. If on the political side his closest parallel is Shelley, that is because both poets drew from eighteenth century naturalism their major doctrines such as faith in natural goodness, the perfectibility of man, the sovereignty of reason, universal benevolence, and the dependence of evil on social institutions.

Freneau's transitional character may be illustrated, perhaps, in his treatment of nature. Although "the Almighty

[1] P. 394.
[2] Pp. 224–225.
[3] P. 398.
[4] P. 353.
[5] Pattee, *op. cit.*, Vol. II, p. 160.
[6] P. 147.

power . . . lives and breathes through all," although the
plant "enjoys" her sleep "with *Reason*, only less complete"[1] than man, Freneau's nature-subjects are seldom
described in minute and individualizing detail. With Dr.
Johnson, whom he read, he seems to have thought that the
poet should be engaged, not in "numbering the streaks of the
tulip," but in "descriptions not descending to minuteness."
Indeed, *May to April* and *The Seasons Moralized*—typical
poems of nature—merely use nature in the eighteenth century conventional and generalized manner in similitudes for
human destinies. Or take his Indians Just as MacPherson
saw in *Ossian* proof of the Shaftesburian doctrine of the
benevolent magnanimity of the natural man, so Freneau
saw proof of his theory in the primitivistic "gen'rous soul"
of the Indian before the advent of the "rav'nous nations,"
as in his early *American Village* and *The Pictures of Columbus*.
This sort of naturalism inspired *The Dying Indian*, simple and
beautiful, and especially *The Indian Burying Ground*, which is
almost his masterpiece as regards delicacy of fancy, felicity
of execution, and suggestiveness. So beautiful is it that the
English poet Campbell borrowed one of its lines. And *The
Scandinavian War Song*, with its "savage notions of valour
and romantic heroism," reminds one of Gray's Norse poems.
But to Freneau the Indian is not only benevolent; he is also
"the murderous Indian," "the cruel Indian," scornful of the
Christian heaven *"where's there's nothing to eat and but little
to steal."* [2] Nor is this puzzling bifurcated attitude toward
the Indian different from his attitude toward the sea, the
domain of which he added to our literature. He shares the
eighteenth century view of the sea as "a commercial highway"
and a savage destroyer. "If it should happen that commerce
grow dull," he will "clew up" his "top-sails" and bid Neptune
"farewell."[3] In contrast think of the romantic Melville's
sea, a "sweet mystery," "the ungraspable phantom of life."
Or think of the gray-bearded Whitman on the beach "as the
old mother sways her to and fro singing her husky song,"
looking out upon the "troops of white-maned racers racing to

[1] P. 378.   [2] P. 401.   [3] P. 388.

the goal," as he associates death with the breaking of the sea, the symbol of change. This mysterious romantic suggestiveness never haunts Freneau, who has the eighteenth century dread of the deep. The sailor treads

> . . . a watery tomb of ocean-green
> And only one frail plank between! [1]

The Hurricane is a typical sea-poem, describing, "while mountains break on either side," the barque, out of control, which "gropes her trackless way" over the "dark abyss." His graphic descriptions, however, of the vaster and more terrifying aspects of the sea, his honest sailor-talk of "studding sails," "sheets and tacks," "booms," as well as plaintive references to a "retreat" to the "solitary wastes of Neptune," foreshadow Cooper and Scott, or Byron, who thrilled with a mysterious kinship in the face of storm and tempest.

Ultimately, Freneau is mainly important according to what Arnold called the "historic estimate" rather than "the real estimate": he is worthy of study as a cross-section of an intensely significant period in our political and literary history, rather than as an intrinsically wise political theorist or a profound creator of poetic beauty. This, however, should not keep us from acknowledging that he is our greatest poet before Bryant and that his genius was thwarted by an age and associates indifferent to "pure poetry," believing, in the words of Madison, "that something more substantial, more durable, more profitable befits our riper age." His chief aesthetic difficulty, it seems to me, is that his expansive sympathy, his enthusiasm for what has been called "the cluttered incoherency of the mundane spectacle," his aversion to restraint—all bequeathed him by naturalism—made him unable to select and focus with concentrated intensity truly significant experience in such a way as to stir the reader's imagination, to suggest a symbolic quality. He can seldom, as Browning said, "do the thing which breeds the thought." In most of his poems, as, for example, in *The Departure, Occasioned by the Removal of Congress from New York*

[1] P. 316.

to Philadelphia, there is absent that focused vision, that arrangement of life carefully planned to produce a desired effect, that order and harmony, which distinguishes art from experience. He is expansive, rather than intense: that sublime Dantean faculty for "one smiting word and then silence" was never Freneau's. Lack of restraint accounts, also, for his too frequently slipshod metrical and rhyming effects.[1] If a good poem is like a pebble dropped into the still waters of the imagination, wakening ripples there that circle and spread until they lap along the shores of infinity, the average poem of Freneau is like a whole handful of pebbles, thrown carelessly into the "waters of the imagination," wakening ripples there which quickly clash in mere confusion.

There is evidence that Freneau was half-ashamed of his satiric muse, "the least engaging of them all,"[2] which has led certain scholars to see in him only the "Poet of the American Revolution," and that he turned to "applied poetry," the effect of which on his countrymen should be taken as a proof of its merit, only because

> An age employ'd in pointing steel
> Can no poetic raptures feel,

[1] Among his rhymes one finds such curiosities as "New Amsterdam" and "horns of a ram," "before you all" and "immemorial," "Britain" and "spit on." His characteristic meter is the iambic, usually in some stanzaic pattern. Occasionally he uses blank verse, as in parts of the excellent *Pictures of Columbus.* M. C. Tyler (*Literary History of the American Revolution,* New York, 1897, Vol. I, p. 180) says, "*The Power of Fancy,* in rhymed tetrameters—alert, elastic, full of music and motion—wholly discards the sing-song, the artificial phraseology, and the stilted movement then so common in English poetry."

[2] Pp. 353–54. Since most of Freneau's so-called satire is far inferior in quality to his "pure poetry," it merits slight aesthetic consideration. Good satire—Swift's, for instance—generally avoids the show of heat or passion, and indirectly, by cool exaggeration or incongruity, makes its object ridiculous. But Freneau's lack of restraint turned most of his satires, which usually lack lightness or humor, into direct, downright abuse, as in the typical lines on Cornwallis:

> "Nature in him disgrac'd the form divine;
> Nature mistook, she meant him for a—swine."

because "these times of rude renown" were indifferent to the "plaintive elegy" and "lyric ode" which were his specialty. Devoted to "mere literature," he wrote, as we have seen, part of a novel; his dramatic fragment *The Spy* recalls Mercy Warren's plays; he defended the theater in half-a-dozen poems; and he hoped that "the fine arts in general will, with the return of peace, find that share of encouragement, which they seem entitled to demand in every nation that makes any pretensions to refinement and civilization."[1] Speaking of the dawning interest in "literature as an expression of the aesthetic mood, literature apart from mere instruction," the conservative Professor Tyler concludes: "The foremost representative of this new literary tendency was Philip Freneau, a true man of genius, the one poet of unquestionable originality granted to America prior to the nineteenth century."[2]

Although the uneven and occasionally crude *House of Night*, a lurid Gothic poem dealing with the Death of Death, spectres and a graveyard, has won deserved attention as "the first distinctly romantic note heard in America," as a fore-shadowing of the work of C. B. Brown, Poe, and Coleridge, its very luridness must not blind us to the fact that it is built around the theme he treats most poetically—the theme of transience:

> Hills sink to plains, and man returns to dust,
> That dust supports a reptile or a flower;
> Each changeful atom by some other nurs'd,
> Takes some new form, to perish in an hour.

Just as his poems of political radicalism were motivated by naturalism, so naturalism determined the choice of this, his master theme. His Lucretian attempt to rationalize death—

> . . . the man exists no more,
> And death is nothing but an empty name;[3]
> . . . if return'd to dread nihility,
> You'll still be happy, for you will not be[4] —

[1] From the "Advertisement" to the edition of 1815.
[2] Tyler, *op. cit.*, Vol. I, p. 11.
[3] P. 295.
[4] P. 223.

and his tendency to found life mainly on sensation, already illustrated, inevitably led to *Reflections on the Mutability of Things* and *On the Vicissitudes of Things:*

> The time is approaching, deny it who may,
>   The days are not very remote,
> When the pageant that glitter'd for many a day,
>   On the stream of oblivion will float.[1]

With the decline of faith in the reality of the world of spirit, which accompanied deism, and with the progressive identification of God and nature, there remained nothing immutable above the stream of sensation, and men became sadly conscious of the truth that sensuous life is fleeting. The naturalist is obsessed with transience:

> The mountains waste, the shores decay,
>   Once purling streams are dead and dry—
> 'Twas Nature's work—'tis nature's play,
>   And Nature says that all must die.[2]

Wordsworth found the need of reinforcing his naturalistic creed with the Christian creed, and "the faith that looks through death." The deist-naturalist Freneau was unable to find that peace which the mystic Vaughan found in his "retreat" from a transient "heaven in sense" to "the way which from this dark and dead abode leads up to God," for to him "God is One," who tended more and more to be merged in sense, and sense is fleeting. Examine his finest poems, such as *The Wild Honey Suckle, The Dying Indian, The Indian Burying Ground, To the Memory of the Brave Americans, The Pyramids of Egypt, Elegiac Stanzas, On a Honey Bee, To a Caty-Did, The Seasons Moralized, The House of Night, On Retirement, The Vanity of Existence, The Man of Ninety, To an Old Man, The Deserted Farmhouse, May to April,* and *The Brook of the Valley,* and in all, as a common denominator, you will find the theme of mutability, transience, or death. Here, fortunately, naturalism presented him with an intrinsically poetical theme, evoking just the requisite emo-

[1] P. 153.   [2] P. 320.

tion to leaven his rather cold rationalism; it is a subject possessing the "grandeur of generality" lacking in Freneau's ephemeral poems on current events. And naturalism also gave him concrete means of rendering this abstract and un-localized eighteenth century theme relatively poetical.[1] Notice his use of "The Wild Honey Suckle," the first fine poem of nature in American literature, as a symbol of transience:

> Smit with those charms, that must decay,
> I grieve to see your future doom;
> They died—nor were those flowers more gay,—
> The flowers that did in Eden bloom:
> Unpitying frosts, and Autumn's power
> Shall leave no vestige of this flower.

Everywhere in his poems of nature we find that haunting sense of the frailty and evanescence of all beautiful things. If in his "Poems of Freedom" Freneau foreshadows the destructive side of Shelley's hope for the perfection of the race, when man shall be

> Sceptreless, free, uncircumscribed, but man
> Equal, unclassed, tribeless, and nationless,
> Exempt from awe, worship, degree, the king
> Over himself; just, gentle, wise,

the theme of his most beautiful "Poems of Romantic Fancy" foreshadows the lyric lament of John Keats for the transient loveliness of a sensuous world,

> Where Beauty cannot keep her lustrous eyes,
> Or new Love pine at them beyond to-morrow.

HARRY HAYDEN CLARK

[1] It should be noted that while naturalism made the poet immerse himself in transience, in the flux, the loss or weakening of the sense of Eternity, of that which changes not, weakened the contrast between that and the flux, and therefore weakened the *poignancy* of the poetic sense of transiency, such as one finds in the great Renaissance poets. Other things being equal, surely the truth makes the best poetry.

NOTE ON THE TEXT

Except where revision has clearly been determined by changes in the political situation rather than by more mature aesthetic insight, the text adopted for each poem is that of the latest known publication or revision which received Freneau's supervision and sanction. Since most of the poems were reprinted, more or less revised, in the two-volume edition of 1809, whereas the edition of 1815 contained only later poems, the major portion of the text is taken from the edition of 1809, and unless otherwise indicated the text of any particular poem is from that edition. All footnotes are by Freneau unless expressly marked otherwise.

An attempt has been made to present the most accurate existing text of Freneau. Every student of the poet must express his gratitude for the pioneer labors of Professor F. L. Pattee, to whom we are indebted for the initial date of publication of most of the poems. Dates following the poems refer to the time of first publication, except when bracketed and preceded by a "w" to indicate that the poem was written earlier. I have personally copied each poem from one of the original, rare, time-browned editions, reproducing not only the idiosyncrasies of spelling, capitalization, and syntax, but also, for the first time, I believe, the original italics and punctuation. Several poems embodying Freneau's neglected naturalism, such as those *On the Religion of Nature* and *On the Universality of the God of Nature*, have been first reprinted here. I have arranged what may, to borrow a scientific analogy, be called Freneau's "applied" poetry in a group entitled *Poems of Freedom*, and his "pure" poetry in another group entitled *Poems of Romantic Fancy*. Within each group the arrangement is roughly chronological. It is hoped that such an arrangement will enable either the historical or the aesthetic reader to follow his peculiar interests without being annoyed by what for his purpose would be irrelevancies.

It is a pleasure to make grateful acknowledgment of the kindness of the officials of the Library of Congress and the libraries of Yale University, the University of Chicago, and the University of Wisconsin in permitting the use of the rare editions necessary for this work.   I wish to record, also, my gratitude to Professors Arthur Beatty and William Ellery Leonard, my colleagues at the University of Wisconsin, who read portions of the Introduction in manuscript, and particularly to Professor Norman Foerster, of the University of North Carolina, who read it all.

H. H. C.

SELECTED READING LIST

I. BIBLIOGRAPHY

Paltsits, V. C. *A Bibliography of the Separate and Collected Works of Philip Freneau.* New York, 1903.

II. TEXTS OF POEMS

The Poems of Philip Freneau. Written chiefly during the late War. Philadelphia, 1786.

The Miscellaneous Works of Mr. Philip Freneau containing his Essays and Additional Poems. Philadelphia, 1788.

Poems Written between the Years 1768 & 1794, by Philip Freneau, of New Jersey: A New Edition, Revised and Corrected by the Author. . . . Monmouth, N. J., 1795.

Poems Written and Published during the American Revolutionary War, and now republished from the original Manuscripts; Interspersed with Translations from the Ancients, and Other Pieces not heretofore in Print. By Philip Freneau. Third edition, 2 vols. Philadelphia, 1809.

A Collection of Poems, on American Affairs, and a variety of other Subjects, chiefly moral and political; written between the Year 1797 and the present Time. By Philip Freneau. . . . 2 vols. New York, 1815.

III. REPRINTS OF POEMS

Smith, John Russell. *Poems on various Subjects, but chiefly illustrative of the Events and Actors in the American War of Independence. By Philip Freneau.* (Reprinted from the rare edition printed at Philadelphia in 1786. With a Preface.) London, 1861.

Duyckinck, Evert A. *Poems relating to the American Revolution. By Philip Freneau.* (With an introductory memoir and notes.) New York, 1865.

Pattee, Fred Lewis. *Poems of Philip Freneau, Poet of the American Revolution.* New Jersey, 1902–1907. (Indispensable for the student of Freneau. Notes indicate place and date of first publication of most of the poems. Introductory 112 pages the most trustworthy biography of Freneau. Bibliography, Vol. III, pp. 407–417, aims "to correct a few omissions and errors in Mr. Paltsits' volume, and to locate copies whose existence he overlooked." The editor lists 119 poems he has omitted.)

IV. EARLY ANTHOLOGIES CONTAINING FRENEAU'S WORK

The Columbian Muse. New York, 1794.

McCarty, William. *Songs, Odes, and Other Poems on National Subjects.* 3 vols. Philadelphia, 1842.

Griswold, Rufus W. *Poets and Poetry of America.* Philadelphia, 1850.

Duyckinck, Evert A. and George L. *Cyclopedia of American Literature,* Vol. I. New York, 1855.

Moore, Frank. *Songs and Ballads of the American Revolution.* New York, 1856.

The American Museum or Repository of Ancient and Modern Fugitive Pieces. Philadelphia, 1787–1792.

V. BIOGRAPHY AND CRITICISM

Austin, Mary S. *Philip Freneau, The Poet of the Revolution. A History of His Life and Times.* Edited by Helen Kearny Vreeland (great-granddaughter of the poet). New York, 1901.

Bowers, Claude G. *Jefferson and Hamilton. The Struggle for Democracy in America.* Boston, 1925.

Clark, Harry H. "Literary Influences upon Philip Freneau," *Studies in Philology,* Vol. XXII, January, 1925.

——. "What Made Freneau the Father of American Poetry?" *Studies in Philology,* Vol. XXVI, January, 1929.

——. "Philip Freneau," *Encyclopedia Britannica.*

——. *The Philosopher of the Forest,* New York, 1929. (A selection of Freneau's prose with an introduction.)

DeLancey, Edward F. "Philip Freneau, the Huguenot Patriot-Poet of the Revolution, and His Poetry," *Proceedings of the Huguenot Society of America,* Vol. II, No. 2, 1891.

Forman, Samuel E. "The Political Activities of Philip Freneau," *Johns Hopkins University Studies in Historical and Political Science,* Series XX, Nos. 9–10. Baltimore, 1902. (A thorough, scholarly study.)

Hustvedt, S. B. "Philippic Freneau," *American Speech,* Vol. IV, October, 1928.

Marble, Mrs. Annie Russell. *Heralds of American Literature.* University of Chicago, 1907.

More, Paul Elmer. "Philip Freneau," *Shelburne Essays*, fifth series. New York, 1908.

Parrington, V. L. *The Colonial Mind, 1620–1800.* New York, 1927.

Patterson, Samuel White. *The Spirit of the American Revolution as Revealed in the Poetry of the Period.* Boston, n. d. (1915).

Payne, G. H. *History of Journalism in the United States.* New York, 1920.

Tyler, Moses Coit. *The Literary History of the American Revolution, 1763–1783.* 2 vols. New York, 1897.

PART ONE
POEMS OF FREEDOM

The
RISING GLORY OF AMERICA.

Being part of a Dialogue pronounced on a public occasion.

ARGUMENT.

The subject proposed—The discovery of America by Columbus—
A philosophical enquiry into the origin of the savages of America
—The first planters from Europe—Causes of their migration to
America—The difficulties they encountered from the jealousy
of the natives—Agriculture descanted on—Commerce and navigation—Science—Future prospects of British usurpation,
tyranny, and devastation on this side the Atlantic—The more
comfortable one of Independence, Liberty and Peace—Conclusion.

Acasto.

Now shall the adventurous muse attempt a theme
More new, more noble, and more flush of fame
Than all that went before—
Now through the veil of ancient days renew
The period famed when first Columbus touched
These shores so long unknown—through various toils,
Famine, and death, the hero forced his way,
Through oceans pregnant with perpetual storms,
And climates hostile to adventurous man.
But why, to prompt your tears, should we resume,
The tale of *Cortez*, furious chief, ordained
With Indian blood to dye the sands, and choak,
Famed *Mexico*, thy streams with dead? or why
Once more revive the tale so oft rehearsed
Of *Atabilipa*, by the thirst of gold,
(Too conquering motive in the human breast.)
Deprived of life, which not Peru's rich ore
Nor *Mexico's* vast mines could then redeem?

3

Better these northern realms demand our song,
Designed by nature for the rural reign,
For agriculture's toil.—No blood we shed
For metals buried in a rocky waste.—
Cursed be that ore, which brutal makes our race
And prompts mankind to shed their kindred blood.

Eugenio.

——But whence arose
That vagrant race who love the shady vale,
And choose the forest for their dark abode?—
For long has this perplext the sages' skill
To investigate.—Tradition lends no aid
To unveil this secret to the human eye,
When first these various nations, north and south,
Possess these shores, or from what countries came,—
Whether they sprang from some primaeval head
In their own lands, like Adam in the east,—
Yet this the sacred oracles deny,
And reason, too, reclaims against the thought:
For when the general deluge drowned the world
Where could their tribes have found security,
Where find their fate, but in the ghastly deep?—
Unless, as others dream, some chosen few
High on the Andes, wrapt in endless snow,
Where winter in his wildest fury reigns,
And subtile aether scarce our life maintains.
But here philosophers oppose the scheme:
This earth, they say, nor hills nor mountains knew
Ere yet the universal flood prevailed;
But when the mighty waters rose aloft,
Roused by the winds, they shook their solid base,
And, in convulsions, tore the deluged world,
'Till by the winds assuaged, again they fell,
And all their ragged bed exposed to view.
    Perhaps far wandering toward the northern pole
The streights of Zembla, and the frozen zone,
And where the eastern Greenland almost joins

America's north point, the hardy tribes
Of banished Jews, Siberians, Tartars wild
Came over icy mountains, or on floats,
First reached these coasts, hid from the world beside.—
And yet another argument more strange,
Reserved for men of deeper thought, and late,
Presents itself to view.—*In Peleg's days.*
(So says the Hebrew seer's unerring pen)
This mighty mass of earth, this solid globe,
Was cleft in twain,—*"divided"* east and west,
While then perhaps the deep Atlantic roll'd,—
Through the vast chasm, and laved the solid world;
And traces indisputable remain
Of this primaeval land now sunk and lost.—
The islands rising in our eastern main
Are but small fragments of this continent,
Whose two extremities were Newfoundland
And St. Helena.—One far in the north,
Where shivering seamen view with strange surprize
The guiding pole-star glittering o'er their heads;
The other near the southern tropic rears
Its head above the waves—Bermuda's isles,
Cape Verd, Canary, Britain, and the Azores,
With fam'd Hibernia, are but broken parts
Of some prodigious waste, which once sustain'd
Nations and tribes, of vanished memory,
Forests and towns, and beasts of every class,
Where navies now explore their briny way.

Leander.

Your sophistry, Eugenio, makes me smile;
The roving mind of man delights to dwell
On hidden things, merely because they're hid:
He thinks his knowledge far beyond all limit,
And boldly fathoms Nature's darkest haunts;—
But for uncertainties, your broken isles,

* *Gen.* X, 25.

Your northern Tartars, and your wandering Jews,
(The flimsy cobwebs of a sophist's brain)
Hear what the voice of history proclaims—
The Carthagenians, ere the Roman yoke
Broke their proud spirits, and enslaved them too,
For navigation were renowned as much
As haughty Tyre with all her hundred fleets,
Full many a league their venturous seamen sailed
Through streight Gibraltar, down the western shore
Of Africa, to the Canary isles:
By them called Fortunate; so Flaccus* sings.
Because eternal spring there clothes the fields
And fruits delicious bloom throughout the year.—
From voyaging here, this inference I draw,
Perhaps some barque with all her numerous crew
Falling to leeward of her destined port,
Caught by the eastern *Trade*, was hurried on
Before the unceasing blast to Indian isles,
Brazil, La Plata, or the coasts more south—
There stranded, and unable to return,
Forever from their native skies estranged
Doubtless they made these virgin climes their own,
And in the course of long revolving years
A numerous progeny from these arose,
And spread throughout the coasts—those whom we call
Brazilians, Mexicans, Peruvians rich,
The tribes of Chili, Patagon, and those
Who till the shores of Amazon's long stream.—
When first the power of Europe here attained,
Vast empires, kingdoms, cities, palaces
And polished nations stock'd the fertile land.
Who has not heard of Cusco, Lima, and
The town of Mexico—huge cities form'd
From Indian architecture; ere the arms
Of haughty Spain disturb'd the peaceful soil.—
But *here*, amid this northern dark domain

* *Hor. Epod.* 16.

No towns were seen to rise.—No arts were here;
The tribes unskill'd to raise the lofty mast,
Or force the daring prow thro' adverse waves,
Gazed on the pregnant soil, and craved alone
Life from the unaided genius of the ground,—
This indicates they were a different race;
From whom descended, 'tis not ours to say—
That power, no doubt, who furnish'd trees, and plants,
And animals to this vast continent,
Spoke into being man among the rest,—
But what a change is here!—what arts arise!
What towns and capitals! how commerce waves
Her gaudy flags, where silence reign'd before!

Acasto.

Speak, learned Eugenio, for I've heard you tell
The dismal story, and the cause that brought
The first adventurers to these western shores!
The glorious cause that urged our fathers first
To visit climes unknown, and wilder woods
Than e'er Tartarian or Norwegian saw,
And with fair culture to adorn a soil
That never felt industrious swain before.

Eugenio.

All this long story to rehearse, would tire;
Besides, the sun towards the west retreats,
Nor can the noblest theme retard his speed,
Nor loftiest verse—not that which sang the fall
Of Troy divine, and fierce Achilles' ire.—
Yet hear a part:—By persecution wronged,
And sacerdotal rage, our fathers came
From Europe's hostile shores to these abodes,
Here to enjoy a liberty in *faith*,
Secure from tyranny and base controul.
For this they left their country and their friends,
And plough'd the Atlantic wave in quest of peace;

And found new shores, and sylvan settlements,
And men, alike unknowing and unknown.
Hence, by the care of each adventurous *chief*
New governments (their wealth unenvied yet)
Were form'd on liberty and virtue's plan.
These searching out uncultivated tracts
Conceived new plans of towns, and capitals,
And spacious provinces—Why should I name
Thee, *Penn*, the Solon of our western lands;
Sagacious legislator, whom the world
Admires, long dead: an infant *colony*,
Nursed by thy care, now rises o'er the rest
Like that tall pyramid in Egypt's waste
Oe'r all the neighbouring piles, they also great.
Why should I name those heroes so well known,
Who peopled all the rest of Canada
To Georgia's farthest coasts, West Florida,
Or Apalachian mountains?—Yet what streams
Of blood were shed! what Indian hosts were slain,
Before the days of peace were quite restored!

Leander.

Yes, while they overturn'd the rugged soil
And swept the forests from the shaded plain
'Midst dangers, foes, and death, fierce Indian tribes
With vengeful malice arm'd, and black design,
Oft murdered, or dispersed, these colonies—
Encouraged, too, by Gallia's hostile sons,
A warlike race, who late their arms display'd,
At *Quebec*, *Montreal*, and farthest coasts
Of *Labrador*, or *Cape Breton*, where now
The British standard awes the subject host.
Here, those brave chiefs, who, lavish of their blood,
Fought in Britannia's cause, in battle fell!—
What heart but mourns the untimely fate of *Wolfe*,
Who, dying, conquered!—or what breast but beats
To share a fate like his, and die like him!

Acasto.

But why alone commemorate the dead,
And pass those glorious heroes by, who yet
Breathe the same air, and see the light with us?—
The dead, Leander, are but empty names,
And they who fall to-day the same to us
As they who fell ten centuries ago!—
Lost are they all that shined on earth before;
Rome's boldest champions in the dust are laid,
Ajax and great Achilles are no more,
And *Philip's* warlike son, an empty shade!—
A *Washington* among our sons of fame
Will rise conspicuous as the morning star
Among the inferior lights—
To distant wilds Virginia sent him forth—
With her brave sons he gallantly opposed
The bold invaders of his country's rights,
Where wild *Ohio* pours the mazy flood,
And mighty meadows skirt his subject streams.—
But now delighting in his elm tree's shade,
Where deep *Potowmac* laves the enchanting shore,
He prunes the tender vine, or bids the soil
Luxuriant harvests to the sun displayed.—
    Behold a different scene—not thus employed
Were *Cortez*, and *Pizarro*, pride of Spain,
Whom blood and murder only satisfied,
And all to glut their avarice and ambition!—

Eugenio.

Such is the curse, Acasto, where the soul
Humane is wanting—but we boast no feats
Of cruelty like Europe's murdering breed—
Our milder epithet is merciful,
And each American, true hearted, learns
To conquer, and to spare; for coward souls
Alone seek vengeance on a vanquished foe.
Gold, fatal gold, was the alluring bait
To Spain's rapacious tribes—hence rose the wars

From Chili to the Caribbean sea,
And Montezuma's Mexican domains:
More blest are we, with whose unenvied soil
Nature decreed no mingling gold to shine,
No flaming diamond, precious emerald,
No blushing sapphire, ruby, chrysolite,
Or jasper red—more noble riches flow
From agriculture, and the industrious swain,
Who tills the fertile vale, or mountain's brow
Content to lead a safe, a humble life,
Among his native hills, romantic shades
Such as the muse of Greece of old did feign,
Allured the Olympian gods from chrystal skies,
Envying such lovely scenes to mortal man.

Leander.

Long has the rural life been justly fam'd,
And bards of old their pleasing pictures drew
Of flowery meads, and groves, and gliding streams:
Hence, old Arcadia—wood-nymphs, satyrs, fauns;
And hence Elysium, fancied heaven below!—
Fair agriculture, not unworthy kings,
Once exercised the royal hand, or those
Whose virtues raised them to the rank of gods.
See old *Laertes** in his shepherd weeds
Far from his pompous throne and court august,
Digging the grateful soil, where round him rise,
Sons of the earth, the tall aspiring oaks,
Or orchards, boasting of more fertile boughs,
Laden with apples red, sweet scented peach,
Pear, cherry, apricot, or spungy plumb;
While through the glebe the industrious oxen draw
The earth-inverting plough.—Those Romans too,
Fabricius and Camillus, loved a life
Of neat simplicity and rustic bliss,

* *Hom. Odyss.* B. 24.

And from the noisy Forum hastening far,
From busy camps, and sycophants, and crowns,
'Midst woods and fields spent the remains of *life*,
Where full enjoyment still awaits the wise.

How grateful, to behold the harvests rise,
And mighty crops adorn the extended plains!—
Fair plenty smiles throughout, while lowing herds
Stalk o'er the shrubby hill or grassy mead,
Or at some shallow river slake their thirst.—
The *inclosure*, now, succeeds the shepherd's care,
Yet milk-white flocks adorn the well stock'd farm,
And court the attention of the industrious swain—
Their fleece rewards him well, and when the winds
Blow with a keener blast, and from the north
Pour mingled tempests through a sunless sky
(Ice, sleet, and rattling hail) secure he sits
Warm in his cottage, fearless of the storm,
Enjoying now the toils of milder moons,
Yet hoping for the spring.—Such are the joys,
And such the toils of those whom heaven hath bless'd
With souls enamoured of a country life.

Acasto.

Such are the visions of the rustic reign—
But this alone, the fountain of support,
Would scarce employ the varying mind of man;
Each seeks employ, and each a different way:
Strip Commerce of her sail, and men once more
Would be converted into savages—
No nation e'er grew social and refined
'Till Commerce first had wing'd the adventurous prow,
Or sent the slow-paced caravan, afar,
To waft their produce to some other clime,
And bring the wished exchange—thus came, of old,
Golconda's golden ore, and thus the wealth
Of *Ophir*, to the wisest of mankind.

Eugenio.

Great is the praise of Commerce, and the men
Deserve our praise, who spread the undaunted sail,
And traverse every sea—their dangers great,
Death still to combat in the unfeeling gale,
And every billow but a gaping grave:—
There, skies and waters, wearying on the eye,
For weeks and months no other prospect yield
But barren wastes, unfathomed depths, where not
The blissful haunt of human form is seen
To cheer the unsocial horrors of the way—
Yet all these bold designs to Science owe
Their rise and glory—Hail, fair Science! thou,
Transplanted from the eastern skies, dost bloom
In these blest regions—Greece and Rome no more
Detain the Muses on *Citheron's* brow,
Or old *Olympus*, crowned with waving woods,
Or *Haemus'* top, where once was heard the harp,
Sweet *Orpheus'* harp, that gained his cause below,
And pierced the souls of Orcus and his bride;
That hushed to silence by its voice divine
Thy melancholy waters, and the gales
O *Hebrus!* that o'er thy sad surface blow.—
No more the maids round Alpheus' waters stray,
Where he with *Arethusa's* stream doth mix,
Or where swift *Tiber* disembogues his waves
Into the Italian sea, so long unsung;
Hither they wing their way, the last, the best
Of countries, where the arts shall rise and grow,
And arms shall have their day—even now we boast
A *Franklin*, prince of all philosophy,
A genius piercing as the electric fire,
Bright as the lightning's flash, explained so well,
By him, the rival of Britannia's sage.*
This is the land of every joyous sound,
Of liberty and life, sweet liberty!

* Newton.

Without whose aid the noblest genius fails,
And Science irretrievably must die.

Leander.

But come, Eugenio, since we know the past—
What hinders to pervade with searching eye
The mystic scenes of dark futurity!
Say, shall we ask what empires yet must rise,
What kingdoms, powers and states, where now are seen
Mere dreary wastes and awful solitude,
Where Melancholy sits, with eye forlorn,
And time anticipates, when we shall spread
Dominion from the north, and south, and west,
Far from the Atlantic to Pacific shores,
And people half the convex of the main!—
A glorious theme!—but how shall mortals dare
To pierce the dark events of future years
And scenes unravel, only known to fate?

Acasto.

This might we do, if warmed by that bright coal
Snatch'd from the altar of cherubic fire
Which touched Isaiah's lips—or if the spirit
Of Jeremy and Amos, prophets old,
Might swell the heaving breast—I see, I see
Freedom's established reign; cities, and men,
Numerous as sands upon the ocean shore,
And empires rising where the sun descends!—
The *Ohio* soon shall glide by many a town
Of note; and where the *Mississippi* stream,
By forests shaded, now runs weeping on,
Nations shall grow, and states not less in fame
Than Greece and Rome of old!—we too shall boast
Our Scipio's, Solon's, Cato's, sages, chiefs
That in the lap of time yet dormant lie,
Waiting the joyous hour of life and light—
O snatch me hence, ye muses, to those days
When, through the veil of dark antiquity,

A race shall hear of us as things remote,
That blossomed in the morn of days—Indeed,
How could I weep that we exist so soon,
Just in the dawning of these mighty times,
Whose scenes are painting for eternity!
Dissentions that shall swell the trump of fame,
And ruin hovering o'er all monarchy!

Eugenio.

Nor shall these angry tumults here subside
Nor murder* cease, through all these provinces,
Till foreign crowns have vanished from our view
And dazzle here no more—no more presume
To awe the spirit of fair Liberty—
Vengeance must cut the thread—and Britain, sure
Will curse her fatal obstinacy for it!
Bent on the ruin of this injured country,
She will not listen to our humble prayers,
Though offered with submission:
Like vagabonds and objects of destruction,
Like those whom all mankind are sworn to hate,
She casts us off from her protection,
And will invite the nations round about,
Russians and Germans, slaves and savages,
To come and have a share in our perdition—
O cruel race, O unrelenting Britain,
Who bloody beasts will hire to cut our throats
Who war will wage with prattling innocence,
And basely murder unoffending women!—
Will stab their prisoners when they cry for quarter,
Will burn our towns, and from his lodging turn
The poor inhabitant to sleep in tempests!—
These will be wrongs, indeed, and all sufficient
To kindle up our souls to deeds of horror,
And give to every arm the nerves of *Sampson*—

* The English massacre at Boston, March 5th, 1770, is here more
particularly glanced at.

These are the men that fill the world with ruin,
And every region mourns their greedy sway,—
Not only for ambition——
But what are this world's goods, that *they* for them
Should exercise perpetual butchery?
What are these mighty riches we possess,
That they should send so far to plunder them—?—
Already have we felt their potent arm—
And ever since that inauspicious day,
When first Sir *Francis Bernard*
His ruffians planted at the *council door,*
And made the assembly room a home for vagrants,
And soldiers, rank and file—e'er since that day
This wretched land, that drinks its children's gore,
Has been a scene of tumult and confusion—!
Are there not evils in the world enough?
Are we so happy that they envy us?
Have we not toiled to satisfy their harpies,
Kings' deputies, that are insatiable;
Whose practice is to incense the royal mind
And make us despicable in his view?—

   Have we not all the evils to contend with
That, in this life, mankind are subject to,
Pain, sickness, poverty, and natural death—
But into every wound that nature gave
They will a dagger plunge, and make them mortal!

                    Leander.

Enough, enough!—such dismal scenes you paint,
I almost shudder at the recollection—
What! are they dogs that they would mangle us?—
Are these the men that come with base design
To rob the hive, and kill the industrious bee!—
To brighter skies I turn my ravished view,
And fairer prospects from the future draw—
Here independent power shall hold her sway,
And public virtue warm the patriot breast:

No traces shall remain of tyranny,
And laws, a pattern to the world beside,
Be here enacted first.—

Acasto.

And when a train of rolling years are past,
(So sung the exiled seer in Patmos isle)
A new Jerusalem, sent down from heaven,
Shall grace our happy earth,—perhaps this land,
Whose ample bosom shall receive, though late,
Myriads of saints, with their immortal king,
To live and reign on earth a thousand years,
Thence called *Millennium.* Paradise anew
Shall flourish, by no second Adam lost,
No dangerous tree with deadly fruit shall grow,
No tempting serpent to allure the soul
From native innocence.—A *Canaan* here,
Another *Canaan* shall excel the old,
And from a fairer Pisgah's top be seen.
No thistle here, nor thorn, nor briar shall spring,
Earth's curse before: the lion and the lamb
In mutual friendship linked, shall browse the shrub,
And timorous deer with softened tygers stray
O'er mead, or lofty hill, or grassy plain;
Another Jordan's stream shall glide along,
And Siloah's brook in circling eddies flow:
Groves shall adorn their verdant banks, on which
The happy people, free from toils and death,
Shall find secure repose. No fierce disease,
No fevers, slow consumption, ghastly plague,
(Fate's ancient ministers) again proclaim
Perpetual war with man: fair fruits shall bloom,
Fair to the eye, and sweeter to the taste;
Nature's loud storms be hushed, and seas no more
Rage hostile to mankind—and, worse than all,
The fiercer passions of the human breast
Shall kindle up to deeds of death no more,
But all subside in universal peace.—

——Such days the world,
And such AMERICA at last shall have
When ages, yet to come, have run their round,
And future years of bliss alone remain.

(A. D. 1775) [W. 1771]

DISCOVERY.

Six thousand years in these dull regions pass'd
'Tis time, you'll say, we knew their bounds at last,
Knew to what skies our setting suns retire,
And where the wintry suns expend their fire;
What land to land protracts the varied scene,
And what extended oceans roll between;
What worlds exist beneath *antarctic* skies,
And from *Pacific* waves what verdant islands rise.

In vain did Nature shore from shore divide:
Art formed a passage and her waves defied:
When his bold plan the master pilot drew
Dissevered worlds stept forward at the view,
And lessening still the intervening space.
Disclosed new millions of the human race.

Proud even of toil, succeeding ages joined
New seas to vanquish, and new worlds to find;
Age following age still farther from the shore,
Found some new wonder that was hid before,
'Till launched at length, with avarice doubly bold,
Their hearts expanding as the world grew old,
Some to be rich, and some to be renowned,
The earth they rifled, and explored it round.

Ambitious Europe! polished in thy pride,
Thine was the art that toil to toil allied
Thine was the gift, to trace each heavenly sphere,
And seize its beams, to serve ambition here:
Hence, fierce *Pizarro* stock'd a world with graves,
Hence *Montezuma* left a race of slaves—
Which project suited best with heaven's decree
To force new doctrines, or to leave them free?—

Religion only feigned to claim a share,
Their riches, not their souls, employed your care—
    Alas! how few of all that daring train
That seek new worlds embosomed in the main,
How few have sailed on virtue's nobler plan,
How few with motives worthy of a man!—
While through the deep-sea waves we saw them go
Where'er they found a *man* they made a foe;
Superior only by superior art,
Forgot the social virtues of the heart,
Forgetting still, where'er they madly ran,
That sacred friendship binds mankind to man,
Fond of exerting power untimely shewn,
The momentary triumph all their own!
Met on the wrecks and ravages of time,
They left no native master of their clime,
His trees, his towns, with hardened front they claimed,
Seized every region that a despot named
And forced the oath that bound him to obey
Some prince unknown, ten thousand miles away.

    Slaves to their passions, man's imperious race,
Born for contention, find no resting place,
And the vain mind, bewildered and perplext,
Makes this world wretched to enjoy the next.
Tired of the scenes that Nature made their own,
They rove to conquer what remains unknown:
Avarice, undaunted, claims whate'er she sees,
Surmounts earth's circle, and foregoes all ease;
Religion, bolder, sends some *sacred* chief
To bend the nations to her own belief.
To their vain standard Europe's sons invite,
Who hold no other *world* can think aright.
Behold their varied tribes, with self applause,
First in religion, liberty, and laws,
And while they bow to cruelty and blood,
Condemn the Indian with his milder god—
Ah, race to justice, truth, and honour blind,
Are thy convictions to convert mankind—!

Vain pride—convince them that your own are just,
Or leave them happy, as you found them first.
    What charm is seen through Europe's realms of strife
That adds new blessings to the savage life?—
On them warm suns with equal splendour shine,
Their each domestic pleasure equals thine,
Their native groves as soft a bloom display,
As self-contented roll their lives away,
And the gay soul, in fancy's visions blest,
Leaves to the care of chance her heaven of rest.—
    What are the arts that rise on Europe's plan
But arts destructive to the bliss of man?
What are all wars, where'er the marks you trace,
But the sad records of our world's disgrace?
Reason degraded from her tottering throne,
And precepts, called divine, observed by none.
    Blest in their distance from that bloody scene,
Why spread the sail to pass the gulphs between?—
If winds can waft to ocean's utmost verge,
And there new islands and new worlds emerge—
If wealth, or war, or science bid thee roam,
Ah, leave religion and thy laws at home,
Leave the free native to enjoy his store,
Nor teach destructive arts, unknown before—
Woes of their own those new found worlds invade,
There, too, fierce passions the weak soul degrade,
Invention there has winged the unerring dart,
There the swift arrow vibrates to the heart,
Revenge and death contending bosoms share,
And pining envy claims her subjects there.—
Are these too few?—then see despotic power
Spends on a throne of logs her busy hour.
Hard by, and half ambitious to ascend,
Priests, interceding with the gods, attend—
Atoning victims at their shrines they lay,
Their crimson knives tremendous rites display,
Or the proud despot's gore remorseless shed,
Through life detested, or adored when dead,

    Born to be wretched, search this globe around,
Dupes to a few the race of man is found!
Seek some new world in some new climate plac'd,
Some gay *Ta-ia** on the watery waste,
Though Nature clothes in all her bright array,
Some proud tormentor steals her charms away:
Howe'er she smiles beneath those milder skies,
Though men decay the monarch never dies!
Howe'er the groves, howe'er the gardens bloom,
A *monarch* and a *priest* is still their doom!

[w. 1772]   1786

A POLITICAL LITANY.

Libera Nos, Domine.—DELIVER US O LORD, *not only from British Dependence, but also,*

FROM a junto that labour with absolute power,
Whose schemes disappointed have made them look sour,
From the lords of the council, who fight against freedom,
Who still follow on where delusion shall lead them.

From the group at St. James's, who slight our petitions,
And fools that are waiting for further submissions—
From a nation whose manners are rough and severe,
From scoundrels and rascals,—do keep us all clear.

From pirates sent out by command of the king
To murder and plunder, but never to swing;
From *Wallace* and *Greaves*, and *Vipers* and *Roses*,†
Who, if heaven pleases, we'll give bloody noses.

From the valiant *Dunmore*, with his crew of banditti,
Who plunder Virginians at *Williamsburg* city,

* Commonly called Otaheite, an Island in the Southern Pacific Ocean, noted for the natural civilization of its inhabitants.

† Captains and ships in the British navy, then employed on the American coast.

From hot-headed *Montague*, mighty to swear,
The little fat man, with his pretty white hair.

From bishops in Britain, who butchers are grown,
From slaves, that would die for a smile from the throne,
From assemblies that vote against *Congress proceedings*,
(Who now see the fruit of their stupid misleadings.)

From *Tryon* the mighty, who flies from our city,
And swelled with importance disdains the committee:
(But since he is pleased to proclaim us his foes,
What the devil care we where the devil he goes.)

From the caitiff, lord *North*, who would bind us in chains,
From a royal king Log, with his tooth-full of brains,
Who dreams, and is certain (when taking a nap)
He has conquered our lands, as they lay on his map.

From a kingdom that bullies, and hectors, and swears,
We send up to heaven our wishes and prayers
That we, disunited, may freemen be still,
And Britain go on—to be damned if she will.

New York, June 1775   1775

TO THE AMERICANS,

On the Rumoured Approach of the Hessian Forces, Waldeckers, &c. (Published 1775)

The blast of death! the infernal guns prepare—
"Rise with the storm and all its dangers share."

Occasioned by General Gage's Proclamation that the
Provinces were in a state of Rebellion, and out of the
King's protection.

REBELS you are—the British champion cries—
Truth, stand thou forth!—and tell the wretch, He lies:—
Rebels!—and see this mock imperial *lord*

Already threats *these rebels* with the CORD.*
The hour draws nigh, the glass is almost run,
When truth will shine, and ruffians be undone;
When this base miscreant will forbear to sneer,
And curse his taunts and bitter insults, *here*.

If to controul the cunning of a knave,
Freedom respect, and scorn the name of SLAVE;
If to protest against a tyrant's laws,
And arm for vengeance in a righteous cause,
Be deemed REBELLION—'tis a harmless thing:
This bug-bear name, like death, *has lost its sting*.

AMERICANS! at freedom's fane adore!
But trust to Britain, and her flag, no more;
The *generous genius* of their isle has fled,
And left a mere impostor in his stead.

If conquered, rebels (their Scotch records show)
Receive no mercy from the *parent* foe; †
Nay, even the grave, that friendly haunt of peace,
(Where Nature gives the woes of man to cease,)
Vengeance will search—and buried corpses there
Be raised, to feast the vultures of the air—
Be hanged on gibbets!—such a war they wage—
Such are the devils that swell our souls with rage!—

If Britain conquers, help us, heavens, to fly:
Lend us your wings, ye ravens of the sky;—
If Britain conquers—we exist no more;
These lands will redden with their children's gore,
Who, turned to slaves, their fruitless toils will moan,
Toils in these fields that once they called their own!

To arms! to arms! and let the murdering sword
Decide, who best deserves the HANGMAN'S CORD:
Nor think the hills of Canada too bleak
When desperate Freedom is the prize you seek;
For *that*, the call of honour bids you go

* See, in the records of American History, about this time, a letter from Gen. Gage to Gen. Washington; with the answer of the latter.
† After the battle of Colloden: See Smollett's History of England, 1745.

O'er frozen lakes and mountains wrapt in snow:
No toils should daunt the nervous and the bold,
They scorn all heat or wave-congealing cold.—
   Haste!—to your tents in iron fetters bring
These SLAVES, that serve a tyrant, and a king;
So just, so virtuous is your cause, I say,
Hell must prevail, if Britain gains the day.

1775

ON A HESSIAN DEBARKATION.

1776.

There is a book, tho' not a book of rhymes,
Where truth severe records a nation's crimes;—
To check such monarchs as with brutal might
Wanton in blood, and trample on the right.

REJOICE, O Death!—Britannia's tyrant sends
From German plains his myriads to our shore;
The Caledonian with the English joined:—
Bring them, ye winds, but waft them back no more.

To these far climes with stately step they come,
Resolved all prayers, all prowess to defy;
Smit with the love of countries not their own,
They come, indeed, to conquer—not to die.

In the slow breeze (I hear their funeral song,)
The dance of ghosts the infernal tribes prepare:
To hell's dark mansions haste, ye abandoned throng,
Drinking from German sculls old *Odin's* beer.

From dire Cesarea,* forced, these slaves of kings,
Quick, let them take their way on eagle's wings:
To thy strong posts, Manhattan's isle, repair,
To meet the vengeance that awaits them there!—

[w. 1776]   1795

* The old Roman name of Jersey.

AMERICA INDEPENDENT;

And Her Everlasting Deliverance from British Tyranny and Oppression.

First published in Philadelphia, by Mr. Robert Bell, in 1778.

To him who would relate the story right,
A mind supreme should dictate, or indite.—
  Yes!—justly to record the tale of fame,
A muse from heaven should touch the soul with flame,
Some powerful spirit, in superior lays,
Should tell the conflicts of these stormy days!

'Tis done! and Britain for her madness sighs—
Take warning, tyrants, and henceforth be wise,
If o'er mankind *man* gives you regal sway,
Take not the rights of human kind away.
  When God from chaos gave this world to be,
Man then he formed, and formed him to be free,
In his own image stampt the favourite race—
How darest thou, tyrant, the fair stamp deface!
When on mankind you fix your abject chains,
No more the image of that God remains;
O'er a dark scene a darker shade is drawn,
His work dishonoured, and our glory gone!
  When first Britannia sent her hostile crew
To these far shores, to ravage and subdue,
We thought them gods, and almost seemed to say
No ball could pierce them, and no dagger slay—
Heavens! what a blunder—half our fears were vain;
These hostile *gods* at length have quit the plain,
On neighbouring isles the storm of war they shun,
Happy, thrice happy, if not quite undone.—
  Yet soon, in dread of some impending woe,
Even from these *islands* shall these ruffians go—
This be their doom, in vengeance for the slain,
To pass their days in poverty and pain;

For such base triumphs, be it still their lot
To triumph only o'er the rebel *Scot*,
And to their insect isle henceforth confined
No longer lord it o'er the human kind.—
   But, by the fates, who still prolong their stay,
And gather vengeance to conclude their day,
Yet, ere they go, the angry Muse shall tell
The treasured woes that in her bosom swell:—
   Proud, fierce, and bold, O Jove! who would not laugh
To see these bullies worshipping a *calf:*
But they are *slaves* who spurn at Reason's rules;
And men once slaves, are soon transformed to fools.—
   To recommend what monarchies have done,
They bring, for witness, David and his son;
How one was brave, the other just and wise,
And hence our plain Republics they despise;
But mark how oft, to gratify their pride,
The people suffered, and the people died;
Though one was wise, and one Goliah slew,
Kings are the choicest curse that man e'er knew!
   Hail, worthy Briton!—how enlarged your fame;
How great your glory, terrible your name;
"Queen of the isles, and empress of the main,"—
Heaven grant you all these mighty things again;
But first insure the gaping crowd below
That you less cruel, and more just may grow:
If fate, vindictive for the sins of man,
Had favour shewn to your infernal plan,
How would your nation have exulted here,
And scorned the widow's sigh, the orphan's tear!
How had your prince, of all bad men the worst,
Laid worth and virtue prostrate in the dust!
A second *Sawney** had he shone to-day,
A world subdued, and murder but his play;
How had that prince, contemning right or law,
Glutted with blood his foul, voracious maw:

---

* Alexander THE GREAT.

In him we see the depths of baseness joined,
Whate'er disgraced the dregs of human kind;
Cain, Nimrod, Nero—fiends in human guise,
Herod, Domitian—these in judgment rise,
And, envious of his deeds, I hear them say
None but a GEORGE could be more vile than they.

  Swoln though he was with wealth, revenge, and pride,
How could he dream that heaven was on his side—
Did he not see, when so decreed by fate,
They placed the crown upon his royal pate,
Did he not see the richest jewel fall—*
Dire was the omen, and astonished all—

  That gem no more shall brighten and adorn;
No more that gem by British kings be worn,
Or swell to wonted heights of fair renown
The fading glories of their boasted crown.

  Yet he to arms, and war, and blood inclined,
(A fair-day warrior with a feeble mind,
Fearless, while others meet the shock of fate,
And dare that death, which clips his thread too late,)
He to the fane (O hypocrite!) did go,
While not an angel there but was his foe,
There did he kneel, and sigh, and sob, and pray,
Yet not to lave his thousand sins away,
Far other motives swayed his spotted soul;
'Twas not for those the secret sorrow stole
Down his pale cheek—'twas vengeance and despair
Dissolved his eye, and planted sorrow there—
How could he hope to bribe the impartial sky
By his base prayers, and mean hypocrisy—
Heaven still is just, and still abhors all crimes,
Not acts like George, the Nero of our times—
What were his prayers—his prayers could be no more
Than a thief's wishes to recruit his store:—
Such prayers could never reach the worlds above;
They were but curses in the ear of Jove;—

* A real event of that day: see REMEMBRANCER of 1777.—

You prayed that conquest might your arms attend,
And crush that freedom virtue did defend,
That the fierce Indian, rousing from his rest,
Might these new regions with his flames invest,
With scalps and tortures aggravate our woe,
And to the infernal world dismiss your foe.

No mines of gold our fertile country yields,
But mighty harvests crown the loaded fields,
Hence, trading far, we gained the golden prize,
Which, though our own, bewitched their greedy eyes—
For that they ravaged India's climes before,
And carried death to Asia's utmost shore—
Clive was your envied slave, in avarice bold—
He mowed down nations for his dearer gold;
The fatal gold could give no true content,
He mourned his murders, and to *Tophet* went.

Led on by lust of lucre and renown,
Burgoyne came marching with his thousands down,
High were his thoughts, and furious his career,
Puffed with self confidence, and pride severe,
Swoln with the idea of his future deeds,
Onward to ruin each advantage leads:
Before his hosts his heaviest curses flew,
And conquered worlds rose hourly to his view:
His wrath, like Jove's, could bear with no controul,
His words bespoke the mischief in his soul;
To *fight* was not this general's only trade,
He shined in writing, and his wit displayed—
To awe the more with titles of command
He told of *forts he ruled* in Scottish land;—
Queen's *colonel* as he was, he did not know
That thorns and *thistles*, mixed with honours, grow;
In Britain's senate, though he held a place,
All did not save him from one long disgrace,
One stroke of fortune that convinced them all
That *men* could conquer, and *lieutenants* fall.

Foe to the rights of man, proud plunderer, say
Had conquest crowned you on that mighty day

When you, to GATES, with sorrow, rage, and shame
Resigned your conquests, honours, arms, and fame,
When at his feet Britannia's wreathes you threw,
And the sun sickened at a sight so new;
Had you been victor—what a waste of woe!
What souls had vanished to where souls do go!
What dire distress had marked your fatal way,
What deaths on deaths disgraced that dismal day!
   Can laurels flourish in a soil of blood,
Or on those laurels can fair honours bud—
Cursed be that wretch who murder makes his trade,
Cursed be all wars that e'er ambition made!
   What murdering *tory* now relieves your grief,
Or plans new conquests for his favourite chief;
Designs still dark employ that ruffian race,
Beasts of your choosing, and our own disgrace,
So vile a crew the world ne'er saw before,
And grant, ye pitying heavens, it may no more:
If ghosts from hell infest our poisoned air,
Those ghosts have entered their base bodies here
Murder and blood is still their dear delight—
Scream round their roofs, ye ravens of the night!
Whene'er they wed, may demons and despair,
And grief and woe, and blackest night be there;
Fiends leagued from hell the nuptial lamp display,
Swift to perdition light them on their way,
Round the wide world their devilish squadrons chace,
To find no realm, that grants one resting place.
   Far to the north, on Scotland's utmost end
An isle there lies, the haunt of every fiend,
No shepherds there attend their bleating flocks
But withered witches rove among the rocks;
'Shrouded in ice, the blasted mountains shew
Their cloven heads, to daunt the seas below;
The lamp of heaven in his diurnal race
There scarcely deigns to unveil his radiant face,
Or if one day he circling treads the sky
He views this island with an angry eye,

Or ambient fogs their broad, moist wings expand
Damp his bright ray, and cloud the infernal land;
The blackening winds incessant storms prolong,
Dull as their night, and dreary as my song;
When stormy winds and gales refuse to blow,
Then from the dark sky drives the unpitying snow;
When drifting snows from iron clouds forbear,
Then down the hail-stones rattle through the air—
There screeching owls, and screaming vultures rest
And not a tree adorns its barren breast;
No peace, no rest the elements bestow,
But seas forever rage, and storms forever blow.
   There, LOYALS, there, with loyal hearts retire,
There pitch your tents, and kindle *there* your fire;
There desert Nature will her stings display,
And fiercest hunger on your vitals prey,
And with yourselves let *John Burgoyne* retire
To reign the monarch, whom your hearts admire.
   Britain, at last to arrest your lawless hand,
Rises the genius of a generous land,
Our injured rights bright Gallia's prince defends,
And from this hour that prince and we are friends,
Feuds, long upheld, are vanished from our view.
Once we were foes—but for the sake of you—
Britain, aspiring Briton, now must bend—
Can she at once with France and us contend,
When we alone, remote from foreign aid,
Her armies captured, and distressed her trade—
Britain and we no more in combat join,
No more, as once, in every sea combine;
Dead is that friendship which did mutual burn,
Fled is the sceptre, never to return;
By sea and land, perpetual foes we meet,
Our cause more honest, and our hearts as great;
Lost are these regions to Britannia's reign,
Nor need these strangers of their loss complain,
Since all, that *here* with greedy eyes they view,
From our own toil, to wealth and empire grew:—

Our hearts are ravished from our former queen
Far as the ocean God hath placed between,
They strive in vain to join this mighty mass,
Torn by convulsions from its native place.
As well might men to flaming *Hecla* join
The huge high *Alps*, or towering *Appenine;*
In vain they send their half-commissioned tribe,
And whom they cannot conquer, strive to bribe;
Their pride and madness burst our union chain,
Nor shall the unwieldy mass unite again.

Nor think that France sustains our cause alone;
With gratitude her helping hand we own,
But hear, ye nations—Truth herself can say
We bore the heat and danger of the day:
She calmly viewed the tumult from afar,
We braved each insult, and sustained the war:
Oft drove the foe, or forced their hosts to yield.
Or left them, more than once, a dear bought field—
'Twas then, at last, on Jersey plains distrest,
We swore to seek the mountains of the west,
There a free empire for our seed obtain,
A terror to the slaves that might remain.

Peace you demand, and vainly wish to find
Old leagues renewed, and strength once more combined—
Yet shall not all your base dissembling art
Deceive the tortures of a bleeding heart—
Yet shall not all your mingled prayers that rise
Wash out your crimes, or bribe the avenging skies;
Full many a corpse lies mouldering on the plain
That ne'er shall see its little brood again:
See, yonder lies, all breathless, cold, and pale,
Drenched in her gore, *Lavinia* of the vale;*
The cruel Indian seized her life away,
As the next morn began her bridal day!—
This *deed* alone our just revenge would claim,
Did not ten thousand more your sons defame.

* Miss *M'Crea*. See histories of the revolutionary war,

Returned, a captive, to my native shore,
How changed I find those scenes that pleased before!
How changed those groves where fancy loved to stray,
When spring's young blossoms bloom'd along the way;
From every eye distils the frequent tear,
From every mouth some doleful tale I hear!
Some mourn a father, brother, husband, friend:
Some mourn, imprisoned in their native land,
In sickly ships what numerous hosts confined
At once their lives and liberties resigned:
In dreary dungeons woeful scenes have passed,
Long in the historian's page the tale will last,
As long as spring renews the flowery wood,
As long as breezes curl the yielding flood!—
Some sent to India's sickly climes afar,
To dig, with slaves, for buried diamonds there,
There left to sicken in a land of woe
Where o'er scorched hills infernal breezes blow,
Whose every blast some dire contagion brings,
Fevers or death on its destructive wings,
'Till fate relenting, its last arrows drew,
Brought death to them, and infamy to you.
Pests of mankind! remembrance shall recall
And paint these horrors to the view of all;
Heaven has not turned to its own works a foe
Nor left to monsters these fair realms below,
Else had your arms more wasteful vengeance spread,
And these gay plains been dyed a deeper red.—
O'er Britain's isle a thousand woes impend,
Too weak to conquer, govern, or defend,
To liberty she holds pretended claim—
The substance we enjoy, and they the name;
Her prince, surrounded by a host of slaves,
Still claims dominion o'er the vagrant waves:
Such be his claims o'er all the world beside,—
An empty nothing—madness, rage and pride.
From Europe's realms fair freedom has retired,
And even in Britain has the spark expired—

Sigh for the change your haughty empire feels,
Sigh for the doom that no disguise conceals!
Freedom no more shall Albion's cliffs survey;
Corruption there has centered all her sway,
Freedom disdains her honest head to rear,
Or herd with nobles, kings, or princes there;
She shuns their gilded spires and domes of state,
Resolved, O Virtue, at thy shrine to wait:
'Midst savage woods and wilds she dares to stray,
And bids uncultured nature bloom more gay.
  She is that glorious and immortal sun,
Without whose ray this world would be undone,
A mere dull chaos, sunk in deepest night,
An abject something, void of form and light,
Of reptiles, worst in rank, the dire abode,
Perpetual mischief, and the dragon's brood.
  Let Turks and Russians glut their fields with blood,
Again let Britain dye the Atlantic flood,
Let all the east adore the sanguine wreathe
And gain new glories from the trade of death—
America! the works of peace be thine,
Thus shalt thou gain a triumph more divine—
To thee belongs a second golden reign,
Thine is the empire o'er a peaceful main;
Protect the rights of human kind below
Crush the proud tyrant who becomes their foe,
And future times shall own your struggles blest,
And future years enjoy perpetual rest.
  American! revenge your country's wrongs;
To you the honour of this deed belongs,
Your arms did once this sinking land sustain,
And saved those climes where Freedom yet must reign—
Your bleeding soil this ardent task demands,
Expel yon' thieves from these polluted lands,
Expect no peace till haughty Britain yields,
'Till humbled Britons quit your ravaged fields—
Still to the charge that routed foe returns,
The war still rages, and the battle burns—

No dull debates, or tedious counsels know,
But rush at once, embodied, on your foe;
With hell-born spite a seven years war they wage,
The pirate *Goodrich*, and the ruffian *Gage*,
Your injured country groans while yet they stay,
Attend her groans, and force their hosts away;
Your mighty wrongs the tragic muse shall trace,
Your gallant deeds shall fire a future race;
To you may kings and potentates appeal,
You may the doom of jarring nations seal;
A glorious empire rises, bright and new!
Firm be the structure, and must rest on you!
Fame o'er the mighty *pile* expands her wings,
Remote from princes, bishops, lords, and kings,
Those fancied gods, who, famed through every shore,
Mankind have fashioned, and like fools, adore.—
Here yet shall heaven the joys of peace bestow,
While through our soil the streams of plenty flow,
And o'er the main we spread the trading sail,
Wafting the produce of the rural vale.

[w. 1778]

On the new

AMERICAN FRIGATE ALLIANCE.

AS Neptune traced the azure main
That owned, so late, proud Britain's reign,
A floating pile approached his car,
The scene of terror and of war.

As nearer still the monarch drew
(Her starry flag displayed to view)
He asked a Triton of his train
"What flag was this that rode the main?

"A ship of such a gallant mien
"This many a day I have not seen,

"To no mean power can she belong,
"So swift, so warlike, stout, and strong.

"See, how she mounts the foaming wave—
"Where other ships would find a grave,
"Majestic, aweful, and serene,
"She sails the ocean, like its queen.—

"Great monarch of the hoary deep,
"Whose trident awes the waves to sleep,
(Replied a Triton of his train)
"This ship, that stems the western main,

"To those new, rising *States* belongs,
"Who, in resentment of their wrongs,
"Oppose proud Britain's tyrant sway,
"And combat her, by land and sea.

"This pile, of such superior fame,
"From their strict *union* takes her name,
"For them she cleaves the briny tide,
"While terror marches by her side.

"When she unfurls her flowing sails,
"Undaunted by the fiercest gales,
"In dreadful pomp she ploughs the main,
"While adverse tempests rage in vain.

"When she displays her gloomy *tier*,
"The boldest foes congeal with fear,
"And, owning her superior might,
"Seek their best safety in their flight.

"But when she pours the dreadful blaze,
"And thunder from her cannon plays,
"The bursting flash, that wings the ball,
"Compells those foes to *strike*, or fall.

"Though she, with her triumphant crew,
"Might to their fate all foes pursue;
"Yet, faithful to the land that bore,
"She stays, to guard her native shore.

"Though she might make the cruisers groan
"That sail within the torrid zone,
"She kindly lends a nearer aid,
"Annoys them here, and guards the trade.

"Now, traversing the eastern main,
"She greets the shores of France and Spain;
"Her gallant flag, displayed to view,
"Invites the old world to the new.

"This task atchieved, behold her go
"To seas congealed with ice and snow,
"To either tropic, and the *line*,
"Where suns with endless fervour shine.

"Not, Argo, on thy decks were found
"Such hearts of brass, as here abound;
"They for their golden fleece did fly,
"These sail—to vanquish tyranny."—

(1778)   1786

On the Death
OF CAPTAIN NICHOLAS BIDDLE,

COMMANDER OF THE RANDOLPH FRIGATE, BLOWN UP
NEAR BARBADOES, 1776.

WHAT distant thunders rend the skies,
What clouds of smoke in columns rise,
    What means this dreadful roar?
Is from his base *Vesuvius* thrown,
Is sky-topt *Atlas* tumbled down,
    Or *Etna's* self no more!

Shock after shock torments my ear;
And lo!—two hostile ships appear,
　　Red lightnings round them glow:
The *Yarmouth* boasts of sixty-four,
The *Randolph* thirty-two—no more—
　　And will she fight this foe!

The *Randolph* soon on Stygian streams
Shall coast along the land of dreams,
　　The islands of the dead!
But Fate, that parts them on the deep,
May save the Briton yet to weep
　　His days of victory fled.

Say, who commands that dismal blaze,
Where yonder starry streamer plays?
　　Does *Mars* with *Jove* engage!
'Tis Biddle wings those angry fires,
Biddle, whose bosom *Jove* inspires,
　　With more than mortal rage.

Tremendous flash!—and hark, the ball
Drives through old *Yarmouth*, flames and all;
　　Her bravest sons expire;
Did Mars himself approach so nigh,
Even Mars, without disgrace, might fly
　　The *Randolph's* fiercer fire.

The Briton views his mangled crew,
"And shall we strike to *thirty-two?*—
　　(Said Hector, stained with gore)
"Shall Britain's flag to *these* descend—
"Rise, and the glorious conflict end,
　　"Britons, I ask no more!"

He spoke—they charged their cannon round,
Again the vaulted heavens resound,
　　The *Randolph* bore it all,

Then fixed her pointed cannons true—
Away the unwieldly vengeance flew;
   Britons, the warriors fall.

The *Yarmouth* saw, with dire dismay,
Her wounded hull, shrouds shot away,
   Her boldest heroes dead—
She saw amidst her floating slain
The conquering *Randolph* stem the main—
   She saw, she turned—and fled!

That hour, blest chief, had she been thine,
Dear *Biddle*, had the powers divine
   Been kind as thou were brave;
But Fate, who doomed thee to expire,
Prepared an arrow, tipt with fire,
   And marked a watery grave,

And in that hour, when conquest came,
Winged at his ship a pointed flame,
   That not even *he* could shun—
The battle ceased, the Yarmouth fled,
The bursting Randolph ruin spread,
   And left her task undone!

1781

GEORGE THE THIRD'S SOLILOQUY.

WHAT mean these dreams, and hideous forms that rise
Night after night, tormenting to my eyes—
No real foes these horrid shapes can be,
But thrice as much they vex and torture me.
   How cursed is he—how doubly cursed am I—
Who lives in pain, and yet who dares not die;
To him no joy this world of Nature brings,
In vain the wild rose blooms, the daisy springs.
Is this a prelude to some new disgrace,
Some baleful omen to my name and race!—

It may be so—ere mighty Caesar died
Presaging Nature felt his doom, and sighed;
A bellowing voice through midnight groves was heard,
And threatening ghosts at dusk of eve appeared—
Ere Brutus fell, to adverse fates a prey,
His evil genius met him on the way,
And so may mine!—but who would yield so soon
A prize, some luckier hour may make my own?
Shame seize my crown ere such a deed be mine—
No—to the last my squadrons shall combine,
And slay my foes, while foes remain to slay,
Or *heaven* shall grant me one successful day.
    Is there a robber close in Newgate hemmed,
Is there a cut-throat, fettered and condemned?
Haste, loyal slaves, to George's standard come,
Attend his lectures when you hear the drum;
Your chains I break—for better days prepare,
Come out, my friends, from prison and from care,
Far to the west I plan your desperate sway,
There 'tis no sin to ravage, burn, and slay.
There, without fear, your bloody aims pursue,
And shew mankind what English thieves can do.
    That day, when first I mounted to the throne,
I swore to let all foreign foes alone.
Through love of peace to terms did I advance,
And made, they say, a shameful league with France.
But different scenes rise horrid to my view,
I charged my hosts to plunder and subdue—
At first, indeed, I thought short wars to wage
And sent some jail-birds to be led by *Gage*,
For 'twas but right, that those we marked for slaves
Should be reduced by cowards, fools, and knaves;
Awhile directed by his feeble hand,
Whose *troops* were kicked and pelted through the land,
Or starved in Boston, cursed the unlucky hour
They left their dungeons for that fatal shore.
    France aids them now, a desperate game I play,
And hostile Spain will do the same, they say;

My armies vanquished, and my heroes fled,
My people murmuring, and my commerce dead,
My shattered navy pelted, bruised, and clubbed,
By Dutchmen bullied, and by Frenchmen drubbed,
My name abhorred, my nation in disgrace,
How should I act in such a mournful case!
My hopes and joys are vanished with my coin,
My ruined army, and my lost Burgoyne!
What shall I do—confess my labours vain,
Or whet my tusks, and to the charge again!
But where's my force—my choicest troops are fled,
Some thousands crippled, and a myriad dead—
If I were owned the boldest of mankind,
And hell with all her flames inspired my mind,
Could I at once with Spain and France contend,
And fight the *rebels* on the world's green end?—
The pangs of *parting* I can ne'er endure,
Yet *part* we must, and part to meet no more!
Oh! blast this *Congress*, blast each upstart STATE,
On whose commands ten thousand captains wait;
From various climes that dire *Assembly* came,
True to their trust, as hostile to my fame,
'Tis these, ah these, have ruined half my sway,
Disgraced my arms, and led my slaves astray—
Cursed be the day, when first I saw the sun,
Cursed be the hour, when I these wars begun:
The fiends of darkness then possessed my mind,
And powers unfriendly to the human kind.
To wasting grief, and sullen rage a prey,
To *Scotland's* utmost verge I'll take my way,
There with eternal storms due concert keep
And while the billows rage, as fiercely weep—
Ye highland lads, my rugged fate bemoan,
Assist me with one sympathizing groan,
For late I find the nations are my foes,
I must submit, and that with bloody nose,
Or, like our James, fly basely from the state,
Or share, what still is worse—old *Charles's* fate.   1779

THE
BRITISH PRISON SHIP
Written 1780.*

CANTO I. *The* CAPTURE.

ASSIST me, CLIO! while in verse I tell
The dire misfortunes that a ship befell,
Which outward bound, to St. Eustatia's shore,
Death and disaster through the billows bore.

FROM Philadelphia's crowded port she came;
For there the builder plann'd her lofty frame,
With wond'rous skill, and excellence of art
He form'd, dispos'd, and order'd every part,
With joy beheld the stately fabric rise
To a stout bulwark of stupendous size,
'Till launch'd at last, capacious of the freight,
He left her to the Pilots, and her fate.

FIRST from her depths the tapering masts ascend,
On whose firm bulk the transverse yards depend,
By shrouds and stays secur'd from side to side
Trees grew on trees, suspended o'er the tide,
Firm to the yards extended, broad and vast
They hung the sails susceptive of the blast,
Far o'er the prow the lengthy bowsprit lay,
Supporting on the extreme the taught Gib-stay,
Twice ten six pounders at their port holes plac'd
And rang'd in rows, stood hostile in the waist:
Thus all prepar'd, impatient for the seas,
She left her station with no adverse breeze,
This her first outset from her native shore,
To sea a stranger, and untry'd before.

FROM the bright radiance that his glories spread
Ere from the east gay Phoebus lifts his head,
From the sweet morn, a kindred name she won,
AURORA call'd, the offspring of the sun,

* Text from the Edition of 1786. [Ed.]

Whose form projecting, the broad prow displays,
Far glittering o'er the wave, a mimic blaze.
   THE gay ship now, in all her pomp and pride,
With sails expanded, flew along the tide;
'Twas thy deep stream, O Delaware, that bore
This pile intended for a southern shore,
(Bound to those isles where endless summer reigns,
Fair fruits, gay blossoms, and enamell'd plains;
Where sloping lawns the roving swain invite,
And the cool morn succeeds the breezy night,
Where each glad day a heaven unclouded brings
And sky-topt mountains teem with golden springs.)
   FROM Cape HENLOPEN, urg'd by favouring gales,
When morn emerg'd, we sea-ward spread our sails,
Then east-south-east explor'd the briny way,
Close to the wind, departing from the bay;
No longer seen the hoarse resounding strand,
With hearts elate we hurried from the land,
Escap'd the dangers of that shelvy ground
To sailors fatal, and for wrecks renown'd—
   THE gale increases as we stem the main,
Now scarce the hills their sky-blue mist retain,
At last they sink beneath the rolling wave
That seems their summits, as they sink, to lave;
Abaft the beam the freshening breezes play,
No mists advancing to deform the day,
No tempests rising o'er the splendid scene,
A sea unruffled, and a heaven serene.
   NOW *Sol's* bright lamp, the heav'n born source of light,
Had pass'd the line of his meridian height,
And westward hung—retreating from the view
Shores disappear'd, and every hill withdrew,
When, still suspicious of some neighbouring foe,
Aloft the Master bade a Seaman go,
To mark if, from the mast's aspiring height
Through all the round a vessel came in sight.
   Too soon the Seaman's glance, extending wide
Far distant in the east a ship espy'd,

Her lofty masts stood bending to the gale,
Close to the wind was brac'd each shivering sail;
Next from the deck we saw the approaching foe,
Her spangled bottom seem'd in flames to glow
When to the winds she bow'd in dreadful haste
And her lee-guns lay delug'd in the waste;
From her top-gallant flow'd an *English Jack;*
With all her might she strove to gain our track,
Nor strove in vain—with pride and power elate
Wing'd on by hell, she drove us to our fate,
No stop, no stay her bloody crew intends,
(So flies a comet with its host of fiends)
Nor oaths, nor prayers arrest her swift career,
Death in her front, and ruin in her rear.

   STRUCK at the sight, the Master gave command
To change our course, and steer toward the land—
Swift to the task the ready sailors run,
And while the word was utter'd, half was done;
As from the south the fiercer breezes rise
Swift from her foe alarm'd AURORA flies,
With every sail extended to the wind
She fled the unequal foe that chac'd behind;
Along her decks dispos'd in close array
Each at its port, the grim artillery lay,
Soon on the foe with brazen throat to roar;
But, small their size, and narrow was their *bore;*
Yet faithful they their destin'd station keep
To guard the barque that wafts them o'er the deep,
Who now must bend to steer a homeward course
And trust her swiftness rather than her force,
Unfit to combat with a powerful foe;
Her decks too open, and her *waist* too low.

   WHILE o'er the wave with foaming prow she flies,
Once more emerging, distant landscapes rise;
High in the air the *starry* streamer plays,
And every sail its various tribute pays:
To gain the land we bore the weighty blast:
And now the wish'd for *cape* appear'd at last;

But the vext foe, impatient of delay,
Prepar'd for ruin, press'd upon her prey;
Near, and more near, in aweful grandeur came
The frigate IRIS, not unknown to fame;
IRIS her name, but HANCOCK once she bore,
Fram'd, and completed on NEW ALBION's shore,
By MANLY lost, the swiftest of the train
That fly with wings of canvas o'er the main.
  Now, while for combat some with zeal prepare,
Thus to the heavens the Boatswain sent his prayer;
"Lift' all ye powers that rule the skies and seas!
"Shower down perdition on such thieves as these,
"Fate strike their hearts with terror and dismay,
"And sprinkle on their powder salt-sea spray!
"May bursting cannon, while his aim he tries,
"Destroy the Gunner, and be-damn his eyes—
"The chief who awes the quarter-deck, may he
"Tripp'd from his stand, be tumbled in the sea.
"May they who rule the *round-top's* giddy height
"Be canted headlong to perpetual night;
"May fiends torment them on a leeward coast,
"And help forsake them when they want it most—
"From their wheel'd engines torn be every gun—
"And now, to sum up every curse in one,
"May latent flames, to save us, intervene,
"And hell-ward drive them from their magazine!"—
  THE Frigate, now, had every sail unfurl'd,
And rush'd tremendous o'er the wat'ry world;
Thus fierce *Pelides*, eager to destroy,
Chac'd the proud Trojan to the gates of Troy—
Swift o'er the waves while hostile they pursue
As swiftly from their fangs AURORA flew,
At length HENLOPEN's cape we gain'd once more,
And vainly strove to force the ship ashore;
Stern fate forbade the barren shore to gain,
Denial sad, and source of future pain!
For then the inspiring breezes ceas'd to blow,
Lost were they all, and smooth the seas below;

By the broad cape becalm'd, our lifeless sails
No longer swell'd their bosoms to the gales;
The ship, unable to pursue her way,
Tumbling about, at her own guidance lay,
No more the helm its wonted influence lends,
No oars assist us, and no breeze befriends;
Mean time the foe, advancing from the sea,
Rang'd her black cannon, pointed on our *lee*,
Then up she *luff'd*, and blaz'd her entrails dire,
Bearing destruction, terror, death, and fire.

    VEXT at our fate, we prim'd a piece, and then
Return'd the shot, to shew them we were men.
Dull night at length her dusky pinions spread,
And every hope to 'scape the foe was fled,
Close to thy cape, Henlopen, though we press'd,
We could not gain thy desert, dreary breast;
Though ruin'd trees beshroud thy barren shore
With mounds of sand half hid, or cover'd o'er,
Though ruffian winds disturb thy summit bare,
Yet every hope and every wish was there,
In vain we sought to reach the joyless strand,
Fate stood between, and barr'd us from the land.

    ALL dead becalm'd, and helpless as we lay,
The ebbing current forc'd us back to sea,
While vengeful IRIS, thirsting for our blood,
Flash'd her red lightnings o'er the trembling flood,
At every flash a storm of ruin came
'Till our shock'd vessel shook through all her frame—
Mad for revenge, our breasts with fury glow
To wreak returns of vengeance on the foe;
Full at his hull our pointed guns we rais'd,
His hull resounded as the cannon blaz'd;
Through his main-top sail one a passage tore,
His sides re-echo'd to the dreadful roar,
Alternate fires dispell'd the shades of night—
But how unequal was this daring fight!
Our stoutest guns threw but a six-pound ball,
Twelve pounders from the foe our sides did maul,

And, while no power to save him intervenes,
A bullet struck our captain of Marines;
Fierce, though he bid defiance to the foe
He felt his death and ruin in the blow,
Headlong he fell, distracted with the wound,
The deck distain'd, and heart blood streaming round.
Another blast, as fatal in its aim,
Wing'd by destruction, through our rigging came,
And, whistling tunes from hell upon its way,
Shrouds, stays, and braces tore at once away,
Sails, blocks, and oars in scatter'd fragments fly—
Their softest language was—SUBMIT, OR DIE.

REPEATED cries throughout the ship resound;
Now every bullet brought a different wound;
'Twixt *wind and water*, one assail'd the side,
Through this aperture rush'd the briny tide—
'Twas then the Master trembled for his crew,
And bade thy shores, O Delaware, adieu!—
And must we yield to yon' destructive ball,
And must our colours to these ruffians fall!—
They fall!—his thunders forc'd our pride to bend,
The lofty topsails with their yards descend,
And the proud foe, such leagues of ocean pass'd,
His wish completed in our woe at last.

CONVEY'D TO YORK, we found, at length, too late,
That Death was better than the prisoner's fate,
There doom'd to famine, shackles and despair,
Condemn'd to breathe a foul, infected air
In sickly hulks, devoted while we lay,
Successive funerals gloom'd each dismal day——
But what on captives British rage can do,
Another Canto, friend, shall let you know.

CANTO II. *The* PRISON SHIP.

THE various horrors of these hulks to tell,
These Prison Ships where pain and horror dwell,
Where death in tenfold vengeance holds his reign,
And injur'd ghosts, yet unaveng'd, complain;

This be my talk—ungenerous Britons, you
Conspire to murder those you can't subdue.—
  WEAK as I am, I'll try my strength to-day
And my best arrows at these hell-hounds play,
To future years one scene of death prolong,
And hang them up to infamy, in song.

  THAT Britain's rage should dye our plains with gore,
And desolation spread through every shore,
None e'er could doubt, that her ambition knew,
This was to rage and disappointment due;
But that those monsters whom our soil maintain'd,
Who first drew breath in this devoted land,
Like famish'd wolves, should on their country prey,
Assist its foes, and wrest our lives away,
This shocks belief—and bids our soil disown
Such friends, subservient to a bankrupt crown,
By them the widow mourns her partner dead,
Her mangled sons to darksome prisons led,
By them—and hence my keenest sorrows rise,
My friend, my guardian, my *Orestes* dies;
Still for that loss must wretched I complain,
And sad *Ophelia* mourn her favourite swain.

  AH! come the day when from this bloody shore
Fate shall remove them to return no more—
To scorch'd Bahama shall the traitors go
With grief and rage, and unremitting woe,
On burning sands to walk their painful round,
And sigh through all the solitary ground,
Where no gay flower their haggard eyes shall see,
And find no shade but from the cypress tree.

  So much we suffer'd from the tribe I hate,
So near they shov'd me to the brink of fate,
When two long months in these dark Hulks we lay
Barr'd down by night, and fainting all the day
In the fierce fervours of the solar beam,
Cool'd by no breeze on Hudson's mountain-stream;
That not unsung these threescore days shall fall
To black oblivion that would cover all!—

No masts or sails these crowded ships adorn,
Dismal to view, neglected and forlorn!
Here, mighty ills oppress the imprison'd throng,
Dull were our slumbers, and our nights too long—
From morn to even along the decks we lay
Scorch'd into fevers by the solar ray;
No friendly *awning* cast a welcome shade,
Once was it promis'd, and was never made;
No favours could these sons of death bestow,
'Twas endless cursing, and continual woe;
Immortal hatred doth their breasts engage,
And this lost empire swells their souls with rage.

Two hulks on Hudson's stormy bosom lie,
Two, farther south, affront the pitying eye—
There, the black SCORPION at her mooring rides,
There, STROMBOLO swings, yielding to the tides;
Here, bulky JERSEY fills a larger space,
And HUNTER, to all hospitals disgrace—
Thou, *Scorpion*, fatal to the crowded throng,
Dire theme of horror and Plutonian song,
Requir'st my lay—thy sultry decks I know,
And all the torments that exist below!
The briny wave that Hudson's bosom fills
Drain'd through her bottom in a thousand rills,
Rotten and old, replete with sighs and groans,
Scarce on the waters she sustain'd her bones;
Here, doom'd to toil, or founder in the tide,
At the moist pumps incessantly we ply'd,
Here, doom'd to starve, like famish'd dogs we tore
The scant allowance, that our tyrants bore.

REMEMBRANCE shudders at this scene of fears—
Still in my view some English brute appears,
Some base-born Hessian slave walks threat'ning by,
Some servile Scot with murder in his eye
Still haunts my sight, as vainly they bemoan
Rebellions manag'd so unlike their *own!*
O may I never feel the poignant pain
To live subjected to such fiends again,

Stewards and *Mates* that hostile Britain bore,
Cut from the gallows on their native shore,
Their ghastly looks and vengeance-beaming eyes
Still to my view in dismal colours rise—
O may I ne'er review these dire abodes,
These piles for slaughter, floating on the floods,—
And you, that o'er the troubled ocean go,
Strike not your standards to this miscreant foe,
Better the greedy wave should swallow all,
Better to meet the death-conducted ball,
Better to sleep on ocean's deepest bed
At once destroy'd and number'd with the dead,
Than thus to perish in the face of day
Where twice ten thousand deaths one death delay.

WHEN to the ocean dives the western sun,
And the scorch'd Tories fire their evening gun,
"Down, rebels, down!" the angry Scotchmen cry,
"Damn'd dogs, descend, or by our broad swords die!"

HAIL, dark abode! what can with thee compare——
Heat, sickness, famine, death, and stagnant air——
Pandora's box, from whence all mischief flew,
Here real found, torments mankind anew!—
Swift from the guarded decks we rush'd along,
And vainly sought repose, so vast our throng:
Three hundred wretches here, denied all light,
In crowded mansions pass the infernal night,
Some for a bed their tatter'd vestments join,
And some on chests, and some on floors recline;
Shut from the blessings of the evening air,
Pensive we lay with mingled corpses there,
Meagre and wan, and scorch'd with heat, below,
We loom'd like ghosts, ere death had made us so—
How could we else, where heat and hunger join'd
Thus to debase the body and the mind,
Where cruel thirst the parching throat invades,
Dries up the man, and fits him for the shades.

No waters laded from the bubbling spring
To these dire ships the British monsters bring—

By planks and ponderous beams completely wall'd
Invain for water, and invain, I call'd—
No drop was granted to the midnight prayer,
To *Dives* in these regions of despair!—
The loathsome cask a deadly dose contains,
Its poison circling through the languid veins;
"Here, *generous* Britain, generous, as you say,
"To my parch'd tongue one cooling drop convey,
"Hell has no mischief like a thirsty throat,
"Nor one tormentor like your *David Sproat.*"*
DULL flew the hours, till, from the East display'd,
Sweet morn dispells the horrors of the shade;
On every side dire objects meet the sight,
And pallid forms, and murders of the night,
The dead were past their pain, the living groan,
Nor dare to hope another morn their own;
But what to them is morn's delightful ray,
Sad and distressful as the close of day,
O'er distant streams appears the dewy green,
And leafy trees on mountain tops are seen,
But they no groves nor grassy mountains tread,
Mark'd for a longer journey to the dead.
BLACK as the clouds that shade St. Kilda's shore,
Wild as the winds that round her mountains roar,
At every post some surly vagrant stands,
Pick'd from the British or the Irish bands,
Some slave from Hesse, some hangman's son at least
Sold and transported, like his brother beast—
Some miscreant Tory, puff'd with upstart pride,
Led on by hell to take the royal side;
Dispensing death triumphantly they stand,
Their musquets ready to obey command;
Wounds are their sport, as ruin is their aim:
On their dark souls compassion has no claim,
And discord only can their spirits please:
Such were our tyrants here, and such were these.

* Commissary of Prisoners at New-York.

INGRATITUDE! no curse like thee is found
Throughout this jarring world's extended round,
Their hearts with malice to our country swell
Because in former days we us'd them well—!
This pierces deep, too deeply wounds the breast;
We help'd them naked, friendless, and distrest,
Receiv'd their vagrants with an open hand,
Bestow'd them buildings, privilege, and land—
Behold the change!—when angry Britain rose,
These thankless tribes became our fiercest foes,
By them devoted, plunder'd, and accurst,
Stung by the serpents whom ourselves had nurs'd.
  BUT such a train of endless woes abound,
So many mischiefs in these hulks are found,
That on them all a poem to prolong
Would swell too high the horrors of my song—
Hunger and thirst to work our woe combine,
And mouldy bread, and flesh of rotten swine,
The mangled carcase, and the batter'd brain,
The doctor's poison, and the captain's cane,
The soldier's musquet, and the steward's debt,
The evening shackle, and the noon-day threat.
  THAT *juice* destructive to the pangs of care
Which Rome of old, nor Athens could prepare.
Which gains the day for many a modern chief
When cool reflection yields a faint relief,
That *charm*, whose virtue warms the world beside,
Was by these tyrants to our use denied,
While yet they deign'd that healthy juice to lade
The putrid water felt its powerful aid;
But when refus'd—to aggravate our pains—
Then fevers rag'd and revel'd through our veins;
Throughout my frame I felt its deadly heat,
I felt my pulse with quicker motions beat:
A pallid hue o'er every face was spread,
Unusual pains attack'd the fainting head,
No physic here, no doctor to assist,
My *name* was enter'd on the sick man's list;

Twelve wretches more the same dark symptoms took,
And these were enter'd on the doctor's book,
The loathsome HUNTER was our destin'd place,
The HUNTER to all hospitals disgrace;
With soldiers sent to guard us on our road,
Joyful we left the SCORPION's dire abode;
Some tears we shed for the remaining crew,
Then curs'd the hulk, and from her sides withdrew.

CANTO III.   *The* HOSPITAL PRISON SHIP.

NOW tow'rd the HUNTER's gloomy sides we came,
A slaughter-house, yet *hospital* in name;
For none came there (to pass through all degrees)
'Till half consum'd, and dying with disease;—
But when too near with labouring oars we ply'd
The *Mate* with curses drove us from the side;
That wretch who, banish'd from the navy crew,
Grown old in blood, did here his trade renew,
His serpent's tongue, when on his *charge* let loose,
Utter'd reproaches, scandal, and abuse,
Gave all to hell who dar'd his *king* disown,
And swore mankind were made for *George* alone:
Ten thousand times, to irritate our woe,
He wish'd us founder'd in the gulph below;
Ten thousand times he brandish'd high his stick,
And swore as often that we were not sick—
And yet so pale!—that we were thought by some
A freight of ghosts from Death's dominions come—
But calm'd at length—for who can always rage,
Or the fierce war of endless passion wage,
He pointed to the stairs that led below
To damps, disease, and varied shapes of woe—
Down to the gloom I took my pensive way,
Along the decks the dying captives lay;
Some struck with madness, some with scurvy pain'd,
But still of putrid fevers most complain'd!
On the hard floors these wasted objects laid,
There toss'd and tumbled in the dismal shade,

There no soft voice their bitter fate bemoan'd,
And Death trode stately, while the victims groan'd;
Of leaky decks I heard them long complain,
Drown'd as they were in deluges of rain,
Deny'd the comforts of a dying bed,
And not a pillow to support the head—
How could they else but pine, and grieve, and sigh,
Detest a wretched life—and wish to die.

  SCARCE had I mingled with this dismal band
When a thin spectre seiz'd me by the hand—
"And art thou come, (death heavy on his eyes)
"And art thou come to these abodes, he cries;
"Why didst thou leave the *Scorpion's* dark retreat,
"And hither haste a surer death to meet?
"Why didst thou leave thy damp infected cell,
"If *that* was purgatory, this is hell—
"We too grown weary of that horrid shade
"Petitioned early for the doctor's aid;
"His aid denied, more deadly symptoms came,
"Weak, and yet weaker, glow'd the vital flame;
"And when disease had worn us down so low
"That few could tell if we were ghosts, or no,
"And all asserted, death would be our fate—
"Then to the doctor we were sent—too late.
"Here wastes away *Autolycus* the brave,
"Here young *Orestes* finds a wat'ry grave,
"Here, gay *Alcander* gay, alas! no more,
"Dies far sequester'd from his native shore;
"He late, perhaps, too eager for the fray,
"Chac'd the vile Briton o'er the wat'ry way
"'Till fortune jealous, bade her clouds appear,
"Turn'd hostile to his fame, and brought him *here*,
  "THUS do our warriors, thus our heroes fall,
"Imprison'd here, base ruin meets them all,
"Or, sent afar to Britain's barbarous shore,
"There die neglected, and return no more:
"Ah rest in peace, poor, injur'd, parted shade,
"By cruel hands in death's dark weeds array'd,

"But happier climes, where suns unclouded shine,
"Light undisturb'd, and endless peace are thine."—
    FROM *Brookland* groves a Hessian doctor came,
Not great his skill, nor greater much his fame;
Fair Science never call'd the wretch her son,
And Art disdain'd the stupid man to own;—
Can you admire that Science was so coy,
Or Art refus'd his genius to employ!—
Do men with brutes an equal dullness share,
Or cuts yon' groveling mole the midway air—
In polar worlds can Eden's blossoms blow,
Do trees of God in barren desarts grow,
Are loaded vines to Etna's summit known,
Or swells the peach beneath the torrid zone—?
Yet still he doom'd his genius to the rack,
And, as you may suppose, was own'd a *quack*.
    HE on his charge the healing work begun
With antimonial mixtures, by the tun,
Ten minutes was the time he deign'd to stay,
The time of grace allotted once a day—
He drencht us well with bitter draughts, 'tis true,
Nostrums from hell, and *cortex* from Peru—
Some with his pills he sent to Pluto's reign,
And some he blister'd with his flies of Spain;
His cream of Tartar walk'd its deadly round,
Till the lean patient at the potion frown'd,
And swore that hemlock, death, or what you will,
Were nonsense to the drugs that stuff'd his bill.—
On those refusing he bestow'd a kick,
Or menac'd vengeance with his walking stick,
Here uncontroul'd he exercis'd his trade,
And grew experienced by the deaths he made,
By frequent blows we from his cane endur'd
He kill'd at least as many as he cur'd,
On our lost comrades built his future fame,
And scatter'd fate, where'er his footsteps came.
    SOME did not seem obedient to his will,
And swore he mingled poison with his pill,

But I acquit him by a fair confession,
He was no Englishman—he was a Hessian—
Although a dunce, he had some sense of sin
Or else the Lord knows where we now had been;
Perhaps in that far country sent to range
Where never prisoner meets with an exchange—
Then had we all been banish'd out of time
Nor I return'd to plague the world with rhyme.

    FOOL though he was, yet candour must confess
Not chief Physician was this dog of Hesse—
One master o'er the murdering tribe was plac'd,
By him the rest were honour'd or disgrac'd;—
Once, and but once, by some strange fortune led
He came to see the dying and the dead—
He came—but anger so deform'd his eye,
And such a faulchion glitter'd on his thigh
And such a gloom his visage darken'd o'er,
And two such pistols in his hands he bore!
That, by the gods!—with such a load of steel
He came, we thought, to murder, not to heal—
Hell in his heart, and mischief in his head,
He gloom'd destruction, and had smote us dead,
Had he so dar'd—but fate with-held his hand—
He came—blasphem'd—and turn'd again to land.

    FROM this poor vessel, and her sickly crew
An English ruffian all his titles drew,
Captain, esquire, commander, too, in chief,
And hence he gain'd his bread, and hence his beef,
But, sir, you might have search'd creation round
Ere such another miscreant could be found—
Though unprovok'd, an angry face he bore,
We stood astonish'd at the oaths he swore;
He swore, till every prisoner stood aghast,
And thought him Satan in a brimstone blast;
He wish'd us banish'd from the public light,
He wish'd us shrouded in perpetual night!
That were he king, no mercy would he show,
But drive all *rebels* to the world below;

That if we *scoundrels* did not scrub the decks
His staff should break our damn'd *rebellious* necks;
He swore, besides, that if the ship took fire
We too should in the pitchy flame expire;
And meant it so—this tyrant I engage
Had lost his breath to gratify his rage.—

IF where he walk'd a captive carcase lay,
Still dreadful was the language of the day—
He call'd us *dogs*, and would have us'd us so,
But vengeance check'd the meditated blow,
The vengeance from our injur'd nation due
To him, and all the base, unmanly crew.

SUCH food they sent, to make complete our woes,
It look'd like carrion torn from hungry crows,
Such vermin vile on every joint were seen,
So black, corrupted, mortified, and lean
That once we try'd to move our flinty chief,
And thus address'd him, holding up the beef:

"SEE, captain, see! what rotten bones we pick,
"What kills the healthy cannot cure the sick:
"Not dogs on such by *Christian* men are fed,
"And see, good master, see, what lousy bread!"

"YOUR meat and bread (this man of flint replied)
"Is not my care to manage or provide—
"But this, damn'd rebel dogs, I'd have you know,
That better than you merit we bestow;
"Out of my sight!"—nor more he deign'd to say,
But whisk'd about, and frowning, strode away.

EACH day, at least three carcases we bore,
And scratch'd them graves along the sandy shore,
By feeble hands the shallow graves were made,
No stone memorial o'er the corpses laid;
In barren sands, and far from home, they lie,
No friend to shed a tear, when passing by;
O'er the mean tombs insulting Britons tread,
Spurn at the sand, and curse the rebel dead.

WHEN to your arms these fatal islands fall,
(For first or last they must be conquer'd all)

Americans! to rites sepulchral just,
With gentlest footstep press this kindred dust,
And o'er the tombs, if tombs can then be found,
Place the green turf, and plant the myrtle round.
    AMERICANS! a just resentment shew,
And glut revenge on this detested foe;
While the warm blood exults the glowing vein
Still shall resentment in your bosoms reign,
Can you forget the greedy Briton's ire,
Your fields in ruin, and your domes on fire,
No age, no sex from lust and murder free,
And, black as night, the hell born refugee!
Must *York* forever your best blood entomb,
And these gorg'd monsters triumph in their doom,
Who leave no art of cruelty untry'd;
Such heavy vengeance, and such hellish pride!
Death has no charms—his realms dejected lie
In the dull climate of a clouded sky,
Death has no charms, except in British eyes,
See, arm'd for death, the infernal miscreants rise,
See how they pant to stain the world with gore,
And millions murder'd, still would murder more;
This selfish race, from all the world disjoin'd,
Perpetual discord spread throughout mankind,
Aim to extend their empire o'er the ball,
Subject, destroy, absorb, and conquer all,
As if the power that form'd us did condemn
All other nations to be slaves to them——
Rouse from your sleep, and crush the thievish band,
Defeat, destroy, and sweep them from the land,
Ally'd like you, what madness to despair,
Attack the ruffians while they linger there;
There *Tryon* sits, a monster all complete
See *Clinton* there with vile *Knyphausen* meet,
And every wretch whom honour should detest
There finds a home—and Arnold with the rest.
Ah! traitors, lost to every sense of shame,
Unjust supporters of a tyrant's claim;

Foes to the rights of freedom and of men,
Flush'd with the blood of thousands you have slain,
To the just doom the righteous skies decree
We leave you, toiling still in cruelty,
Or on dark plans in future herds to meet,
Plans form'd in hell, and projects half complete:
The years approach that shall to ruin bring
Your lords, your chiefs, your miscreant of a king
Whose murderous acts shall stamp his name accurs'd,
And his last triumphs more than damn the first.

1781

On

THE MEMORABLE VICTORY,

Obtained by the gallant Captain Paul Jones, of *Le Bon Homme Richard*, (or father Richard) over the *Seraphis*, of 44 guns, under the command of Captain Pearson:

*First published in Mr. Francis Bailey's
Freeman's Journal, Philadelphia, 1781.*

O'ER the rough main with flowing sheet
The guardian of a numerous fleet,
  Seraphis from the Baltic came;
A ship of less tremendous force
Sailed by her side the self-same course,
  Countess of Scarborough was her name.

And now their native coasts appear,
Britannia's hills their summits rear
  Above the German main:
Fond to suppose their dangers o'er,
They southward coast along the shore,
  Thy waters, gentle Thames, to gain.

Full forty guns Seraphis bore,
And Scarborough's Countess twenty-four,
  Manned with Old England's boldest tars—

What flag that rides the Gallic seas
Shall dare attack such piles as these,
   Designed for tumults and for wars!

Now from the top-mast's giddy heights
A seaman cried—"Four sail in sight
   "Approach with favouring gales;"
Pearson, resolved to save the fleet,
Stood off to sea, these ships to meet,
   And closely braced his shivering sails.

With him advanc'd the Countess bold,
Like a black tar in wars grown old:
   And now these floating piles drew nigh;
But, muse, unfold, what chief of fame
In the other warlike squadron came,
   Whose standards at his mast head fly.

'Twas Jones, brave JONES, to battle led
As bold a crew as ever bled
   Upon the sky-surrounded main;
The standards of the western world
Were to the willing winds unfurled,
   Denying Britain's tyrant reign.

The *Good-Man-Richard* led the line;
The *Alliance* next: with these combine
   The Gallic ship they *Pallas* call:
The *Vengeance*, armed with sword and flame,
These to attack the Britons came—
   But *two* accomplished all.

Now Phoebus sought his pearly bed:
But who can tell the scenes of dread,
   The horrors of that fatal night!
Close up these floating castles came;
The Good Man Richard bursts in flame;
   Seraphis trembled at the sight.

She felt the fury of *her* ball:
Down, prostrate down, the Britons fall;
  The decks were strewed with slain:
Jones to the foe his vessel lashed;
And, while the black artillery flashed,
  Loud thunders shook the main.

Alas! that mortals should employ
Such murdering engines, to destroy
  That frame by heaven so nicely joined;
Alas! that e'er the god decreed
That brother should by brother bleed,
  And pour'd such madness in the mind.

But thou, brave Jones, no blame shalt bear;
The rights of men demand thy care:
  For *these* you dare the greedy waves—
No tyrant, on destruction bent
Has planned thy conquests—thou art sent
  To humble tyrants and their slaves.

See!—dread Seraphis flames again—
And art thou, *Jones*, among the slain,
  And sunk to Neptune's caves below—
He lives—though crowds around him fall,
Still he, unhurt, survives them all;
  Almost alone he fights the foe.

And can thy ship these strokes sustain?
Behold thy brave companions slain,
  All clasped in ocean's dark embrace.
"STRIKE, OR BE SUNK!"—the Briton cries—
"SINK, IF YOU CAN!"—the chief replies,
  Fierce lightnings blazing in his face.

Then to the side three guns he drew,
(Almost deserted by his crew)
  And charged them deep with woe:

By *Pearson's* flash he aim'd hot balls;
His main-mast totters—down it falls—
  O'erwhelming half below.

Pearson as yet disdained to yield,
But scarce he secret fears concealed,
  And thus was heard to cry—
"With hell, not mortals, I contend;
"What art thou—human or a fiend,
  "That dost my force defy?

"Return, my lads, the fight renew!"
So called bold Pearson to his crew;
  But called, alas! in vain;
Some on the decks lay maimed and dead;
Some to their deep recesses fled,
  And more were shrouded in the main.

Distressed, forsaken, and alone,
He hauled his tattered standard down,
  And yielded to his gallant foe;
Bold *Pallas* soon the *Countess* took,—
Thus both their haughty colours struck,
  Confessing what the brave can do.

But, Jones, too dearly didst thou buy
These ships possest so gloriously,
  Too many deaths disgraced the fray:
Thy barque that bore the conquering flame,
That the proud Briton overcame,
  Even she forsook thee on thy way;

For when the morn began to shine,
Fatal to her, the ocean brine
  Poured through each spacious wound;
Quick in the deep she disappeared,
But Jones to friendly Belgia steered,
  With conquest and with glory crowned.

Go on, great man, to scourge the foe,
And bid the haughty Britons know
    They to our *Thirteen Stars* shall bend;
The *Stars* that clad in dark attire,
Long glimmered with a feeble fire,
    But radiant now ascend.

Bend to the Stars that flaming rise
On western worlds, more brilliant skies.
    Fair Freedom's reign restored.
So when the Magi, come from far,
Beheld the God-attending Star,
    They trembled and adored.

1781

TO

LORD CORNWALLIS,

AT YORK-VIRGINIA, *October* 8, 1781.*

HAIL, great destroyer (equall'd yet by none)
Of countries not thy master's, nor thine own;
Hatch'd by some demon on a stormy day,
Satan's best substitute to burn and slay;
Confin'd at last, hemm'd in by land and sea
Burgoyne himself was but a type of thee!
LIKE his, to freedom was thy deadly hate,
Like his thy baseness, and be his thy fate:
To you, like him, no prospect Nature yields
But ruin'd wastes and desolated fields—
Invain you raise the interposing wall,
And hoist those standards that, like you, must fall,
In you conclude the glories of your race,
Complete your monarch's, and your own disgrace.
    What has your lordship's pilfering arms attain'd?—
Vast stores of *plunder*, but no STATE regain'd—

* Text from the Edition of 1786. [Ed.]

That may return, though you perhaps may groan,
Restore it, ruffian, for 'tis not your own—
Then, lord and soldier, headlong to the brine
Rush down at once—the devil and the swine.
    WOULD'ST thou at last with *Washington* engage,
Sad object of his pity, not his rage?
See, round thy posts how terribly advance
The chiefs, the armies, and the fleets of France,
Fight while you can, for warlike *Rochambeau*
Aims at your head his last decisive blow,
Unnumber'd ghosts, from earth untimely sped,
Can take no rest till you, like them, are dead—
Then die, my Lord; that only chance remains
To wash away dishonourable stains,
For small advantage would your capture bring,
The *plundering servant of a bankrupt king*.

[w. 1781]   1786

ON THE FALL OF

GENERAL EARL CORNWALLIS,*

Who, with above seven thousand Men, surrendered themselves
prisoners of war, to the renowned and illustrious General
GEORGE WASHINGTON, commander in chief of the allied
armies of France and America, on the memorable 19th of
October, 1781.

> "Give us the proudest prisoner of the Goths,
> "That we may hew his limbs, and on a pile
> "*Ad manes fratrum* sacrifice his flesh,
> "Before this earthly prison of their bones;
> "That so the shadows be not unappeas'd,
> "Nor we disturb'd with prodigies on earth."
>   Shakespeare's *Titus Andronicus*. Act. I. Scene II.

———

A CHIEFTAIN join'd with Howe, Burgoyne, and Gage,
Once more, nor this the last, provokes my rage—

    * Text from the Edition of 1786. [Ed.]

Who saw these Nimrods first for conquest burn!
Who has not seen them to the dust return?
This ruffian next, who scour'd our ravag'd fields,
Foe to the human race, Cornwallis yields!—
None e'er before essay'd such desperate crimes,
Alone he stood, arch-butcher of the times,
Rov'd uncontroul'd this wasted country o'er,
Strew'd plains with dead, and bath'd his jaws with gore?

'TWAS thus the wolf, who sought by night his prey,
And plunder'd all he met with on his way,
Stole what he could, and murder'd as he pass'd,
Chanc'd on a trap, and lost his head at last.

WHAT pen can write, what human tongue can tell
The endless murders of this man of hell!
Nature in him disgrac'd the form divine;
Nature mistook, she meant him for a—swine:
That eye his forehead to her shame adorns;
Blush! nature, blush—bestow him tail and horns!—
By him the orphans mourn—the widow'd dame
Saw ruin spreading in the wasteful flame;
Gash'd o'er with wounds beheld with streaming eye
A son, a brother, or a consort, die!—
Through ruin'd realms bones lie without a tomb,
And souls be sped to their eternal doom,
Who else had liv'd, and seen their toils again
Bless'd by the genius of the rural reign.

BUT turn your eyes, and see the murderer fall,
Then say—"Cornwallis has atchiev'd it all."—
Yet he preserves the honour and the fame
That vanquish'd heroes only ought to claim—
Is he a hero!—Read, and you will find
Heroes are beings of a different kind:—
Compassion to the worst of men is due,
And mercy heaven's first attribute, 'tis true;
Yet most presume it was *too nobly* done
To grant mild terms to *Satan's first-born son.*

CONVINC'D we are, no foreign spot of earth
But Britain only, gave this reptile birth.

That white-cliff'd isle, the vengeful dragon's den,
Has sent us monsters where we look'd for men.
When memory paints their horrid deeds anew,
And brings these murdering miscreants to your view,
Then ask the leaders of these bloody bands,
Can they expect compassion at our hands?—
　　BUT may this year, the glorious eighty-one,
Conclude successful, as it first begun;
This brilliant year their total downfall see,
And what Cornwallis *is*, may Clinton *be*.

　　O COME the time, nor distant be the day,
When our bold navy shall its wings display;
Mann'd by our sons, to seek that barbarous shore,
The wrongs revenging that their fathers bore:
As Samuel hew'd the tyrant Agag down,
So hew the wearer of the British crown;
Unpitying, next his hated offspring slay,
Or into foreign lands the fiends convey:
Give them their turn to pine and die in chains,
'Till not one monster of the race remains.

　　THOU, who resid'st on those thrice happy shores,
Where white rob'd peace her envied blessings pours,
Stay, and enjoy the pleasures that she yields;
But come not, stranger, to our wasted fields.
For warlike hosts on every plain appear,
War damps the beauties of the rising year:
In vain the groves their bloomy sweets display;
War's clouded winter chills the charms of May:
Here human blood the trampled harvest stains;
Here bones of men yet whiten all the plains;
Seas teem with dead; and our unhappy shore
Forever blushes with its children's gore.

　　BUT turn your eyes—behold the tyrant fall,
And think—Cornwallis has atchiev'd it all.—

　　ALL mean revenge Americans disdain,
Oft have they prov'd it, and now prove again;
With nobler fires their generous bosoms glow;
Still in the captive they forget the foe:—

But when a *nation* takes a wrongful cause,
And hostile turns to heaven's and nature's laws;
When, sacrificing at ambition's shrine,
Kings slight the mandates of the power divine,
And devastation spread on every side,
To gratify their malice or their pride,
And send their slaves their projects to fulfil,
To wrest our freedom, or our blood to spill:—
Such to forgive, is virtue too sublime;
For even compassion has been found a crime.

    A PROPHET once, for miracles renown'd,
Bade *Joash* smite the arrows on the ground—
Taking the mystic shafts, the prince obey'd,
Thrice smote them on the earth—and then he stay'd—
    GRIEV'D when he saw full victory deny'd,
"Six times you should have smote," the prophet cry'd,
"Then had proud *Syria* sunk beneath thy power;
"Now thrice you smite her—but shall smite no more."

    CORNWALLIS! thou art rank'd among the great;
Such was the will of all-controuling fate.
As mighty men, who liv'd in days of yore,
Were figur'd out some centuries before;
So you with them in equal honour join,
Your great precursor's name was Jack Burgoyne!
Like you was he, a man in arms renown'd,
Who, hot for conquest, sail'd the ocean round;
This, this was he, who scour'd the woods for praise,
And burnt down cities* to describe the blaze!

    So, while on fire, his harp Rome's tyrant strung,
And as the buildings flam'd, old Nero sung.

    WHO would have guess'd the purpose of the fates,
When that *proud boaster* bow'd to conquering Gates!—
Then sung the sisters† as the wheel went round,
(Could we have heard the invigorating sound)

---

* Charlestown, near Boston. See his letter on that occasion.
† The *Parcae*, or *Fates*, who, according to the Heathen mythology
were three in number.

Thus surely did the fatal sisters sing—
"When just four years do this same season bring,
"And in his annual journey, when the sun
"Four times completely shall his circuit run,
"An *angel* then shall rid you of your fears,
"By binding *Satan* for a thousand years,
"Shall lash the serpent to the infernal shore,
"To waste the nations, and deceive no more,
"Make wars and blood, and tyranny to cease,
"And hush the fiends of Britain into peace."

JOY to your lordship, and your high descent,
You are the Satan that the *sisters* meant.
Too soon you found your race of ruin run,
Your conquests ended, and your battles done!
But that to live is better than to die,
And life you chose, though life with infamy,
You should have climb'd your loftiest vessel's deck,
And hung a millstone round your halter'd neck—
Then plung'd forever to the wat'ry bed,
Hell in your heart, and vengeance on your head.

ALL must confess, that in regard to you,
'Twas wrong to rob the devil of his due—
For Hayne, for Hayne! no death but thine atones;
For thee, Cornwallis, how the gallows groans!
That injur'd man's, and all the blood you've shed,
That blood shall rest on your devoted head;
Asham'd to live, and yet afraid to die,
Your courage slacken'd as the foe drew nigh—
Ungrateful wretch, to yield your *favourite band*
To chains and prisons in a hostile land:
To the wide world your *Negro friends* to cast
And leave your *Tories* to be hang'd at last!—
You should have fought with horror and amaze,
'Till scorch'd to cinders in the cannon blaze,
'Till all your host of Beelzebubs was slain,
Doom'd to disgrace no human shape again—
As if from hell this horned host he drew,
Swift from the South the embodied ruffians flew;

Destruction follow'd at their *cloven* feet,
'Till you, Fayette, constrain'd them to retreat,
And held them close, till thy fam'd squadron came,
De Grasse, completing their eternal shame.

WHEN the loud cannon's unremitting glare
And red hot balls compell'd *you* to despair,
How could you stand to meet your generous foe?
Did not the sight confound your soul with woe?—
In thy great soul what god-like virtues shine,
What inborn greatness, WASHINGTON, is thine!—
Else had no prisoner trod these lands to-day,
All, with his lordship, had been swept away,
All doom'd alike death's vermin to regale,
Nor one been left to tell the dreadful tale!
But his own terms the vanquish'd murderer nam'd—
He nobly gave the miscreant all he claim'd,
And bade Cornwallis, conquer'd and distress'd,
Bear all his torments in his tortur'd breast.

Now curs'd with life, a *foe* to man and God,
Like *Cain*, I drive you to the land of *Nod*.
He with a brother's blood his hands did stain,
One brother he, you have a thousand slain.
And, O! may heaven affix some public *mark*
To know Cornwallis—may he *howl* and *bark!*—
On eagle's wings explore your downward flight
To the deep horrors of the darkest night,
Where, wrapt in shade on ocean's utmost bound,
No longer sun, nor moon, nor stars are found;
Where never light her kindling radiance shed,
But the dark comets rove with all their *dead,**
Doom'd through the tracks of endless space to run
No more revolving to confound the sun.

SUCH horrid deeds your spotted soul defame
We grieve to think your shape and ours the same!
Enjoy what comfort in this life you can,
The form you have, not feelings of a man;

* See Whiston's Hypothesis.

Haste to the rocks, thou curse to human kind,
There thou may'st wolves and brother tygers find;
Eternal exile be your righteous doom
And gnash your dragon's teeth in some sequester'd gloom
Such be the end of each relentless foe
Who feels no pity for another's woe—
So may they fall—even you, though much too late,
Shall curse the day you languish'd to be great;
Haste from the torments of the present life—
Quick, let the halter end thee or the knife;
So may destruction rush with speedy wing,
Low as yourself to drag your cruel king,
His head torn off, his hands, his feet, and all,
Deep in the dust may Dagon's image fall;
His stump alone escape the vengeful steel,
Sav'd but to grace the gibbet or the wheel.

1781

TO THE
MEMORY

Of the brave AMERICANS, under General GREENE, in
South Carolina, who fell in the action of *September* 8,
1781.*

AT Eutaw springs the valiant died:
Their limbs with dust are cover'd o'er—
Weep on, ye springs, your tearful tide;
How many heroes are no more!

If in this wreck of ruin, they
Can yet be thought to claim a tear,
O smite thy gentle breast, and say
The friends of freedom slumber here!

* Text from the edition of 1795. [Ed.]

Thou, who shalt trace this bloody plain,
If goodness rules thy generous breast,
Sigh for the wasted rural reign;
Sigh for the shepherds, sunk to rest!

Stranger, their humble graves adorn;
You too may fall, and ask a tear:
'Tis not the beauty of the morn
That proves the evening shall be clear—

They saw their injur'd country's woe;
The flaming town, the wasted field;
Then rush'd to meet the insulting foe;
They took the spear—but left the shield,

Led by thy conquering genius, GREENE,
The Britons they compell'd to fly:
None distant view'd the fatal plain,
None griev'd, in such a cause, to die—

But, like the Parthian, fam'd of old,
Who, flying, still their arrows threw;
These routed Britons, full as bold,
Retreated, and retreating slew.

Now rest in peace, our patriot band;
Though far from Nature's limits thrown,
We trust, they find a happier land,
A brighter sun-shine of their own.

1781

ARNOLD'S DEPARTURE.*

WITH evil omens from the harbour sails
The ill-fated ship that worthless ARNOLD bears,
God of the southern winds, call up thy gales,
And whistle in rude fury round his ears.

* *Imitated from* Horace. [Text from the edition of 1795.—Ed.]

With horrid waves insult his vessel's sides,
And may the east wind on a leeward shore
Her cables snap, while she in tumult rides,
And shatter into shivers every oar,

And let the north wind to her ruin haste,
With such a rage, as when from mountains high
He rends the tall oak with his weighty blast,
And ruin spreads, where'er his forces fly.

May not one friendly star that night be seen;
No Moon, attendant, dart one glimmering ray
Nor may she ride on oceans more serene
Than Greece, triumphant, found that stormy day,

When angry Pallas spent her rage no more
On vanquish'd Ilium, then in ashes laid,
But turn'd it on the barque that Ajax bore,*
Avenging thus her temple, and the maid.

When toss'd upon the vast Atlantic main
Your groaning ship the southern gales shall tear,
How will your sailors sweat, and you complain
And meanly howl to Jove, that will not hear!

But if, at last, upon some winding shore
A prey to hungry cormorants you lie,
A wanton goat to every stormy power,†
And a fat lamb, in sacrifice, shall die.

Dec. 1782   1782

* Ajax the younger, son of Oileus, king of the Locrians. He debauched Cassandra in the temple of Pallas, which was the cause of his misfortune, on his return from the siege of Troy.
† The *Tempests* were Goddesses among the Romans.

THE POLITICAL BALANCE;
OR, THE FATES OF BRITAIN AND AMERICA
COMPARED:

A TALE.

Deciding Fates, in Homer's stile, we shew,
And bring contending gods once more to view.

AS Jove the Olympian (who both I and you know,
Was brother to Neptune, and husband to Juno)
Was lately reviewing his papers of state,
He happened to light on the records of FATE.

In Alphabet order this volume was written—
So he opened at B, for the article Britain—
She struggles so well, said the god, I will see
What the sisters in Pluto's dominions decree.

And, first, on the top of a column he read
"Of a king, with a mighty soft place in his head,
"Who should join in his temper the ass and the mule,
"The third of his name, and by far the worst fool:

"His reign shall be famous for multiplication,
"The sire and the king of a *whelp* generation:
"But such is the will and the purpose of fate,
"For each child he begets he shall forfeit a *State:*

"In the course of events, he shall find to his cost
"That he cannot regain what he foolishly lost;
"Of the nations around he shall be the derision,
"And know, by experience, the rule of Division."

So Jupiter read—a god of first rank—
And still had read on—but he came to a blank:
For the Fates had neglected the rest to reveal—
They either forgot it, or chose to conceal:

When a leaf is torn out, or a blot on a page
That pleases our fancy, we fly in a rage—
So, curious to know what the Fates would say next,
No wonder if Jove, disappointed, was vext.

But still, as true genius not frequently fails,
He glanced at the *Virgin*, and thought of the *Scales;*
And said, "To determine the will of the Fates,
"One scale shall weigh *Britain*, the other the *States.*"

Then turning to Vulcan, his maker of thunder,
Said he, "My dear Vulcan, I pray you look yonder,
"Those *creatures* are tearing each other to pieces,
"And, instead of abating, the carnage increases.

"Now, as you are a blacksmith, and lusty stout ham-eater,
"You must make me a globe of a shorter diameter;
"The world in abridgement, and just as it stands
"With all its proportions of waters and lands;

"But its various divisions must so be designed,
"That I can unhinge it whene'er I've a mind—
"How else should I know what the portions will weigh,
"Or which of the combatants carry the day?"

Old Vulcan complied, (we've no reason to doubt it)
So he put on his apron and strait went about it—
Made center, and circles as round as a pancake,
And here the Pacific, and there the Atlantic.

An axis he hammered, whose ends were the poles,
(On which the whole body perpetually rolls)
A brazen meridian he added to these,
Where four times repeated were ninety degrees.

I am sure you had laughed to have seen his droll attitude,
When he bent round the surface the circles of latitude,
The zones, and the tropics, meridians, equator,
And other fine things that are drawn on salt water.

Away to the southward (instructed by Pallas)
He placed in the ocean the Terra Australis,
New Holland, New Guinea, and so of the rest—
AMERICA lay by herself in the west:

From the regions where winter eternally reigns,
To the climes of Peru he extended her plains;
Dark groves, and the zones did her bosom adorn,
And the *Crosiers*,* new burnished, he hung at Cape Horn.

The weight of two oceans she bore on her sides,
With all their convulsions of tempests and tides;
Vast lakes on her surface did fearfully roll,
And the ice from her rivers surrounded the pole.

Then Europe and Asia he northward extended,
Where under the Arctic with Zembla they ended;
(The length of these regions he took with his garters,
Including Siberia, the land of the Tartars).

In the African clime (where the cocoa-nut tree grows)
He laid down the desarts, and even the negroes,
The shores by the waves of four oceans embraced,
And elephants strolling about in the waste.

In forming East India, he had a wide scope,
Beginning his work at the cape of Good Hope;
Then eastward of that he continued his plan,
'Till he came to the empire and isles of Japan.

Adjacent to Europe he struck up an island,
(One part of it low, but the other was high land)
With many a comical creature upon it,
And one wore a hat, and another a bonnet.

Like emmits or ants in a fine summer's day,
They ever were marching in battle array,

* Stars, in the form of a cross, which mark the South Pole in
Southern latitudes.

Or skipping about on the face of the brine,
Like witches in egg-shells (their ships of the line.)

These poor little creatures were all in a flame,
To the lands of America, urging their claim,
Still biting, or stinging, or spreading their sails;
(For Vulcan had formed them with stings in their tails.)

So poor and so lean, you might count all their ribs,*
Yet were so enraptured with crackers and squibs,
That Vulcan with laughter almost split asunder,
"Because they imagined their crackers were thunder."

Due westward from these, with a channel between,
A servant to slaves, Hibernia was seen,
Once crowded with monarchs, and high in renown,
But all she retained was the Harp and the Crown!

Insulted forever by nobles and priests,
And managed by bullies, and governed by beasts,
She looked!—to describe her I hardly know how—
Such an image of death in the scowl on her brow:

For scaffolds and halters were full in her view,
And the fiends of perdition their cutlasses drew:
And axes and gibbets around her were placed,
And the demons of murder her honours defaced—
With the blood of the WORTHY her mantle was stained,
And hardly a trace of her beauty remained.

Her genius, a female, reclined in the shade,
And, sick of oppression, so mournfully played,
That Jove was uneasy to hear her complain,
And ordered his blacksmith to loosen her chain:

Then tipt her a wink, saying, "Now is your time,
"(To *rebel* is the sin, to *revolt* is no crime)

* Their national debt being now above £200,000,000 sterling.

"When your fetters are off, if you dare not be free
"Be a slave and be damned, but complain not to me."

But finding her timid, he cried in a rage—
"Though the doors are flung open, she stays in the cage!
"Subservient to Britain then let her remain,
"And her freedom shall be, *but the choice of her chain.*"

At length, to discourage all stupid pretensions,
Jove looked at the globe, and approved its dimensions,
And cried in a transport—"Why what have we here!
"Friend Vulcan, it is a most beautiful sphere!

"Now while I am busy in taking apart
"This globe that is formed with such exquisite art,
"Go, Hermes, to Libra, (you're one of her gallants)
"And ask, in my name, for the loan of her balance."

Away posted Hermes, as swift as the gales,
And as swiftly returned with the ponderous scales,
And hung them aloft to a beam in the air,
So equally poised, they had turned with a hair.

Now Jove to COLUMBIA his shoulders applied,
But aiming to lift her, his strength she defied—
Then, turning about to their godships, he says—
"A BODY SO VAST is not easy to raise;

"But if you assist me, I still have a *notion*
"Our *forces, united,* can put her in motion,
"And swing her aloft, (though alone I might fail)
"And place her, in spite of her bulk, in our scale;

"If six years together the Congress have strove,
"And more than *divided the empire with Jove;*
"With a Jove like myself, who am *nine* times as great,
"You can join, like their soldiers, to heave up this weight."

So to it they went, with handspikes and levers,
And upward she sprung, with her mountains and rivers!
Rocks, cities, and islands, deep waters and shallows,
Ships, armies, and forests, high heads, and fine fellows:

"Stick to it!" cries Jove "now heave one and all!
"At least we are lifting *one-eighth of the ball!*"
"If backward she tumbles—then trouble begins,
"And then have a care, my dear boys, of your shins!"

When gods are determined what project can fail?
So they gave a hard shove, and she mounted the scale;
Suspended aloft, Jove viewed her with awe—
And the *gods*,* for their *pay*, had a hearty—huzza!

But Neptune bawled out— "Why Jove you're a noddy,
"Is Britain sufficient to poise that vast body?
"'Tis nonsense such castles to build in the air—
"As well might an oyster with Britain compare."

"Away to your waters, you blustering bully,"
Said Jove, "or I'll make you repent of your folly,
"Is Jupiter, Sir, to be tutored by you?—
"Get out of my sight, for I know what to do!"

Then searching about with his fingers for Britain,
Thought he, "this same island I cannot well hit on!
The devil take him who first called her the GREAT:
"If she was—she is *vastly* diminished of late!"

Like a man that is searching his thigh for a flea,
He peeped and he fumbled, but nothing could see;
At last he exclaimed—"I am surely upon it—
"I think I have hold of a Highlander's bonnet."

But finding his error, he said with a sigh,
"This bonnet is only the island of Skie,†

* American soldiers.
† An Island on the north-west of Scotland.

So away to his *namesake* the PLANET he goes,
And borrowed *two moons* to hang on his nose.

Through these, as through glasses, he saw her quite clear,
And in rapture cried out—"I have found her—she's here!
"If this be not Britain, then call me an ass,
"She *looks like a gem in an ocean of glass.*

"But faith, she's so small I must mind how I shake her;
"In a box I'll enclose her, for fear I should break her:
"Though a god, I might suffer for being aggressor,
"Since scorpions, and vipers, and hornets possess her;

"The white cliffs of Albion I think I descry,
"And the hills of Plinlimmon appear rather nigh—
"But, Vulcan, inform me what creatures are these,
"That smell so of onions, and garlick, and cheese?"

Old Vulcan replied—"Odds splutter a nails!
"Why, these are the Welch, and the country is Wales!
"When Taffy is vext, no devil is ruder—
"Take care how you trouble the offspring of TUDOR!

"On the crags of the mountains *hur* living *hur* seeks,
"*Hur* country is planted with garlick and leeks;
"So great is *hur* choler, beware how you teaze *hur*,
"For these are the Britons—unconquered by Caesar."

"But now, my dear Juno, pray give me my mittens,
"(These insects I am going to handle are Britons)
"I'll draw up their isle with a finger and thumb,
"As the doctor extracts an old tooth from the gum."

Then he raised her aloft—but to shorten our tale,
She looked like a CLOD in the opposite scale—
Britannia so small, and Columbia so large—
A ship of first rate, and a ferryman's barge!

Cried Pallas to Vulcan, "Why, Jove's in a dream—
"Observe how he watches the turn of the beam!
"Was ever a mountain outweighed by a grain?
"Or what is a drop when compared to the main?"

But Momus alledged—"in my humble opinion,
"You should add to Great-Britain her foreign dominion,
"When this is appended, perhaps she will rise,
"And equal her rival in weight and in size."

"Alas! (said the monarch), your project is vain,
"But little is left of her foreign domain;
"And, scattered about in the liquid expanse,
"That little is left to the mercy of France;

"However, we'll lift them, and give her fair play"—
And soon in the scale with their mistress they lay;
But the gods were confounded and struck with surprise,
And Vulcan could hardly believe his own eyes!

For (such was the purpose and guidance of fate)
Her foreign dominions diminished her weight—
By which it appeared, to Britain's disaster,
Her foreign possessions were changing their master.

Then, as he replaced them, said Jove with a smile—
"COLUMBIA shall never be ruled by an isle—
"But vapours and darkness around her may rise,
"And tempests conceal her awhile from our eyes;

"So locusts in Egypt their squadrons display,
"And rising, disfigure the face of the day;
"So the moon, at her full, has a frequent eclipse,
"And the sun in the ocean diurnally dips.

"Then cease your endeavours, ye vermin of Britain—
(And here, in derision, their island he spit on)

"'Tis madness to seek what you never can find,
"Or to think of uniting what nature disjoined;

"But still you may flutter awhile with your wings,
"And spit out your venom and brandish your stings:
"Your hearts are as black, and as bitter as gall,
"A curse to mankind—and a blot on the BALL."*

                                        April 1782

* It is hoped that such a sentiment may not be deemed wholly il-
liberal. Every candid person will certainly *draw a line between a brave
and magnanimous people, and a most vicious and vitiating government.*
Perhaps the following extract from a pamphlet lately published in
London and republished at Baltimore (June, 1809) by Mr. *Bernard
Dornin*, will place the preceding sentiment in a fair point of view:
"A better spirit than exists in the English people, never existed
in any people in the world; it has been misdirected, and squandered
upon party purposes in the most degrading and scandalous manner;
they have been led to believe that they were benefiting the commerce
of England by destroying the commerce of America, that they were
defending their sovereign by perpetuating the bigoted oppression
of their fellow subjects; their rulers and their guides have told them
that they would equal the vigour of France by equalling her atrocity,
and they have gone on, wasting that opulence, patience and courage,
which if husbanded by prudent, and moderate counsels, might have
proved the salvation of mankind. The same policy of turning the
good qualities of Englishmen to their own destruction, which made
Mr. Pitt omnipotent, continues his power to those who resemble
him only in his vices; advantage is taken of the loyalty of Englishmen, to make them meanly submissive; their piety is turned into
persecution; their courage into useless and obstinate contention;
they are plundered because they are ready to pay, and soothed into
asinine stupidity because they are full of virtuous patience. If
England must perish at last, so let it be: that event is in the hands
of God; we must dry up our tears, and submit. But that England
should perish swindling and stealing; that it should perish waging
war against lazar-houses and hospitals, that it should perish per-
secuting with monastic bigotry; that it should calmly give itself
up to be ruined by the flashy arrogance of one man, and the narrow
fanaticism of another; these events are within the power of human
beings, but I did not think that the magnanimity of Englishmen
would ever stoop to such degradations."

BARNEY'S INVITATION.

COME all ye lads who know no fear,
To wealth and honor with me steer
In the HYDER ALI privateer,
 Commanded by brave BARNEY.

She's new and true, and tight and sound,
Well rigged aloft, and all well found—
Come away and be with laurel crowned,
 Away—and leave your lasses.

Accept our terms without delay,
And make your fortunes while you may,
Such offers are not every day
 In the power of a jolly sailor.

Success and fame attend the brave,
But death the coward and the slave,
Who fears to plow the Atlantic wave,
 To seek the bold invaders.

Come, then, and take a cruising bout,
Our ship sails well, there is no doubt,
She *has* been tried both in and out,
 And answers expectation.

Let no proud foes whom Europe bore,
Distress our trade, insult our shore—
Teach them to know their reign is o'er,
 Bold Philadelphia sailors!

We'll teach them how to sail so near,
Or to venture on the Delaware,
When we in warlike trim appear
 And cruise without Henlopen.

Who cannot wounds and battle dare
Shall never clasp the blooming fair;

The brave alone their charms should share,
  The brave are their protectors.

With hand and heart united all,
Prepared to conquer or to fall,
Attend, my lads, to honours call,
  Embark in our HYDER ALI.

From an Eastern prince she takes her name,
Who, smit with Freedom's sacred flame,
Usurping Britons brought to shame,
  His country's wrongs avenging;

See, on her stern the waving stars—
Inured to blood, inured to wars,
Come, enter quick, my jolly tars,
  To scourge these warlike Britons.

Here's grog enough—then drink a bout,
I know your hearts are firm and stout;
American blood will never give out,
  And often we have proved it.

Though stormy oceans round us roll,
We'll keep a firm undaunted soul,
Befriended by the cheering bowl,
  Sworn foes to melancholy:

While timorous landsmen lurk on shore,
'Tis ours to go where cannons roar—
On a coasting cruise we'll go once more,
  Despisers of all danger;

And Fortune still, who crowns the brave,
Shall guard us over the gloomy wave
A fearful heart betrays a knave;
  Success to HYDER ALI.

1786

SONG,

On Captain Barney's Victory over the Ship *General Monk. April 26, 1782.*

O'ER the waste of waters cruising,
  Long the GENERAL MONK had reigned;
All subduing, all reducing,
  None her lawless rage restrained:
Many a brave and hearty fellow
  Yielding to this warlike foe,
When her guns began to bellow
  Struck his humbled colours low.

But grown bold with long successes,
  Leaving the wide watery way,
She, a stranger to distresses,
  Came to cruise within Cape May:
"Now we soon (said captain Rogers)
  "Shall their men of commerce meet;
"In our hold we'll have them lodgers,
  "We shall capture half their fleet.

"Lo! I see their van appearing—
  "Back our topsails to the mast—
"They toward us full are steering
  "With a gentle western-blast;
"I've a list of all their cargoes,
  "All their guns, and all their men:
"I am sure these modern Argo's
  "Cant escape us one in ten:

"Yonder comes the charming SALLY
  "Sailing with the GENERAL GREENE—
"First we'll fight the HYDER ALI,
  "Taking her is taking them:
"She invites to give us battle,
  "Bearing down with all her sail—

"Now, boys, let our cannon rattle!
  "To take her we cannot fail.

"Our eighteen guns, each a nine pounder,
  "Soon shall terrify this foe;
"We shall maul her, we shall wound her,
  "Bringing rebel colours low."
While he thus anticipated
  Conquests that he could not gain,
He in the Cape May channel waited
  For the ship that caused his pain.

Captain Barney then preparing,
  Thus addressed his gallant crew—
"Now, brave lads, be bold and daring,
  "Let your hearts be firm and true;
"This is a proud English cruiser,
  "Roving up and down the main,
"We must fight her—must reduce her,
  "Though our decks be strewed with slain.

"Let who will be the survivor,
  "We must conquer or must die,
"We must take her up the river,
  "Whate'er comes of you or I:
"Though she shews most formidable
  "With her eighteen pointed nines,
"And her quarters clad in sable,
  "Let us baulk her proud designs.

"With four nine pounders, and twelve sixes
  "We will face that daring band;
"Let no dangers damp your courage,
  "Nothing can the brave withstand.
"Fighting for your country's honour,
  "Now to gallant deeds aspire;
"Helmsman, bear us down upon her,
  "Gunner, give the word to fire!"

Then yard arm and yard arm meeting,
  Strait began the dismal fray,
Cannon mouths, each other greeting,
  Belched their smoky flames away:
Soon the langrage, grape and chain shot,
  That from BARNEY'S cannons flew,
Swept the MONK, and cleared each round top,
  Killed and wounded half her crew.

Captain Rogers strove to rally:
  But they from their quarters fled,
While the roaring HYDER ALI
  Covered o'er his decks with dead.
When from *their* tops their dead men tumbled,
  And the streams of blood did flow,
Then their proudest hopes were humbled
  By their brave *inferior* foe.

All aghast, and all confounded,
  They beheld their champions fall,
And their captain, sorely wounded,
  Bade them quick for quarters call.
Then the MONK'S proud flag descended,
  And her cannon ceased to roar;
By her crew no more defended,
  She confessed the contest o'er.

Come, brave boys, and fill your glasses,
  You have humbled one proud foe,
No brave action this surpasses,
  Fame shall tell the nations so—
Thus be Britain's woes completed,
  Thus abridged her cruel reign,
'Till she ever, thus defeated,
  Yields the sceptre of the main.

1782

A PICTURE OF THE TIMES,

With Occasional Reflections.

STILL round the world triumphant Discord flies,
Still angry kings to bloody contest rise;
Hosts bright with steel, in dreadful order placed,
And ships contending on the watery waste;
Distracting demons every breast engage,
Unwearied nations glow with mutual rage;
Still to the charge the routed Briton turns,
The war still rages and the battle burns;
See, man with man in deadly combat join,
See, the black navy form the flaming line;
Death smiles alike at battles lost or won—
Art does for him what Nature would have done.

Can scenes like these delight the human breast?—
Who sees with joy humanity distrest?
Such tragic scenes fierce passion might prolong,
But slighted Reason says, they must be wrong.

Cursed be the day, how bright soe'er it shined,
That first made kings the masters of mankind;
And cursed the wretch who first with regal pride
Their equal rights to equal men denied;
But cursed, o'er all, who first to slavery broke
Submissive bowed and owned a monarch's yoke:
Their servile souls his arrogance adored
And basely owned a brother for a lord;
Hence wrath, and blood, and feuds and wars began,
And man turned monster to his fellow man.

Not so that age of innocence and ease
When men, yet social, knew no ills like these;
Then dormant yet, Ambition (half unknown)
No rival murdered to possess a throne;
No seas to guard, no empires to defend—
Of some small tribe the father and the friend.
The hoary sage beneath his sylvan shade
Imposed no laws but those which reason made;

On peace, not war, on good, not ill intent,
He judged his brethren by their own consent;
Untaught to spurn those brethren to the dust;
In virtue firm, and obstinately just,
For him no navies roved from shore to shore,
No slaves were doomed to dig the glittering ore;
Remote from all the vain parade of state,
No slaves in scarlet sauntered at his gate,
Nor did his breast the angry passions tear,
He knew no murder and he felt no fear.

Was this the patriarch sage—Then turn your eyes
And view the contrast that our age supplies;
Touched from the life, we trace no ages fled,
I draw no curtain that conceals the dead;
To distant Britain let the view be cast,
And say, the present far exceeds the past;
Of all the plagues that e'er the world have cursed,
Name George, the tyrant, and you name the worst!

What demon, hostile to the human kind,
Planted these fierce disorders in the mind?
All urged alike, one phantom we pursue,
But what has war with human kind to do?
In death's black shroud our bliss can ne'er be found;
'Tis madness aims the life-destroying wound,
Sends fleets and armies to these ravaged shores
Plots constant ruin, but no peace restores.

O dire Ambition!—thee these horrors suit:
Lost to the human, she assumes the brute;
She, proudly vain, or insolently bold,
Her heart revenge, her eye intent on gold,
Swayed by the madness of the present hour
Lays worlds in ruin for *extent of power;*
That shining bait, which dropt in folly's way
Tempts the weak mind, and leads the heart astray!

Thou happiness! still sought but never found,
We, in a circle, chace thy shadow round;
Meant all mankind in different forms to bless,
Which yet possessing, we no more possess:

Thus far removed and painted on the eye
Smooth verdant fields seem blended with the sky,
But where they both in fancied contact join
In vain we trace the visionary line;
Still as we chace, the empty circle flies,
Emerge new mountains or new oceans rise.

[1782]

To

A CONCEALED ROYALIST

On a Virulent Attack *

*"We have force to crumble you into dust, although you were as hard
as rocks, adamant, or jasper."*

WHEN round the bark the howling tempest raves
Tossed in the conflict of a thousand waves,
The lubber landsmen weep, complain, and sigh,
And on the pilot's skill, or heaven, rely;
Lurk in their holes, astonished and aghast,
Dreading the moment that must be their last.
    The tempest done—their terror also ceases,
And up they come, and shew their *shameless* faces,
At once *feel bold*, and tell the pilot, too,
He did no more than they—themselves—*could do!*
    A FOE TO TYRANTS! ONE *your pen* restores:—
There is a TYRANT WHOM YOUR SOUL ADORES:
And every line *you write* too plainly shows,
Your heart is hostile to that TYRANT'S FOES.
    What, worse than folly, urged this genius dull
With CHURCHILL's wreathes to shade his leaden scull:
So, midnight darkness union claims with light:
So oil and water in one mass unite:—
No more your rage in *plundered verse* repeat,
Sink into prose—even there no *safe retreat,*

* Addressed to Eleazer Oswald, editor of the *Independent Gazette*,
who had been waging war on the *Freeman's Journal* during the
summer of 1782. [Ed.]

REED'S patriot fame to distant years may last,
When *rancorous reptiles* to the *dogs* are cast,
Or, where oblivion spreads her weary wings,
Lost in the lumber of forgotten things;
And none shall ask, nor wish to know, nor care,
Who—what their names—or when they lived—or where.

1782

Occasioned

By GENERAL WASHINGTON'S

Arrival in Philadelphia, on his way to his residence in
Virginia. (December, 1783)

1

THE great, unequal conflict past,
The Briton banished from our shore,
Peace, heav'n-descended, comes at last,
And hostile nations rage no more;
From fields of death the weary swain
Returning, seeks his native plain.

2

In every vale she smiles serene,
Freedom's bright stars more radiant rise,
New charms she adds to every scene,
Her brighter sun illumes our skies;
Remotest realms admiring stand,
And hail the *Hero* of our land:

3

He comes!—the Genius of these lands—
Fame's thousand tongues his worth confess,
Who conquered with his suffering bands,
And grew immortal by distress:
Thus calms succeed the stormy blast,
And valour is repaid at last.

4

O *Washington!*—thrice glorious name,
What due rewards can man decree—
Empires are far below thine aim,
And sceptres have no charms for thee;
Virtue alone has your regard,
And she must be your great reward.

5

Encircled by extorted power,
Monarchs must envy thy *Retreat*,
Who cast, in some ill-fated hour,
Their country's freedom at their feet;
'Twas yours to act a nobler part
For injured Freedom had thy heart.

6

For ravaged realms and conquered seas
Rome gave the great imperial prize,
And, swelled with pride, for feats like these,
Transferred her heroes to the skies:—
A brighter scene your deeds display,
You gain those heights a different way.

7

When *Faction* reared her bristly head,
And joined with tyrants to destroy,
Where'er you marched the monster fled,
Timorous her arrows to employ:
Hosts caught from you a bolder flame,
And despots trembled at your name.

8

Ere war's dread horrors ceased to reign,
What leader could your place supply?—
Chiefs crowded to the embattled plain,
Prepar'd to conquer or to die—

Heroes arose—but none like you
Could save our lives and freedom too.

9

In swelling verse let kings be read,
And princes shine in polished prose;
Without such aid your triumphs spread
Where'er the convex ocean flows,
To Indian worlds by seas embraced,
And Tartar, tyrant of the waste.

10

Throughout the east you gain applause,
And soon the *Old World*, taught by you,
Shall blush to own her barbarous laws,
Shall learn instruction from the *New:*
Monarchs shall hear the humble plea,
Nor urge too far the proud decree.

11

Despising pomp and vain parade,
At home you stay, while France and Spain
The secret, ardent wish conveyed,
And hailed you to their shores in vain:
In *Vernon's* groves you shun the throne,
Admired by kings, but seen by none.

12

Your fame, thus spread to distant lands,
May envy's fiercest blasts endure,
Like Egypt's pyramids it stands,
Built on a basis more secure;
Time's latest age shall own in you
The patriot and the statesman too.

13

Now hurrying from the busy scene,
Where thy *Potowmack's* waters flow,
May'st thou enjoy thy rural reign,

And every earthly blessing know;
Thus HE* whom Rome's proud legions swayed,
Returned, and sought his sylvan shade.

14

Not less in wisdom than in war
Freedom shall still employ your mind,
Slavery shall vanish, wide and far,
'Till not a trace is left behind;
Your counsels not bestowed in vain,
Shall still protect this infant reign.

15

So, when the bright, all-cheering sun
From our contracted view retires,
Though folly deems his race is run,
On other worlds he lights his fires!
Cold climes beneath his influence glow,
And frozen rivers learn to flow.

16

O say, thou great, exalted name!
What Muse can boast of equal lays,
Thy worth disdains all vulgar fame,
Transcends the noblest poet's praise,
Art soars, unequal to the flight,
And genius sickens at the height.

17

For States redeemed—our western reign
Restored by thee to milder sway,
Thy conscious glory shall remain
When this great globe is swept away,
And *all* is lost that pride admires,
And all the pageant scene expires.

1783

* Cincinnatus.

On the
EMIGRATION TO AMERICA
and
Peopling the Western Country

TO western woods, and lonely plains,
Palemon from the crowd departs,
Where Nature's wildest genius reigns,
To tame the soil, and plant the arts—
What wonders there shall freedom show,
What mighty STATES successive grow!

From Europe's proud, despotic shores
Hither the stranger takes his way,
And in our new found world explores
A happier soil, a milder sway,
Where no proud despot holds him down,
No slaves insult him with a crown.

What charming scenes attract the eye,
On wild Ohio's savage stream!
There Nature reigns, whose works outvie
The boldest pattern art can frame;
There ages past have rolled away,
And forests bloomed but to decay.

From these fair plains, these rural seats,
So long concealed, so lately known,
The unsocial Indian far retreats,
To make some other clime his own,
When other streams, less pleasing flow,
And darker forests round him grow.

Great Sire* of floods! whose varied wave
Through climes and countries takes its way,
To whom creating Nature gave
Ten thousand streams to swell thy sway!
* Mississippi.

No longer shall *they* useless prove,
Nor idly through the forests rove;

Nor longer shall your princely flood
From distant lakes be swelled in vain,
Nor longer through a darksome wood
Advance, unnoticed, to the main,
Far other ends, the heavens decree—
And commerce plans new freights for thee.

While virtue warms the generous breast,
There heaven-born freedom shall reside,
Nor shall the voice of war molest,
Nor Europe's all-aspiring pride—
There Reason shall new laws devise,
And order from confusion rise.

Forsaking kings and regal state,
With all their pomp and fancied bliss,
The traveller owns, convinced though late,
No realm so free, so blest as this—
The east is half to slaves consigned,
Where kings and priests enchain the mind.

O come the time, and haste the day,
When man shall man no longer crush,
When Reason shall enforce her sway,
Nor these fair regions raise our blush,
Where still the *African* complains,
And mourns his yet unbroken chains.

Far brighter scenes a future age,
The muse predicts, these States will hail,
Whose genius may the world engage,
Whose deeds may over death prevail,
And happier systems bring to view,
Than all the eastern sages knew.

[1784]   1785

LITERARY IMPORTATION.

However we wrangled with Britain awhile
We think of her now in a different stile,
And many fine things we receive from her isle;
Among all the rest,
Some demon possessed
Our dealers in knowledge and sellers of sense
To have a good *bishop* imported from thence.

The words of *Sam Chandler** were thought to be vain,
When he argued so often and proved it *so plain*
"That Satan must flourish till bishops should reign:"
Though he went to the wall
With his project and all,
Another bold Sammy,† in bishop's array,
Has got something more than his pains for his pay.

It seems we had spirit to humble a throne,
Have genius for science inferior to none,
But hardly encourage a plant of our own:
If a college be planned,
'Tis all at a stand
'Till in Europe we send at a shameful expense,
To send us a book-worm to teach us some sense.

Can we never be thought to have learning or grace
Unless it be brought from that horrible place
Where tyranny reigns with her impudent face;
And popes and pretenders,
And sly faith-defenders
Have ever been hostile to reason and wit,
Enslaving a world that shall conquer them yet.

* Who laboured for the establishment of an American Episcopacy, previously to the revolutionary war.

† Freneau refers here to Bishop Samuel Seabury of Connecticut, the first Anglican bishop in America. [Ed.]

'Tis folly to fret at the picture I draw:
And I say what was said by a *Doctor Magraw;**
"If they give us their Bishops, they'll give us their law."
How that will agree
With such people as we,
Let us leave to the learned to reflect on awhile,
And say what they think in a handsomer stile.

[w. 1786]   1788

STANZAS

Written at the foot of Monte Souffriere, near the Town of Basseterre, Guadaloupe.

THESE Indian isles, so green and gay
In summer seas by nature placed—
Art hardly told us where they lay,
'Till tyranny their charms defaced:
    Ambition here her efforts made,
    And avarice rifled every shade.

Their genius wept, his sons to see
By foreign arms untimely fall,
And some to distant climates flee,
Where later ruin met them all:
    He saw his sylvan offspring bleed,
    That *envious natures* might succeed.

The CHIEF, who first o'er untried waves
To these fair islands found his way,
Departing, left a race of slaves,
Cortez, your mandate to obey,
    And these again, if fame says true,
    To extirpate the vulgar crew.

No more to Indian coasts confined,
The PATRON, thus, indulged his grief;

* A noted practitioner in physic, formerly of N. York.

And to regret his heart resigned,
To see some proud European chief,
   Pursue the harmless Indian race,
   Torn by his dogs in every chace.—

Ah, what a change! the ambient deep
No longer hears the lover's sigh;
But wretches meet, to wail and weep
The loss of their dear liberty:
   Unfeeling hearts possess these isles,
   Man frowns—and only nature smiles.

Proud of the vast extended shores
The haughty Spaniard calls his own,
His selfish heart restrains his stores,
To other climes but scarcely known:
   His Cuba lies a wilderness,
   Where slavery digs what slaves possess.

Jamaica's sweet, romantic vales
In vain with golden harvests teem;
Her endless spring, her fragrant gales
More than Elysian magic seem:
   Yet what the soil profusely gave
   Is there denied the toiling slave.

Fantastic joy and fond belief
Through life support the galling chain;
Hope's airy prospects banish griefs,
And bring his native lands again:
   His native groves a heaven display,
   The funeral is the *jocund* day.

For man oppressed and made so base,
In vain from Jove fair virtue fell;
Distress be-glooms the toiling race,
They have no motive to excel:
   In death alone their miseries end,
   The tyrant's dread—is their best friend.

How great THEIR praise let *truth* declare,
Who touched with honour's sacred flame,
Bade freedom to *some coasts* repair
To urge the slaves's neglected claim;
 And scorning interest's *swinish* plan,
 Gave to mankind *the rights of man*.

Ascending there, may freedom's sun
In all his force serenely clear,
A long, unclouded circuit run,
Till little tyrants disappear;
 And a new race, not bought or sold,
 Rise from the ashes of the old.—

1787

Epistle

to

THE PATRIOTIC FARMER.

THUS, while new laws the stubborn STATES reclaim,
And most for pensions, some for honours aim,
YOU, who first aimed a shaft at GEORGE'S crown,
And marked the way to conquest and renown,
While from the vain, the lofty, and the proud,
Retiring to your groves, you shun the crowd,—
Can toils, like your's, in cold oblivion end,
Columbia's patriot, and her earliest friend?
 Blest, doubly blest, from public scenes retired,
Where public welfare all your bosom fired;
Your life's best days in studious labours past
Your deeds of virtue make your bliss at last;
When all things fail, the soul must rest on these!—
May heaven restore you to your favourite trees,
And calm content, best lot to man assigned,
Be heaven's reward to your exalted mind.
 When her base projects you beheld, with pain,
And early doomed an end to Britain's reign.

When rising nobly in a generous cause
(Sworn foe to tyrants and imported laws)
Thou DICKINSON! the patriot and the sage,
How much we owed to your convincing page:*
That page—the check of tyrants and of knaves,
Gave birth to heroes who had else been slaves,
Who, taught by you, denied a monarch's sway;
And if they brought him low—you planned the way.

Though in this glare of pomp you take no part
Still must your conduct warm each generous heart:
What, though you shun the patriot vain and loud,
While hosts neglect, that once to merit bowed,
Shun those gay scenes, where recent laurels grow,
The mad PROCESSION, and the painted show;
In days to come, when pomp and pride resign,
Who would not change his proudest wreathes for thine,
In fame's fair fields such well-earned honours share,
And DICKINSON confess unrivalled there!

(1788)

ON THE PROSPECT

OF

A REVOLUTION IN FRANCE

"Now, at the feast they plan the fall of Troy;
"The stern debate ATRIDES *hears with joy."*
—*Hom. Odys.*

BORNE on the wings of time another year
Sprung from the past, begins its proud career:
From that bright spark which first illumed these lands,
See Europe kindling, as the blaze expands,
Each gloomy tyrant, sworn to chain the mind,
Presumes no more to trample on mankind:

* The Farmer's Letters, and others of his truly valuable writings.

Even potent LOUIS trembles on his throne,
The generous prince who made our cause his own,
More equal rights his injured subjects claim,
No more a country's strength—that country's shame;
Fame starts astonished at such prizes won,
And rashness wonders how the work was done.
   Flushed with new life, and brightening at the view,
Genius, triumphant, moulds the world anew;
To these far climes in swift succession moves
Each art that Reason owns and sense approves.
What though his age is bounded to a span
Time sheds a conscious dignity on man,
Some happier breath his rising passions swells,
Some kinder genius his bold arm impels,
Dull superstition from the world retires,
Disheartened zealots haste to quench their fires;
One equal rule o'er twelve* vast STATES extends,
Europe and Asia join to be our friends,
Our active flag in every clime displayed
Counts stars on colours that shall never fade;
A far famed chief o'er this vast whole presides
Whose motto HONOR is—whom VIRTUE guides;
His walks forsaken in Virginia's groves
Applauding thousands bow where'er HE moves,
Who laid the basis of this EMPIRE sure
Where public faith should public peace secure.
   Still may she rise, exalted in her aims,
And boast to every age her patriot names,
To distant climes extend her gentle sway,
While choice—not force—bids every heart obey:
Ne'er may she fail when Liberty implores,
Nor want true valour to defend her shores,
'Till Europe, humbled, greets our western wave,
And owns an equal—whom she wished a slave.

1790

* At this time, Rhode-Island was not a member of the general Confederation of the American States. (1788.)

THE DISTREST THEATRE.*

HEALTH to the Muse!—and fill the glass,—
Heaven grant her soon some better place,
Than earthen floor and fabric mean,
Where disappointment shades the scene:

There as I came, by rumour led,
I sighed and almost wished her dead;
Her visage stained with many a tear,
No HALLAM and no HENRY here!

But what could all their art attain?—
When pointed laws the stage restrain
The prudent Muse obedience pays
To sleepy squires, that damn all plays.

Like thieves they hang beyond the town,
They shove her off—to please the gown;—
Though Rome and Athens owned it true,
The stage might mend our morals *too*.

See, *Mopsus* all the evening sits
O'er bottled beer, that drowns his wits;
Were Plays allowed, he might at least
Blush—and no longer act the beast.

See, *Marcia*, now from guardian free,
Retailing scandal with her tea;—
Might she not come, nor danger fear
From *Hamlet's* sigh, or *Juliet's* tear.

The world but acts the player's part†—
(So says the motto of their art)—
That world in vice great lengths is gone
That fears to see its picture drawn.

* Harmony Hall, at Charleston, now demolished.
† *Totus Mundus agit Histrionem.*

Mere vulgar actors cannot please;
The streets supply enough of these;
And what can wit or beauty gain
When sleepy dullness joins their train?

A *State* betrays a homely taste,
By which the stage is thus disgraced,
Where, drest in all the flowers of speech,
Dame virtue might her precepts teach.

Let but a dancing bear arrive,
A pig, that counts you four, or five—
And Cato, with his moral strain
May strive to mend the world in vain.

1791

The New England
SABBATH–DAY CHACE.

(Written Under the Character of HEZEKIAH SALEM.)

ON a fine Sunday morning I mounted my steed
And southward from HARTFORD had meant to proceed;
My baggage was stow'd in a cart very snug,
Which RANGER, the gelding, was destined to lug;
With his harness and buckles, he loom'd very grand,
And was drove by young DARBY, a lad of the land—
On land, or on water, most handy was he,
A jockey on shore, and a sailor at sea,
He knew all the roads, he was so very keen
And the *Bible* by heart, at the age of fifteen.
  As thus I jogg'd on, to my saddle confined,
With *Ranger* and *Darby* a distance behind;
At last in full view of a steeple we came
With a *cock* on the spire (I suppose he was game;
A dove in the pulpit may suit your grave people,
But always remember—a cock on the steeple)
Cries Darby—"Dear master, I beg you to stay;
Believe me, there's danger in driving this way;

Our deacons on Sundays have power to arrest
And lead us to church—if your honour thinks best—
Though still I must do them the justice to tell,
They would choose you should pay them the fine full as well."

The fine (said I) Darby, how much may it be—
A shilling or sixpence?—why, now let me see,
Three shillings are all the small pence that remain
And to change a half joe would be rather PROFANE.
Is it more than three shillings, the fine that you speak on;
What say you good Darby—will that serve the deacon.

"Three shillings (cried Darby) why, master, you're jesting!
Let us *luff* while we can and make sure of our *westing*—
Forty shillings, excuse me, is too much to pay
It would take my month's wages—that's all I've to say.
By taking *this road* that inclines to the right
The squire and the sexton may bid us good night,
If once to old Ranger I give up the rein
The parson himself may pursue us in vain."

"Not I, my good Darby (I answer'd the lad)
Leave the church on the left! they would think we were mad;
I would sooner rely on the heels of my steed,
And pass by them all like a *Jehu* indeed:—
As long as I'm able to lead in the race
Old Ranger, the gelding, will go a good pace,
As the deacon pursues, he will fly like a swallow,
And you in the cart must, undoubtedly, follow."

Then approaching the church, as we pass'd by the door
The sexton peep'd out, with a saint or two more,
A deacon came forward and waved us his hat,
A signal to drop him some money—mind that!—

"Now, Darby, (I halloo'd) be ready to skip,
Ease off the curb bridle—give Ranger the whip:
While you have the rear, and myself lead the way,
No doctor or deacon shall catch us this day."

By this time the deacon had mounted his poney
And chaced for the sake of our souls and—our money:
The saint, as he followed, cried—"Stop them, halloo!"
As swift as he followed, as swiftly we flew—

"Ah master! (said Darby), I very much fear
We must drop him some money to check his career,
He is gaining upon us and waves with his hat
There's nothing, dear master, will stop him but that.
Remember the Beaver (you well know the fable)
Who flying the hunters as long as he's able,
When he finds that his efforts can nothing avail
But death and the puppies are close to his tail,
Instead of desponding at such a dead lift
He bites off *their object*, and makes a free gift—
Since fortune all hope of escaping denies
Better give them a little, than lose the whole prize."
But scarce had he spoke, when we came to a place
Whose muddy condition concluded the chace,
Down settled the cart—and old Ranger stuck fast
Aha! (said the Saint) have I catch'd ye at last?

Caetera desunt.

1790

On the Death of

DR. BENJAMIN FRANKLIN.

THUS, some tall tree that long hath stood
The glory of its native wood,
By storms destroyed, or length of years,
Demands the tribute of our tears.

The pile, that took long time to raise,
To dust returns by slow decays:
But, when its destined years are o'er,
We must regret the loss the more.

So long accustomed to your aid,
The world laments your exit made;
So long befriended by your art,
Philosopher, 'tis hard to part!—

When monarchs tumble to the ground,
Successors easily are found:
But, matchless FRANKLIN! what a few
Can hope to rival such as you,
Who seized from kings their sceptred pride,
And turned the lightning's darts aside *

1790

EPISTLE

From DR. FRANKLIN (deceased) to his Poetical Pane-
gyrists, on some of their Absurd Compliments.

"GOOD Poets, who so full of pain,
Are you sincere—or do you feign?
Love for your tribe I never had,
Nor penned three stanzes, good or bad.

At funerals, sometimes, grief appears,
Where legacies have purchased tears:
'Tis folly to be sad for nought,
From me you never gained a groat.

To better trades I turned my views,
And never meddled with the muse;
Great things I did for rising States,
And kept the lightning from some pates.

This grand discovery, you adore it,
But ne'er will be the better for it:
You still are subject to those fires,
For poets' houses have no spires.

Philosophers are famed for pride;
But, pray, be modest—when I died,
No "sighs disturbed old ocean's bed,"
No "Nature wept" for Franklin dead!

* Eripuit coelo fulmen, sceptrumque tyrannis!

That day, on which I left the coast,
A beggar-man was also lost:
If "Nature wept," you must agree
She wept for *him*—as well as *me*.

There's reason even in telling lies—
In such profusion of her "sighs,"
She was too sparing of a tear—
In Carolina, all was clear:

And, if there fell some snow and sleet,
Why must it be my winding sheet?
Snows oft have cloathed the *April* plain,
Have melted, and will melt again.

Poets, I pray you, say no more,
Or say what Nature said before;
That reason should your pens direct,
Or else you pay me no respect.

Let reason be your constant rule,
And Nature, trust me, is no fool—
When to the dust great men she brings,
"MAKE HER DO—SOME UNCOMMON THINGS."

1790

THE DEPARTURE:

Occasioned by the Removal of Congress from New-York to Philadelphia.—(1790.)

FROM Hudson's banks, in proud array,
(Too mean to claim a longer stay)
Their new ideas to improve,
Behold the *generous* Congress move!

Such thankless conduct much we feared,
When Timon's coach stood ready geered,

And HE—the foremost on the floor,
Stood pointing to the Delaware shore,

So long confined to *little things*,
They sigh to be where *Bavius* sings,
Where *Sporus* builds his splendid pile,
And *Bufo's* tawdry Seasons smile.

New chaplains, now, shall ope their jaws,
New salaries grease unworthy paws:
Some reverend man, that turtle carves,
Will fatten, while the solder starves.

The YORKER asks—but asks in vain—
"What demon bids them 'move again?
"Whoever 'moves must suffer loss,
"And rolling stones collect no moss.

"Have we not paid for chaplains' prayers,
"That heaven might smile on state affairs?—
"Put some things up, pulled others down,
"And raised our streets through half the town?

"Have we not, to our utmost, strove
"That Congress might not hence remove—
"At dull debates no silence broke,
"And walked on tip-toe while they spoke?

"Have we not toiled through cold and heat,
"To make the FEDERAL PILE complete—
"Thrown down our FORT, to give them air,
"And sent our guns, the devil knows where?

"Times change! but Memory still recalls
"The DAY, when ruffians scaled their walls—
"Sovereigns besieged by angry men,
"Mere prisoners in the town of PENN?

"Can they forget when, half afraid,
"The timorous COUNCIL* lent no aid;
"But left them to the rogues that rob,
"The tender mercies of the mob?

"Oh! if they can, their lot is cast;
"One hundred miles will soon be passed—
"THIS DAY the FEDERAL DOME is cleared,
"To Paulus'-Hook the barge is steered,
"Where Timon's coach stands ready geered!"

[1790]   1795

THE AMERICAN SOLDIER.

(A Picture from the Life)

> " *To serve with love,*
> *And shed your blood,*
> *Approved may be above,*
> *And here below*
> (*Examples shew*)
> *'Tis dangerous to be good.*"
>
> LORD OXFORD.

DEEP in a vale, a stranger now to arms,
Too poor to shine in courts, too proud to beg,
He, who once warred on Saratoga's plains,
Sits musing o'er his scars, and wooden leg.

Remembering still the toil of former days,
To *other* hands he sees his earnings paid;—
They share the due reward—*he* feeds on praise,
Lost in the abyss of want, misfortune's shade.

Far, far from domes where splendid tapers glare,
'Tis his from dear bought peace no wealth to win,
Removed alike from courtly cringing 'squires,
The great-man's *Levee*, and the proud man's grin.

* See the history of those times.

Sold are those arms which once on Britons blazed,
When, flushed with conquest, to the charge they came;
That power repelled, and *Freedom's* fabrick raised,
She leaves her soldier—*famine* and a *name!* (1790)

1795

Occasioned by
A LEGISLATION BILL

Proposing a Taxation upon Newspapers.

"'Tis time to tax the News, (Sangrado cries)
"Subjects were never good that were too wise:
"In every hamlet, every trifling town,
"Some sly, designing fellow sits him down,
"On spacious folio prints his weekly mess,
"And spreads around this poison of his Press.
"Hence, to the WORLD the streams of scandal flow,
"Disclosing secrets, that it should not know,
"Hence courtiers strut with libels on their backs;—
"And shall not news be humbled by a tax!

"Once (*'tis most true*) such papers did some good,
"When British chiefs arrived in angry mood:
"By them enkindled, every heart grew warm,
"By them excited, all were taught to arm,
"When *some*, retiring to Britannia's clime,
"Sat brooding o'er the vast events of time;
"Doubtful which side to take, or what to say,
"Or who would win, or who would lose the day.

"Those times are past; (and past experience shews)
"The well-born sort alone, should read the news,
"No common herds should get behind the scene
"To view the movements of the state machine:
"One paper only, filled with courtly stuff,
"One paper, for one country is enough,
"Where incense offered at Pomposo's shrine
"Shall prove his house-dog and himself divine."

1791

To the
PUBLIC.*

THIS age is so fertile of mighty events,
That people complain, with some reason, no doubt,
Besides the time lost, and besides the expence,
With reading the papers they're fairly worn out:
The past is no longer an object of care,
The present consumes all the time they can spare.

Thus grumbles the reader, but still he reads on
With his pence and his paper unwilling to part.
He sees the world passing, men going and gone,
Some riding in coaches, and some in a cart:
For a peep at the farce a subscription he'll give,—
Revolutions must happen, and printers must live:

For a share of your favour we aim with the rest:
To enliven the scene we'll exert all our skill,
What we have to impart shall be some of the best,
And MULTUM IN PARVO our text, if you will;
Since we never admitted a clause in our creed,
That the greatest employment of life is—to read.

The king of the French and the queen of the North
At the head of the play, for the season, we find:
From the spark that we kindled, a flame has gone forth
To astonish the world and enlighten mankind:
With a code of new doctrines the universe rings,
And PAINE is addressing strange sermons to kings.

    Thus launch'd, as we are, on the ocean of news,
In hopes that your pleasure our pains will repay,
All honest endeavours the author will use

* Text from the edition of 1795. This poem appeared in the first
number of the *National Gazette*, Oct. 31, 1791. [Ed.]

To furnish a feast for the grave and the gay:
At least he'll essay such a track to pursue
That the world shall approve—and his news shall be true.

1791

LINES
WRITTEN ON A PUNCHEON OF JAMAICA SPIRITS.

WITHIN these wooden walls, confined,
The ruin lurks of human kind;
More mischiefs here, united, dwell,
And more diseases haunt this cell
Than ever plagued the Egyptian flocks,
Or ever cursed Pandora's box.

Within these prison-walls repose
The seeds of many a bloody nose;
The chattering tongue, the horrid oath;
The fist for fighting, nothing loth;
The passion quick, no words can tame,
That bursts like sulphur into flame;
The nose with diamonds glowing red,
The bloated eye, the broken head!

Forever fastened be this door—
Confined within, a thousand more
Destructive fiends of hateful shape,
Even now are plotting an escape,
Here, only by a cork restrained,
In slender walls of wood contained,
In all their dirt of death reside
Revenge, that ne'er was satisfied;
The tree that bears the deadly fruit
Of murder, maiming, and dispute;
ASSAULT, that innocence assails,
The IMAGES of gloomy jails
The GIDDY THOUGHT, on mischief bent,
The midnight hour, in folly spent,

ALL THESE *within this cask appear,*
And JACK, *the hangman, in the rear!*
　　Thrice happy he, who early taught
By Nature, ne'er this poison sought;
Who, friendly to his own repose,
Treads under foot this worst of foes,—
He, with the purling stream content,
The beverage quaffs that Nature meant;
In Reason's scale his actions weighed,
His spirits want no foreign aid—
Not swell'd too high, or sunk too low,
Placid, his easy minutes flow;
Long life is his, in vigour pass'd,
Existence, welcome to the last,
A spring, that never yet grew stale—
Such virtue lies in—ADAM'S ALE!

1792

A WARNING TO AMERICA.

REMOVED from Europe's feuds, a hateful scene
(Thank heaven, such wastes of ocean roll between)
Where tyrant kings in bloody schemes combine,
And each forbodes in tears, *Man is no longer mine!*
Glad we recall the DAY that bade us first
Spurn at their power, and shun their wars accurst;
Pitted and gaffed no more for England's glory
Nor made the tag-rag-bobtail of their story.

Something still wrong in every system lurks,
Something imperfect haunts all human works—
Wars must be hatched, unthinking men to fleece,
Or we, *this day*, had been in perfect peace,
With double bolts our Janus' temple shut,
Nor terror reigned through each back-woods-man's hut,
No rattling drums assailed the peasant's ear
Nor Indian yells disturbed our sad frontier,
Nor *gallant chiefs*, 'gainst Indian hosts combined
Scaped from the trap—*to leave their tails behind.*

Peace to all feuds!—and come the happier day
When Reason's sun shall light us on our way;
When erring man shall all his RIGHTS retrieve,
No despots rule him, and no priests deceive,
Till then, Columbia!—watch each stretch of power,
Nor sleep too soundly at the midnight hour,
By flattery won, and lulled by soothing strains,
Silenus took his nap—and waked in chains—
In a soft dream of smooth delusion led
Unthinking Gallia bowed her drooping head
To tyrants' yokes—and met such brusies there,
As now must take three ages to repair;
Then keep the paths of dear bought freedom clear,
Nor slavish systems grant admittance here.

(1792)

On the

FOURTEENTH OF JULY,

a Day ever Memorable to Regenerated France.*

BRIGHT DAY, that did to France restore
What priests and kings had seiz'd away,
That bade her generous sons disdain
The fetters that their fathers wore,
The titled slave, a tyrant's sway,
That ne'er shall curse her soil again!

Bright day! a partner in thy joy,
COLUMBIA hails the rising sun,
She feels her toils, her blood repaid,
When fiercely frantic to destroy,
(Proud of the laurels he had won)
The Briton, here unsheath'd his blade.

By traitors driven to ruin's brink
Fair Freedom dreads united knaves,
The world must fall if she must bleed;—

* Text from the edition of 1795. [Ed.]

And yet, by heaven! I'm proud to think
The world was ne'er subdued by slaves—
Nor shall the hireling herd succeed.

Boy! fill the generous goblet high;
Success to France, shall be the toast:
The fall of kings the fates foredoom,
The crown decays, its' splendours die;
And they, who were a nation's boast,
Sink, and expire in endless gloom.

Thou, stranger, from a distant shore,*
Where fetter'd men their rights avow,
Why on this joyous day so sad?
Louis insults with chains no more,—
Then why thus wear a clouded brow,
When every manly heart is glad?

Some passing days and rolling years
May see the *wrath of kings* display'd,
Their wars to prop the tarnish'd crown;
But orphans' groans, and widows' tears,
And justice lifts her shining blade
To bring the tottering bauble down.   (1792)

TO CRISPIN O'CONNER,

A BACK-WOODSMAN,

(Supposed to be written by Hezekiah Salem)

WISE was your plan when twenty years ago
From *Patrick's isle* you first resolved to stray,
Where lords and knights, as thick as rushes grow,
And vulgar folks are in each other's way;

Where mother-country acts the step-dame's part,
Cuts off, by aid of hemp, each petty sinner,
And twice or thrice in every score of years
Hatches sad wars to make her brood the thinner.

* Addressed to the Aristocrats from Hispaniola.

How few aspire to quit the ungrateful soil
That starves the plant it had the strength to bear:
How many stay, to grieve, and fret, and toil,
And view the plenty that they must not share.

This you beheld, and westward set your nose,
Like some bold prow, that ploughs the Atlantic foam,
   —And left less venturous weights, like famished crows,
To feed on hog-peas, hips, and haws, at home.

Safe landed here, not long the coast detained
Your wary steps:—but wandering on, you found
Far in the west, a paltry spot of land,
That no man envied, and that no man owned.

A woody hill, beside a dismal bog—
This was your choice; nor were you much to blame:
And here, responsive to the croaking frog,
You grubbed, and stubbed, and feared no landlord's claim.

An axe, and adze, a hammer, and a saw;
These were the tools, that built your humble shed:
A cock, a hen, a mastiff, and a cow:
These were your *subjects*, to this desert led.

Now times are changed—and labour's nervous hand
Bids harvests rise where briars and bushes grew;
The dismal bog, by lengthy sluices drained,
Supports no more hoarse captain Bull Frog's crew.—

Prosper your toil!—but, friend, had you remained
In lands, where starred and gartered nobles shine,
When you had, thus, to sixty years attained,
What different fate, 'Squire Crispin, had been thine!

Nine pence a day, coarse fare, a bed of boards,
The midnight loom, high rents, and excised beer;
Slave to dull squires, kings' brats, and huffish lords,
(Thanks be to Heaven) not yet in fashion here!

1792

CRISPIN'S ANSWER.

MUCH pleased am I, that you approve
Freedom's blest cause that brought me here:
Ireland I loved—but there they strove
To make me bend to KING and PEER.

I could not bow to noble knaves,
Who EQUAL RIGHTS to men deny:
Scornful, I left a land of slaves,
And *hither* came, my axe to ply:

The axe has well repaid my toil—
No king, no priest, I yet espy
To tythe my hogs, to tax my soil,
And suck my whiskey bottle dry.

In foreign lands what snares are laid!
There royal rights all right defeat;
They taxed my sun, they taxed my shade,
They taxed the offal that I eat.

They taxed my hat, they taxed my shoes,
Fresh taxes still on taxes grew;
They would have taxed my very nose,
Had I not fled, dear friends, to you.

1792

To SHYLOCK AP-SHENKIN.*

SINCE the day I attempted to print a gazette,
This Shylock Ap-Shenkin does nothing but fret:
Now preaching and screeching, then nibbling and scribbling,
Remarking and barking, and whining and pining,
   And still in a pet,
From morning 'till night, with my humble gazette.

* Text from the edition of 1795. [Ed.]

Instead of whole columns our page to abuse,
Your readers would rather be treated with News:
While wars are a-brewing, and kingdoms undoing,
While monarchs are falling, and princesses squalling,
While France is reforming, and Irishmen storming—
In a glare of such splendour, what folly to fret
At so humble a thing as a poet's GAZETTE!

No favours I ask'd from your friends in the EAST:
On your wretched soup-meagre I left them to feast;
So many base lies you have sent them in print,
That scarcely a man at our paper will squint:—
And now you begin (with a grunt and a grin,
With the bray of an ass, and a visage of brass,
With a quill in your hand and a LIE in your mouth)
To play the same trick on the men of the SOUTH!

One Printer for CONGRESS (some think) is enough,
To flatter, and lie, to palaver, and puff,
To preach up in favour of monarchs and titles,
And garters, and ribbands, to prey on our vitals:
Who knows but Pomposo will give it in fee,
Or make mister Shenkin the Grand Patentee!!!
Then take to your scrapers, ye Republican Papers,
No rogue shall go snacks—and the News-Paper Tax
Shall be puff'd to the skies, as a measure most wise—
So, a spaniel, when master is angry, and kicks it,
Sneaks up to his shoe, and submissively licks it.

                                        1792

To

MY BOOK.*

SEVEN years are now elaps'd, dear rambling volume,
Since, to all knavish wights a foe,
I sent you forth to vex and gall 'em,
Or drive them to the shades below.

          * Text from the edition of 1795. [Ed.]

With spirit, still, of DEMOCRATIC proof,
And still despising Shylock's canker'd hoof:
What doom the fates intend, is hard to say,
Whether to live to some far-distant day,
Or sickening in your prime,
In this bard-baiting clime,
Take pet, make wings, say prayers, and flit away.

"Virtue, order, and religion,*
"Haste, and seek some other region;
"Your plan is laid, to hunt them down,
'Destroy the mitre, rend the gown,
'And that vile hag, Philosophy, restore"—
Did ever volume plan so much before?
For seven years past, a host of busy foes
Have buzz'd about your nose,
White, black, and grey, by night and day;
Garbling, lying, singing, sighing:
These eastern gales a cloud of insects bring
That fluttering, snivelling, whimpering—on the wing—
And, wafted still as discord's demon guides,
Flock round the flame, that yet shall singe their hides.

Well!—let the fates decree whate'er they please:
Whether you're doom'd to drink oblivion's cup,
Or Praise-God Barebones eats you up,
This I can say, you've spread your wings afar,
Hostile to garter, ribbon, crown, and star;
Still on the people's, still on Freedom's side,
With full determin'd aim, to baffle every claim
Of well-born wights, that aim to mount and ride.

1792

* When this poem was first published in the *National Gazette*,
August 4, 1792, a note called attention to the following attack: "The
National Gazette is—the vehicle of party spleen and opposition to the
great principles of order, virtue, and religion." Gaz. U. States. It
should be carefully noted, then, that Freneau is in these words quot-
ing—in paraphrase—Fenno's attack and ridiculing it. [Ed.]

To a PERSECUTED PHILOSOPHER.*

AS ARISTIPPUS once, with weary feet,
Pursued his way through polish'd ATHENS street,
Minding no business but his own;
Out rush'd a set of whelps
With sun-burnt scalps,
(Black, red, and brown,)
That nipt his heels, and nibbled at his gown:

While, with his staff, he kept them all at bay
Some yelp'd aloud, some howl'd in dismal strain,
Some wish'd the sage to bark again:—
Even little Shylock seem'd to say,
"Answer us, sir, in your best way:—
"We are, 'tis true, a snarling crew,
"But with our jaws have gain'd applause,
"And—sir—can worry such as you."

The sage beheld their spite with steady eye,
And only stopp'd to make this short reply:
"Hark ye, my dogs, I have not learn'd to yelp,
Nor waste my breath on every lousy whelp;
Much less, to write, or stain my wholesome page
In answering puppies—bursting with their rage:
Hence to your straw!—such contest I disdain:
        Learn this, ('tis not amiss)
        For men I keep a pen,
        For dogs, a cane!

1792

TO AN
ANGRY ZEALOT:

[IN ANSWER TO SUNDRY VIRULENT CHARGES.]†

IF of RELIGION I have made a sport,
Then why not cite me to the BISHOP'S COURT?

* Text from the edition of 1795. [Ed.]
† Text from the edition of 1795. [Ed.]

Fair to the world let every page be set,
And prove your charges from all I've said and writ:—
What if this heart no narrow notions bind,
Its pure good-will extends to all mankind:
Suppose I ask no portion from your feast,
Nor heaven-ward ride behind your parish priest,
Because I wear not Shylock's Sunday face
Must I, for that, be loaded with disgrace?

The time has been,—the time, I fear, is now,
When holy phrenzy would erect her brow,
Round some poor wight with painted devils meet,
And worse than Smithfield blaze through every street;
But wholesome laws prevent such horrid scenes,
No more afraid of deacons and of deans,
In this new world our joyful PSALM we sing
THAT EVEN A BISHOP IS A HARMLESS THING! *

1792

On the

Demolition

of the

FRENCH MONARCHY.

FROM Bourbon's brow the crown remov'd,
Low in the dust is laid;
And, parted now from all she loved,
MARIA's † beauties fade:

What shall relieve her sad distress,
What power recall that former state

* In the *National Gazette* for September 26, 1792, the above poem
was prefaced as follows: "It is asserted in Mr. Russell's (Boston)
Columbian Centinel of Sept. 12 (and copied into Mr. Fenno's *Gazette
of the United States* of last Saturday) that 'the Clergy of this country
are constantly vilified, and *religion* ridiculed through the medium
of the *National Gazette*. . . .' " [Ed.]

† Maria Antoinette, late queen of France.

When drinking deep her seas of bliss,
She smiled, and look'd so sweet!
With aching heart and haggard eye
She views the palace,* towering high,
Where, once, were passed her brightest days,
And nations stood, in wild amaze,
Louis! to see you eat.

This gaudy vision to restore
Shall fate its laws repeal,
Or cruel despots rise once more
To plan a new BASTILLE!
Will, *from their sheathes, ten thousand blades*†
In glittering vengeance start
To mow down slaves, and slice off heads,
Taking a monarch's part?—
Ah no!—the heavens this hope refuse;
Despots! they send you no such news—
Nor *Conde*, fierce, nor *Frederick*, stout,
Nor *Catherine* brings this work about,
Nor *Brunswick's* warlike art:

Nor HE ‡ that once, with fire and sword,
This western world alarmed:
Throughout our clime whose thunders roared,
Whose legions round us swarmed—
Once more his tyrant arm invades
A race § that dare be free:
His Myrmidons, with murdering blades,
In one base cause agree!—
Ill fate attend on every scheme
That tends to darken REASON's beam:
And rising with gigantic might

* Thuilleries—within view of which the royal family of France were at this time imprisoned.—1792.
† Alluding to Mr. Edmund Burke's rant upon this subject.
‡ George III.
§ The French Republicans.

In VIRTUE's cause, I see unite
Worlds, under FREEDOM's TREE!

Valour, at length, by Fortune led,
The RIGHTS OF MAN restores;
And GALLIA, now from bondage freed,
Her rising sun adores:
On EQUAL RIGHTS, her fabric planned,
Storms idly round it rave,
Nor longer breathes in Gallic land
A monarch, or a slave!
At distance far, and self-removed
From all he owned and all he loved,
See!—turned his back on Freedom's blaze,
In foreign lands the emigrant strays,
Or finds an early grave!

Enrolled with these—and close immur'd,
The gallant chief * is found,
He, whom admiring crowds adored,
Through either world renowned,
Here, bold in arms, and firm in heart,
He helped to gain our cause,
Yet could not from a tyrant part,
But, turned to embrace his laws!—
Ah! hadst thou stay'd in fair Auvergne,†
And Truth from PAINE vouchsafed to learn;
There, happy, honoured, and retired,
Both hemispheres had still admired,
Still crowned you with applause.

See! doomed to fare on famished steeds,
The rude Hungarians fly;
Brunswick, with drooping courage leads
Death's meagre family:

* La Fayette; at this time in the Prussian prison of Spandau.
† The province of France, where the Marquis's family estate lay.

In dismal groups, o'er hosts of dead,
Their madness they bemoan,
No friendly hand to give them bread,
No THIONVILLE their own!
The Gaul, enraged as they retire,
Hurls at their heads his blaze of fire—
What hosts of *Frederick's reeking* crew
Dying, have bid the world adieu,
To dogs their flesh been thrown!
Escaped from death, a mangled train
In scatter'd bands retreat:
Where, bounding on Silesia's plain,
The Despot * holds his seat;
With feeble step, I see them go
The heavy news to tell
Where *Oder's* lazy waters flow,
Or glides the swift *Moselle;*
Where *Rhine* his various journey moves
Through marshy lands and ruined groves,
Or, where the vast *Danubian* flood
(So often stained by Austrian Blood)
Foams with the autumnal swell.

But will they not some tidings bear
Of Freedom's sacred flame,
And shall not groaning millions hear
The long abandoned name?—
Through ages past, their spirits broke,
I see them spurn old laws,
Indignant, burst the Austrian yoke,
And clip the Eagle's † claws:
From shore to shore, from sea to sea
They join, to set the wretched free,
And, driving from the servile court
Each titled slave—they help support
THE DEMOCRATIC CAUSE!

* The Monarch of Prussia.
† The imperial standard of Germany.

O FRANCE! the world to thee must owe
A debt they ne'er can pay:
The RIGHTS OF MAN you bid them know,
And kindle REASON'S DAY!
COLUMBIA, in your friendship blest,
Your gallant deeds shall hail—
On the same ground our fortunes rest,
Must flourish, or must fail:
But—should all Europe's slaves combine
Against a cause so fair as thine,
And ASIA aid a league so base—
Defeat would all their arms disgrace,
And Liberty Prevail!

*First published in the National Gazette, Philadelphia, Decem-
ber 19, 1792.*

On the

FRENCH REPUBLICANS.*

THESE gallant men, that some so much despise
Did not, like mushrooms, spring up in a night:
By them instructed, France again shall rise,
And every Frenchman learn his native right.
American! when in your country's cause
You march'd, and dar'd the English lion's jaws,
Crush'd Hessian slaves, and made their hosts retreat,
Say, were you not Republican—complete?

Forever banish'd, now, be prince and king,
To Nations and to Laws our reverence due:
And let not language to my memory bring,
A word that might recall the infernal crew,
Monarch!—henceforth I blot it from my page,
Monarchs and slaves too long disgrace this age;
But thou, Republican, that SOME disclaim,
Shalt save a world, and damn a tyrant's fame.

* Text from the edition of 1795. [Ed.]

Friends to Republics, cross the Atlantic brine,
Low in the dust see regal splendour laid:
Hopeless forever, sleeps the Bourbon line
Long practis'd adepts in the murdering trade!
With patriot care the nation's will expressing
Republicans shall prove all Europe's blessing,
Pull from his height each blustering Noble down
And chace all modern Tarquins from the throne.

1795

On

MR. PAINE'S RIGHTS OF MAN.

THUS briefly sketched the sacred RIGHTS OF MAN,
How inconsistent with the ROYAL PLAN!
Which for itself exclusive honour craves,
Where some are masters born, and millions slaves.
With what contempt must every eye look down
On that base, childish bauble called a *crown*,
The gilded bait, that lures the crowd, to come,
Bow down their necks, and meet a slavish doom;
The source of half the miseries men endure,
The quack that kills them, while it seems to cure.
    Roused by the REASON of his manly page,
Once more shall PAINE a listening world engage:
From Reason's source, a bold reform he brings,
In raising up *mankind*, he pulls down *kings*,
Who, source of discord, patrons of all wrong,
On blood and murder have been fed too long:
Hid from the world, and tutored to be base,
The curse, the scourge, the ruin of our race,
Their's was the task, a dull designing few,
To shackle beings that they scarcely knew,
Who made this globe the residence of slaves,
And built their thrones on systems formed by knaves
—Advance, bright years, to work their final fall,
And haste the period that shall crush them all.

Who, that has read and scann'd the historic page
But glows, at every line, with kindling rage,
To see by them the rights of men aspersed,
Freedom restrain'd, and Nature's law reversed,
Men, ranked with beasts, by monarchs *will'd* away,
And bound young fools, or madmen to obey:
Now driven to wars, and now oppressed at home,
Compelled in crowds o'er distant seas to roam,
From India's climes the plundered prize to bring
To glad the strumpet, or to glut the king.
   COLUMBIA, hail! immortal be thy reign:
Without a king, we till the smiling plain;
Without a king, we trace the unbounded sea,
And traffic round the globe, through each degree;
Each foreign clime our honour'd flag reveres,
Which asks no monarch, to support the STARS:
Without a *king*, the laws maintain their sway,
While honour bids each generous heart obey.
Be ours the task the ambitious to restrain,
And this great lesson teach—that kings are vain;
That warring realms to certain ruin haste,
That kings subsist by war, and wars are waste:
So shall our nation, form'd on Virtue's plan,
Remain the guardian of the Rights of Man,
A vast Republic, famed through every clime,
Without a king, to see the end of time.

                             [1792] 1795

ODE TO LIBERTY.*

"O Toi, dont l'auguste lumiere!" &c.

THOU LIBERTY! celestial light
So long conceal'd from Gallic lands,
Goddess, in ancient days ador'd
By Gallia's conquering bands:
Thou LIBERTY! whom savage kings
Have plac'd among forbidden things,
Tho' still averse that man be free,
Secret, they bow to Liberty—
O, to my accents lend an ear,
Blest object of each tyrant's fear,
While I to modern days recall
The Lyric muse of ancient Gaul.

Ere yet my willing voice obeys
The transports of the heart,
The goddess to my view displays
The temple rear'd in ancient days,
Fit subject for the muse's art.
Now, round the world I cast my eye,
With pain, its ruins I descry:
This temple once to Freedom rais'd
Thermopylae! in thy fam'd strait—
I see it to the dust debas'd,
And servile chains, its fate!

In those fair climes, where freedom reign'd,
Two thousand years degrade the Grecian name,
I see them still enslav'd, enchain'd;
But France from Rome and Athens caught the flame—
A temple now to heaven they raise
Where nations bound in ties of peace
With olive-boughs shall throng to praise
The gallant Gaul, that bade all discord cease.

* Text from the edition of 1795. Freneau's note indicates that
the ode is a translation "from the original, of M. Pichon." Accord-

(ORIGINAL)

O TOI, dont l'auguste lumiere
Si long tems avait fui nos yeux!
Toi, jadis l'idols premiere
De mes invincibles ayeux,
LIBERTE, *qu'un tyran sauvage,*
A l'infant meme qu'il t'outrage
Honore par des voeux secrets;
A mes accens prete l'oreille,
Aujourdhui ma muse reveille
L'antique lutte des vieux Français.

Avant que ma voix obeisse
Au transport que saisit mes sens,
Montre moi, deesse propice
Un temple digne de mes chants!
Mon oeil a parcouru la terre
J'y trouve a peine la ponissiere
D'un dome a ton nom consacré:
Un tyran siege aux Thermopyles
Et sous les chaines les plus viles
Le capitole est encombré.

Vingt siecles de honte et de chaines
Ont pese sur ces lieux divins;
C'est nous qui de Rome et de l'Athenes
Resusciterons les destins,
Français, soyons seuls notre exemple
Qu'a ma voix on eleve un temple
Ou tous les peuples a jamais
Depouillant des haines sauvauges
Viennent de palmes et d'homages
Couronner les heroes Français.

ing to the Philadelphia *General Advertiser* (May 21, 1793), the original was read by Citizen Duponceau at a "Republican dinner" given Genêt May 18, and Citizen Freneau was asked to render a translation. [Ed.]

Before this Pantheon, fair and tall,
The piles of darker ages fall,
And freemen here no longer trace
The monuments of man's disgrace;
Before its porch, at Freedom's tree
Exalt the CAP OF LIBERTY,
The cap* that once Helvitia knew
(The terror of that tyrant crew)
And on our country's altar trace
The features of each honour'd face—
The men that strove for equal laws,
Or perish'd, martyrs in their cause.

Ye gallant chiefs, above all praise,
Ye Brutuses of ancient days!
Tho' fortune long has strove to blast,
Your virtues are repaid at last.
Your heavenly feasts awhile forbear
And deign to make my song your care;
My lyre a bolder note attains,
And rivals old Tyrtoeus' strains;
The ambient air returns the sound,
And kindles rapture all around.

With thee begins the lofty theme,
Eternal NATURE—power supreme,
Who planted FREEDOM in the mind,
The first great right of all mankind:
Too long presumptuous folly dar'd
To veil our race from thy regard;
Tyrants on ignorance form'd their plan.
And made *their* crimes, the crimes of man,
Let victory but befriend our cause
And reason deign to dictate laws;
At once mankind their rights reclaim
And honour pay to thy great name.—

* Which owes its origin to William Tell, the famous deliverer of Switzerland.

Devant ce Pantheon sublime
Brisez ces palais infamans
De nos opprobres et du crime
Honteux et cruels monumens,
Au pied de ses nobles portiques
Plantez ces bonnets Helvetiques
Devenus la terreur des rois:
Et sur l'autel de la patrie
Gravez l'honorable effigie
Des martyrs sacres de nos droits.

Vous m'entendez, manes augustes
De Thrasibule et de Brutus!
Les Destins trop long tems injustes
Couronnent enfin vos vertus—
Paraissez, ombres adorées
Venez de vos fetes sacrées
Remplir les sublimes concerts
Deja ma lyre transportee
Rivale des chants de Tyrtée
De ses sons etonne les airs.

C'est par toi que l'hymne commence
Maitre supreme, etre eternal!
Toi qui sis de l'independance
Le premier besoin du mortel.
Long tems l'ignorance et l'audace
Couvrirent ton auguste face,
Du masque impur de leurs forfaits
Un seul combat, une victoire
Venge nos droits et rend ta glorie
Plus eclatante que jamais.

But O! what cries our joys molest,
What discord drowns sweet music's feast!
What demon, from perdition, leads
Night, fire and thunder o'er our heads!
In northern realms, prepar'd for fight
A thousand savage clans unite.—
To avenge a faithless Helen's doom
All Europe's slaves, determin'd, come
Freedom's fair fabric to destroy
And wrap in flames our modern Troy!

These these are they—the murdering bands,
Whose blood, of old, distain'd our lands,
By our forefathers chac'd and slain,
The monuments of death remain:
Hungarians, wet with human blood,
Ye Saxons fierce, so oft subdued
By ancient Gauls on Gallic plains,
Dread, dread the race that still remains:
Return, and seek your dark abodes
Your dens and caves in northern woods,
Nor stay to tell each kindred ghost
What thousands from your tribes are lost.

A fiend* from hell, of murderous brood,
Stain'd with a hapless husband's blood,
Unites with Danube† and the Spree,†
Who arm to make the French their prey:
To check their hosts and chill with fear,
Frenchmen, advance to your frontier.
There dig the ETERNAL TOMB of kings,
Or *Poland's Fate* each monster brings,
Mows millions down, your cause defeats,
And ISMAEL'S HORRID SCENE‡ repeats.

*Catharine the 2nd, present empress of Russia, who deposed her husband Peter the 3d, and deprived him of life in July 1762, while in prison.

† Two great rivers of Germany; here metaphorically designating the Austrian and Prussian powers.

‡ The Turkish fortress of Ismael, in 1786, stormed by the Russian

Mais quels cris viennent de nos fetes
Troubler les choeurs majestueux?
Quel demon porte sur nos tetes
La nuit, le tonnerre, et les feux?
Verrons nous des hordes sauvages
Inonder encore nos rivages,
Des torrens du Septentrion
Et pour venger une autre Helene
Toute la force Europeene
Investit une autre Ilion.

C'etoient ces bandes homicides
Dont le sang verse tant de fois
De mes ancetres intrepides
Atteste encore les exploits—
Fiers Saxons, Hongres sanguinaires,
Esclaves jadis de mes peres,
Craignez leurs braves descendans
Rentrez en vos cavernes sombres,
Ou craignez d'avertir leurs ombres
Des revoltes de vos enfans.

Une Tisiphone egarée
Teinte encore du sang d'un epoux
Avec le Danube et la Sprée:
S'unit et s'arme contre nous
A ces despotes sanguinaires:
Français, volez sur vos frontieres
Creuser un eternel tombeau:
Ou craignez pour votre patrie,
Et l'opprobe de Varsovie
Et les horreurs d'Ismailon!

army. After carrying it by assault, upwards of 30,000 persons, men, women, and children were slaughtered by the Russian barbarians, in less than three hours.

Ye nations brave, so long rever'd,
Whom Rome, in all her glory, fear'd;
Whose stubborn souls no tyrant broke
To bow the neck to Caesar's yoke—
SCYTHIANS! whom Romans never chain'd;
GERMANS! that unsubdued remain'd,
Ah! see your sons, a sordid race,
With despots leagu'd, to their disgrace
Aid the base cause that you abhor,
And hurl on France the storm of war.

Our bold attempts shape modern Rome,
She bids her kindred despots come;
From Italy her forces draws
To waste their blood in TARQUIN'S CAUSE:
A hundred hords of foes advance,
Embodying on the verge of France;
'Mongst these, to guide the flame of war,
I see Porsenna's * just a score.
While from the soil, by thousands, spring
SCEVOLA's † to destroy each king.

O Rome! what glory you consign
To those who court your ancient fame!
Frenchmen, like Romans, now shall shine,
And copying them, their ancient honours claim.
O France, my native clime, my country dear,
While, youth remains, may I behold you free,
Each tyrant crush'd, no threatening despot near
    To endanger Liberty!
By you unfetter'd be all human kind,
    No slaves on earth be known
And man be blest, in friendship join'd,
    From Tyber to the Amazon!

1793

* An ancient king of Etruria: who took Tarquin's part against the Romans.

† *Scevola*, who attempted the life of Porsenna in his own camp, but failed.

Et vous qu'au sort de ses conquetes
Rome craignit pour ses remparts,
Peuples dont les augustes tetes
S'indignant du joug des Cesars,
Scythes aux fers inaccessibles,
Fiers Germains, Teutons invincibles,
Voyez vos laches descendans
D'une main vile et sanguinaire
Sur les bienfaiteurs de la terre
Lancer la foudre des tyrans.

Ainsi, par des faits heroiques
Rome allarmant tous ses voisins
Vit tous les peuples Italiques
Vendre leurs bras a ses Tarquins.
Sur ses frontieres investies
Avec cent hordes ennemies
La France voit vingt Porsennas:
Contre tant de liberticides
Nos phalanges tyrannicides
Vomiront mille Scevolas.

O Rome! tu leguas ta glorie
Aux peuples faits pour l'imiter!
C'est nous Français que la victoire
Au meme faite veut porter!
O France, O ma chere patrie!
Puisse je au printems de ma vie
Te voir les despotes soumis:
Et que par toi l'univers libre
De l'Amazone jusq'au Tibre
N'offre que des peuples amis!

ODE *

GOD save the Rights of Man!
Give us a heart to scan
Blessings so dear:
Let them be spread around
Wherever man is found,
And with the welcome sound
Ravish his ear.

Let us with France agree,
And bid the world be free,
While tyrants fall!
Let the rude savage host
Of their vast numbers boast—
Freedom's almighty trust
Laughs at them all!

Though hosts of slaves conspire
To quench fair Gallia's fire,
Still shall they fail:
Though traitors round her rise,
Leagu'd with her enemies,
To war each patriot flies,
And will prevail.

No more is valour's flame
Devoted to a name,
Taught to adore—
Soldiers of LIBERTY
Disdain to bow the knee,
But teach EQUALITY
To every shore.

The world at last will join
To aid thy grand design,
Dear Liberty!

* Text from the edition of 1795. [Ed.]

To Russia's frozen lands
The generous flame expands:
On Afric's burning sands
Shall man be free!

In this our western world
Be Freedom's flag unfurl'd
Through all its shores!
May no destructive blast
Our heaven of joy o'ercast,
May Freedom's fabric last
While time endures.

If e'er her cause require!
Should tyrants e'er aspire
To aim their stroke,
May no proud despot daunt—
Should he his standard plant,
Freedom will never want
Her hearts of oak!

[w. 1793]   1795

On the Death

of a

REPUBLICAN PRINTER:

[By his Partner and Successor.] *

LIKE Sybils' leaves, abroad he spread
His sheets, to awe the aspiring crew:
Stock-jobbers fainted while they read;
Each hidden scheme display'd to view—
Who could such doctrines spread abroad
So long, and not be clapper-claw'd!

Content with slow uncertain gains,
With heart and hand prepar'd he stood

* Text from the edition of 1795. [Ed.]

To send his works to distant plains,
And hills beyond the Ohio-flood—
And, since he had no time to lose,
Preach'd whiggish lectures with his news.

Now death, with cold unsparing hand,
(At whose decree even CAPETS fall)
From life's poor glass has shook his sand,
And sent him, fainting, to the wall—
Because he gave you some sad wipes,
O Mammon! seize not thou his types.

What shall be done, in such a case?
Shall I, because my partner fails,
Call in his bull-dogs from the chace
To loll their tongues and drop their tails—
No, faith—the title-hunting crew
No longer fly than we pursue.

1793

On The
ANNIVERSARY

Of the storming of the Bastille, at Paris.   July 14th, 1789.*

THE chiefs that bow to Capet's reign,
In mourning, now, their weeds display;
But we, that scorn a monarch's chain,
Combine to celebrate the DAY
    Of Freedom's birth that put the seal,
    And laid in dust the proud Bastille.

To Gallia's rich and splendid crown,
This mighty *Day* gave such a blow
As Time's recording hand shall own
No former *age* had power to do:

* Text from the edition of 1795. [Ed.]

No single gem some Brutus stole,
But instant ruin seiz'd the whole.

Now tyrants rise, once more to bind
In royal chains a nation freed—
Vain hope! for they, to death consign'd,
Shall soon, like perjur'd Louis, bleed:
   O'er every king, o'er every queen
   Fate hangs the sword, and guillotine.

"Plung'd in a gulf of deep distress
France turns her back—(so traitors say)
Kings, priests, and nobles, round her press,
Resolv'd to seize their destin'd prey:
   Thus Europe swears (in arms combin'd)
   Te Poland's doom is France consign'd."

Yet those, who now are thought so low
From conquests that were *basely* gain'd,
Shall rise tremendous from the blow
And free TWO WORLDS, that still are chain'd,
   Restrict the Briton to his isle,
   And Freedom plant in every soil.

Ye sons of this degenerate clime,
Haste, arm the barque, expand the sail;
Assist to speed that golden time
When Freedom rules, and monarchs fail;
   All left to France—*new powers* may join,
   And help to crush the cause divine.

Ah! while I write, dear France ALLIED,
My ardent wish I scarce restrain,
To throw these Sybil leaves aside,
And fly to join you on the main:
   Unfurl the topsail for the chace
   And help to crush the tyrant race!

1793

To
SHYLOCK AP–SHENKIN.*

(IN REPLY TO BIG LOOKS AND MENACES.)

BECAUSE some pumpkin-shells and lobster claws,
Thrown o'er his garden walls by Crab-tree's duke,
Have chanc'd to light within your meagre jaws,
(A dose, at which all honest men would puke:)

Because some treasury-luncheons you have gnaw'd,
Like rats, that prey upon the public store:
Must you, for that, your crude stuff belch abroad,
And vomit lies on all that pass your door!

To knavery's tribe my verse still fatal found,
Alike to kings and cobblers gives their due:
Spruce tho' you be, your heels may drum the ground,
And make rare pass-time for the sportive crew.

Why all these hints of menace, dark and sad,
What is my crime, that that Ap-Shenkin raves?
No secret-service-money have I had
For waging two years' war with fools and knaves.

Abus'd at court, unwelcome to the GREAT—
This page of mine no well-born aspect wears:
On honest yeomen I repose its fate,
CLODHOPPER's dollar is as good as theirs.

Why wouldst thou then with ruffian hand destroy
A wight, that wastes his ink in Freedom's cause:
Who, to the last, his arrows will employ
To publish Freedom's rights, and guard her laws!

* Text from the edition of 1795. Hamilton, in anonymous letters
in Fenno's *Gazette*, had accused Freneau of receiving Federal money
from Jefferson as a reward for attacking the Federal government.
[Ed.]

O thou! that hast a heart so flinty hard
Thus oft, too oft, a poet to rebuke,
From those that rhyme you ne'er shall meet regard;
Of CRAB-TREE's dutchy—you shall be no DUKE.

1795

To a
NOISY POLITICIAN.*

SINCE Shylock's BOOK has walk'd the circles here,
What numerous blessings to our country flow!
Whales on our shores have run aground,
Sturgeons are in our rivers found;
Nay, ships have on the Delaware sail'd,
A sight most new!
Wheat has been sown, harvests have grown,
And Shylock held strange dialogues with Sue.

On coaches, now, gay coats of arms are wore
By some, who hardly had a coat before:
Silk gowns instead of homespun, now, are seen,
And, sir, 'tis true ('twixt me and you)
Thas some have grown prodigious fat,
That were prodigious lean!

1795

Addressed to a
POLITICAL SHRIMP,

or, Fly upon the Wheel.†

THE man that doth an Elephant pursue
Whose capture gains a mighty price,
Amidst the chace, heeds not the barking crew,
Or lesser game of rats and mice.

---

* Text from the edition of 1795. [Ed.]
† Text from the edition of 1795. [Ed.]

On ocean's waste who chace the royal flag
Stop not to take the privateer;
Who mean to seize the steed, neglect the nag;
No squirrel-hunter kills a deer.

Reptile! your venom ever spits in vain—
To honours's coat no drop adheres:—
To court!—return to Britain's tyrant reign,
White-wash her *king*, and scowr her *peers*.

Some scheming knaves, that strut in *courtly* guise,
May vile abuse, through you, impart—
But they that on no *Treasury* lean, despise
Your venal pen—your canker'd heart.

1795

To

MY BOOK.*

UNHAPPY Volume!—doom'd by fate
To meet with unrelenting hate
From those who can their venom spit,
Yet condescend to steal your wit:
While Shylock, with malicious spirit,
Allows you not a grain of merit,
While he an idle pomp assumes,
Let him return his borrowed plumes,
And you will find the insect creeping,
With not a feather worth the keeping.

1795

On the

DEATH OF CATHARINE II.†

EMPRESS OF ALL THE RUSSIAS.

CONFUSION to that iron sway
Which bids the brute, not man, obey,

* Text from the edition of 1795. [Ed.]
† Text from the edition of 1815. [Ed.]

And dooms him to Siberian soil,
Chains, whips, and vassalage, and toil.

This female wolf, whom wolves did nurse,
So long of polar worlds the curse,
This Catharine, skill'd in royal arts,
To the dark world at last departs.

In style, the second of her name,
She to the crown by treason came;
To Peter, drowsy, royal drone,
She gave a prison for a throne.

She would have sent her Tartar bands
To waste and ravage gallic lands,
She would have sent her legions o'er,
Columbia! to invade your shore!—

But, even in conquest, she foresaw
Destruction to despotic law;
She fear'd, in hordes returning home,
That liberty would with them come.

She fear'd the savage from the den
Would see and learn the rights of men;
And hence, in time, destruction bring
To hell's viceregents—queen and king.

No thanks to her! she fear'd her beasts,
Enslaved by kings, enslaved by priests,
Even if all freedom they o'er ran,
Would learn the dignity of man;

And kept them home, and held them there,
Oppression's iron reign to bear;
And never meet a beam of light,
Involved in worse than Zembla's night.

Now she is dead, and Paul will rise
As fierce as she, but not as wise;
He may his barbarous millions send,
He may the fall of France intend;

But they who see with keener eye
Will see them faint, will see them fly;
With hostile step will see them come
To turn their backs, or meet their doom.

1815

PREFATORY LINES TO A PERIODICAL PUBLICATION.*

WHEREVER this volume may chance to be read
For the feast of good humor a table I spread;
Here are dishes by dozens; whoever will eat
Will have no just cause to complain of the treat.

If the best of the market is not to be had
I'll help you to nothing that's seriously bad;
To sense and to candor no place I refuse,
Pick here and pick there, and wherever you choose.

If I give you a frolic I hope for no fray;
My style I adapt to the taste of the day,
The feast of amusement we draw from all climes,
The best we can give in a run of hard times.

The guest, whom the pepper of satire may bite
Is wrong, very wrong, if he shows us his spite;
Should a fit of resentment be-ruffle his mind,
Sit still, I would tell him, be calm and resign'd.

In the service of freedom forever prepared,
We have done our endeavor the goddess to guard;

* Text from the edition of 1815. These lines appeared originally, in a somewhat different version, in the first number of the *Time-Piece*, March 13, 1797. [Ed.]

This idol, whom reason should only adore,
And banish'd from Europe, to dwell on our shore.

In a country like this, exalted by fame,
The trade of an author importance may claim
Which monarchs would never permit them to find,
Whose views are to chain and be-darken the mind.

Ye sons of Columbia! our efforts befriend;
To you all the tyrants of Europe shall bend
Till reason at length shall illume the ball
And man from his state of debasement recall.

Republics of old, that are sunk in the dust,
Could once like our own, of their liberty boast;
Both virtue and wisdom in Athens appear'd,
Each eye saw their charms, and all bosoms revered.

But as virtue and morals fell into disgrace
Pride, splendour, and folly stept into their place;
Where virtues domestic no longer were known,
Simplicity lost, and frugality flown.

Where virtues, that always a republic adorn,
Were held in contempt, or were laugh'd into scorn,
There, tyrants and slaves were the speedy effect
Of virtue dishonor'd or fall'n to neglect:

Then tyrants and slaves, the worst plagues of this earth,
From the lapse of good manners were hatch'd into birth;
And soon the base maxim all popular grew,
And allowed, that the many were made for the few.

From the fate of republics, or Athens, or Rome,
'Tis time we should learn a sad lesson at home—
From their faults and their errors a warning receive,
And steer from the shoals where they both found a grave.

Columbians! forever may freedom remain,
And virtue for ever that freedom maintain;
To these, all attracting, all views should submit
All labors of learning, all essays of wit.

'Tis time a new system of things was embraced
To prevail on a planet so often debased;
As here, with our freedom, that system began,
Here, at least keep it pure—for the honor of man.

1797

THE REPUBLICAN FESTIVAL:

In Compliment to Colonel Munroe, on his return to America, 1797.*

AS late at a feast that she gave to MUNROE,
    Her mark of attention to show,
Young liberty gave her libations to flow,
    To honor where honor is due.

Return'd from the country that trampled on crowns
    Where high in opinion he stood,
Dark malice attack'd him, with sneers, and with frowns,
    But he met the applause of the good.

To the *knight of the sceptre* unwelcome he came
    But freedom his merit confess'd—
He look'd at their malice, and saw it was fame,
    And pity forgave them the rest.

Good humor, and pleasure, and friendship did join,
    And reason the pleasure increased;
And the hero, who captured the British Burgoyne,
    Presided and honor'd the feast.

On a broomstick from hell, with a quill in his hand,
    Baal-Zephou came riding the air;

* Text from the edition of 1815. [Ed.]

He look'd, and he saw that among the whole band
  Not a single apostate was there.

Disappointed, he sigh'd, but still hover'd about
  Till the *toasts*, with a vengeance, began—
He met the first *four;* when the next they gave out*
  To his cavern he fled back again.

In liberty's temple, the petulant cur
  Could see not a man but he hates;
With a curse on her cause, and a sneer, and a spur
  He fled from the frown of a GATES.

[w. 1797]   1815

TO DUNCAN DOOLITTLE,

A *"half-starved"* Democrat.†

DUNCAN, with truth it may be said,
Your mouth was made for rye or barley bread;
What claim have *you* to halls of state,
Whose business is to stand and wait,
  Subserviant to command?
What right have you to white-bread, superfine,
Who were by nature destin'd for *"a swine"*—
  As said good Edmund Burke,
  The drudge of Britain's dirty work,
Whose mighty pamphlets rous'd the royal band!

When passing by a splendid dome of pride
By speculation built (and built so vast
That there a *standing army* might reside)
Say, Duncan, stood you not aghast,

---

  * Public censure, arm'd with the spear of Ithurial: may it discover
the demons of tyranny, wherever they lurk, and pursue them to their
native obscurity.
  † Text from the *Time-Piece*, October 20, 1797.

When gazing up (like fox that look'd for grapes)
You saw so many things in curious shapes,
   Trees rang'd along the table,
   And sugar-columns, far above the rabble,
   With roses *blooming* in *October,*
   And wisdom's figures—dull and sober.
Ah! how you smack'd your lips, and look'd so wishful
When pigs and poultry—many a lovely dish-full,
   Imparted to your nose the savoury scent
   For royal noses—not for Duncan's—meant.

For things like these, you, caitiff, were not born—
   A pewter spoon was for your chops intended;
Some shins of beef, and garlands made of thorn—
   On things like these has Freedom's feast depended.
Though in the days of fight you musquet carried,
   Or wandered up and down, a cannon-hauling,
Better you might in Jericho have tarried
   And *rebel-starving* made your *loyal* calling.
Among our far-fam'd chieftains that are *dead*
(Like beer set by in mug without a lid,
And sure, a half-gill glass I'll put it all in)
I'll toast your health—yes, to the very brim
And to the little gaping world proclaim
   You are a *Hero fallen:*
One of the wights who dar'd all death, or wound,
And warr'd for two and sixpence in the pound.

Of *public virtue* you're a rare example—
   Go, mind your hoe, your pick-ax, or your spade;
A hut of six foot square shall be your *"temple,"*
   And all your honour—strutting on parade.
   But pray, beware of *public good;*
   It will not always find you food,
   And if your son should anything inherit,
   Bequeath him not your *public spirit,*
But sixpence, to be train'd to SAWING WOOD.

1797

The MILLENNIUM—

To a Ranting field Orator.*

WITH aspect wild, in ranting strain
　You bring the brilliant period near,
When monarchy will close her reign
　And wars and warriors disappear;
　　The lion and the lamb will stray,
　　And, social, walk the woodland way.

I fear, with superficial view
　You contemplate dame nature's plan:—
She various forms of being drew,
　And made the common tyrant—man:
　　She form'd them all with wise design,
　　Distinguish'd each, and drew the line.

Observe the lion's visage bold
　His iron tooth, his murderous claw,
His aspect cast in anger's mould;
　The strength of steel is in his paw:
　　Could he be meant with lambs to stray
　　Or feed along the woodland way?

Since first his race on earth began
　War was his trade and war will be:
And when he quits that ancient plan
　With milder natures to agree,
　　He will be changed to something new
　　And have some other part to do.

One system see through all this frame,
　Apparent discord still prevails;
The forest yields to active flame,
　The ocean swells with stormy gales;
　　No season did the God decree
　　When leagued in friendship these should be.

* Text from the edition of 1815. [Ed.]

And do you think that human kind
  Can shun the all-pervading law—
That passion's slave we ever find—
  Who discord from their nature draw:—
    Ere discord can from man depart
    He must assume a different heart.

Yet in the slow advance of things
  A time may come our race may rise,
By reason's aid to stretch their wings,
  And see the light with other eyes;
    And when the ancient mist is pass'd;
    To find their nature changed at last,

The sun himself, the powers ordain,
  Should in no perfect circle stray;
He shuns the equatorial plane,
  Prefers an odd serpentine way,
    And lessens yearly, sophists prove,
    His angle in the voids above.

When moving in his ancient line,
  And no oblique ecliptic near,
With some new influence he may shine
  But you and I will not be here
    To see the lion shed his teeth
    Or kings forget the trade of death—

[w. 1797]   1815

To the
SCRIBE OF SCRIBES.*

BY the gods of the poets, Apollo and Jove,
By the muse who directs me, the spirits that move,
I council you, Peter, once more, to retire
Or satire shall pierce, with her arrows of fire.

* Text from the edition of 1815. [Ed.]

Be careful to stop in your noisy career,
Or homeward retreat, for your danger is near:
The clouds are collecting to burst on your head,
Their sulphur to dart, or their torrents to shed.

Along with the tears, I foresee you will weep,
In the cave of oblivion I put you to sleep;—
This dealer in scandal, this bladder of gall,
This sprig of Parnassus must go to the wall.

From a star of renown in the reign of night
He has dwindled away to a little *rush-light:*
Then snuff it, and snuff it, while yet it remains
And PETER will leave you to snuff for your pains.—

1815

TO THE
AMERICANS OF THE UNITED STATES.

First published November, 1797.*

MEN of this passing age!—whose noble deeds
Honour will bear above the *scum* of Time:
Ere this eventful century expire,
Once more we greet you with our humble rhyme:
Pleased, if we meet your smiles, but—if denied,
Yet, with YOUR sentence, we are satisfied.

Catching our subjects from the varying scene
Of human things; a mingled work we draw,
Chequered with fancies odd, and figures strange,
Such, as no *courtly* poet ever saw;
Who writ, beneath some GREAT MAN's cieling placed;
Travelled no lands, nor roved the watery waste.

* Text from the edition of 1809, where this poem stands as an introduction to Volume II. [Ed.]

To seize some *features* from the faithless past;
Be this our care—before the century close:
The colours strong!—for, if we deem aright,
The *coming age will be an age of prose:*
When *sordid cares* will break the muses' dream,
And COMMON SENSE be ranked in seat supreme,

Go, now, dear book; once more expand your wings:
Still to the cause of man *severely true:*
Untaught to flatter *pride*, or fawn on kings;—
Trojan, or Tyrian,*—*give them both their due.—*
*When they are right, the cause of both we plead,
And both will please us well,—if both will read.*

1797

To the
DEMOCRATIC COUNTRY EDITORS.

On a Charge of Bribery

You, Journalists, are bribed—that's clear,
And paid French millions by the year;
We see it in the coats you wear;

Such damning, such convincing proof
Of such a charge, is strong enough—
Your suits are made of costly stuff.

Dear boys! you lodge in mansions grand—
In time you'll *own six feet of land*,
Where now the sexton has command.

Your lodging is in garret high;
But where your best possessions lie,
Yourselves know best—and HIM on high.

And have you had a foreign bribe?—
Then, why so lean?—shall we describe
The leanness of your honest tribe?

* Tros, Tyriusque mihi nullo discrimine agetur.—Virg.

Why did you not with *Tories* join
To hold the British king divine—
And all his mandates *very fine?*

Then had your faces shined with fat—
Then had you worn the gold-laced hat—
And—said your *lessons—very pat.*—

Your lives are, *now*, continual trial,
Existence, constant self-denial,
To keep down *some*, who would be *royal.*

For public good you wear out types,
For public good you get *dry wipes*—
For public good you may get—*stripes.*

One half your time in *Federal court*,
On libel charge—you're made a sport—
You pay your fees—nor dare retort.—

All pleasure you are sworn to shun;
Are always cloistered, like a nun,
And glad to hide from *Ragman's* dun.—

All night you sit by glare of lamp,
Like Will o' Wisp in vapoury swamp,
To write of armies and the camp.—

You write—compile—compile and write,
'Till you have nearly lost your sight—
Then off to jail; and so, good night.

Turned out as poor as Christ-church rat,
Once more the trade you would be at
Which never yet made lean man fat.

You send your journals far and wide,
And though undone, and though belied;
You choose to take the patriot side.

Your works are in Kentucky found;
And there your politics go round—
And there you trust them many a pound.—

At home, to folks residing near,
You grant a credit, *half a year;*
And pine, mean while, on cakes and beer.

The time elapsed when *friends* should pay,
You urge your dun from day to day;
And so you must—and so you may.

One customer begins to fret,
And tells the dunner in a pet,
"Plague take the Printer and his debt:

"Ungrateful man—go hang—go burn—
"I *read* his paper night and morn,
"And now experience *this return!*

"Sir! was I not among the first
"Who did my name on paper trust,
"To help this Journalist accursed?

"Thus am I used for having *signed:*
"But I have spirit, he shall find—
"Ah me! the baseness of mankind!"

Thus, on you strive with constant pain,
The kindest tell you, *call again!*—
And you their humble dupe remain.

Who aims to prosper—should be sold—
If bribes are offered, take the gold,
Nor live to be forever fooled.

SALEM.
1809

REFLECTIONS

On the Mutability of Things—1798.*

THE time is approaching, deny it who may,
    The days are not very remote,
When the pageant that glitter'd for many a day,
    On the stream of oblivion will float.

The times are advancing when matters will turn,
    And some, who are now in the shade,
And pelted by malice, or treated with scorn,
    Will pay, in coin that was paid:

The time it will be, when the people aroused,
    For better arrangements prepare,
And firm to the cause, that of old they espoused,
    Their steady attachment declare:

When tyrants will shrink from the face of the day,
    Or, if they presume to remain,
To the tune of *peccavi*, a solo will play,
    And lower the royalty strain:

When government favors to flattery's press
    Will halt on their way from afar,
And people will laugh at the comical dress
    Of the knights of the garter and star:

When a *monarch*, new fangled, with lawyer and scribe,
    In junto will cease to convene,
Or take from old England a pitiful bribe,
    To pamper his "highness serene;"

When virtue and merit will have a fair chance
    The loaves and the fishes to share,
And *Jefferson*, you to your station advance,
    The man from the president's chair:

      * Text from the 1815 edition. [Ed.]

When honesty, honor, experience, approved,
  No more in disgrace will retire;
When fops from the places of trust are removed
  And the leaders of faction retire.

[w. 1798]   1815

The
POLITICAL WEATHERCOCK.

'TIS strange that things upon the ground
Are commonly most steady found
    While those in station proud
Are turned and twirled, or twist about,
Now here and there, now in or out,
    Mere playthings to a cloud.

See yonder influential man,
So late the stern Republican
    While *interest* bore him up;
See him recant, abjure the cause,
See *him* support tyrannic laws,
    The dregs of slavery's cup!

Thus, on yon' steeple towering high,
Where clouds and storms distracted fly,
    The weather-cock is placed;
Which only while the storm does blow
Is to one point of compass true,
    Then veers with every blast.

But things are so appointed here
That weather-cocks on high appear,
    On pinnacle displayed,
While SENSE, and WORTH, and reasoning wights,
And they who plead for HUMAN RIGHTS,
    Sit humble in the shade.

                                          1809

REFLECTIONS

**ON THE GRADUAL PROGRESS OF NATIONS FROM DEMO-
CRATICAL STATES TO DESPOTIC EMPIRES.***

Mantua vae miserae nimium vicina Cremonae!   Virgil.

OH fatal day! when to the Atlantic shore
European despots sent the doctrine o'er,
That man's vast race was born to lick the dust;
Feed on the Winds, or toil through life accurst;
Poor and despised, that rulers might be great
And swell to monarchs, to devour the state.

Whence came these ills, or from what causes grew,
This vortex vast, that only spares the few,
Despotic sway, where every plague combined,
Distracts, degrades, and swallows up mankind;
Takes from the intellectual sun its light,
And shrouds the world in universal night?

Accuse not nature for the dreary scene,
That glooms her stage or hides her heaven serene,
She, equal still in all her varied ways,
An equal blessing to the world displays.
The suns that now on northern climates glow,
Will soon retire to melt Antarctic snow,
The seas she robb'd to form her clouds and rain,
Return in rivers to that source again;
But man, wrong'd man, borne down, deceived and vex'd,
Groans on through life, bewilder'd and perplex'd;
No suns on him but suns of misery shine,
Now march'd to war, now grovelling in the mine.
Chain'd, fetter'd, prostrate, sent from earth a slave,
To seek rewards in worlds beyond the grave.

If in her general system, just to all,
We nature an impartial parent call,

* Text from the edition of 1815. [Ed.]

Why did she not on man's whole race bestow,
Those fine sensations angels only know;
Who, sway'd by reason, with superior mind
In nature's state all nature's blessings find,
Which shed through all, does all their race pervade,
In streams not niggard by a despot made?

Leave this a secret in great nature's breast,
Confess that all her works tend to the best,
Or own that man's neglected culture here
Breeds all the mischiefs that we feel or fear.
In all, except the skill to rule her race,
Man, wise and skillful, gives each part its place:
Each nice machine he plans, to reason true,
Adapting all things to the end in view,
But taught in this, the art himself to rule
His sense is folly, and himself a fool.

Where social strength resides, there rests, 'tis plain,
The power, mankind to govern and restrain:
This strength is not but in the social plan
Controling all, the common good of man,
That power concentred by the general voice,
In honest men, an honest people's choice,
With frequent change, to keep the patriot pure,
And from vain views of power the heart secure:
Here lies the secret, hid from Rome or Greece,
That holds a state in awe, yet holds in peace.

See through the world, in ages now retired,
Man foe to man, as policy required:
At some proud tyrant's nod what millions rose,
To extend their sway, and make a world their foes.
View Asia ravaged, Europe drench'd with blood,
In feuds whose cause no nation understood.
The cause we fear, of so much misery sown,
Known at the helm of state, and there alone.

Left to himself, wherever man is found,
In peace he aims to walk life's little round;
In peace to sail, in peace to till the soil,
Nor force false grandeur from a brother's toil.
All but the base, designing, scheming, few,
Who seize on nations with a robber's view,
With crowns and sceptres awe his dazzled eye,
And priests that hold the artillery of the sky;
These, these, with armies, navies, potent grown,
Impoverish man and bid the nations groan.
These with pretended balances of states
Keep worlds at variance, breed eternal hates,
Make man the poor base slave of low design,
Degrade his nature to its last decline,
Shed hell's worse blots on his exalted race,
And make them poor and mean, to make them base.

Shall views like these assail our happy land,
Where embryo monarchs thirst for wide command,
Shall a whole nation's strength and fair renown
Be sacrificed, to prop a tottering throne,
That, ages past, the world's great curse has stood,
Has throve on plunder, and been fed on blood.—
Americans! will you control such views?
Speak—for you must—you have no hour to lose.

1815

STANZAS

TO AN ALIEN, WHO AFTER A SERIES OF PERSECUTIONS EMIGRATED TO THE SOUTHWESTERN COUNTRY.—1799*—

REMOTE, beneath a sultry star
Where Mississippi flows afar
I see you rambling, God knows where.

Sometimes, beneath a cypress bough
When met in dreams, with spirits low,
I long to tell you what I know.

* Text from the edition of 1815. [Ed.]

How matters go, in this our day,
When monarchy renews her sway,
And royalty begins her play.

I thought you wrong to come so far
Till you had seen our western star
Above the mists ascended clear.

I thought you right, to speed your sails
If you were fond of loathesome jails,
And justice with uneven scales.

And so you came and spoke too free
And soon they made you bend the knee,
And lodged you under lock and key.

Discharged at last, you made your peace
With all you had, and left the place
With empty purse and meagre face.—

You sped your way to other climes
And left me here to teaze with rhymes
The worst of men in worst of times.

Where you are gone the soil is free
And freedom sings from every tree,
"Come quit the crowd and live with me!"

Where I must stay, no joys are found;
Excisemen haunt the hateful ground,
And chains are forged for all around.

The scheming men, with brazen throat,
Would set a murdering tribe afloat
To hang you for the lines you wrote.

If you are safe beyond their rage
Thank heaven, and not our ruling sage,
Who shops us up in jail and cage.

Perdition seize that odious race
Who, aiming at distinguish'd place,
Would life and liberty efface;

With iron rod would rule the ball
And, at their shrine, debase us all,
Bid devils rise and angels fall.

Oh wish them ill, and wish them long
To be as usual in the wrong
In scheming for a chain too strong.

So will the happy time arrive
When coming home, if then alive,
You'll see them to the devil drive.

[w. 1799]   1815

STANZAS

To the memory of General WASHINGTON, *who died December 14,* 1799.

Terra tegit, populus moeret, coelum habet! *

DEPARTING with the closing age
    To virtue, worth, and freedom true,
The chief, the patriot, and the sage
    To Vernon bids his last adieu:
        To reap in some exalted sphere
        The just rewards of virtue here.

Thou, Washington, by heaven design'd
    To act a part in human things
That few have known among mankind,
    And far beyond the task of kings;
        We hail you now to heaven received,
        Your mighty task on earth achieved.

* Text from the edition of 1815. [Ed.]

While sculpture and her sister arts,
  For thee their choicest wreaths prepare,
Fond gratitude her share imparts
  And begs thy bones for burial there;
    Where, near Virginia's northern bound
    Swells the vast pile on federal ground.

To call from their obscure abodes
  The grecian chief, the roman sage,
The kings, the heroes, and the gods
  Who flourish'd in time's earlier age,
    Would be to class them not with you,—
    Superior far, in every view.

Those ancients of ferocious mould,
  Blood their delight, and war their trade,
Their oaths profaned, their countries sold,
  And fetter'd nations prostrate laid;
    Could these, like you, assert their claim
    To honor and immortal fame?

Those monarchs, proud of pillaged spoils,
  With nations shackled in their train,
Returning from their desperate toils
  With trophies,—and their thousands slain;
    In all they did no traits are known
    Like those that honor'd Washington.

Who now will save our shores from harms,
  The task to him so long assign'd?
Who now will rouse our youth to arms
  Should war approach to curse mankind?
    Alas! no more the word you give,
    But in your precepts you survive.

Ah, gone! and none your place supply,
  Nor will your equal soon appear;

But that great name can only die
　When memory dwells no longer here,
　　When man and all his systems must
　　Dissolve, like you, and turn to dust.

[w. 1799]　　　　　　　　　　　　　1815

STANZAS

Upon the Same Subject with the Preceding.*

THE chief who freed these suffering lands
From Britain's bold besieging bands,
The hero, through all countries known,—
The guardian genius of his OWN,

Is gone to that celestial *bourne*
From whence no traveller can return,
Where Scipio and where Trajan went;
And heaven reclaims the soul it lent.

Each heart with secret wo congeals;
Down the pale cheek moist sorrow steals,
And all the nobler passions join
To mourn, remember, and resign.

O ye, who carve the marble bust
To celebrate poor human dust,
And from the silent shades of death
Retrieve the form but not the breath,

Vain is the attempt by force of art
To impress his image on the heart:
It lives, it glows, in every breast,
And tears of millions paint it best.

Indebted to his guardian care,
And great alike in peace and war,
The loss they feel these STATES deplore,—
Their friend . . . . their father . . . . is no more.

*Text from the edition of 1815. [Ed.]

What will they do to avow their grief?
No sighs, no tears, afford relief;
Dark mourning weeds but ill express
The poignant wo that all confess;
Nor will the monumental stone
Assuage one tear—relieve one groan.

O Washington! thy honor'd dust
To parent nature we entrust;
Convinced that your exalted mind
Still lives, but soars beyond mankind,
Still acts in virtue's sacred cause,
Nor asks from man his vain applause.

In raptures with a theme so great,
While thy famed actions they relate,
Each future age from thee shall know
All that is good and great below;
Shall glow with pride to hand thee down
To latest time, to long renown,
The brightest name on freedom's page,
And the first honor of our age.

1815

STANZAS

*Occasioned by certain absurd, extravagant, and even
blasphemous panegyrics and encomiums on the character of the late gen. Washington, that appeared in
several pamphlets, journals, and other periodical publications, in January, 1800.**

NO tongue can tell, no pen describe
The phrenzy of a numerous tribe,
Who, by distemper'd fancy led,
Insult the memory of the dead.

* Text from the edition of 1815. [Ed.]

Of old, there were in every age
Who stuff'd with gods the historian's page,
And raised beyond the human sphere
Some who, we know, were mortal here.

Such was the case, we know full well,
When darkness spread her pagan spell;
Mere insects, born for tombs and graves,
They changed into celestial knaves;
Made some, condemn'd to tombs and shrouds,
Lieutenant generals in the clouds.

In journals, meant to spread the news,
From state to state—and we know whose—
We read a thousand idle things
That madness pens, or folly sings.

Was, Washington, your conquering sword
Condemn'd to such a base reward?
Was trash, like that we now review,
The tribute to your valor due?

One holds you *more than mortal kind*,
One holds you *all ethereal mind*,
This puts you in your saviour's seat,
That makes you *dreadful in retreat*.

One says *you are become a star*,
One makes you *more resplendent, far;*
One sings, that, when to death you bow'd,
Old mother nature *shriek'd aloud*.

We grieve to see such pens profane
The first of chiefs, the first of men.—
To Washington—a man—who died,
As *abba father* well applied?

Absurdly, in a frantic strain,
Why ask him not for *sun* and *rain?*—

We sicken at the vile applause
That bids him *give the ocean laws.*

Ye patrons of the ranting strain,
What *temples have been rent in twain?*
What fiery chariots have been sent
To dignify the sad event?—

O, ye profane, irreverent few,
Who reason's medium never knew:
On you she never glanced her beams;
You carry all things to extremes.

Shall they, who spring from parent earth,
Pretend to more than mortal birth?
Or, to the omnipotent allied,
Control his heaven, or join his side?

O, is there not some chosen curse,
Some vengeance due, with lightning's force
That far and wide destruction spreads,
To burst on such irreverent heads!

Had they, in life, be-praised him so,
What would have been the event, I know
He would have spurn'd them, with disdain,
Or rush'd upon them, with his cane.

He was no god, ye flattering knaves,
He *own'd no world, he ruled no waves;*
But—and exalt it, if you can,
He was the upright, HONEST MAN.

This was his glory, this outshone
Those attributes you doat upon:
On this strong ground he took his stand,
Such virtue saved a sinking land.

[w. 1800]   1815

ON THE ABUSE OF HUMAN POWER

As exercised over opinion.*

WHAT human power shall dare to bind
The mere opinions of the mind?
Must man at that tribunal bow
Which will no range to thought allow,
But his best powers would sway or sink,
And idly tells him what to THINK?

Yes! there are such, and such are taught
To fetter every power of thought;
To chain the mind, or bend it down
To some mean system of their own,
And make religion's sacred cause
Amenable to human laws.

Has human power the simplest claim
Our hearts to sway, our thoughts to tame;
Shall she the rights of heaven assert,
Can she to falsehood truth convert,
Or truth again to falsehood turn,
And at the test of reason spurn?

All human sense, all craft must fail
And all its strength will nought avail,
When it attempts with efforts blind
To sway the independent mind,
Its spring to break, its pride to awe,
Or give to private judgment, law.

Oh impotent! and vile as vain,
They, who would native thought restrain!
As soon might they arrest the storm
Or take from fire the power to warm,
As man compel, by dint of might,
Old darkness to prefer to light.

* Text from the edition of 1815. [Ed.]

No! leave the mind unchain'd and free,
And what they ought, mankind will be,
No hypocrite, no lurking fiend,
No artist to some evil end,
But good and great, benign and just,
As God and nature made them first.

1815

STANZAS

On the decease of Thomas Paine, who died at New
York, on the 8*th* of June, 1809.*

PRINCES and kings decay and die
  And, instant, rise again:
But this is not the case, trust me,
  With men like THOMAS PAINE.

In vain the democratic host
  His *equal* would attain:
For years to come they will not boast
  A second Thomas Paine.

Though many may his name assume;
  Assumption is in vain;
For every man has not *his* plume—
  Whose name is *Thomas Paine.*

Though heaven bestow'd on all its sons
  Their *proper* share of brain,
It gives to few, ye simple ones,
  The mind of Thomas Paine.

To tyrants and the tyrant crew,
  Indeed, he was the bane;
He writ, and gave them all their due,
  And signed it,—THOMAS PAINE.

* Text from the edition of 1815. [Ed.]

Oh! how we loved to see him write
　　And curb the race of Cain!
They hope and wish that Thomas P——
　　May never rise again.

What idle hopes!—yes—such a man
　　May yet appear again.—
When *they* are dead, they die for aye:
　　—Not so with Thomas Paine.

1815

On the
SYMPTOMS OF HOSTILITIES.

—1809— *

BUT will they once more be engaged in a war,
　　Be fated to discord again?
A peace to the nations will nothing restore
But the challenge of death and a deluge of gore!
　　A modern crusade
　　Is undoubtedly made:—
With treaties rejected, and treaties renew'd,
A permanent treaty they never conclude.

And who is to blame? we submissively ask—
Did nature predestine this curse to mankind;
　　Or is it the cruel detestable task
That tyrants impose, with their minions combined?
　　We are anxious to know
　　The source of our wo
In a world where the blessings of nature abound
Why discord, the bane of her blessings, is found.

Must our freedom, our labors, our commerce, our all
　　Be tamely surrender'd, to tyrants convey'd;

* Text from the edition of 1815. [Ed.]

Must the flag of the country disgracefully fall,
   To be torn by the dogs of the *slaughtering trade?*
    Does no one reply,
    With a tear in his eye,
It must be the case, if we do not resent
What monarchs have menaced and tyranny meant.

Not a ship, or a barque, that departs from the shore
   But her cargo is plunder'd, her sailors are slain,
Or arriving in England, we see them no more,
   Condemn'd in the court of deceit and chicane,
    Where their wicked decrees
    And their costs and their fees
Have ruin'd the merchant—mechanics half fed,
And sailors uncaptured are begging their bread.

To reason with tyrants is surely absurd;
   To argue with them is to preach to the deaf:
They argue alone by the length of the sword;
   Their honor the same as the word of a thief.
    In such to confide
    When a cause they decide,
Is the wolf and the lamb (if the tale we recall)
Where the weakest and meekest must go the wall.

But an englishman's throat is expanded so wide
   Not the ocean itself is a mess for his maw:
And missions there are, and a scoundrel employ'd
   To divide, and to rule by the florentine law: *
    New-England must join
    In the knavish design,
As some have predicted to those who believe 'em;
—The event is at hand—may the devil deceive 'em.

With an empire at sea and an empire on land,
   And the system projected, monopolization,

* Nicholas Machiavel's maxim, *divide et impera;* divide and govern.
He was a native of Florence, in Italy.

The *western republic* no longer will stand
　　Than answers the views of a desperate nation,
　　　　Who have shackled the east,
　　　　Made the native a beast,
And are scheming to give us—the matter is clear—
A man of their own for the president's chair.

Then arouse from your slumbers, ye men of the west,
　　Already the indian his hatchet displays;
Ohio's frontier, and Kentucky distrest;
　　The village, and cottage, are both in a blaze:—
　　　　Then indian and english
　　　　No longer distinguish,
They bribe, and are bribed, for a warfare accurst;
Of the two, we can hardly describe which is worst.

In the court of king Hog was a council convened,
　　In which they agreed we are growing too strong:
They snuffed and grunted, and loudly complained
　　The sceptre would fall, if they suffer'd it long;
　　　　To cut up our *trade*
　　　　Was an object, they said,
The nearest and dearest of all in their view;
Not a fish should be caught if old England said, No!

Then arouse from your slumbers, ye men of the west,
　　A war is approaching, there's room to suppose;
The rust on your guns we abhor and detest,
　　So brighten them up—we are coming to blows
　　　　With the queen of the ocean
　　　　The *prop of devotion,*
The bulwark of all that is truly divine;
A motto she often has put on her sign.

[w. 1809]   1815

LINES
ADDRESSED TO MR. JEFFERSON,

On his retirement from the presidency of the United States.
—1809.*

PRAESENTI TIBI MATUROS LARGIMUR HONORES—*Hor.*

To you, great sir, our heartfelt praise we give,
And your ripe honors yield you—while you live.

AT length the year, which marks his course, expires,
And JEFFERSON from public life retires;
That year, the close of years, which own his claim,
And give him all his honors, all his fame.
Far in the heaven of fame I see him fly,
Safe in the realms of immortality:
On EQUAL WORTH his honor'd mantle falls,
Him, whom Columbia her true patriot calls;
Him, whom we saw her codes of freedom plan,
To none inferior in the ranks of man.

When to the helm of state your country call'd
No danger awed you and no fear appall'd;
Each bosom, faithful to its country's claim,
Hail'd JEFFERSON, that long applauded name;
All, then, was dark, and wrongs on wrongs accrued
Our treasures wasted, and our strength subdued;
What seven long years of war and blood had gain'd,
Was lost, abandon'd, squander'd, or restrain'd:
Britania's tools had schemed their *easier* way,
To conquer, ruin, pillage, or betray;
Domestic traitors, with exotic, join'd,
To shackle this *last refuge* of mankind;
Wars were provoked, and *France* was made our foe,
That George's race might govern all below,

* Text from the edition of 1815. [Ed.]

O'er this wide world, uncheck'd, unbounded, reign,
Seize every clime, and subjugate the main.

    All this was seen—and rising in your might,
By genius aided, you reclaim'd our right,
That RIGHT, which conquest, arms, and valor gave
To this young nation—not to live a slave.

    And what but toil has your long service seen?
Dark tempests gathering o'er a sky serene—
For wearied years no mines of wealth can pay,
No fame, nor all the plaudits of that day,
Which now returns you to your rural shade,
The sage's heaven, for contemplation made,
Who, like the ROMAN, in their country's cause
Exert their valor, or enforce its laws,
And late retiring, every wrong redress'd,
Give their last days to solitude and rest.

    This great reward a generous nation yields—
REGRET attends you to your native fields;
Their grateful thanks for every service done,
And hope, your thorny race of care is run.

    From your sage counsels what effects arise!
The vengeful briton from our waters flies;
His thundering ships no more our coasts assail,
But seize the advantage of the western gale.
Though bold and bloody, warlike, proud, and fierce,
They shun your vengeance for a MURDERED PEARCE,
And starved, dejected, on some meagre shore,
Sigh for the country they shall rule no more.

    Long in the councils of your native land,
We saw you cool, unchanged, intrepid, stand:
When the firm CONGRESS, still too firm to yield,
Stay'd masters of the long contested field,

Your wisdom aided, what their counsels framed—
By you the murdering savages were tamed—
That INDEPENDENCE we had sworn to gain,
By you asserted (nor DECLARED in vain)
We seized, triumphant, from a tyrant's throne,
And Britain totter'd when the work was done.

You, when an angry *faction* vex'd their age,
Rose to your place at once, and check'd their rage;
The envenom'd shafts of malice you defied,
And turn'd all projects of revolt aside:—
We saw you libell'd by the *worst of men*,
While hell's red lamp hung quivering o'er his pen,
And fiends congenial every effort try
To blast that merit which shall never die—

These had their hour, and traitors wing'd their flight,
To aid the screechings of distracted night.
Vain were their hopes—the poison'd darts of hell,
Glanced from your flinty shield, and harmless fell.

All this you bore—beyond it all you rose,
Nor ask'd despotic laws to crush your foes.
Mild was your language, temperate though severe;
And not less potent than ITHURIEL'S SPEAR
To touch the infernals in their loathesome guise,
Confound their slanders and detect their lies.

All this you braved—and, now, what task remains,
But silent walks on solitary plains:
To bid the vast luxuriant harvest grow,
The slave be happy and secured from wo—
To illume the statesmen of the times to come
With the bold spirit of primeval Rome;
To taste the joys your long tried service brings,
And look, with pity, on the cares of kings:—
Whether, with NEWTON, you the heavens explore,
And trace through nature the creating power,
Or, if with mortals you reform the age,

(Alike, in all, the patriot and the sage)
May peace and soft repose, attend you, still,
In the lone vale, or on the cloud-capp'd hill,
While smiling plenty decks the abundant plain,
And hails ASTREA to the world again.

[w. 1809]   1815

On the

BRITISH COMMERCIAL DEPREDATIONS.*

AS gallant ships as ever ocean stemm'd—
A thousand ships are captured, and condemn'd!
Ships from our shores, with native cargoes fraught,
And sailing to the very shores they ought:
And yet at peace!—the wrong is past all bearing;
The very comets† are the war declaring:
Six thousand seamen groan beneath your power,
For years immured, and prisoners to this hour:

Then England come! a sense of wrong requires
To meet with thirteen stars your thousand fires;
On your own seas the conflict to sustain,
Or drown them, with your commerce in the main!

True do we speak, and who can well deny,
That England claims all water, land, and sky
Her power expands—extends through every zone,
Nor bears a rival—but must rule alone.
To enforce her claims, a thousand sails unfurl'd
Pronounce their *home* the cock-pit of the world;
The modern *Tyre*, whose fiends and lions prowl,
A tyrant navy, which in time must howl.‡

---

* Text from the edition of 1815. [Ed.]
† A large comet appeared for several months, about this time.
‡ Howl, ye ships of Tarshish, &c.—Ezekiel.

Heaven send the time—the world obeys her *nod:*
Her nods, we hope, the sleep of death forbode;
Some mighty change, when plunder'd thrones agree,
And plunder'd countries, to make commerce free.

1815

MILITARY RECRUITING

TO A RECRUIT FOND OF SEGAR SMOKING.—

————Ex fumo dare lucem
Cogitat, ut speciosa dehinc miracula promat.—*Hor.*

WHEN first I arrived to the age of a man
    And met the distraction of care,
As the day to a close rather sorrowful ran
    Yet I smiled and I smoked my segar:
        O, how sweet did it seem
        What a feast, what a dream
What a pleasure to smoke the segar!

In vain did the din of the females assail
    Or the noise of the carts in the street,
With a spanish segar and a pint of good ale
    I found my enjoyment complete:
        Old care I dismiss'd
        While I held in my fist
The pitcher, and smoked the segar.

What a world are we in, if we do not retire,
    And, at times, to the tavern repair
To read the gazette, by a hickory fire,
    With a sixpence or shilling to spare,
        To handle the glass
        And an evening pass
With the help of a lively segar.

The man of the closet, who studies and reads,
    And prepares for the wars of the bar;

The priest who harangues, or the lawyer who pleads,
  What are they without the segar?
    What they say may be right,
    But they give no delight
  Unless they have smoked the segar.

The farmer still plodding, who follows his plough,
  A calling, the first and the best,
Would care not a fig for the sweat on his brow
  If he smoked a segar with the rest:
    To the hay-loft alone
    I would have it unknown,
  For *there* a segar I detest.

The sailor who climbs and ascends to the yard
  Bespatter'd and blacken'd with tar,
Would think his condition uncommonly hard
  If he did not indulge the segar,
    To keep them in trim
    While they merrily swim
  On the ocean, to countries afar.

The soldier *untry'd* in the midst of the smoke,
  The havoc and carnage of war,
Would stand to his cannon, as firm as a rock,
  Would they let him but smoke his segar:
    Every gun in the fort
    Should make its report
  From the fire which illumes the segar.

Come, then, to the tavern, ye sons of the sword,
  No fear of a wound or a scar;
If your money is gone, your account will be scored
  By the lady who tends at the bar:
    And this I can say,
    Not a cent need you pay
  For the use of the social segar.

1815

On the
LAKE EXPEDITIONS.*

WHERE Niagara's awful roar
Convulsive shakes the neighboring shore,
Alarm'd I heard the trump of war,
    Saw legions join!

And such a blast, of old, they blew,
When southward from St. Lawrence flew
The indian, to the english true,
    Led by Burgoyne.

United *then*, they sail'd *Champlain*,
United now, they march again,
A land of freedom to profane
    With savage yell.

For this they scour the mountain wood;
Their errand, death, their object, blood:
For this they stem thy subject flood,
    O stream Sorel!

Who shall repulse the hireling host,
Who force them back through snow and frost,
Who swell the lake with thousands lost,
    Dear freedom? say!—

Who but the sons of freedom's land,
Prepared to meet the bloody band;
Resolved to make a gallant stand
    Where lightnings play.

Their squadrons, arm'd with gun and sword,
Their legions, led by knight and lord
Have sworn to see the reign restored
    Of George, the goth;

    * Text from the edition of 1815. [Ed.]

Whose mandate, from a vandal shore,
Impels the sail, directs the oar,
And, to extend the flames of war,
    Employs them both.

                                        1815

The

BATTLE OF LAKE ERIE

September 10, 1813*

"TO clear the lake of *Perry's* fleet
And make his flag his winding sheet
This is my object—I repeat—"
    —Said Barclay, flush'd with native pride,
To some who serve the british crown:—
But *they*, who dwell beyond the moon,
Heard this bold menace with a frown,
    Nor the rash sentence ratified.

Ambition so bewitch'd his mind,
And royal smiles had so combined
With skill, to act the part assign'd
    He for no contest cared, a straw;
The ocean was too narrow far
To be the seat of naval war;
He wanted lakes, and room to spare,
    And all to yield to Britain's law.

And thus he made a sad mistake;
Forsooth he must possess the lake,
As merely made for England's sake
    To play her pranks and rule the roast;
Where she might govern, uncontrol'd,
An unmolested empire hold,
And keep a fleet to fish up gold,
    To pay the troops of George Provost.

    * Text from the edition of 1815. [Ed.]

The ships approach'd, on either side,
And Erie, on his bosom wide
Beheld two hostile navies ride,
    Each for a combat well prepared:
The lake was smooth, the sky was clear,
The martial drum had banish'd fear,
And death and danger hover'd near,
    Though both were held in disregard.

From lofty heights their colors flew,
And Britain's standard all in view,
With frantic valor fired the crew
    That mann'd the guns of queen Charlotte.
"And we must *Perry's* squadron take,
And England shall command the lake;—
And you must fight for Britain's sake,
    (Said Barclay) sailors, will you not?"

Assent they gave with heart and hand;
For never yet a braver band
To fight a ship, forsook the land,
    Than Barclay had on board that day;—
The guns were loosed the game to win,
Their muzzles gaped a dismal grin,
And out they pulled their tompion pin,
    The bloody game of war to play.

But Perry soon, with flowing sail,
Advanced, determined to prevail,
When from his bull-dogs flew the hail
    Directed full at queen Charlotte.
His wadded guns were aim'd so true,
And such a weight of ball they threw,
As, Barclay said, he never knew
    To come, before, so scalding hot!

But still, to animate his men
From gun to gun the warrior ran

And blazed away and blazed again—
  Till *Perry's* ship was half a wreck:
They tore away both tack and sheet,—
Their victory might have been complete,
Had *Perry* not, to shun defeat
  In lucky moment left his deck.

Repairing to another post,
From another ship he fought their host
And soon regain'd the fortune lost,
  And down, his flag the briton tore:
With loss of arm and loss of blood
Indignant, on his decks he stood
To witness Erie's crimson flood
  For miles around him, stain'd with gore!

Thus, for dominion of the lake
These captains did each other rake,
And many a widow did they make;—
  Whose is the fault, or who to blame?—
The briton challenged with his sword,
The yankee took him at his word,
With spirit laid him close on board—
  They're ours—he said—and closed the game.

1815

The
VOLUNTEER'S MARCH.*

July, 1814.

Dulce est pro patria mori.

YE, whom Washington has led,
Ye, who in his footsteps tread,

* This little ode, with the addition of two new stanzas is somewhat altered from one of Robert Burns' compositions, and applied to an american occasion: the original being Bruce's supposed address to his army, a little before the battle of Bannockbourne. [Text from the edition of 1815.—Ed.]

Ye, who death nor danger dread,
　Haste to glorious victory.

Now's the day and now's the hour;
See the British navy lour,
See approach proud George's power,
　England! chains and slavery.

Who would be a traitor knave?
Who would fill a coward's grave?
Who so base to be a slave?
　Traitor, coward, turn and flee.

Meet the tyrants, one and all;
Freemen stand, or freemen fall—
At Columbia's patriot call,
　At her mandate, march away!

Former times have seen them yield,
Seen them drove from every field,
Routed, ruin'd and repell'd—
　Seize the spirit of those times!

By oppression's woes and pains—
By our sons in servile chains
We will bleed from all our veins
　But they shall be—shall be free.

O'er the standard of their power
Bid Columbia's eagle tower,
Give them hail in such a shower
　As shall blast them—horse and man!

Lay the proud invaders low,
Tyrants fall in every foe;
Liberty's in every blow,
　Forward! let us do or die.

1815

The
BATTLE OF STONINGTON

ON THE SEABOARD OF CONNECTICUT; *

*In an attack upon the town and a small fort of two guns, by
the Ramillies, seventy-four gun ship, commanded by sir Thomas
Hardy; the Pactolus, 38 gun ship, Despatch, brig of 22 guns,
and a razee, or bomb ship.—August, 1814.*

FOUR gallant ships from England came
Freighted deep with fire and flame,
And other things we need not name,
    To have a dash at Stonington.

Now safely moor'd, their work begun;
They thought to make the yankees run,
And have a mighty deal of fun
    In stealing sheep at Stonington.

A deacon, then popp'd up his head
And parson Jones's sermon read,
In which the reverend doctor said
    That they must fight for Stonington.

A townsman bade them, next, attend
To sundry resolutions penn'd,
By which they promised to defend
    With sword and gun, old Stonington.

The ships advancing different ways,
The britons soon began to blaze,
And put th' old women in amaze,
    Who fear'd the loss of Stonington.

The yankees to their fort repair'd,
And made as though they little cared
For all that came—though very hard
    The cannon play'd on Stonington.

    * Text from the edition of 1815. [Ed.]

The *Ramillies* began the attack,
Despatch came forward—bold and black—
And none can tell what kept them back
    From setting fire to Stonington.

The bombardiers with bomb and ball,
Soon made a farmer's barrack fall,
And did a cow-house sadly maul
    That stood a mile from Stonington.

They kill'd a goose, they kill'd a hen,
Three hogs they wounded in a pen—
They dash'd away, and pray what then?
    This was not taking Stonington.

The shells were thrown, the rockets flew,
But not a shell, of all they threw,
Though every house was full in view,
    Could burn a house in Stonington.

To have their turn they thought but fair;—
The yankees brought two guns to bear,
And, sir, it would have made you stare,
    This smoke of smokes at Stonington.

They bored Pactolus through and through,
And kill'd and wounded of her crew
So many, that she bade adieu
    T' the gallant boys of Stonington.

The brig Despatch was hull'd and torn—
So crippled, riddled, so forlorn,
No more she cast an eye of scorn
    On th' little fort at Stonington.

The Ramillies gave up th' affray
And, with her comrades, sneak'd away—
Such was the valor, on that day,
    Of british tars near Stonington.

But some assert, on certain grounds,
(Besides the damage and the wounds)
It cost the king ten thousand pounds
   To have a dash at Stonington.

1815

On the

CONFLAGRATIONS AT WASHINGTON; *

August 24, 1814

    ——Jam deiphobi dedit ampla ruinam,
Vulcano superante, domus; jam proximus ardet
Ucalegon.—*Virgil*.

Now, George the third rules not alone,
For George the vandal shares the throne,
True flesh of flesh and bone of bone.

God save us from the fangs of both;
Or, one a vandal, one a goth,
May roast or boil us into froth.

Likes danes, of old, their fleet they man
And rove from *Beersheba* to *Dan*,
To burn, and beard us—where they can.

They say, at George the fourth's command
This vagrant host was sent, to land
And leave in every house—a brand.

An idiot only would require
Such war—the worst they could desire—
The felon's war—the war of fire.

The warfare, now, th' invaders make
Must surely keep us all awake,
Or life is lost for freedom's sake.

    * Text from the edition of 1815. [Ed.]

They said to Cockburn, "honest Cock!
To make a noise and give a shock
Push off, and burn their navy dock:

"Their capitol shall be emblazed!
How will the *buckskins* stand amazed,
And curse the day its walls were raised!"

Six thousand heroes disembark—
Each left at night his floating ark
And *Washington* was made their mark.

That few would fight them—few or none—
Was by their leaders clearly shown—
And "*down*," they said, "*with Madison!*"

How close they crept along the shore!
As closely as if *Rodgers* saw her—
A frigate to a seventy-four.

A veteran host, by veterans led,
With *Ross* and *Cockburn* at their head—
They came—they saw—they burnt—and fled.

But not unpunish'd they retired;
They something paid, for all they fired,
In soldiers kill'd, and chiefs expired.

Five hundred veterans bit the dust,
Who came, inflamed with lucre's lust—
And so they waste—and so they must.

They left our congress naked walls—
Farewell to towers and capitols!
To lofty roofs and splendid halls!

To courtly domes and glittering things,
To folly, that too near us clings,
To courtiers who—'tis well—had wings.

Farewell to all but glorious war,
Which yet shall guard *Potomac's* shore,
And honor lost, and fame restore.

To conquer armies in the field
Was, once, the surest method held
To make a hostile country yield.

The mode is this, now acted on;
In conflagrating *Washington,*
They held our independence gone!

Supposing *George's* house at Kew,
Were burnt, (as we intend to do,)
Would that be burning England too?

Supposing, near the silver *Thames*
We laid in ashes their *saint James,*
Or *Blenheim* palace wrapt in flames;

Made Hampton Court to fire a prey,
And meanly, then, to sneak away,
And never ask them, what's to pay?

Would that be conquering London town?
Would that subvert the english throne,
Or bring the royal system down?

With all their glare of guards or guns,
How would they look like simpletons,
And not at all the *lion's sons!*

Supposing, then, we take our turn
And make it public law, to burn,
Would not old english honor spurn

At such a mean insidious plan
Which only suits some savage clan—
And surely not—the english man!

A doctrine has prevail'd too long;
A king, they hold, *can do no wrong*—
Merely a pitch-fork, without prong:

But de'il may trust such doctrines, more,—
One king, that wrong'd us, long before,
Has wrongs, by hundreds, yet in store.

He wrong'd us forty years ago;
He wrongs us yet, we surely know;
He'll wrong us till he gets a blow

That, with a vengeance, will repay
The mischiefs we lament this day,
This burning, damn'd, infernal play;

Will send *one city* to the sky,
Its buildings low and buildings high,
And buildings—built the lord knows why;

Will give him an eternal check
That breaks his heart or breaks his neck,
And plants our standard on QUEBEC.

1815

To
THE LAKE SQUADRONS.*

THE brilliant task to you assign'd
Asks every effort of the mind,
And every energy, combined,
    To crush the foe.

Sail where they will, you must be there;
Lurk where they can, you will not spare
The blast of death—but all things dare
    To bring them low.

* Text from the edition of 1815. [Ed.]

To wield his thunders on *Champlain*,
Macdonough leads his gallant train,
And, his great object to sustain,
      Vermont unites

Her hardy youths and veterans bold
From shelter'd vale and mountain cold,
Who fought, to guard, in days of old
      Their country's rights.

That country's wrongs are all your own
And to the world the word is gone—
Her independence must to none
      Be sign'd away.

Be to the nation's standards true,
To Britain, and to Europe shew
That you can fight and conquer too,
      And prostrate lay.

That bitter foe, whose thousands rise
No more to fight us *in disguise*,
But count our freedom for their prize,
      If valor fails:

Beneath your feet let fear be cast,
Remember deeds of valor past,
And nail your colors to the mast
      And spread your sails.

In all the pride and pomp of war
Let thunders from the cannon roar,
And lightnings flash from shore to shore,
      To wing the ball.

Let *Huron* from his slumbers wake,
Bid *Erie* to his centre shake,
Till, foundering in *Ontario's* lake,
      You swamp them all!

1815

ROYAL CONSULTATIONS;

Relative to the Disposal of

LORD WELLINGTON'S ARMY.*

SAID the goth to the vandal, the prince to the king,
Let us do a mad action, to make the world ring:
With Wellington's army we now have the means
To make a bold stroke and exhibit new scenes.

A stroke at the *states* is my ardent desire,
To waste, and harass them with famine and fire;
My vengeance to carry through village and town,
And even to batter their capitol down.

The vandal then answer'd, and said to the goth,
Dear George, with yourself I am equally wroth:
Of Wellington's army dispose as you please,
It is best, I presume, they should go beyond seas;
For, should they come *home*, I can easily show
The hangman will have too much duty to do.

So, away came the bruisers, and when they came here
Some mischief they did, where no army was near:
They came to *correct* and they came to chastise
And to do all the evils their heads could devise.

At Washington city, they burnt and destroy'd
Till among the big houses they made a huge void;
Then back to their shipping they flew like the wind,
But left many more than five hundred behind
Of wounded and dead, and others say, double;
And thus was the hangman excused from some trouble.

Alexandria beheld them in battle array;
Alexandria they plunder'd a night and a day.
Then quickly retreated, with moderate loss,
Their forces conducted by Cockburn and Ross.

* Text from the edition of 1815. [Ed.]

At Baltimore, next, was their place of attack;
But Baltimore drove them repeatedly back;
There *Rodgers* they saw, and their terror was such,
They saw they were damn'd when they saw him approach.

The forts were assail'd by the strength of their fleet,
And the forts, in disorder beheld them retreat
So shatter'd and crippled, so mangled and sore,
That the tide of *Patapsco* was red with their gore.

Their legions by land no better succeeded—
In vain they manoeuvered, in vain they paraded,
Their hundreds on hundreds were strew'd on the ground,
Each shot from the rifles brought death or a wound.
One shot from a buckskin completed their loss,
And their legions no longer were headed by *Ross!*

Where they mean to go next, we can hardly devise,
But home they would go if their master was wise.

Yet folly so long has directed their course;
Such madness is seen in the waste of their force,
Such weakness and folly, with malice combined,
Such rancor, revenge, and derangement of mind,
That, all things consider'd, with truth we may say,
Both *Cochrane* and *Cockburn* are running away.*

To their regent, the prince, to their master the king
They are now on the way, they are now on the wing,
To tell them the story of loss and disaster,
One begging a pension, the other a plaister.
Let them speed as they may, to us it is plain
They will patch up their hulks for another campaign,
Their valor to prove, and their havoc to spread
When Wellington's army is *missing* or dead.

1815

* About this time, September, 1814, the admirals Cochrane and
Cockburn quitted the coast of the United States in their respective
flag ships.

PART TWO

POEMS OF ROMANTIC FANCY

The
HISTORY
of the
PROPHET JONAH

Versified (or rather paraphrased) from the sacred
writings.

Canto I.

IN ages past, when smit with warmth sublime,
Their bards foretold the dark events of time,
And piercing forward through the mystic shade,
Kings yet to come, and chiefs unborn survey'd,
Amittai's son perceiv'd, among the rest,
The mighty flame usurp his labouring breast:—
For thus, in dreams, the voice unerring came
Of Him, who lives through every age the same:
  "Arise! and o'er the intervening waste,
"To Nineveh's imperial turrets haste;
"That mighty town to ruin I decree,
"Proclaim destruction, and proclaim from me:
"Too long it stands, to God and man a foe,
"Without one virtue left to shield the blow;
"Guilt, black as night, their speedy ruin brings,
"And hottest vengeance from the King of Kings."
  The prophet heard—but dared to disobey,
(Weak as he was) and fled a different way;
In Joppa's port a trading ship he found
Far o'er the main to distant Tarshish bound:

193

The price of passage to her chief he paid,
And there conceal'd with wandering sailors stay'd,
His purpose fixt, at once perverse and blind,
To leave his country, and his God behind.

But He who spread the ocean's vast expanse,
And views all nature with a single glance,
Forth from its prison bade the tempest fly—
The tempest swell'd the ocean to the sky;
The trembling barque, as the fierce billow knocks,
Scarce bears the fury of repeated shocks;
Her crew distrest, astonish'd and afraid,
Each to his various god in anguish pray'd,
Nor trust alone to penitence and prayer,
They clear the decks, and for the worst prepare,
The costly lading to the deep they throw,
That lighter o'er the billows she may go,
Nor with regret the wealthy cargo spared,
For wealth is nothing when with life compared.

But to the ship's remotest chambers fled
There pensive Jonah droop'd his languid head,
And, new to all the dangers of the deep,
Had sunk, dejected, in the arms of sleep—
'Twas then the master broke the prophet's rest,
And thus exclaim'd, and smote his frantic breast—
"O sleeper, from thy stupid slumbers rise,
"At such an hour can sleep invade thine eyes?—
"If ever thou to heaven didst send a prayer,
"Now send thy warmest supplications there,
"Perhaps thy God may pity our distress,
"And save us, foundering in this dark abyss."

Thus warn'd, the seer his vows repentant paid—
Meantime, the seamen to their fellows said:
"No common waves our shatter'd vessel rend,
"There must be *one* for whom these storms impend,
"Some wretch we bear, for whom these billows rise,
"Foe to the gods, and hated by the skies;
"Come, since the billows all our arts defy,
"Come, let the lot decide for whom we die."

Instant the lots amidst the vase they threw
And the markt lot dejected Jonah drew!

Then thus their chief the guilty man address'd,
"Say, for what crime of thine are we distrest?
"What is thy country, what thy calling, say,
"Whence dost thou come, what potentate obey?
"Unfold it all, nor be the truth deny'd."—
The master spoke, and Jonah thus reply'd:

"A Hebrew I, from neighbouring regions came,
"A Jewish prophet, of no vulgar fame:
"That God I fear who spread this raging sea,
"Who fixt the shores by his supreme decree,
"And reigns throughout immeasurable space,
"His footstool earth, the heaven his dwelling place.
"But I, regardless of his high command,
"His mandate slighting, fled my native land,
"Fool that I was, from Joppa's port to fly,
"Who thought to shun his all-pervading eye!
"For this the tempest rends each tatter'd sail,"
"For this your vessel scarce supports the gale!

The seamen heard, distracted and dismay'd;
When thus again their trembling pilot said:
"How couldst thou thus, ungenerous as thou art,
"Affront thy patron, and with us depart?—
"Lo! for thy crimes, and not our own, we die;
"Mark, how the wild waves threaten from on high,
"Our sails in fragments flit before the blast,
"Scarce to its station we confine the mast;
"What shall we do, unhappy man, declare,
"How shall we act, or how direct our prayer,
"That angry Neptune may his rage restrain,
"And hush once more these tumults of the main?"

The seer reply'd, "The means are in your power
"To still the tempest in this dreadful hour:—
"High on the sea-beat prow will I ascend,
"And let the boldest of your crew attend
"To plunge me headlong from that giddy steep
"Down to the bosom of the unfathom'd deep;

"So shall the ocean from its raging cease,
"And the fierce tempest soon he hush'd to peace:—
"'Tis for my crimes this angry ocean raves,
"'Tis for my sin we plough these fearful waves;
"Dislodge me soon—the storm shall then decay,
"Which still grows louder while on board I stay."
   Thus he—but they, to save their vagrant guest,
Refus'd as yet to grant his strange request,
And though aloft on mountain waves they ride,
And the tost galley reels from side to side,
Yet to their breasts they drew the sweepy oar,
And vainly strove to gain the distant shore:
The ruffian winds refuse that wish'd retreat,
And fiercer o'er the decks the billows beat.
   Then to the skies the chief his prayer addrest,
"Thou Jove supreme, the greatest and the best!
"Because thy sovereign pleasure doth require
"That death alone must satisfy thine ire,
"O spare us for thy dying prophet's sake,
"Nor let us perish for the life we take;
"If we are wrong, his lot was thy decree,
"And thou hast done as it seem'd best to thee."
   Then from the summit of the washy prow,
They plunged the prophet to the depths below,
And straight the winds, and straight the billows cease,
And every threatening surge lay hush'd in peace;
The trembling crew adore the Power Supreme
Who kindly thus from ruin rescued them;
Their vows they send to his imperial throne,
And victims offer to this God unknown.

Canto II.

When from the prow's intimidating height
They plung'd the prophet to the realms of night,
Not long he languished in the briny deep,
In death's cold arms not yet decreed to sleep.—
Jehovah saw him, from the abodes of bliss,
Sunk to the bottom of the vast abyss,

And bade a whale, the mightiest of the kind,
His prophet in these dismal mansions find—
The hostile form, approaching through the wave,
Receiv'd him living to a living grave,
Where three long days in dark distress he lay,
And oft repenting, to his God did pray—
The power benign, propitious to his prayer,
Bade the huge fish to neighbouring shores repair—
Instant the whale obey'd the high command,
And cast him safe on Palestina's strand.
   The prophet then his past transgressions mourn'd,
And grateful, thus to heaven this thanks return'd:
"Afflicted from the depths of hell I pray'd,
"The dark abyss of everlasting shade:
"My God in mercy heard the earnest prayer,
"And dying Jonah felt thy presence there.
"Because I dared thy mandate disobey,
"Far didst thou plunge me from the face of day:
"In the vast ocean, where no land is found,
"The mighty waters closed thy prophet round:
"On me the waves their utmost fury spent,
"And all thy billows o'er my body went,
"Yet then, surrounded by the dismal shade,
"Thus to my MAKER from the depths I said:
"Though hid beneath the caverns of the main,
"To thy blest temple will I look again,
"Though from thy sight to utter darkness thrown,
"Still will I trust, and trust on thee alone—
"With anguish deep I felt the billows roll,
"Scarce in her mansion stay'd my frighted soul;
"About my head were wrapt the weeds of night,
"And darkness, mingled with no ray of light;
"I reached the caves the briny ocean fills,
"I reached the bases of the infernal hills,
"Earth, with her bars, encompass'd me around,
"Yet, from the bottom of the dark profound
"Where life no more the swelling vein supplies,
"And death reposes, didst thou bid me rise.

"When fainting nature bow'd to thy decree, ⎫
"And the lone spirit had prepar'd to flee, ⎬
"Then from my prison I remember'd thee, ⎭
"My prayer towards thy heavenly temple came,
"The temple sacred to JEHOVAH's name.—
"Unhappy they, who vanities pursue,
"And lies believing, their own souls undo—
"But to thine ear my grateful song shall rise,
"For thee shall smoke the atoning sacrifice,
"My vows I'll pay at thy imperial throne,
"Since my salvation was from thee alone."

Canto III.

Once more the voice to humbled Jonah came
Of HIM, who lives through every age the same:
"Arise! and o'er the intervening waste
"To Nineveh's exalted turrets haste,
"And what to thee my SPIRIT shall reveal,
"That preach—nor dare the sacred truth conceal—
"To desolation I that town decree;
"Proclaim destruction, and proclaim from me."
Obedient to JEHOVAH's high command,
The prophet rose, and left Judea's land,
And now he near the spiry city drew,
(Euphrates pass'd, and rapid Tigris too:)
So vast the bulk of this prodigious place,
Three days were scant its lengthy streets to trace;
But as he enter'd, on the first sad day,
Thus he began his tidings of dismay:
    "O NINEVEH! to heaven's decree attend!
"Yet forty days, and all thy glories end;
"Yet forty days, the skies protract thy fall,
"And desolation then shall bury all,
"Thy proudest towers their utter ruin mourn,
"And domes and temples unextinguished burn!
"O Nineveh! the GOD of armies dooms
"Thy thousand streets to never-ending glooms:

"Through mouldering fanes the hollow winds shall roar,
"And vultures scream where monarchs lodg'd before!
"Thy guilty sons shall bow beneath the sword,
"Thy captive matrons own a foreign lord.—
"Such is the vengeance that the heavens decree,
"Such is the ruin that must bury thee!"
  The people heard, and smit with instant fear,
Believ'd the fatal warnings of the seer:
This sudden ruin so their souls distrest,
That each with sackcloth did his limbs invest,
From him that glitter'd on the regal throne,
To him that did beneath the burden groan—
  Soon to their monarch came this voice of fate,
Who left his throne and costly robes of state,
And o'er his limbs a vest of sackcloth drew,
And sate in ashes, sorrowful to view—
His lords and nobles, now repentant grown,
With equal grief their various sins bemoan.
And through the city sent this loud decree,
With threatening back'd, and dreadful penalty:
  "Ye Ninevites! your wonted food refrain,
"Nor touch, ye beasts, the herbage of the plain,
"Let all that live be humbled to the dust,
"Nor taste the waters, though ye die of thirst:
"Let men and beasts the garb of sorrow wear,
"And beg yon' skies these guilty walls to spare:
"Let all repent the evil they pursue,
"And curse the mischief that their hands would do—
"Perhaps that GOD, who leans to mercy still,
"And sent a prophet to declare his will,
"May yet the vengeance he designs, adjourn,
"And, ere we perish, from his anger turn."
  JEHOVAH heard, and pleas'd beheld at last
Their deep repentance for transgressions past,
With pity moved, he heard the earnest prayer
Of this vast city, humbled in despair;
Though justly due, his anger dies away,
He bids the angel of destruction stay:—

The obedient angel hears the high command,
And sheathes the sword, he drew to smite the land.

Canto IV.

But anger swell'd the haughty prophet's breast,
Rage burn'd within, and robb'd his soul of rest;
Such was *his* pride, *he* wish'd they all in flame
Might rather perish than belie *his* fame,
And GOD's own bolts the tottering towers assail,
And millions perish, than *his* word should fail.
Then to the heavens he sent this peevish prayer—
(Vain, impious man, to send such pinings there):
"While yet within my native land, I stay'd,
"This would at last reward my toil, I said,
"Destruction through the Assyrian streets to cry,
"And then the event my mission falsify;
"For this I strove to shun thy sight before,
"And sought repose upon a foreign shore;
"I knew thou wert so gracious and so kind,
"Such mercy sways thy all creating mind,
"Averse thy bolts of vengeance to employ,
"And still relenting when you should'st destroy,
"That when I had declar'd thy sacred will,
"Thou would'st not what I prophesy'd fulfill,
"But leave me thus to scorn, contempt, and shame,
"A lying prophet, blasted in my fame—
"And now, I pray thee, grant my last request,
"O take my life, so wretched and unblest!
"If here I stay, 'tis but to grieve and sigh;
"Then take my life—'tis better for to die?"

"Is it thy place to swell with rage and pride,"
(Thus to his pining prophet, God reply'd)
"Say is it just thy heart should burn with ire
"Because *yon' city* is not wrapt in fire?
"What if I choose its ruin to delay,
"And send destruction on some future day,
"Must thou, for that, with wasting anguish sigh,
"And, hostile to my pleasure, wish to die?"

Then Jonah parted from the mourning town,
And near its eastern limits sate him down,
A booth he builded with assiduous care,
(Form'd of the cypress boughs that flourish'd there)
And anxious now beneath their shadow lay,
Waiting the issue of the fortieth day—
As yet uncertain if the Power Divine
Or would to mercy, or to wrath incline—
    Meantime the leaves that roof'd this arbour o'er,
Shrunk up and faded, sheltered him no more;
    But GOD ordain'd a thrifty gourd to rise,
To screen his prophet from the scorching skies;
High o'er his head aspired the spreading leaf,
Too fondly meant to mitigate his grief,
So close a foliage o'er his head was made,
That not a beam could pierce the happy shade:
The wondering seer perceiv'd the branches grow
And bless'd the shadow that reliev'd his woe;
    But when the next bright morn began to shine
(So God ordain'd) a worm attack'd the vine,
Beneath his bite its goodly leaves decay,
And wasting, withering, die before the day!
Then as the lamp of heaven still higher rose
From eastern skies a sultry tempest blows,
The vertic sun as fiercely pour'd his ray,
And beam'd around insufferable day.
How beat those beams on Jonah's fainting head!
How oft he wish'd a place among the dead!
All he could do, was now to grieve and sigh,
His life detest, and beg of God to die.
    Again, JEHOVAH to his prophet said,
"Art thou so angry for thy vanish'd shade—
"For a mere shadow dost thou well to grieve,
"For this poor loss would'st thou thy being leave?"—
    "My rage is just, (the frantic prophet cry'd),
"My last, my only comfort is deny'd—
"The spreading vine that form'd my leafy bower;
"Behold it vanish'd in the needful hour!

"To beating winds and sultry suns a prey,
"My fainting spirit droops and dies away—
"Give me a mansion in my native dust,
"For though I die with rage, my rage is just."
    Once more the Almighty deign'd to make reply—
"Does this lost *gourd* thy sorrow swell so high,
"*Whose* friendly shade not to thy toil was due,
"Alone it sprouted and alone it grew;
"A night beheld its branches waving high,
"And the next sun beheld those branches die;
"And should not pity move the LORD of all
"To spare the vast Assyrian capital,
"Within whose walls uncounted myriads stray,
"Their Father I, my sinful offspring they?—
"Should they not move the creating mind
"With six score thousand of the infant kind,
"And herds untold that graze the spacious field,
"For whom yon' meads their stores of fragrance yield;
"Should I this royal city wrap in flame,
"And slaughter millions to support thy fame,
"When now repentant to their God they turn,
"And their past follies, low in ashes, mourn?—
"Vain thoughtless wretch, recall thy weak request,
"Death never came to man a welcome guest;—
"Why wish to die—what madness prompts thy mind?
"Too long the days of darkness thou shalt find;
"Life was a blessing by thy Maker meant,
"Dost thou despise the blessings he has lent—
"Enjoy my gifts while yet the seasons run
"True to their months, and social with the sun;
"When to the dust my mandate bids thee fall,
"All these are lost, for death conceals them all—
"No more the sun illumes the sprightly day,
"The seasons vanish, and the stars decay:
"The trees, the flowers, no more thy sense delight,
"Death shades them all in ever-during night.
"Then think not long the little space I lent—
"Of thy own sins, like Nineveh, repent;

"Rejoice at last the mighty change to see,
"And bear with them as I have borne with thee."

[w. 1768]   1786

Debemur morti nos nostraque!—

The
PYRAMIDS OF EGYPT
A Dialogue
Written in 1769.

Scene. Egypt.
Persons. Traveller, Genius, Time.

Traveller.

WHERE are those far-famed piles of human grandeur,
Those sphinxes, pyramids, and Pompey's pillar,
That bid defiance to the arm of TIME—
Tell me, dear GENIUS, for I long to see them.

Genius.

At Alexandria rises Pompey's pillar,
Whose date is but of yesterday, compared
With those prodigious fabricks that you see
O'er yonder distant plain—upon whose breast
Old Nile hath never roll'd his swelling stream,
The only plain so privileged in Egypt;
These pyramids may well excite your wonder;
They are of most remote antiquity,
Almost coeval with those cloud-crown'd hills
That westward from them rise—long ere the age
That saw old Babel's tower aspiring high,
Then first the sage Egyptian architects
These ancient turrets to the heavens rais'd:—
But Babel's tower is gone, and these remain!

Traveller.

Old Rome I thought unrival'd in her years,
At least the remnants that we find at Rome,—
Deep are they sunk in dark antiquity;—
But these, you tell me, are of older date.

Genius.

Talk not of Rome!—Before they lopt a bush
From the seven hills where Rome, earth's empress, stood,
These pyramids were old—their birth-day is
Beyond tradition's reach, or history.

Traveller.

Then let us haste toward those piles of wonder
That scorn to bend beneath this weight of years—
Lo! to my view, the aweful mansions rise
The pride of art, the sleeping place of death!
Are these the four prodigious monuments
That so astonish every generation—
Let us examine this, the first and greatest—
A secret horror, chills my breast, dear Genius,
To touch these monuments that are so ancient,
The fearful property of ghosts and death!—
And of such mighty bulk, that I presume
A race of giants were the architects.————
Since these proud fabricks to the heavens were rais'd
How many generations have decay'd,
How many monarchies to ruin pass'd!
How many empires had their rise and fall!
While these remain—and promise to remain
As long as yonder sun, that gilds their summits,
Or moon or stars their wonted circuits run.

Genius.

————————————————————The time will come
When these stupendous piles you deem immortal,
Worn out with age, shall moulder on their bases,

And down, down, low to endless ruin verging,
O'erwhelm'd by dust, be seen and known no more!—
Ages ago, in dark oblivion's lap
Had they been shrouded, but the atmosphere
In these parch'd climates, hostile to decay,
Is pregnant with no rain, that by its moisture
Might waste their bulk in such excess of time,
And prove them briefly mortal.—
'Twas on this plain the ancient Memphis stood,
Her walls encircled these tall pyramids—
But where is Pharaoh's palace, where the domes
Of Egypt's haughty lords? all, all are gone,
And like the phantom snows of a May morning,
Left not a vestige to remember them!

Traveller.

How shall I reach the vertex of this pile—
How shall I clamber up its shelving sides?
I scarce endure to glance towards the summit,
It seems among the clouds—When wast thou rais'd
O work of more than mortal majesty—
Was this produced by persevering man,
Or did the gods erect this pyramid?

Genius.

Nor gods, nor giants rais'd this pyramid—
It was the toil of mortals like yourself,
That swell'd it to the skies——
Seest thou yon' little door?   Through that they pass'd,
Who rais'd so high this aggregate of wonders!
What cannot tyrants do,
When they have subject nations at their will,
And the world's wealth to gratify ambition!
Millions of slaves beneath their labours fainted
Who here were doom'd to toil incessantly,
And years elaps'd while groaning myriads strove
To raise this mighty tomb—and but to hide
The worthless bones of an Egyptian king.—

O wretch, might not a humbler tomb have done,
Could nothing but a pyramid inter thee?

Traveller.

Perhaps old Israel's race, when here oppress'd,
Rais'd, in their years of bondage, this dread pile.

Genius.

Before the Jewish patriarchs saw the light,
While yet the globe was in its infancy
These were erected to the pride of man—
Five thousand years have run their tedious round
Since these smooth stones were on each other laid,
Five thousand more may run as dull a round
Ere Egypt sees her pyramids decay'd.

Traveller.

But suffer me to enter, and behold
The interior wonders of this edifice.

Genius.

'Tis darkness all, with hateful silence join'd—
Here drowsy bats enjoy a dull repose,
And marble coffins, vacant of their bones,
Shew where the royal dead in ruin lay!
By every pyramid a temple rose
Where oft, in concert, those of ancient time
Sung to their goddess ISIS hymns of praise;
But these are fallen!—their columns too superb
Are levell'd with the dust—nor these alone—
Where is thy vocal statue, *Memnon*, now,
That, once, responsive to the morning beams,
Harmoniously to father Phoebus sung!
Where is the image that in past time stood
High on the summit of yon' pyramid?
Still may you see its polish'd pedestal—
Where art thou ancient Thebes?——all buried low,
All vanish'd! crumbled into mother dust,

And nothing of antiquity remains
But these huge pyramids, and yonder hills.

Time.

Old Babel's tower hath felt my potent arm,
I ruin'd *Ecbatan* and *Babylon*,
Thy huge Colossus, *Rhodes*, I tumbled down,
And on these pyramids I smote my scythe;
But they resist its edge——then let them stand.—
But I can boast a greater feat than this,
I long ago have shrouded those in death
Who made these structures rebels to my power—
But, O return!—These piles are not immortal!
This earth, with all its belts of hills and mountains,
Shall perish by my hand——then how can these,
These hoary-headed pyramids of Egypt,
That are but dwindled moates upon her body,
That on a little, little spot of ground
Extinguish the dull radiance of the sun,
Be proof to death and me?—Traveller return—
There's nought but GOD immortal—HE alone
Exists secure, when Genius, and *Time*,
(Time not immortal, but a viewless point
In the vast circle of eternity)
Are swallowed up, and, like the pyramids,
Leave not an atom for their monument!

[w. 1769]   1786

The POWER of FANCY.*

Written 1770.

WAKEFUL, vagrant, restless thing,
Ever wandering on the wing,
Who thy wondrous source can find,
FANCY, regent of the mind;
A spark from Jove's resplendent throne,
But thy nature all unknown.

* Text from the edition of 1786. [Ed.]

THIS spark of bright, celestial flame,
From Jove's seraphic altar came,
And hence alone in man we trace,
Resemblance to the immortal race.

Ah! what is all this mighty WHOLE,
These suns and stars that round us roll!
What are they all, where'er they shine,
But *Fancies* of the Power Divine!
What is this *globe*, these *lands*, and *seas*,
And *heat*, and *cold*, and *flowers*, and *trees*,
And *life*, and *death*, and *beast*, and *man*,
And *time*,—that with the *sun* began—
But thoughts on reason's scale combin'd,
Ideas of the Almighty mind?

On the surface of the brain
Night after night she walks unseen,
Noble fabrics doth she raise
In the woods or on the seas,
On some high, steep, pointed rock,
Where the billows loudly knock
And the dreary tempests sweep
Clouds along the uncivil deep.

Lo! she walks upon the moon,
Listens to the chimy tune
Of the bright, harmonious spheres,
And the song of angels hears;
Sees this earth a distant star,*
Pendant, floating in the air;
Leads me to some lonely dome,
Where Religion loves to come,
Where the bride of Jesus dwells,
And the deep ton'd organ swells
In notes with lofty anthems join'd,
Notes that half distract the mind.

Now like lightning she descends
To the prison of the fiends,

* Milton's Paradise Lost, B. II, v. 1052.

Hears the rattling of their chains,
Feels their never ceasing pains—
But, O never may she tell
Half the frightfulness of hell.

   Now she views Arcadian rocks,
Where the shepherds guard their flocks,
And, while yet her wings she spreads,
Sees chrystal streams and coral beds,
Wanders to some desert deep,
Or some dark, enchanted steep,
By the full moonlight doth shew
Forests of a dusky blue,
Where, upon some mossy bed,
Innocence reclines her head.

   SWIFT, she stretches o'er the seas
To the far off Hebrides,
Canvas on the lofty mast
Could not travel half so fast—
Swifter than the eagle's flight
Or instantaneous rays of light!
Lo! contemplative she stands
On Norwegia's rocky lands—
Fickle Goddess, set me down
Where the rugged winters frown
Upon Orca's howling steep,
Nodding o'er the northern deep,
Where the winds tumultuous roar,
Vext that *Ossian* sings no more.
Fancy, to that land repair,
Sweetest Ossian slumbers there;
Waft me far to southern isles
Where the soften'd winter smiles,
To Bermuda's orange shades,
Or Demarara's lovely glades;
Bear me o'er the sounding cape,
Painting death in every shape,
Where daring *Anson* spread the sail
Shatter'd by the stormy gale—

Lo! she leads me wide and far,
Sense can never follow her—
Shape thy course o'er land and sea,
Help me to keep pace with thee,
Lead me to yon' chalky cliff,
Over rock and over reef,
Into Britain's fertile land,
Stretching far her proud command.
Look back and view, thro' many a year,
Caesar, Julius Caesar, there.

Now to Tempe's verdant wood,
Over the mid ocean flood
Lo! the islands of the sea
—Sappho, Lesbos mourns for thee:
Greece, arouse thy humbled head,
Where are all thy mighty dead,
Who states to endless ruin hurl'd
And carried vengeance through the world?—
Troy, thy vanish'd pomp resume,
Or, weeping at thy Hector's tomb,
Yet those faded scenes renew,
Whose memory is to *Homer* due.
Fancy, lead me wandering still
Up to Ida's cloud-topt hill;
Not a laurel there doth grow
But in vision thou shalt show,—
Every sprig on Virgil's tomb
Shall in livelier colours bloom,
And every triumph Rome has seen
Flourish on the years between.

Now she bears me far away
In the east to meet the day,
Leads me over Ganges' streams,
Mother of the morning beams—
O'er the ocean hath she ran,
Places me on *Tinian;*
Farther, farther in the east,
Till it almost meets the west,

Let us wandering both be lost
On Taitis sea-beat coast,
Bear me from that distant strand,
Over ocean, over land,
To California's golden shore—
Fancy, stop, and rove no more.

   Now, tho' late, returning home,
Lead me to *Belinda's* tomb;
Let me glide as well as you
Through the shroud and coffin too,
And behold, a moment, there,
All that once was good and fair—
Who doth here so soundly sleep?
Shall we break this prison deep?—
Thunders cannot wake the maid,
Lightnings cannot pierce the shade,
And tho' wintry tempests roar,
Tempests shall disturb no more.

   YET must those eyes in darkness stay,
That once were rivals to the day—?
Like heaven's bright lamp beneath the main
They are but set to rise again.

   FANCY, thou the muses' pride,
In thy painted realms reside
Endless images of things,
Fluttering each on golden wings,
Ideal objects, such a store,
The universe could hold no more:
Fancy, to thy power I owe
Half my happiness below;
By thee Elysian groves were made,
Thine were the notes that Orpheus play'd;
By thee was Pluto charm'd so well
While rapture seiz'd the sons of hell—
Come, O come—perceiv'd by none,
You and I will walk alone.

[W. 1770]   1786

THE PRAYER OF ORPHEUS.

SAD monarch of the world below,
Stern guardian of this drowsy shade,
Through these unlovely realms I go
To seek a captive thou hast made.
O'er Stygian waters have I pass'd,
Contemning Jove's unjust decree,
And reached thy sable court at last
To find my lost Eurydicè.

Of all the nymphs, so deckt and drest
Like Venus of the starry train,
She was the loveliest and the best,
The pride and glory of the plain.
O free from thy despotic sway
This nymph of heaven-descended charms,
Too soon she came this dusky way——
Restore thy captive to my arms.

As by a stream's fair verdant side
In myrtle shades she rov'd along,
A serpent stung my blooming bride,
This brightest of the female throng—
The venom hastening thro' her veins
Forbade the freezing blood to flow.
And thus she left the Thracian plains
For these dejected groves below.

Even thou mays't pity my sad pain,
Since Love, as ancient stories say,
Forced thee to leave thy native reign,
And in Sicilian meadows stray:
Bright Proserpine thy bosom fired,
For her you sought unwelcome light,
Madness and love in you conspired
To seize her to the shades of night.

But if, averse to my request,
The banished nymph, for whom I mourn,

Must in Plutonian chambers rest,
And never to my arms return——
Take Orpheus too—his warm desire
Can ne'er be quench'd by your decree:
In life or death he must admire,
He must adore Eurydicè.

The
AMERICAN VILLAGE, &c.*

WHERE yonder stream divides the fertile plain,
Made fertile by the labours of the swain;
And hills and woods high tow'ring o'er the rest,
Behold a village with fair plenty blest:
Each year tall harvests crown the happy field;
Each year the meads their stores of fragrance yield,
And ev'ry joy and ev'ry bliss is there,
And healthful labour crowns the flowing year.

   Though *Goldsmith* weeps in melancholy strains,
Deserted Auburn and forsaken plains,
And mourns his village with a patriot sigh,
And in that village sees Britannia die:
Yet shall this land with rising pomp divine,
In it's own splendour and Britannia's shine.
O muse, forget to paint her ancient woes,
Her Indian battles, or her Gallic foes;
Resume the pleasures of the rural scene,
Describe the village rising on the green,
It's harmless people, born to small command,
Lost in the bosom of this western land:
So shall my verse run gentle as the floods,
So answer all ye hills, and echo all ye woods;
So glide ye streams in hollow channels pent,
Forever wasting, yet not ever spent.

 * Text taken from a photostatic copy of the very rare pamphlet
edition owned by The Library of Congress. [Ed.]

Ye clust'ring boughs by hoary thickets borne!
Ye fields high waving with eternal corn!
Ye woodland nymphs the tender tale rehearse,
The fabled authors of immortal verse:
Ye Dryads fair, attend the scene I love,
And Heav'n shall centre in yon' blooming grove.
What tho' thy woods, AMERICA, contain
The howling forest, and the tiger's den,
The dang'rous serpent, and the beast of prey,
Men are more fierce, more terrible than they.
No monster with it's vile contagious breath,
No flying scorpion darting instant death;
No pois'nous adder, burning to engage,
Has half the venom or has half the rage.
What tho' the Turk protests to heav'n his ire,
With lift up hand amidst his realms of fire;
And Russia's Empress sends her fleets afar,
To aid the havock of the burning war:
Their rage dismays not, and their arms in vain,
In dreadful fury bathe with blood the plain;
Their terrors harmless, tho' their story heard,
How this one conquer'd, or was nobly spar'd:
Vain is their rage, to us their anger vain,
The deep Atlantic raves and roars between.

To yonder village then will I descend,
There spend my days, and there my ev'nings spend;
Sweet haunt of peace whose mud' wall'd sides delight,
The rural mind beyond the city bright:
Their tops with hazles or with alders wove,
Remurmur magic to the neighb'ring grove;
And each one lab'ring in his own employ,
Comes weary home at night, but comes with joy:
The soil which lay for many thousand years
O'er run by woods, by thickets and by bears;
Now reft of trees, admits the chearful light,
And leaves long prospects to the piercing sight;
Where once the lynx nocturnal sallies made,

And the tall chestnut cast a dreadful shade:
No more the panther stalks his bloody rounds,
Nor bird of night her hateful note resounds;
Nor howling wolves roar to the rising moon,
As pale arose she o'er yon eastern down.
Some prune their trees, a larger load to bear
Of fruits nectarine blooming once a year:
See groaning waggons to the village come
Fill'd with the apple, apricot or plumb;
And heavy beams suspended from a tree,
To press their juice against the winter's day:
Or see the plough torn through the new made field,
Ordain'd a harvest, yet unknown to yield.
The rising barn whose spacious floor receives
The welcome thousands of the wheaten sheaves,
And spreads it's arms to take the plenteous store,
Sufficient for its master and the poor:
For as Eumoeus us'd his beggar guest
The great Ulysses in his tatters drest:
So here fair Charity puts forth her hand,
And pours her blessing o'er the greatful land:
No needy wretch the rage of winter fears,
Secure he sits and spends his aged years,
With thankful heart to gen'rous souls and kind,
That save him from the winter and the wind.

A LOVELY island once adorn'd the sea,
Between New-Albion and the Mexic' Bay;
Whose sandy sides wash'd by the ocean wave,
Scarce heard a murmur but what ocean gave:
Small it's circumference, nor high it's coast,
But shady woods the happy isle could boast;
On ev'ry side new prospects catch'd the eye,
There rose blue mountains to the arched sky:
Here thunder'd ocean in convulsive throws,
And dash'd the island as it's waters rose:
Yet peaceful all within, no tumults there,
But fearless steps of the unhunted hare;

And nightly chauntings of the fearless dove,
Or blackbird's note, the harbinger of love.
So peaceful was this haunt that nature gave,
Still as the stars, and silent as the grave;
No loud applause there rais'd the patriot breast,
No shouting armies their mad joy confest,
For battles gain'd, or trophies nobly won,
Or nations conquer'd near the rising sun;
No clam'rous crews, or wild nocturnal cheer,
Or murd'rous ruffians, for no men were here.
On it's east end a grove of oak was seen,
And shrubby hazels fill'd the space between;
Dry alders too, and aspin leaves that shook
With ev'ry wind, conspir'd to shade a brook,
Whose gentle stream just bubbling from the ground,
Was quickly in the salter ocean drown'd:
Beyond whose fount, the center of the isle,
Wild plumb trees flourish'd on the shaded soil.
In the dark bosom of this sacred wood,
Had fate but smil'd, some village might have stood
Secluded from the world, and all it's own,
Of other lands unknowing, and unknown.
Here might the hunter have destroy'd his prey,
Transfix'd the goat before the dawn of day;
And trudging homeward with his welcome load,
The fruit of wand'rings thro' each by-way road:
Thrown down his burthen with the needless sigh,
And gladly feasted his small family.
Small fields had then suffic'd, and grateful they,
The annual labours of his hands to pay;
And free his right to search the briny flood
For fish, or slay the creatures of the wood.

THUS spent his days in labour's pleasant pain,
Had liv'd and dy'd the homely shepherd swain:
Had seen his children and his children's heirs,
The fruit of love and memory of years
To agriculture's first fair service bent,

The work of mortals, and their great intent.
So had the Sire his days of pleasure known,
And wish'd to change no country for his own:
So had he with his fair endearing wife,
Pass'd the slow circle of a harmless life;
With happy ignorance divinely blest,
The path, the centre and the home of rest.
Long might the sun have run his bright career,
And long the moon her mantled visage rear;
And long the stars their nightly vigils kept,
And spheres harmonious either sung or wept:
He had not dream'd of worlds besides his own,
And thought them only stars, beyond the moon;
Enjoy'd himself, nor hear'd of future hell,
Or heav'n, the recompence of doing well;
Had scarcely thought of an eternal state,
And left his being in the hands of fate.—
O had this isle such souls sublime contain'd,
And there for ages future sons remain'd:
But envious time conspiring with the sea,
Wash'd all it's landscapes, and it's groves away.
It's trees declining, stretch'd upon the sand,
No more their shadows throw across the land.
It's vines no more their clust'ring beauty show,
Nor sturdy oaks embrace the mountain's brow.
Bare sands alone now overwhelm the coast,
Lost in it's grandeur, and it's beauty lost.

    THUS, tho' my fav'rite isle to ruin gone,
Inspires my sorrow, and demands my moan;
Yet this wide land it's place can well supply
With landscapes, hills and grassy mountains high.
O HUDSON! thy fair flood shall be my theme,
Thy winding river, or thy glassy stream;
On whose tall banks tremendous rocks I spy,
Dread nature in primaeval majesty.
Rocks, to whose summits clouds eternal cling,
Or clust'ring birds in their wild wood notes sing.

Hills, from whose sides the mountain echo roars,
Rebounding dreadful from the distant shores;
Or vallies, where refreshing breezes blow,
And rustic huts in fair confusion grow,
Safe from the winds, secur'd by mountains high,
That seem to hide the concave of the sky;
To whose top oft' the curious hind ascends,
And wonders where the arch'd horizon bends;
Pleas'd with the distant prospects rising new,
And hills o'er hills, a never ending view.
Through various paths with hasty step he scours,
And breathes the odours of surrounding flow'rs,
Caught from their bosoms by the fragrant breath,
Of western breezes, or the gale of death.*
Then low descending, seeks the humble dome,
And centres all his pleasures in his home,
'Till day returning, brings the welcome toil,
To clear the forest, or to tame the soil;
To burn the woods, or catch the tim'rous deer,
To scour the thicket, or contrive the snare.

SUCH was the life our great fore-fathers led,
The golden season now from BRITAIN fled,
E'er since dread commerce stretch'd the nimble sail,
And sent her wealth with ev'ry foreign gale.—
Strange fate, but yet to ev'ry country known,
To love all other riches but it's own.
Thus fell the mistress of the conquer'd earth,
GREAT ROME, who ow'd to ROMULUS her birth,
Fell to the monster LUXURY, a prey,
Who forc'd a hundred nations to obey.
She whom nor mighty CARTHAGE could withstand,
Nor strong JUDEA's once thrice holy land:
She all the west, and BRITAIN could subdue,
While vict'ry with the ROMAN eagles flew;
She, she herself eternal years deny'd,
Like ROME she conquer'd, but by ROME she dy'd:

* South wind.

But if AMERICA, by this decay,
The world itself must fall as well as she.
No other regions latent yet remain,
This spacious globe has been research'd in vain.
Round it's whole circle oft' have navies gone,
And found but sea or lands already known.
When she has seen her empires, cities, kings,
Time must begin to flap his weary wings;
The earth itself to brighter days aspire,
And wish to feel the purifying fire.

NOR think this mighty land of old contain'd
The plund'ring wretch, or man of bloody mind:
Renowned SACHEMS once their empires rais'd
On wholesome laws; and sacrifices blaz'd.
The gen'rous soul inspir'd the honest breast,
And to be free, was doubly to be blest:
'Till the east winds did here COLUMBUS blow,
And wond'ring nations saw his canvas flow.
'Till here CABOT descended on the strand,
And hail'd the beauties of the unknown land;
And rav'nous nations with industrious toil,
Conspir'd to rob them of their native soil:
Then bloody wars, and death and rage arose,
And ev'ry tribe resolv'd to be our foes.
Full many a feat of them I could rehearse,
And actions worthy of immortal verse:
Deeds ever glorious to the INDIAN name,
And fit to rival GREEK or ROMAN fame,
But one sad story shall my Muse relate,
Full of paternal love, and full of fate;
Which when ev'n yet the northern shepherd hears,
It swells his breast, and bathes his face in tears,
Prompts the deep groan, and lifts the heaving sigh,
Or brings soft torrents from the female eye.

FAR in the arctic skies, where HUDSON'S BAY
Rolls it's cold wave and combats with the sea,
A dreary region lifts it's dismal head,

True sister to the regions of the dead.
Here thund'ring storms continue half the year,
Or deep-laid snows their joyless visage rear:
Eternal rocks, from whose prodigious steep
The angry tiger stuns the neighb'ring deep;
While through the wild wood, or the shrouded plain,
The moose deer seeks his food, but often seeks in vain.
Yet in this land, froze by inclement skies,
The Indian huts in wild succession rise;
And daily hunting, when the short-liv'd spring
Shoots joyous forth, th' industrious people bring
Their beaver spoils beneath another sky,
PORT NELSON and each BRITISH factory:
In slender boats from distant lands they sail,
Their small masts bending to the inland gale,
On traffic sent to gain the little store,
Which keeps them plenteous, tho' it keeps them poor.
Hither CAFFRARO in his flighty boat,
One hapless spring his furry riches brought;
And with him came, for sail'd he not alone,
His consort COLMA, and his little son.
While yet from land o'er the deep wave he plough'd,
And tow'rds the shore with manly prowess row'd.
His barque unfaithful to it's trusted freight,
Sprung the large leak, the messenger of fate;
But no lament or female cry was heard,
Each for their fate most manfully prepar'd,
From bubbling waves to send the parting breath
To lands of shadows, and the shade of death.
O FATE! unworthy such a tender train,
O day, lamented by the Indian swain!
Full oft' of it the strippling youth shall hear,
And sadly mourn their fortune with a tear:
The Indian maids full oft' the tale attend,
And mourn their COLMA as they'd mourn a friend.

NOW while in waves the barque demerg'd they strive,
Dead with despair, tho' nature yet alive:

Forth from the shore a friendy brother flew,
In one small boat, to save the drowning crew.
He came, but in his barque of trifling freight,
Could save but two, and one must yield to fate.
O dear CAFFRARO, said the hapless wife,
O save our son, and save thy dearer life:
'Tis thou canst teach him how to hunt the doe,
Transfix the buck, or tread the mountain snow,
Let me the sentence of my fate receive,
And to thy care my tender infant leave.
He sigh'd, nor answer'd, but as firm as death,
Resolv'd to save her with his latest breath:
And as suspended by the barque's low side,
He rais'd the infant from the chilling tide,
And plac'd it safe; he forc'd his COLMA too
To save herself, and what could mortal do?
But nobly scorning life, she rais'd her head
From the flush'd wave, and thus divinely said:

  Of life regardless, I to fate resign,
But thou, CAFFRARO, art forever mine.
O let thy arms no future bride embrace,
Remember COLMA, and her beauteous face,
Which won thee youthful in thy gayest pride,
With captives, trophies, victors at thy side;
Now I shall quick to blooming regions fly,
A spring eternal, and a nightless sky,
Far to the west, where radiant SOL descends,
And wonders where the arch'd horizon ends:
There shall my soul thy lov'd idea keep;
And 'till thy image comes, unceasing weep.
There, tho' the tiger is but all a shade,
And mighty panthers but the name they had;
And proudest hills, and lofty mountains there,
Light as the wind, and yielding as the air;
Yet shall our souls their ancient feelings have,
More strong, more noble than this side the grave.
There lovely blossoms blow throughout the year,

And airy harvests rise without our care:
And all our sires and mighty ancestors,
Renown'd for battles and successful wars,
Behold their sons in fair succession rise,
And hail them happy to serener skies.
There shall I see thee too, and see with joy
Thy future charge, my much lov'd Indian boy:
The thoughtless infant, whom with tears I see,
Once sought my breast, or hung upon my knee;
Tell him, ah tell him, when in manly years,
His dauntless mind, nor death nor danger fears,
Tell him, ah tell him, how thy COLMA dy'd,
His fondest mother, and thy youthful bride:
Point to my tomb thro' yonder furzy glade,
And show where thou thy much lov'd COLMA laid.
O may I soon thy blest resemblance see,
And my sweet infant all reviv'd in thee.
'Till then I'll haunt the bow'r or lonely shade,
Or airy hills for contemplation made,
And think I see thee in each ghostly shoal,
And think I clasp thee to my weary soul.
Oft, oft thy form to my expecting eye,
Shall come in dreams with gentle majesty;
Then shall I joy to find my bliss began
To love an angel, whom I lov'd a man!
She said, and downward in the hoary deep
Plung'd her fair form to everlasting sleep;
Her parting soul it's latest struggle gave,
And her last breath came bubbling thro' the wave.

THEN sad CAFFRARO all his grief declares,
And swells the torrent of the gulph with tears;
And senseless stupid to the shore is borne
In death-like slumbers, 'till the rising morn,
Then sorrowing, to the sea his course he bent
Full sad, but knew not for what cause he went,
'Till, sight distressing, from the lonely strand,
He saw dead COLMA wafting to the land.

Then in a stupid agony of pray'r,
He rent his mantle, and he tore his hair;
Sigh'd to the stars, and shook his honour'd head,
And only wish'd a place among the dead!
O had the winds been sensible of grief,
Or whisp'ring angels come to his relief;
Then had the rocks not echo'd to his pain,
Nor hollow mountains answer'd him again:
Then had the floods their peaceful courses kept,
Nor the sad pine in all it's murmurs wept;
Nor pensive deer stray'd through the lonely grove,
Nor sadly wept the sympathising dove.——
Thus far'd the sire through his long days of pain,
Or with his offspring rov'd the silent plain;
'Till years approaching, bow'd his sacred head
Deep in the dust, and sent him to the dead:
Where now perhaps in some strange fancy'd land,
He grasps the airy bow, and flies across the strand;
Or with his COLMA shares the fragrant grove,
It's vernal blessings, and the bliss of love.

FAREWELL lamented pair, and whate'er state
Now clasps you round, and sinks you deep in fate;
Whether the fiery kingdom of the sun,
Or the slow wave of silent Acheron,
Or Christian's heaven, or planetary sphere,
Or the third region of the cloudless air;
Or if return'd to dread nihility,
You'll still be happy, for you will not be.

Now fairest village of the fertile plain,
Made fertile by the labours of the swain;
Who first my drowsy spirit did inspire,
To sing of woods, and strike the rural lyre:
Who last shou'd see me wand'ring from thy cells,
And groves of oak where contemplation dwells,
Wou'd fate but raise me o'er the smaller cares,
Of Life unwelcome and distressful years,

Pedantic labours and a hateful ease,
Which scarce the hoary wrinkled sage cou'd please.
Hence springs each grief, each long reflective sigh,
And not one comfort left but poetry.
Long, long ago with her I could have stray'd,
To woods, to thickets or the mountain shade;
Unfit for cities and the noisy throng,
The drunken revel and the midnight song;
The gilded beau and scenes of empty joy,
Which please a moment and forever die.
Here then shall center ev'ry wish, and all
The tempting beauties of this spacious ball:
No thought ambitious, and no bold design,
But heaven born contemplation shall be mine.
In yonder village shall my fancy stray,
Nor rove beyond the confines of to-day;
The aged volumes of some plain divine,
In broken order round my hut shou'd shine;
Whose solemn lines should soften all my cares,
And sound devotion to th' eternal stars:
And if one sin my rigid breast did stain,
Thou poetry shou'dst be the darling sin;
Which heav'n without repentance might forgive,
And which an angel might commit and live:
And where yon' wave of silent water falls,
O'er the smooth rock or Adamantine walls:
The summer morns and vernal eves should see,
MILTON, immortal bard my company;
Or SHAKESPEARE, DRYDEN, each high sounding name,
The pride of BRITAIN, and one half her fame:
Or him who wak'd the fairy muse of old,
And pleasing tales of lands inchanted told.
Still in my hand, he his soft verse shou'd find
His verse, the picture of the poets mind:
Or heav'nly POPE, who now harmonious mourns,
"Like the rapt seraph that adores and burns."
Then in sharp satire, with a giant's might,
Forbids the blockhead and the fool to write:

And in the centre of the bards be shown
The deathless lines of godlike ADDISON;
Who, bard thrice glorious, all delightful flows,
And wrapt the soul of poetry in prose.
   Now cease, O muse, thy tender tale to chaunt,
The smiling village, or the rural haunt;
New scenes invite me, and no more I rove,
To tell of shepherds, or the vernal grove.

1772

THE DESERTED FARM-HOUSE.

THIS antique dome the insatiate tooth of time
   Now level with the dust has almost laid;—
Yet ere 'tis gone, I seize my humble theme
   From these low ruins, that his years have made.

Behold the unsocial hearth! where once the fires
   Blazed high, and soothed the storm-stay'd traveller's woes;
See! the weak roof, that abler props requires,
   Admits the winds, and swift descending snows.

Here, to forget the labours of the day,
   No more the swains at evening hours repair,
But wandering flocks assume the well known way
   To shun the rigours of the midnight air.

In yonder chamber, half to ruin gone,
   Once stood the ancient housewife's curtained bed—
Timely the prudent matron has withdrawn,
   And each domestic comfort with her fled.

The trees, the flowers that her own hands had reared,
   The plants, the vines, that were so verdant seen,—
The trees, the flowers, the vines have disappear'd,
   And every plant has vanish'd from the green.

So sits in tears on wide Campania's plain
   ROME, once the mistress of a world enslaved;

That triumph'd o'er the land, subdued the main,
   And Time himself, in her wild transports, braved.

So sits in tears on Palestina's shore
   The Hebrew town, of splendour once divine—
Her kings, her lords, her triumphs are no more;
   Slain are her priests, and ruin'd every shrine.

Once, in the bounds of this deserted room,
   Perhaps some swain nocturnal courtship made,
Perhaps some *Sherlock* mused amidst the gloom;
   Since Love and Death forever seek the shade.

Perhaps some miser, doom'd to discontent,
   Here counted o'er the heaps acquired with pain;
He to the dust—his gold, on traffick sent,
   Shall ne'er disgrace these mouldering walls again.

Nor shall the glow-worm fopling, sunshine bred,
   Seek, at the evening hour this wonted dome—
Time has reduced the fabrick to a shed,
   Scarce fit to be the wandering beggar's home.

And none but I its dismal case lament—
   None, none but I o'er its cold relics mourn,
Sent by the muse—(the time perhaps misspent)—
   To write dull stanzas on this dome forlorn.

                                        1775

THE CITIZEN'S RESOLVE.

"Far be the dull and heavy day
"And toil, and restless care, from me—
"Sorrow attends on loads of gold,
"And kings are wretched, I am told.
"Soon from the noisy town removed
"To such wild scenes as Plato* lov'd,

* In place of "Plato" Freneau wrote "Shenstone" in the 1786
edition. This edition also bears the note, "Written 1770." [Ed.]

"Where, placed the leafless oaks between,
"Less haughty grows the winter green,
"There, Night, will I (lock'd in thy arms,
"Sweet goddess of the sable charms)
"Enjoy the dear, delightful dreams
"That fancy prompts by shallow streams,
"Where wood nymphs walk their evening round,
"And fairies haunt the moonlight ground.
　　"Beneath some mountain's towering height
"In cottage low I hail the night,
"Where jovial swains with heart sincere
"Welcome the new returning year;—
"Each tells a tale or chaunts a song
"Of her, for whom he sigh'd so long,
"Of Cynthia fair, or Delia coy,
"Neglecting still her love-sick boy—
"While, near, the hoary headed sage
"Recalls the feats of youth's gay age,
"All that in past time e'er was seen,
"And many a frolic on the green,
"How champion he with champions met,
"And fiercely they did combat it—
"Or how, full oft, with horn and hound
"They chaced the deer the forest round—
"The panting deer as swiftly flies,
"Yet by the well-aimed musquet dies!
　　"Thus pass the evening hours away,
"Unnoticed dies the parting day;
"Unmeasured flows that happy juice,
"Which mild October did produce,
"No surly sage, too frugal found,
"No niggard housewife deals it round:
"And deep they quaff the inspiring bowl
"That kindles gladness in the soul.—
　　"But now the moon, exalted high,
"Adds lustre to the earth and sky,
"And in the mighty ocean's glass
"Admires the beauties of her face—

"About her orb you may behold
"The circling stars that freeze with cold—
"But they in brighter seasons please,
"Winter can find no charms in these,
"While less ambitious, we admire,
"And more esteem domestic fire.

 "O could I there a mansion find
"Suited exactly to my mind
"Near that industrious, heavenly train
"Of rustics honest, neat, and plain;
"The days, the weeks, the years to pass
"With some good-natured, longing lass,
"With her the cooling spring to sip,
"And seize, at will, her damask lip;
"The groves, the springs, the shades divine,
"And all Arcadia should be mine!

 "Steep me, steep me, some poppies deep
"In beechen bowl, to bring on sleep;
"Love hath my soul in fetters bound,
"Through the dull night no sleep I found;—
"O gentle sleep! bestow thy dreams
"Of fields, and woods, and murmuring streams,
"Dark, tufted groves, and grottoes rare,
"And Flora, charming Flora, there.

 "Dull Commerce, hence, with all thy train
"Of debts, and dues, and loss, and gain;
"To hills, and groves, and purling streams,
"To nights of ease, and heaven-born dreams,
"While wiser Damon hastes away,
"Should I in this dull city stay,
"Condemn'd to death by slow decays
"And care that clouds my brightest days?

 "No—by *Silenus'* self I swear,
In "rustic shades I'll kill that care."

 So spoke *Lysander*, and in haste
His clerks discharg'd, his goods re-cased,
And to the western forests flew
With fifty airy schemes in view;

His ships were set to public sale—
But what did all that change avail?—
In three short months, sick of the *heavenly train*,
In three short months—he moved to town again.

1786

THE DYING ELM.

SWEET, lovely Elm, who here dost grow
Companion of unsocial care,
Lo! thy dejected branches die:
Amidst this torrid air—
Smit by the sun or blasting moon,
Like fainting *flowers*, their verdure gone.

Thy withering leaves, that drooping hang,
Presage thine end approaching nigh;
And lo! thy amber tears distill,
Attended with that last departing sigh—
O charming tree! no more decline,
But be thy shades and love-sick whispers mine.

Forbear to die—this weeping eve
Shall shed her little drops on you,
Shall o'er thy sad disaster grieve,
And wash your wounds with pearly dew,
Shall pity you, and pity me,
And heal the langour of my tree!

Short is thy life, if thou so soon must fade,
Like angry Jonah's gourd at Nineveh,
That, in a night, its bloomy branches spread,
And perished with the day.—
    Come, then, revive, sweet lovely Elm, lest I,
Thro' vehemence of heat, like Jonah, wish to die.

1779

ON RETIREMENT:

A HERMIT's house beside a stream
With forests planted round,
Whatever it to you may seem
More real happiness I deem
Than if I were a monarch crown'd.

A cottage I could call my own
Remote from domes of care;
A little garden, wall'd with stone,
The wall with ivy overgrown,
A limpid fountain near,

Would more substantial joys afford,
More real bliss impart
Than all the wealth that misers hoard,
Than vanquished worlds, or worlds restored—
Mere cankers of the heart!

Vain foolish man! how vast thy pride,
How little can thy wants supply!—
'Tis surely wrong to grasp so wide—
We act as if we only had
To triumph—not to die!

1786

The
PICTURES OF COLUMBUS,
The Genoese *

Picture I.

Columbus *making* Maps.†

AS o'er his charts Columbus ran,
Such disproportion he survey'd,

---

* Text from the edition of 1788. [Ed.]
† History informs us this was his original profession: and from the
disproportionate vacancy observable in the drafts of that time be-

He thought he saw in art's mean plan
   Blunders that Nature never made;
The *land* in one poor corner placed,
And all beside, a swelling waste!—
"It can't be so," Columbus said;

"This world on paper idly drawn,
"O'er one small tract so often gone
"The pencil tires; in this void space
"Allow'd to find no resting place.

"But copying Nature's bold design,
"If true to her, no fault is mine:
"Perhaps in these moist regions dwell
"Forms wrought like man, and lov'd as well.

"Yet to the west what lengthen'd seas!
"Are no gay islands found in these,
"No sylvan worlds that Nature meant
"To balance Asia's vast extent?

"As late a mimic globe I made
"(Imploring Fancy to my aid)
"O'er these wild seas a shade I threw,
"And a new world my pencil drew.

"But westward plac'd, and far away
"In the deep seas this country lay
"Beyond all climes already known,
"In Neptune's bosom plac'd alone.

"Who knows but he that hung this ball
"In the clear void, and governs all,
"On those dread scenes, remote from view,
"Has trac'd his great idea too.

tween Europe and Asia to the west, it is most probable he first took
the idea of another continent, lying in a parallel direction to, and
existing between both.

"What can these idle charts avail—
"O'er real seas I mean to sail;
"If fortune aids the grand design,
"Worlds yet unthought of shall be mine.

"But how shall I this country find!
"Gay, painted picture of the mind!
"Religion * holds my project vain,
"And owns no worlds beyond the main.

"'Midst yonder hills long time has stay'd
"In sylvan cells a wondrous maid,
"Who things to come can truly tell,
"Dread mistress of the magic spell.

"Whate'er the depths of time can shew
"All pass before her in review,
"And all events her eyes survey,
"'Till time and nature both decay.

"I'll to her cave, enquiring there
"What mighty things the fates prepare;
"Whether my hopes and plans are vain,
"Or I must give new worlds to Spain."

Picture II.

The Cell of an Inchantress.

Inchantress.

Who dares attempt this gloomy grove
Where never shepherd dream'd of love,
And birds of night are only found,
And poisonous weeds bestrew the ground:
Hence, stranger, take some other road,
Nor dare prophane my dark abode;
The winds are high, the moon is low—
Would you enter?—no, no, no:—

* The Inquisition made it criminal to assert the existence of the Antipodes.

Columbus.

Sorceress of mighty power! *
Hither at the midnight hour
Over hill and dale I've come,
Leaving ease and sleep at home:
With daring aims my bosom glows;
Long a stranger to repose,
I have come to learn from you
Whether phantoms I pursue,
Or if, as reason would persuade,
New worlds are on the ocean laid—
Tell me, wonder-working maid,
Tell me, dire inchantress, tell,
Mistress of the magic spell!

Inchantress.

The staring owl her note has sung;
With gaping snakes my cave is hung;
Of maiden hair my bed is made,
Two winding sheets above it laid;
With bones of men my shelves are pil'd,
And toads are for my supper boil'd;
Three ghosts attend to fill my cup,
And four to serve my pottage up;
The crow is waiting to say grace:—
Wouldst thou in such a dismal place
The secrets of thy fortune trace?

Columbus.

Though death and all his dreary crew
Were to be open'd on my view,
I would not from this threshold fly
'Till you had made a full reply.

* The fifteenth century was, like many of the preceding, an age of
superstition, cruelty, and ignorance. When this circumstance therefore is brought into view, the mixture of truth and fiction will not
appear altogether absurd or unnatural. At any rate, it has ever been
tolerated in this species of poetry.

Open wide this iron gate,
I must read the book of fate:
Tell me, if beyond the main
Islands are reserv'd for Spain;
Tell me, if beyond the sea
Worlds are to be found by me:
Bid your spirits disappear,
Phantoms of delusive fear,
These are visions I despise,
Shadows and uncertainties.

Inchantress.

Must I, then, yield to your request!
Columbus, why disturb my rest!—
For this the ungrateful shall combine,
And hard misfortune shall be thine;—
For this the base reward remains
Of cold neglect and galling chains! *
In a poor solitude forgot,
Reproach and want shall be the lot
Of him that gives new worlds to Spain,
And westward spreads her golden reign.

Before you came to vex my bower
I slept away the evening hour,
Or watch'd the rising of the moon,
With hissing vipers keeping tune,
Or galloping along the glade
Took pleasure in the lunar shade,
And gather'd herbs, or made a prize
Of horses tails and adders eyes:
Now open flies the iron gate,
Advance, and read the book of fate!
On thy design what woes attend!

* In 1498 he was superseded in his command at Hispaniola, and sent home in irons. Soon after finishing his fourth voyage, finding himself neglected by the Court of Spain after all his services, he retired to Valladolid, in Old Castile, where he died on the 20th of May, A.D. 1506.

The nations at the ocean's end,
No longer destin'd to be free,
Shall owe distress and death to thee!
The seats of innocence and love
Shall soon the scenes of horror prove;
But why disturb these Indian climes,
The pictures of more happy times!
Has avarice, with unfeeling breast,
Has cruelty thy soul possess'd?
May ruin on thy boldness wait!—
Advance, and read the book of fate.

WHEN vulture, fed but once a week,
And ravens three together shriek,
And skeleton for vengeance cries,
Then shall the fatal curtain rise!
Two lamps in yonder vaulted room,
Suspended o'er a brazen tomb,
Shall lend their glimmerings, as you pass,
To find your fortune in that glass
Whose wondrous virtue is, to show
Whate'er the inquirer wants to know.

Picture III.

The Mirror.

Columbus.

Strange things I see, bright mirror, in thy breast:—
There *Perseverance* stands, and nobly scorns
The gabbling tongue of busy *calumny:*
Proud *Erudition* in a scholar's garb
Derides my plans and grins a jeering smile.
Hypocrisy, clad in a doctor's gown,
A western continent deems heresy:
The princes, kings, and nobles of the land
Smile at my projects, and report me mad:
One royal woman only stands my friend,
Bright *Isabell*, the lady of our hearts,
Whom avarice prompts to aid my purposes,

And love of toys—weak female vanity!—
She gains her point!—three slender barques I see
(Or else the witch's glass deceives mine eye)
Rigg'd trim, and furnish'd out with stores and men,
Fitted for tedious journeys o'er the main:
Columbus—ha!—their motions he directs;
Their captains come, and ask advice from him,
Holding him for the soul of resolution.
Now, now we launch from *Palos!* prosperous gales
Impel the canvas: now the far fam'd streight
Is pass'd, the pillars of the son of Jove,
Long held the limits of the paths of men:
Ah! what a waste of ocean here begins,
And lonely waves, so black and comfortless!
Light flies each bounding galley o'er the main;
Now *Lancerota* gathers on our view,
And Teneriffe her clouded summit rears:
Awhile we linger at these islands fair
That seem the utmost boundaries of the world,
Then westward aiming on the unfathom'd deep
Sorrowing, with heavy hearts we urge our way.
Now all is discontent—such oceans pass'd,
No land appearing yet, dejects the most;
Yet, fertile in expedients, I alone
The mask of mild content am forc'd to wear:
A thousand signs I see, or feign to see,
Of shores at hand, and bottoms underneath,
And not a bird that wanders o'er the main,
And not a cloud that traverses the sky
But brings me something to support their hopes:
All fails at last!—so frequently deceiv'd
They growl with anger—mad to look at death
They gnash their teeth, and will be led no more;
On me their vengeance turns: they look at me
As their conductor to the realms of ruin:
Plot after plot discover'd, not reveng'd,
They join against their chief in mutiny:
They urge to plunge him in the boiling deep

As one, the only one that would pursue
Imaginary worlds through boundless seas:—
The scene is chang'd—Fine islands greet mine eye,
Cover'd with trees, and beasts, and yellow men;
Eternal summer through the vallies smiles
And fragrant gales o'er golden meadows play!—
Inchantress, 'tis enough!—now veil your glass—
The curtain falls—and I must homeward pass.

Picture IV.

Columbus *addresses King* Ferdinand.

Prince and pride of Spain! while meaner crowns,
Pleas'd with the shadow of monarchial sway,
Exact obedience from some paltry tract
Scarce worth the pain and toil of governing,
Be thine the generous care to send thy fame
Beyond the knowledge, or the guess of man.
    This gulphy deep (that bounds our western reign
So long by civil feuds and wars disgrac'd)
Must be the passage to some other shore
Where nations dwell, children of early time,
Basking in the warm sunshine of the south,
Who some false deity, no doubt, adore,
Owning no virtue in the potent cross:
What honour, sire, to plant your standards there,*
And souls recover to our holy faith
That now in paths of dark perdition stray
Warp'd to his worship by the evil one!
    THINK not that Europe and the Asian waste,
Or Africa, where barren sands abound,
Are the sole gems in Neptune's bosom laid:
Think not the world a vast extended plain:
See yond' bright orbs, that through the ether move,
All globular; this earth a globe like them
Walks her own rounds, attended by the moon,

---

* It is allowed by most historians, that Ferdinand was an implicit
believer and one of the most superstitious bigots of his age.

Bright comrade, but with a borrowed lustre bright.
If all the surface of this mighty round
Be one wide ocean of unfathom'd depth
Bounding the little space already known,
Nature must have forgot her wonted wit
And made a monstrous havock of proportion.
If her proud depths were not restrain'd by lands,
And broke by continents of vast extent
Existing somewhere under western skies,
Far other waves would roll before the storms
Than ever yet have burst on Europe's shores,
Driving before them deluge and confusion.
    But Nature will preserve what she has plann'd:
And the whole suffrage of antiquity,
Platonic dreams, and reason's plainer page
All point at something that we ought to see
Buried behind the waters of the west,
Clouded with the shadows of uncertainty.
The time is come for some sublime event
Of mighty fame:—mankind are children yet,
And hardly dream what treasures they possess
In the dark bosom of the fertile main,
Unfathom'd, unattempted, unexplor'd.
These, mighty prince, I offer to reveal,
And by the magnet's aid, if you supply
Ships and some gallant hearts, will hope to bring
From distant climes, news worthy of a king.

Picture V.

Ferdinand *and his* First Minister.

Ferdinand.

What would this madman have, this odd projector!
A wild address I have to-day attended,
Mingling its folly with our great affairs,
Dreaming of islands and new hemispheres
Plac'd on the ocean's verge, we know not where—
What shall I do with this petitioner?

Minister.

Even send him, sire, to perish in his search:
He has so pester'd me these many years
With idle projects of discovery—
His name—I almost dread to hear it mention'd:
He is a Genoese of vulgar birth
And has been round all Europe with his plans
Presenting them to every potentate;
He lives, 'tis said, by vending maps and charts,
And being us'd to sketch imagin'd islands
On that blank space that represents the seas,
His head at last grows giddy with this folly,
And fancied isles are turned to real lands
With which he puzzles me perpetually:
What pains me too, is, that our royal lady
Lends him her ear, and reads his mad addresses,
Oppos'd to reason and philosophy.

Ferdinand.

He acts the devil's part in Eden's garden;
Knowing the man was proof to his temptations
He whisper'd something in the ear of Eve,
And promis'd much, but meant not to perform.

Minister.

I've treated all his schemes with such contempt
That any but a rank, mad-brain'd enthusiast,
Pushing his purpose to extremities,
Would have forsook your empire, royal sir,
Discourag'd, and forgotten long ago.

Ferdinand.

Has he so long been busy at his projects?—
I scarcely heard of him till yesterday:
A plan pursued with so much obstinacy
Looks not like madness:—wretches of that stamp
Survey a thousand objects in an hour,

In love with each, and yet attach'd to none
Beyond the moment that it meets the eye—
But him I honour, tho' in beggar's garbs,
Who has a soul of so much constancy
As to bear up against the hard rebuffs,
Sneers of great men, and insolence of power,
And through the opposition of them all
Pursues his object:—Minister, this man
Must have our notice:—Let him be commissioned
Viceroy of all the lands he shall discover,
Admiral and general in the fleets of Spain;
Let three stout ships be instantly selected,
The best and strongest ribb'd of all we own,
With men to mann them, patient of fatigue:
But stay, attend! how stands our treasury?—

Minister.

Empty—even to the bottom, royal sir!
We have not coin for bare necessities,
Much less, so pardon me, to spend on madmen.

Picture VI.

Columbus *addresses Queen* Isabella.

While Turkish queens, dejected, pine,
Compell'd sweet freedom to resign;
And taught one virtue, *to obey,*
Lament some eastern tyrant's sway,

Queen of our hearts, bright Isabel!
A happier lot to you has fell,
Who makes a nation's bliss your own,
And share the rich Castilian throne.

Exalted thus, beyond all fame,
Assist, fair lady, that proud aim
Which would your native reign extend
To the wide world's remotest end.

From science, fed by busy thought,
New wonders to my view are brought:
The vast abyss beyond our shore
I deem impassable no more.

Let those that love to dream or sleep
Pretend no limits to the deep:
I see beyond the rolling main
Abounding wealth reserv'd for Spain.

From Nature's earliest days conceal'd,
Men of their own these climates yield,
And scepter'd dames, no doubt, are there,
Queens like yourself, but not so fair.

But what should most provoke desire
Are the fine pearls that they admire,
And diamonds bright and coral green
More fit to grace a Spanish queen.

Their yellow shells, and virgin gold,
And silver, for our trinkets sold,
Shall well reward this toil and pain,
And bid our commerce shine again.

As men were forc'd from Eden's shade
By errors that a woman made,
Permit me at a woman's cost
To find the climates that we lost.

He that with you partakes command,
The nation's hope, great Ferdinand,
Attends, indeed, to my request,
But wants no empires in the west.

Then, queen, supply the swelling sail,
For eastward breathes the steady gale
That shall the meanest barque convey
To regions richer than Cathay.*

* The ancient name for China.

Arriv'd upon that flowery coast
Whole towns of golden temples boast,
While these bright objects strike our view
Their wealth shall be reserv'd for you.

Each swarthy king shall yield his crown,
And smiling lay their sceptres down,
When they, not tam'd by force of arms,
Shall hear the story of your charms.

Did I an empty dream pursue
Great honour still must wait on you,
Who sent the lads of Spain to keep
Such vigils on the untravell'd deep,

Who fix'd the bounds of land and sea,
Trac'd Nature's works through each degree,
Imagin'd some unheard of shore
But prov'd that there was nothing more.

YET happier prospects, I maintain,
Shall open on your female reign,
While ages hence with rapture tell
How much they owe to Isabell!

Picture VII.

Queen Isabella's *Page of Honour writing a reply to* Columbus.

Your yellow shells, and coral green,
And gold, and silver—not yet seen,
Have made such mischief in a woman's mind
The queen could almost pillage from the crown,
And add some costly jewels of her own,
Thus sending you that charming coast to find
Where all these heavenly things abound,
Queens in the west, and chiefs renown'd.
But then no great men take you by the hand,
Nor are the nobles busied in your aid;

The clergy have no relish for your scheme,
And deem it madness—one archbishop said
You were bewilder'd in a paltry dream
That led directly to undoubted ruin,
Your own and other men's undoing:—
And our confessor says it is not true,
And calls it heresy in you
Thus to assert the world is round,
And that Antipodes are found
Held to the earth, we can't tell how.—
    But you shall sail; I heard the queen declare
That mere geography is not her care;—
And thus she bids me say,
"Columbus, haste away,
"Hasten to Palos, and if you can find
"Three barques, of structure suited to your mind,
"Strait make a purchase in the royal name;
"Equip them for the seas without delay,
"Since long the journey is (we heard you say)
"To that rich country which we wish to claim.—
"Let them be small!—for know the crown is poor
"Though basking in the sunshine of renown.
"Long wars have wasted us: the pride of Spain
"Was ne'er before so high, nor purse so mean;
"Giving us ten years' war, the humbled *Moor*
"Has left us little else but victory:
"Time must restore past splendor to our reign."

Picture VIII.

Columbus *at the Harbour* of Palos, *in Andalusia.*

Columbus.

    In three small barques to cross so vast a sea,
Held to be boundless, even in learning's eye,
And trusting only to a magic glass,
Which may have represented things untrue,
Shadows and visions for realities!—
It is a bold attempt!—Yet I must go,

Travelling the surge to its great boundary;
Far, far away beyond the reach of men,
Where never galley spread her milk-white sail
Or weary pilgrim bore the Christian name!
   But though I were confirm'd in my design
And saw the whole event with certainty,
How shall I so exert my eloquence,
And hold such arguments with vulgar minds
As to convince them I am not an idiot
Chasing the visions of a shatter'd brain,
Ending in their perdition and my own?
The world, and all its wisdom is against me;
The dreams of priests; philosophy in chains;
False learning swoln with self-sufficiency;
Men seated at the helm of royalty
Reasoning like school-boys;—what discouragements!
Experience holds herself mine enemy,
And one weak woman only hears my story!—
I'll make a speech—"Here jovial sailors, here!
"Ye that would rise beyond the rags of fortune,
"Struggling too long with hopeless poverty,
"Coasting your native shores on shallow seas,
"Vex'd by the gallies of the Ottoman;
"Now meditate with me a bolder plan,
"Catching at fortune in her plentitude!
"He that shall undertake this voyage with me
"Shall be no longer held a vulgar man:
"Princes shall wish they had been our companions,
"And Science blush she did not go along
"To learn a lesson that might humble pride
"Now grinning idly from a pedant's cap,
"Lurking behind the veil of cowardice.

   "FAR in the west a golden region lies
"Unknown, unvisited for many an age,
"Teeming with treasures to enrich the brave.
"Embark, embark—Columbus leads the way—
"Why, friends, existence is alike to me

"Dear and desireable with other men;
"What good could I devise in seeking ruin?
"Embark, I say; and he that sails with me
"Shall reap a harvest of immortal honour:
"Wealthier he shall return than they that now
"Lounge in the lap of principalities,
"Hoarding the gorgeous treasures of the east."—
　Alas, alas! they turn their backs upon me,
And rather choose to wallow in the mire
Of want, and torpid inactivity,
Than by one bold and masterly exertion
Themselves ennoble, and enrich their country!

Picture IX.

A Sailor's Hut, *near the Shore*

Thomas *and* Susan

Thomas.

I wish I was over the water again!
　'Tis a pity we cannot agree;
When I try to be merry 'tis labour in vain,
　You always are scolding at me;
Then what shall I do
With this termagant Sue;
　Tho' I hug her and squeeze her
　I never can please her—
Was there ever a devil like you!

Susan.

If I was a maid as I now am a wife
　With a sot and a brat to maintain,
I think it should be the first care of my life,
　To shun such a drunkard again:
Not one of the crew
Is so hated by Sue;
　Though they always are bawling,
　And pulling and hauling—
Not one is a puppy like you.

Thomas.

Dear Susan, I'm sorry that you should complain:
There is nothing indeed to be done;
If a war should break out, not a sailor in Spain
Would sooner be found at his gun:
Arriving from sea
I would kneel on one knee,
And the plunder presenting
To Susan relenting—
Who then would be honour'd like me!

Susan.

To-day as I came by the sign of the *ship*,
A mighty fine captain was there,
He was asking for sailors to take a small trip,
But I cannot remember well where:
He was hearty and free,
And if you can agree
To leave me, dear honey,
To bring me some money!—
How happy—indeed—I shall be!

Thomas.

The man that you saw not a sailor can get,
'Tis a captain Columbus, they say;
To fit out a ship he is running in debt,
And our wages he never will pay:
Yes, yes, it is he,
And, Sue, do ye see,
On a wild undertaking
His heart he is breaking—
The devil may take him for me!

Picture X.

Bernardo, *a Spanish Friar, in his canonicals.*

Did not our holy book most clearly say
This earth is built upon a pillar'd base;

And did not REASON add convincing proofs
That this huge world is one continued plain
Extending onward to immensity,
Bounding with oceans these abodes of men,
I should suppose this dreamer had some hopes,
Some prospects built on probability.
What says our lord the pope—he cannot err—
He says, *our world is not orbicular,*
And has rewarded some with chains and death
Who dar'd defend such wicked heresies.
But we are turning heretics indeed!—
A foreigner, an idiot, an impostor,
An infidel (since he dares contradict
What our most holy order holds for truth)
Is pouring poison in the royal ear;
Telling him tales of islands in the moon,
Leading the nations into dangerous errors,
Slighting instruction from our brotherhood!—
O Jesu! Jesu! what an age is this!

Picture XI.

Orosio, *a Mathematician, with his scales and compasses.*

   This persevering man succeeds at last!
The last gazette has publish'd to the world
That *Ferdinand* and *Isabella* grant
Three well-rigg'd ships to *Christopher Columbus;*
And have bestow'd the noble titles too
Of *Admiral* and *Vice-Roy*—great indeed!—
Who will not now project, and scrawl on paper—
Pretenders now shall be advanc'd to honour;
And every pedant that can frame a problem,
And every lad that can draw parallels
Or measure the subtension of an angle,
Shall now have ships to make discoveries.
   THIS simple man would sail he knows not where;
Building on fables, schemes of certainty;—

Visions of *Plato*, mix'd with idle tales
Of later date, intoxicate his brain:
Let him advance beyond a certain point
In his fantastic voyage, and I foretell
He never can return: ay, let him go!—
There is a line towards the setting sun
Drawn on an ocean of tremendous depth,
(Where nature plac'd the limits of the day)
Haunted by dragons, fond of solitude,
Red serpents, fiery forms, and yelling hags,
Fit company for mad adventurers.—
There, when the sun descends, 'tis horror all;
His angry globe through vast abysses gliding
Burns in the briny bosom of the deep
Making a havoc so detestable,
And causing such a wasteful ebullition
That never island green, or continent
Could find foundation, there to grow upon.

Picture XII.

Columbus *and a* Pilot.

Columbus.

To take on board the sweepings of a jail
Is inexpedient in a voyage like mine,
That will require most patient fortitude,
Strict vigilance and staid sobriety,
Contempt of death on cool reflection founded,
A sense of honour, motives of ambition,
And every sentiment that sways the brave,—
Princes should join me now!—not those I mean
Who lurk in courts, or revel in the shade
Of painted ceilings:—those I mean, more worthy,
Whose daring aims and persevering souls,
Soaring beyond the sordid views of fortune,
Bespeak the lineage of true royalty.

Pilot.

A fleet arrived last month at Carthagene
From Smyrna, Cyprus, and the neighboring isles:
Their crews, releas'd from long fatigues at sea,
Have spent their earnings in festivity,
And hunger tells them they must out again.
Yet nothing instantly presents itself
Except your new and noble expedition:
The fleet must undergo immense repairs,
And numbers will be unemploy'd a while:
I'll take them in the hour of dissipation
(Before reflection has made cowards of them,
Suggesting questions of impertinence)
When desperate plans are most acceptable,
Impossibilities are possible,
And all the spring and vigour of the mind
Is strain'd to madness and audacity:
If you approve my scheme, our ninety men
(The number you pronounce to be sufficient)
Shall all be enter'd in a week, at most.

Columbus.

Go, pilot, go—and every motive urge
That may put life into this expedition.
Early in August we must weigh our anchors.
Time wears apace—bring none but willing men,
So shall our orders be the better borne,
The people less inclin'd to mutiny.

Picture XIII.

Discontents *at Sea.*

Antonio.

DREADFUL is death in his most gentle forms!—
More horrid still on this mad element,
So far remote from land—from friends remote!
So many thousand leagues already sail'd

In quest of visions!—what remains to us
But perishing in these moist solitudes;
Where many a day our corpses on the sea
Shall float unwept, unpitied, unentomb'd!
O fate most terrible!—undone Antonio!
Why didst thou listen to a madman's dreams,
Pregnant with mischief—why not, comrades, rise!—
See, Nature's self prepares to leave us here;
The needle, once so faithful to the pole,
Now quits his object and bewilders us;
Steering at random, just as chance directs—
O fate most terrible! undone Antonio!—

Hernando.

Borne to creation's utmost verge, I saw
New stars ascending, never view'd before!
Low sinks the bear!—O land, my native land,
Clear springs and shady groves! why did I change
Your aspect fair for these infernal wastes,
Peopled by monsters of another kind;
Ah me! design'd not for the view of man!

Columbus.

Cease, dastards, cease; and be inform'd that man
Is nature's lord, and wields her to his will;
If her most noble works obey our aims,
How much more so ought worthless scum, like you,
Whose whole existence is a morning dream,
Whose life is sunshine on a wintry day,
Who shake at shadows, struck with palsied fear:
Measuring the limit of your lives by distance.

Antonio.

Columbus, hear! when with the land we parted
You *thirty days* agreed to plough the main,
Directing westward.—Thirty have elaps'd,
And thirty more have now begun their round,
No land appearing yet, nor trace of land,

But distant fogs that mimic lofty isles,
Painting gay landscapes on the vapourish air,
Inhabited by fiends that mean our ruin—
You persevere, and have no mercy on us—
Then perish by yourself—we must return—
And know, our firm resolve is fix'd for Spain;
In this resolve we are unanimous.

Juan de Villa-Real *to* Columbus.

(*A Billet.*)

"I heard them over night a plot contriving
"Of fatal purpose—have a care Columbus!—
"They have resolv'd, as on the deck you stand,
"Aiding the vigils of the midnight hour,
"To plunge you headlong in the roaring deep,
"And slaughter such as favour your design
"Still to pursue this western continent."

Columbus, solus.

Why, nature, hast thou treated those so ill,
Whose souls, capacious of immense designs,
Leave ease and quiet for a nation's glory,
Thus to subject them to these little things,
Insects, by heaven's decree in shapes of men!
But so it is, and so we must submit,
Bending to thee, the heaven's great chancellor!
But must I fail!—and by timidity!
Must thou to thy green waves receive me, Neptune,
Or must I basely with my ships return,
Nothing accomplish'd!—not one pearl discover'd,
One bit of gold to make our queen a bracelet,
One diamond for the crown of Ferdinand!
How will their triumph be confirm'd, who said
That I was mad!—Must I then change my course,
And quit the country that would strait appear,
If one week longer we pursued the sun!—
The witch's glass was not delusion, sure!—
All this, and more, she told me to expect!—

(To the crew)

"Assemble, friends; attend to what I say:
"Signs unequivocal, at length, declare
"That some great continent approaches us:
"The sea no longer glooms unmeasur'd depths,
"The setting sun discovers clouds that owe
"Their origin to fens and woodland wastes,
"Not such as breed on ocean's salt domain:—
"Vast flocks of birds attend us on our way,
"These all have haunts amidst the watry void,
"Sweet scenes of ease, and sylvan solitude,
"And springs, and streams that we shall share with them.
"Now, hear my most importunate request:
"I call you all my friends; you are my equals,
"Men of true worth and native dignity,
"Whose spirits are too mighty to return
"Most meanly home, when nothing is accomplish'd—
"Consent to sail our wonted course with me
"But one week longer, and if that be spent,
"And nought appear to recompence our toil,
"Then change our course and homeward haste away—
"Nay, homeward not!—for that would be too base—
"But to some negro coast, where we may hide,
"And never think of Ferdinand again."

Hernando.

One week!—too much—it shall not be, **Columbus!**
Already are we on the verge of ruin,
Warm'd by the sunshine of another sphere,
Fann'd by the breezes of the burning zone,
Launch'd out upon the world's extremities!—
Who knows where one week more may carry us?

Antonio.

Nay, talk not to the traitor!—base Columbus,
To thee our ruin and our deaths we owe!
Away, away!—friends!—men at liberty,
Now free to act as best befits our case,

Appoint another pilot to the helm,
And *Andalusia* be our port again!

Columbus.

Friends, is it thus you treat your admiral,
Who bears the honours of great Ferdinand,
The royal standard, and the arms of Spain!
Three days allow me—and I'll show new worlds.

Hernando.

Three days!—one day will pass too tediously—
But in the name of all our crew, Columbus,
Whose speaker and controuler I am own'd;
Since thou indeed art a most gallant man,
Three days we grant—but ask us not again!

Picture XIV.

Columbus *at* Cat Island.

Columbus, solus.

Hail, beauteous land! the first that greets mine eye
Since, bold, we left the cloud capp'd *Teneriffe*,
The world's last limit long suppos'd by men,—
Tir'd with dull prospects of the watry waste
And midnight dangers that around us grew,
Faint hearts and feeble hands and traitors vile,
Thee, *Holy Saviour*, on this foreign land
We still adore, and name this coast from thee! *
In these green groves who would not wish to stay
Where guardian nature holds her quiet reign,
Where beardless men speak other languages,
Unknown to us, ourselves unknown to them.

———

Antonio.

In tracing o'er the isle no gold I find—
Nought else but barren trees and craggy rocks

* He called the island San Salvador (Holy Savior).   It lies about
90 miles S. E. from Providence.

Where screaming sea-fowl mix their odious loves,
And fields of burning marle, where devils play
And men with copper skins talk barbarously;—
What merit has our chief in sailing hither,
Discovering countries of no real worth!
Spain has enough of barren sands, no doubt,
And savages in crowds are found at home;—
Why then surmount the world's circumference
Merely to stock us with this Indian breed?

Hernando.

Soft!—or Columbus will detect your murmuring—
This new found isle has re-instated him
In all our favours—see you yonder sands?—
Why, if you see them, swear that they are gold,
And gold like this shall be our homeward freight,
Gladding the heart of Ferdinand the great,
Who, when he sees it, shall say smilingly,
"Well done, advent'rous fellows, you have brought
"The treasure we expected and deserv'd!"—
Hold!—I am wrong—there goes a savage man
With gold suspended from his ragged ears:
I'll brain the monster for the sake of gold;
There, savage, try the power of Spanish steel—
'Tis of *Toledo* *—true and trusty stuff!
He falls! he falls! the gold, the gold is mine!
First acquisition in this golden isle!—

Columbus, solus.

Sweet sylvan scenes of innocence and ease,
How calm and joyous pass the seasons here!
No splendid towns or spiry turrets rise,
No lordly palaces—no tyrant kings
Enact hard laws to crush fair freedom here;
No gloomy jails to shut up wretched men;
All, all are free!—here God and nature reign;

* The best steel-blades in Spain are manufactured at *Toledo* and *Bilboa.*

Their works unsullied by the hands of men.—
Ha! what is this—a murder'd wretch I see,
His blood yet warm—O hapless islander,
Who could have thus so basely mangled *thee*,
Who never offer'd insult to our shore—
Was it for those poor trinkets in your ears
Which by the custom of your tribe you wore,—
Now seiz'd away—and which would not have weigh'd
One poor piastre!
Is this the fruit of my discovery!
If the first scene is murder, what shall follow
But havock, slaughter, chains and devastation
In every dress and form of cruelty!
O injur'd Nature, whelm me in the deep,
And let not Europe hope for my return,
Or guess at worlds upon whose threshold now
So black a deed has just been perpetrated!—
We must away—enjoy your woods in peace,
Poor, wretched, injur'd, harmless islanders;—
On *Hayti's* * isle you say vast stores are found
Of this destructive gold—which without murder
Perhaps, we may possess!—away, away!
And southward, pilots, seek another isle,
Fertile they say, and of immense extent:
There we may fortune find without a crime.

Picture XV.

Columbus *in a Tempest, on his return to Spain.*

The storm hangs low; the angry lightning glares
And menaces destruction to our masts;
The *Corposant* † is busy on the decks,
The soul, perhaps, of some lost admiral

* This island is now called Hispaniola.

† A vapour common at sea in bad weather, something larger and
rather paler than the light of a candle; which, seeming to rise out of
the sea, first moves about the decks, and then ascends or descends the
rigging in proportion to the increase or decrease of the storm. Superstition formerly imagined them to be the souls of drowned men.

Taking his walks about most leisurely,
Foreboding we shall be with him to-night:
See, now he mounts the shrouds—as he ascends
The gale grows bolder!—all is violence!
Seas, mounting from the bottom of their depths,
Hang o'er our heads with all their horrid curls
Threatening perdition to our feeble barques,
Which three hours longer cannot bear their fury,
Such heavy strokes already shatter them;
Who can endure such dreadful company!—
Then, must we die with our discovery!
Must all my labours, all my pains, be lost,
And my new world in old oblivion sleep?—
My name forgot, or if it be remember'd,
Only to have it said, "He was a madman
"Who perish'd as he ought—deservedly——
"In seeking what was never to be found!"—
Let's obviate what we can this horrid sentence,
And, lost ourselves, perhaps, preserve our name.
'Tis easy to contrive this painted casket,
(Caulk'd, pitch'd, secur'd with canvas round and round)
That it may float for months upon the main,
Bearing the freight within secure and dry:
In this will I an abstract of our voyage,
And islands found, in little space enclose:
The western winds in time may bear it home
To Europe's coasts: or some wide wandering ship
By accident may meet it toss'd about,
Charg'd with the story of another world.

Picture XVI.

Columbus *visits the* Court *at Barcelona.*

Ferdinand.

Let him be honour'd like a God, who brings
Tidings of islands at the ocean's end!
In royal robes let him be straight attir'd,
And seated next ourselves, the noblest peer.

Isabella.

The merit of this gallant deed is mine:
Had not my jewels furnish'd out the fleet
Still had this world been latent in the main—
Since on this project every man look'd cold,
A woman, as his patroness, shall shine;
And through the world the story shall be told,
A woman gave new continents to Spain.

Columbus.

A world, great prince, bright queen and royal lady,
Discover'd now, has well repaid our toils;
We to your bounty owe all that we are;
Men of renown and to be fam'd in story.
Islands of vast extent we have discover'd
With gold abounding: see a sample here
Of those most precious metals we admire;
And *Indian* men, natives of other climes,
Whom we have brought to do you princely homage,
Owning they hold their diadems from you.

Ferdinand.

To fifteen sail your charge shall be augmented:
Hasten to *Palos*, and prepare again
To sail in quest of this fine golden country,
The *Ophir*, never known to Solomon;
Which shall be held the brightest gem we have,
The richest diamond in the crown of Spain.

Picture XVII.

Columbus *in* Chains.

Are these the honours they reserve for me,
Chains for the man that gave new worlds to Spain!
Rest here, my swelling heart!—O kings, O queens,
Patrons of monsters,* and their progeny,

* During his third voyage, while in San Domingo, such unjust representations were made of his conduct to the Court of Spain, that a

Authors of wrong, and slaves to fortune merely!
Why was I seated by my prince's side,
Honour'd, caress'd like some first peer of Spain?
Was it that I might fall most suddenly
From honour's summit to the sink of scandal!
'Tis done, 'tis done!—what madness is ambition!
What is there in that little breath of men,
Which they call *Fame*, that should induce the brave
To forfeit ease and that domestic bliss
Which is the lot of happy ignorance,
Less glorious aims, and dull humility.—
Whoe'er thou art that shalt aspire to honour,
And on the strength and vigour of the mind
Vainly depending, court a monarch's favour,
Pointing the way to vast extended empire;
First count your pay to be ingratitude,
Then chains and prisons, and disgrace like mine!
Each wretched pilot now shall spread his sails,
And treading in my footsteps, hail new worlds,
Which, but for me, had still been empty visions.

Picture XVIII.

Columbus at Valladolid. *

I

How sweet is sleep, when gain'd by length of toil!
No dreams disturb the slumbers of the dead—
To snatch existence from this scanty soil,
Were these the hopes deceitful fancy bred;
And were her painted pageants nothing more
Than this life's phantoms by delusion led?

new admiral, Bovadilla, was appointed to supersede him, who sent
Columbus home in irons.
   * After he found himself in disgrace with the Court of Spain, he
retired to Vallodolid, a town of Old Castile, where he died, it is said,
more of a broken heart than any other disease, on the 20th of May,
1506.

2

The winds blow high: one other world remains;
Once more without a guide I find the way;
In the dark tomb to slumber with my chains—
Prais'd by no poet on my funeral day,
Nor even allow'd one dearly purchas'd claim—
My new found world not honour'd with my name.

3

Yet, in this joyless gloom while I repose,
Some comfort will attend my pensive shade,
When memory paints, and golden fancy shows
My toils rewarded, and my woes repaid;
When empires rise where lonely forests grew,
Where Freedom shall her generous plans pursue.

4

To shadowy forms, and ghosts and sleepy things,
Columbus, now with dauntless heart repair;
You liv'd to find new worlds for thankless kings,
Write this upon my tomb—yes—tell it there—
Tell of those chains that sullied all my glory—
Not mine, but their's—ah, tell the shameful story.

[W. 1774]   1778

THE SILENT ACADEMY.

SUBJECTED to despotic sway,
Compelled all mandates to obey,
Once in this dome I humbly bowed,
A member of the murmuring crowd,
Where *Pedro Blanco* held his reign,
The tyrant of a small domain.
  By him a numerous herd controuled,
The smart, the stupid, and the bold,
Essayed some little share to gain
Of the vast treasures of his brain—

Some learned the Latin, some the Greek,
And some in flowery style to speak—
Some writ their themes, while others read,
And some with Euclid stuffed the head—
Some toiled in verse, and some in prose,
And some in logick sought repose—
Some learned to cypher, some to *draw*,
And some began to study LAW.

But all is ruined, all is done,
The tutor to the shades is gone,
And all his pupils, led astray,
Have each found out a different way.

Some are in chains of wedlock bound,
And some are hanged and some are drowned;
Some are advanced to posts and places,
And some in pulpits screw their faces;
Some at the bar a living gain,
Perplexing what they should explain;
To soldiers turned, a bolder band
Repel the invaders of the land;
Some to the arts of physic bred,
Despatch their patients to the dead;—
Some plough the land, and some the sea,
And some are slaves, and some are free;
Some court the great, and some the muse,
And some subsist by mending shoes——
While others—but so vast the throng,
The Cobblers shall conclude my song.

1786

THE VERNAL AGUE.

WHERE the pheasant roosts at night,
Lonely, drowsy, out of sight,
Where the evening breezes sigh
Solitary, there stray I.

Close along a shaded stream,
Source of many a youthful dream,

Where branchy cedars dim the day
There I muse, and there I stray.

Yet, what can please amid this bower,
That charmed the eye for many an hour!
The budding leaf is lost to me,
And dead the bloom on every tree.

The winding stream, that glides along,
The lark, that tunes her early song,
The mountain's brow, the sloping vale,
The murmuring of the western gale,

Have lost their charms!—the blooms are gone!
Trees put a darker aspect on,
The stream disgusts that wanders by,
And every zephyr brings a sigh.

Great guardian of our feeble kind!—
Restoring Nature, lend thine aid!
And o'er the features of the mind
Renew those colours, that must fade,
  When vernal suns forbear to roll,
  And endless winter chills the soul.

1786

A SATIRE

In Answer to a Hostile Attack.*

(First written and published 1775.)

LONG have I sat on this disastrous shore,
And, sighing, sought to gain a passage o'er
To Europe's towns, where, as our travellers say,
Poets may flourish, or, perhaps they may;
But such abuse has from your coarse pen fell
I think I may defer my voyage as well;

* Entitled *MacSwiggen* in the edition of 1786.   [Ed.]

Why should I far in search of honour roam,
And dunces leave to triumph here at home?
  Great Jove in wrath a spark of genius gave,
And bade me drink the mad Pierian wave,
Hence came these rhimes, with truth ascrib'd to me,
That swell thy little soul to cruelty:
If thus, tormented at these slightly lays,
You strive to blast what ne'er was meant for praise,
How will you bear the more exalted rhyme,
By labour polished, and matured by time?
  Devoted madman! what inspired thy rage,
Who bade thy foolish muse with me engage?
Against a wind-mill would you try thy might,
Against a castle would a pigmy fight?
What could thy slanderous pen with malice arm
To injure him, who never did you harm?
Have we from you been urgent to attain
The mean ideas of your barren brain?
Have I been seen in borrowed clothes to shine,
And, when detected, *swear by Jove they are mine?*
O miscreant, hostile to thine own repose,
From thy own malice thy destruction flows!
  Blessed be our western world—its scenes conspire
To raise a poet's fancy and his fire,
Lo, blue-topt mountains to the skies ascend!
Lo, shady forests to the breezes bend!
See mighty streams meandering to the main!
See lambs and lambkins sport on every plain!
The spotted herds in flowery meadows see!
But what, ungenerous wretch, are these to thee?—
You find no charms in all that nature yields,
Then leave me to my grottoes and the fields:
I interfere not with your vast design—
Pursue your studies, and I'll follow mine,
Pursue, well pleas'd, your theologic schemes,
Attend professors, and correct your themes,
Still some dull nonsense, low-bred wit invent,
Or prove from scripture what it never meant,

Or far through law, that land of scoundrels, stray,
And truth disguise through all your mazy way;
Wealth you may gain, your clients you may squeeze,
And by long cheating, learn to live at ease;
If but in *Wood* or *Littleton* well read,
The devil shall help you to your daily bread.

O waft me far, ye muses of the west—
Give me your green bowers and soft seats of rest—
Thrice happy in those dear retreats to find
A safe retirement from all human kind—
Though dire misfortunes every step attend,
The muse, still social, still remains a friend—
In solitude her converse gives delight,
With gay poetic dreams she cheers the night,
She aids me, shields me, bears me on her wings,
In spite of growling whelps, to high, exalted things,
Beyond the miscreants that my peace molest,
Miscreants, with dullness and with rage opprest.

Hail, great BRIGHT GENIUS, foe to honest fame,
Patron of dunces, and thyself the same,
You dream of conquest—tell me, how, or whence?
Act like a man and combat me with sense—
This evil have I known, and known but once,
Thus to be galled and slandered by a dunce,
Saw rage and weakness join their dastard plan
To crush the shadow, not attack the man.

What swarms of vermin from the sultry south
Like frogs surround thy pestilential mouth—
Clad in the gard of *sacred sanctity*,
What madness prompts thee to invent a lie?
Thou base defender of a wretched crew,
Thy tongue let loose on those you never knew,
The human spirit with the brutal joined,
The imps of *Orcus* in thy breast combined,
The genius barren, and the wicked heart,
Prepared to take each trifling miscreant's part,
The turn'd up nose, the monkey's foolish face,
The scorn of reason, and *your sire's disgrace*—

Assist me, gods, to drive this dog of rhyme
Back to the torments of his native clime,
Where dullness mingles with her native earth,
And rhymes, not worth the pang that gave them birth!
Where did he learn to write or talk with men—
A senseless blockhead, with a scribbling pen—
In vile acrostics thou may'st please the fair,
Not less than with thy looks and powdered hair,
But strive no more with rhyme to daunt your foes,
Or, by the flame that in my bosom glows,
The muse on you shall her worst fury spend,
And *hemp*, or *water*, thy vile being end.

Aspers'd like me, who would not grieve and rage!
Who would not burn, GIANT, to engage?
Him and his friends, a mean, designing race,
I, singly I, must combat face to face—
Alone I stand to meet the foul-mouth'd train,
Assisted by no poets of the plain,
Whose timerous Muses cannot swell their theme
Beyond a meadow or a purling stream—
Were not my breast impervious to despair,
And did not *Clio* reign unrivalled there,
I must expire beneath the ungenerous host,
And dullness triumph o'er a poet lost.

Rage gives me wings, and fearless prompts me on
To conquer brutes the world should blush to own;
No peace, no quarter to such imps I lend,
Death and perdition on each line I send;
Bring all the wittlings that your host supplies,
A cloud of nonsense and a storm of lies—
Your kitchen wit—SANGRADO's loud applause
That wretched rhymer with his lanthorn jaws—
His deep-set eyes forever on the wink,
His soul extracted from the public sink—
All such as he, to my confusion call—
And though ten myriads—I despise them all.

Come on *dear satyrist*, come—your muse is willing,
Your prose is merry, but your verse is killing—

Come on, attack me with that whining prose,
Your beard is red, and swine-like is your nose,
Like burning brush your bristly head of hair,
The ugliest image of a Greenland bear—
Come on—attack us with your choicest rhimes,
Sound void of sense betrays the unmeaning chimes—
Come, league your forces; all your wit combine,
Your wit not equal to the bold design—
The heaviest arms the muse can give, I wield,
To stretch a green goose floundering on the field,
'Swiggen, who, aided by some spurious muse,
But bellows nonsense, and but writes abuse,
Insect! immortal and unfading grown,
But by no deeds or merits of *its* own—
So, when some hateful monster sees the day,
In spirits we preserve it from decay,
But for what end, it is not hard to guess—
Not for its value, but its *ugliness*.

  Now, by the winds which shake thy rubric mop,
(That nest of witches, or that barber's shop)
Great Satirist hear—Be wise in times to come,
A dunce by nature, bid thy muse be dumb,
Lest you, devoted to the infernal skies,
Descend, like Lucifer, no more to rise—
Sick of all feuds, to reason I appeal
From wars of *paper*, and from wars of *steel*,
Let others *here* their hopes and wishes end,
I to the sea with weary steps descend,
Quit the mean conquest that such swine might yield,
And leave *one poet* to enjoy the field.
In distant isles some happier scene we choose,
And court in softer shades the unwilling muse,
Thrice happy there, through peaceful plains to rove,
Or the cool verdure of the Orange grove,
Safe from the miscreants that my peace molest,
Miscreants, with dullness and with rage opprest.

[w. 1775]   1786

The
HOUSE of NIGHT
A Vision*

Advertisement——This Poem is founded upon the authority of Scripture, inasmuch as these sacred books assert, that *the last enemy that shall be conquered is Death.* For the purposes of poetry he is here personified, and represented as on his dying bed. The scene is laid at a solitary palace, (the time midnight) which, tho' before beautiful and joyous, is now become sad and gloomy, as being the abode and receptacle of Death. Its owner, an amiable, majestic youth, who had lately lost a beloved consort, nevertheless with a noble philosophical fortitude and humanity, entertains him in a friendly manner, and by employing Physicians, endeavours to restore him to health, altho' an enemy; convinced of the excellence and propriety of that divine precept, *If thine enemy hunger, feed him; if he thirst, give him drink.* He nevertheless, as if by a spirit of prophecy, informs this (fictitiously) wicked being of the certainty of his doom, and represents to him in a pathetic manner the vanity of his expectations, either of a reception into the abodes of the just, or continuing longer to make havock of mankind upon earth. The patient finding his end approaching, composes his epitaph, and orders it to be engraved on his tombstone, hinting to us thereby, that even Death and Distress have vanity; and would be remembered with honour after he is no more, altho' his whole life has been spent in deeds of devastation and murder. He dies at last in the utmost agonies of despair, after agreeing with the avaricious Undertaker to intomb his bones. This reflects upon the inhumanity of those men, who, not to mention an enemy, would scarcely cover a departed friend with a little dust, without the certainty of a reward for so doing. The circumstances of his funeral are then recited, and the visionary and fabulous part of the poem disappears. It concludes with a few reflexions on the impropriety of a too great attachment to the present life, and incentives to such moral virtue as may assist in conducting us to a better.

————

I.

TREMBLING I write my dream, and recollect
A fearful vision at the midnight hour;

* Text from the edition of 1786. [Ed.]

So late, Death o'er me spread his sable wings,
Painted with fancies of malignant power!

2.

Such was the dream the sage Chaldean saw
Disclos'd to him that felt heav'n's vengeful rod,
Such was the ghost, who through deep silence cry'd,
Shall mortal man—be juster than his God.

3.

Let others draw from smiling skies their theme,
And tell of climes that boast unfading light,
I draw a darker scene, replete with gloom,
I sing the horrors of the *House of Night.*

4.

Stranger, believe the truth experience tells,
Poetic dreams are of a finer cast
Than those which o'er the sober brain diffus'd,
Are but a repetition of some action past.

5.

Fancy, I own thy power—when sunk in sleep
Thou play'st thy wild delusive part so well
You lift me into immortality,
Depict new heavens, or draw scenes of hell.

6.

By some sad means, when Reason holds no sway,
Lonely I rov'd at midnight o'er a plain
Where murmuring streams and mingling rivers flow,
Far to their springs, or seek the sea again.

7.

Sweet vernal May! tho' then thy woods in bloom
Flourish'd, yet nought of this could Fancy see,
No wild pinks bless'd the meads, no green the fields,
And naked seem'd, to stand each lifeless tree:

8.

Dark was the sky, and not one friendly star
Shone from the zenith or horizon, clear,
Mist sate upon the woods, and darkness rode
In her black chariot, with a wild career.

9.

And from the woods the late resounding note
Issued of the loquacious *Whip-poor-will*,*
Hoarse, howling dogs, and nightly roving wolves
Clamour'd from far off clifts invisible.

10.

Rude, from the wide extended *Chesapeke*
I heard the winds the dashing waves assail,
And saw from far, by pictures fancy form'd,
The black ship travelling through the noisy gale.

11.

At last, by chance and guardian fancy led,
I reach'd a noble dome, rais'd fair and high,
And saw the light from upper windows flame,
Presage of mirth and hospitality.

12.

And by that light around the dome appear'd
A mournful garden of autumnal hue,
Its lately pleasing flowers all drooping stood
Amidst high weeds that in rank plenty grew.

13.

The Primrose there, the violet darkly blue,
Daisies and fair Narcissus ceas'd to rise,

---

* A Bird peculiar to America, of a solitary nature, who never sings but in the night. Her note resembles the name given to her by the country people.

Gay spotted pinks their charming bloom withdrew,
And Polyanthus quench'd its thousand dyes.

14.

No pleasant fruit or blossom gaily smil'd.
Nought but unhappy plants and trees were seen,
The yew, the myrtle, and the church-yard elm,
The cypress, with its melancholy green.

15.

There cedars dark, the osier, and the pine,
Shorn tamarisks, and weeping willows grew,
The poplar tall, the lotos, and the lime,
And pyracantha did her leaves renew.

16.

The poppy there, companion to repose,
Display'd her blossoms that began to fall,
And here the purple amaranthus rose
With mint strong-scented, for the funeral.

17.

And here and there with laurel shrubs between
A tombstone lay, inscrib'd with strains of woe,
And stanzas sad, throughout the dismal green,
Lamented for the dead that slept below.

18.

Peace to this awful dome!—when strait I heard
The voice of men in a secluded room,
Much did they talk of death, and much of life,
Of coffins, shrouds, and horrors of a tomb.

19.

Pathetic were their words, and well they aim'd
To explain the mystic paths of providence,
Learn'd were they all, but there remain'd not I
To hear the upshot of their conference.

20.

Meantime from an adjoining chamber came
Confused murmurings, half distinguish'd sounds,
And as I nearer drew, disputes arose
Of surgery, and remedies for wounds.

21.

Dull were their feuds, for they went on to talk
Of *Anchylosis*,* and the shoulder blade,
Os Femoris, * *Trochanters* *—and whate'er
Has been discuss'd by Cheselden or Meade:

22.

And often each, to prove his notion true
Brought proofs from Galen or Hippocrates—
But fancy led me hence—and left them so,
Firm at their points of hardy No and Yes.

23.

Then up three winding stairs my feet were brought
To a high chamber, hung with mourning sad,
The unsnuff'd candles glar'd with visage dim,
'Midst grief, in ecstacy of woe run mad.

24.

A wide leaf'd table stood on either side,
Well fraught with phials, half their liquids spent,
And from a couch, behind the curtain's veil,
I heard a hollow voice of loud lament.

25.

Turning to view the object whence it came,
My frighted eyes a horrid form survey'd;

* *Anchylosis*—a morbid contraction of the joints. *Os Femoris*—
the thigh bone. *Trochanters*—two processes in the upper part of
the thigh bone, otherwise called *rotator major et minor*, in which the
tendons of many muscles terminate.

Fancy, I own thy power—Death on the couch,
With fleshless limbs, at rueful length, was laid.

26.

And o'er his head flew jealousies and cares,
Ghosts, imps, and half the black Tartarian crew,
Arch-angels damn'd, nor was their Prince remote,
Borne on the vaporous wings of Stygian dew.

27.

Around his bed, by the dull flambeaux' glare,
I saw pale phantoms—Rage to madness vext,
Wan, wasting grief, and ever musing care,
Distressful pain, and poverty perplext.

28.

Sad was his countenance, if we can call
That *countenance*, where only bones were seen
And eyes sunk in their sockets, dark and low,
And teeth, that only show'd themselves to grin.

29.

Reft was his scull of hair, and no fresh bloom
Of cheerful mirth sate on his visage hoar:
Sometimes he rais'd his head, while deep-drawn groans
Were mixt with words that did his fate deplore.

30.

Oft did he wish to see the daylight spring,
And often toward the window lean'd to hear,
Fore-runner of the scarlet-mantled morn,
The early note of wakeful *Chanticleer*.

31.

Thus he—But at my hand a portly youth
Of comely countenance, began to tell,

"That this was Death upon his dying bed,
"Sullen, morose, and peevish to be well;

32.

"Fix't is his doom—the miscreant reigns no more
"The tyrant of the dying or the dead;
"This night concludes his all-consuming reign,
"Pour out, ye heav'ns, your vengeance on his head.

33.

"But since, my friend, (said he), chance leads you here,
"With me this night upon the sick attend,
"You on this bed of death must watch, and I
"Will not be distant from the fretful fiend.

34.

"Before he made this lofty pile his home,
"In undisturb'd repose I sweetly slept,
"But when he came to this sequester'd dome
"'Twas then my troubles came, and then I wept:

35.

"Twice three long nights, in this sad chamber, I,
"As though a brother languish'd in despair,
"Have 'tended faithful round his gloomy bed,
"Have been content to breathe this loathsome air.

36.

"A while relieve the languors that I feel,
"Sleep's magic forces close my weary eyes;
"Soft o'er my soul unwonted slumbers steal,
"Aid the weak patient till you see me rise.

37.

"But let no slumbers on your eye-lids fall,
"That if he ask for powder or for pill

"You may be ready at the word to start,
"And still seem anxious to perform his will.

38.

"The bleeding Saviour of a world undone
"Bade thy compassion rise toward thy foe;
"Then, stranger, for the sake of Mary's son,
"Thy tears of pity on this wretch bestow.

39.

"'Twas he that stole from my adoring arms
"*Aspasia*, she the loveliest of her kind,
"Lucretia's virtue, with a Helen's charms,
"Charms of the face, and beauties of the mind.

40.

"The blushy cheek, the lively, beaming eye,
"The ruby lip, the flowing jetty hair,
"The stature tall, the aspect so divine,
"All beauty, you would think, had center'd there.

41.

"Each future age her virtues shall extol,
"Nor the just tribute to her worth refuse;
"Fam'd, to the stars URANIA bids her rise,
"Theme of the moral, and the tragic Muse.

42.

"Sweet as the fragrance of the vernal morn,
"Nipt in its bloom this faded flower I see;
"The inspiring angel from that breast is gone,
"And life's warm tide forever chill'd in thee!

43.

"Such charms shall greet my longing soul no more,
"Her lively eyes are clos'd in endless shade,
"Torpid, she rests on yonder marble floor;
"Approach, and see what havock DEATH has made.

44.

"Yet, stranger, hold—her charms are so divine,
"Such tints of life still on her visage glow,
"That even in death this slumbering bride of mine
"May seize thy heart, and make thee wretched too.

45.

"O shun the sight—forbid thy trembling hand
"From her pale face to raise the enshrouding lawn,—
"Death claims thy care, obey his stern command,
"Trim the dull tapers, for I see no dawn!"

46.

So said, at Death's left side I sate me down,
The mourning youth toward his right reclin'd;
Death in the middle lay, with all his groans,
And much he toss'd and tumbled, sigh'd and pin'd.

47.

But now this man of hell toward me turn'd.
And strait, in hideous tone, began to speak,
Long held he sage discourse, but I forebore
To answer him, much less his news to seek.

48.

He talk'd of tomb-stones and of monuments,
Of Equinoxial climes and India shores,
He talk'd of stars that shed their influence,
Fevers and plagues, and all their noxious stores.

49.

He mention'd, too, the guileful *calenture,**
Tempting the sailor on the deep sea main,

* *Calenture*—an inflammatory fever, attended with a delirium, common in long voyages at sea, in which the diseased persons fancy the sea to be green fields and meadows, and, if they are not hindered, will leap overboard.

That paints gay groves upon the ocean floor,
Beckoning her victim to the faithless scene.

50.

Much spoke he of the myrtle and the yew,
Of ghosts that nightly walk the church-yard o'er,
Of storms that through the wint'ry ocean blow
And dash the well-mann'd galley on the shore,

51.

Of broad-mouth'd cannons, and the thunderbolt,
Of sieges and convulsions, dearth and fire,
Of poisonous weeds—but seem'd to sneer at these
Who by the laurel o'er him did aspire.

52.

Then with a hollow voice thus went he on,
"Get up, and search, and bring, when found, to me,
"Some cordial, potion, or some pleasant draught,
"Sweet, slumb'rous poppy, or the mild Bohea.

53.

"But hark, my pitying friend!—and, if you can,
"Deceive the grim physician at the door—
"Bring half the mountain springs—ah! hither bring
"The cold rock water from the shady bower.

54.

"For till this night such thirst did ne'er invade,
"A thirst provok'd by heav'n's avenging hand;
"Hence bear me, friends, to quaff, and quaff again
"The cool wave bubbling from the yellow sand.

55.

"To these dark walls with stately step I came,
"Prepar'd your drugs and doses to defy;
"Smit with the love of never dying fame,
"I came, alas! to conquer—not to die!"

56.

Glad, from his side I sprang, and fetch'd the draught,
Which down his greedy throat he quickly swills,
Then on a second errand sent me strait,
To search in some dark corner for his pills.

57.

Quoth he, "These pills have long compounded been,
"Of dead men's bones and bitter roots, I trow;
"But that I may to wonted health return,
"Throughout my lank veins shall their substance go."

58.

So down they went—He rais'd his fainting head
And oft in feeble tone essay'd to talk;
Quoth he, "Since remedies have small avail,
"Assist unhappy Death once more to walk."

59.

Then slowly rising from his loathsome bed,
On wasted legs the meagre monster stood,
Gap'd wide, and foam'd, and hungry seem'd to ask,
Tho' sick, an endless quantity of food.

60.

Said he, "The sweet melodious flute prepare,
"The anthem, and the organ's solemn sound,
"Such as may strike my soul with ecstacy,
"Such as may from yon' lofty wall rebound.

61.

"Sweet music can the fiercest pains assuage,
"She bids the soul to heav'n's blest mansions rise,
"She calms despair, controuls infernal rage
"And deepest anguish, when it hears her, dies.

62.

"And see, the mizzling, misty midnight reigns,
"And no soft dews are on my eye-lids sent—!

"Here, stranger, lend thy hand; assist me, pray,
"To walk a circuit of no large extent."—

63.

On my prest shoulders leaning, round he went,
And could have made the boldest spectre flee,
I led him up stairs, and I led him down,
But not one moment's rest from pain got he.

64.

Then with his dart, its cusp unpointed now,
Thrice with main strength he smote the trembling floor;
The roof resounded to the fearful blow,
And *Cleon* started, doom'd to sleep no more.

65.

When thus spoke Death, impatient of controul,
"Quick, move, and bring from yonder black bureau
"The sacred book that may preserve my soul
"From long damnation, and eternal woe.

66.

"And with it bring—for you may find them there,
"The works of holy authors, dead and gone,
"The sacred *tome* of moving Drelincourt,
"Or what more solemn Sherlock mus'd upon:

67.

"And read, my Cleon, what these sages say,
"And what the sacred Penman hath declar'd,
"That when the wicked leaves his odious way,
"His sins shall vanish, and his soul be spar'd."

68.

But he, unmindful of the vain command,
Reason'd with Death, nor were his reasonings few:
Quoth he—"My Lord, what frenzy moves your brain,
"Pray, what, my Lord, can Sherlock be to you,

69.

"Or all the sage divines that ever wrote,
"Grave Drelincourt, or heaven's unerring page;
"These point their arrows at your hostile breast,
"And raise new pains that time must ne'er assuage.

70.

"And why should thus thy woe disturb my rest?
"Much of Theology I once did read,
"And there 'tis fixt, sure as my God is so,
"That Death shall perish, tho' a God should bleed.

71.

"The martyr, doom'd the pangs of fire to feel,
"Lives but a moment in the sultry blast;
"The victim groans, and dies beneath the steel,
"But thy severer pains shall always last.

72.

"O miscreant vile, thy age has made thee doat—
"If peace, if sacred peace were found for you,
"Hell would cry out, and all the damn'd arise
"And, more deserving, seek for pity too.

73.

"Seek not for Paradise—'tis not for thee,
"Where high in heaven its sweetest blossoms blow,
"Nor even where, gliding to the Persian main
"Thy waves, Euphrates, through the garden flow!

74.

"Bloody has been thy reign, O man of hell,
"Who sympathiz'd with no departing groan;
"Cruel wast thou, and hardly dost deserve
"To have *Hic Jacet* stampt upon thy stone.

75.

"He that could build his mansion o'er the tombs,
"Depending still on sickness and decay,

"May dwell unmov'd amidst these drowsier glooms,
"May laugh the dullest of these shades away.

76.

"Remember how with unrelenting ire
"You tore the infant from the unwilling breast—
"ASPASIA fell, and CLEON must expire,
"Doom'd by the impartial God to endless rest:

77.

"In vain with stars he deck'd yon' spangled skies,
"And bade the mind to heaven's bright regions soar,
"And brought so far to my admiring eyes
"A glimpse of glories that shall blaze no more!

78.

"Even now to glut thy devilish wrath, I see
"From eastern realms a wasteful army rise:
"Why else those lights that tremble in the north?
"Why else yon' comet blazing through the skies?

79.

"Rejoice, O fiend; Britannia's tyrant sends
"From German plains his myriads to our shore.
"The fierce Hibernian with the Briton join'd—
"Bring them, ye winds!—but waft them back no more.

80.

"To you, alas! the fates in wrath deny
"The comforts to *our* parting moments due,
"And leave you here to languish and to die,
"Your crimes too many, and your tears too few.

81.

"No cheering voice to thee shall cry, Repent!
"As once it echoed through the wilderness—
"No patron died for thee—damn'd, damn'd art thou
"Like all the devils, nor one jot the less.

82.

"A gloomy land, with sullen skies is thine,
"Where never rose or amaranthus grow,
"No daffodils, nor comely columbine,
"No hyacinths nor asphodels for you.

83.

"The barren trees that flourish on the shore
"With leaves or fruit were never seen to bend,
"O'er languid waves unblossom'd branches hang,
"And every branch sustains some vagrant fiend.

84.

"And now no more remains, but to prepare
"To take possession of thy punishment,
"That's thy inheritance, that thy domain,
"A land of bitter woe, and loud lament.

85.

"And oh that HE, who spread the universe,
"Would cast one pitying glance on thee below;
"Millions of years in torments thou might'st fry,
"But thy eternity!—who can conceive its woe!"

86.

He heard, and round with his black eye-balls gaz'd,
Full of despair, and curs'd, and rav'd, and swore:
"And since this is my doom," said he, "call up
"Your wood-mechanics to my chamber door:

87.

"Blame not on me the ravage to be made;
"Proclaim,—even Death abhors such woe to see
"I'll quit the world, while decently I can,
"And leave the work to George my deputy."

88.

Up rush'd a band, with compasses and scales
To measure his slim carcase, long and lean—

"Be sure," said he, "to frame my coffin strong,
"You, master workman, and your men, I mean:

89.

"For if the Devil, so late my trusty friend,
"Should get one hint where I am laid, from you,
"Not with my soul content, he'd seek to find
"That mouldering mass of bones, my body, too!

90.

"Of hardest ebon let the plank be found,
"With clamps and ponderous bars secur'd around,
"That if the box by Satan should be storm'd,
"It may be able for resistance found."

91.

"Yes," said the master workman, "noble Death,
"Your coffin shall be strong—that leave to me—
"But who shall these your funeral dues discharge?
"Nor friends nor pence you have, that I can see."

92.

To this said Death—"You might have ask'd me, too,
"Base caitiff, who are my executors,
"Where my estate, and who the men that shall
"Partake my substance, and be call'd my heirs.

93.

"Know, then, that hell is my inheritance,
"The devil himself my funeral dues must pay—
"Go—since you must be paid—go, ask of him,
"For he has gold, as fabling poets say."

94.

Strait they retir'd—when thus he gave me charge,
Pointing from the light window to the west,
"Go three miles o'er the plain, and you shall see
"A burying-yard of sinners dead, unblest.

95.

"Amid the graves a spiry building stands
"Whose solemn knell resounding through the gloom
"Shall call thee o'er the circumjacent lands
"To the dull mansion destin'd for my tomb.

96.

"There, since 'tis dark, I'll plant a glimmering light
"Just snatch'd from hell, by whose reflected beams
"Thou shalt behold a tomb-stone, full eight feet,
"Fast by a grave, replete with ghosts and dreams.

97.

"And on that stone engrave this epitaph,
"Since Death, it seems, must die like mortal men;
"Yes—on that stone engrave this epitaph,
"Though all hell's furies aim to snatch the pen.

98.

"Death in this tomb his weary bones hath laid,
"Sick of dominion o'er the human kind—
"Behold what devastations he hath made,
"Survey the millions by his arm confin'd.

99.

"Six thousand years has sovereign sway been mine,
"None, but myself, can real glory claim;
"Great Regent of the world I reign'd alone,
"And princes trembled when my mandate came.

100.

"Vast and unmatch'd throughout the world, my fame
"Takes place of gods, and asks no mortal date—
"No; by myself, and by the heavens, I swear,
"Not Alexander's name is half so great.

101.

"Nor swords nor darts my prowess could withstand,
"All quit their arms, and bow'd to my decree,

"*Even mighty* JULIUS *died beneath my hand,*
"*For slaves and Caesars were the same to me!*

102.

"*Traveller, wouldst thou his noblest trophies seek,*
"*Search in no narrow spot obscure for those;*
"*The sea profound, the surface of all land*
"*Is moulded with the myriads of his foes.*"

103.

Scarce had he spoke, when on the lofty dome
Rush'd from the clouds a hoarse resounding blast—
Round the four eaves so loud and sad it play'd
As though all musick were to breathe its last.

104.

Warm was the gale, and such as travellers say
Sport with the winds on Zaara's waste;
Black was the sky, a mourning carpet spread,
Its azure blotted, and its stars o'ercast!

105.

Lights in the air like burning stars were hurl'd,
Dogs howl'd, heaven mutter'd, and the tempest blew,
The red half-moon peeped from behind a cloud
As if in dread the amazing scene to view.

106.

The mournful trees that in the garden stood
Bent to the tempest as it rush'd along,
The elm, the myrtle, and the cypress sad
More melancholy tun'd its bellowing song.

107.

No more that elm its noble branches spread,
The yew, the cypress, or the myrtle tree,
Rent from the roots the tempest tore them down,
And all the grove in wild confusion lay.

108.

Yet, mindful of his dread command, I part
Glad from the magic dome—nor found relief;
Damps from the dead hung heavier round my heart,
While sad remembrance rous'd her stores of grief.

109.

O'er a dark field I held my dubious way
Where Jack-a-lanthorn walk'd his lonely round,
Beneath my feet substantial darkness lay,
And screams were heard from the distemper'd ground.

110.

Nor look'd I back, till to a far off wood
Trembling with fear, my weary feet had sped—
Dark was the night, but at the inchanted dome
I saw the infernal windows flaming red.

111.

And from within the howls of Death I heard,
Cursing the dismal night that gave him birth,
Damning his ancient sire, and mother sin,
Who at the gates of hell, accursed, brought him forth.

112.

(For fancy gave to my enraptur'd soul
An eagle's eye, with keenest glance to see,
And bade those distant sounds distinctly roll,
Which, waking, never had affected me.)

113.

Oft his pale breast with cruel hand he smote,
And tearing from his limbs a winding sheet,
Roar'd to the black skies, while the woods around,
As wicked as himself, his words repeat.

114.

Thrice tow'rd the skies his meagre arms he rear'd,
Invok'd all hell, and thunders on his head,

Bid light'nings fly, earth yawn, and tempests roar,
And the sea wrap him in its oozy bed.

115.

"My life for one cool draught!—O, fetch your springs,
"Can one unfeeling to my woes be found!
"No friendly visage comes to my relief,
"But ghosts impend, and spectres hover round.

116.

"Though humbled now, dishearten'd and distrest,
"Yet, when admitted to the peaceful ground,
"With heroes, kings, and conquerors I shall rest,
"Shall sleep as safely, and perhaps as sound."

117.

Dim burnt the lamp, and now the phantom Death
Gave his last groans in horror and despair—
"All hell demands me hence,"—he said, and threw
The red lamp hissing through the midnight air.

118.

Trembling, across the plain my course I held,
And found the grave-yard, loitering through the gloom.
And, in the midst, a hell-red, wandering light,
Walking in fiery circles round the tomb.

119.

Among the graves a spiry building stood,
Whose tolling bell, resounding through the wood,
Sung doleful ditties to the adjacent wood,
And many a dismal drowsy thing it said.

120.

This fabrick tall, with towers and chancels grac'd,
Was rais'd by sinners' hands, in ages fled;
The roof they painted, and the beams they brac'd,
And texts from scripture o'er the walls they spread:

121.

But wicked were their hearts, for they refus'd
To aid the helpless orphan, when distrest,
The shivering, naked stranger they mis-us'd,
And banish'd from their doors the starving guest.

122.

By laws protected, cruel and prophane,
The poor man's ox these monsters drove away;—
And left *Distress* to attend *her* infant train,
No friend to comfort, and no bread to stay.

123.

But heaven look'd on with keen, resentful eye,
And doom'd them to perdition and the grave,
That as they felt not for the wretch distrest,
So heaven no pity on their souls would have.

124.

In pride they rais'd this building tall and fair,
Their hearts were on perpetual mischief bent,
With pride they preach'd, and pride was in their prayer,
With pride they were deceiv'd, and so to hell they went.

125.

At distance far approaching to the tomb,
By lamps and lanthorns guided through the shade,
A coal-black chariot hurried through the gloom,
Spectres attending, in black weeds array'd

126.

Whose woeful forms yet chill my soul with dread,
Each wore a vest in Stygian chambers wove,
Death's kindred all—Death's horses they bestrode,
And gallop'd fiercely, as the chariot drove.

127.

Each horrid face a grizly mask conceal'd,
Their busy eyes shot terror to my soul

As now and then, by the pale lanthorn's glare,
I saw them for their parted friend condole.

128.

Before the hearse Death's chaplain seem'd to go,
Who strove to comfort, what he could, the dead;
Talk'd much of *Satan*, and the land of woe,
And many a chapter from the scriptures read.

129.

At last he rais'd the swelling anthem high,
In dismal numbers seem'd he to complain;
The captive tribes that by *Euphrates* wept,
Their song was jovial to his dreary strain.

130.

That done, they plac'd the carcase in the tomb,
To dust and dull oblivion now resign'd,
Then turn'd the chariot tow'rd the House of Night,
Which soon flew off, and left no trace behind.

131.

But as I stoop'd to write the appointed verse,
Swifter than thought the airy scene decay'd;
Blushing the morn arose, and from the east
With her gay streams of light dispell'd the shade.

132.

What is this *Death*, ye deep read sophists, say?—
Death is no more than one unceasing change;
New forms arise, while other forms decay,
Yet all is LIFE throughout creation's range.

133.

The towering *Alps*, the haughty *Appenine*,
The *Andes*, wrapt in everlasting snow,
The *Apalachian* and the *Ararat*
Sooner or later must to ruin go.

134.

Hills sink to plains, and man returns to dust,
That dust supports a reptile or a flower;
Each changeful atom by some other nurs'd
Takes some new form, to perish in an hour.

135.

Too nearly join'd to sickness, toils, and pains,
(Perhaps for former crimes imprison'd here)
True to itself the immortal soul remains,
And seeks new mansions in the starry sphere.

136.

When Nature bids thee from the world retire,
With joy thy lodging leave, a fated guest;
In Paradise, the land of thy desire,
Existing always, always to be blest.

1779

The
JAMAICA FUNERAL.*

1776

———

1

ALCANDER died—the rich, the great, the brave;
Even such must yield to heaven's severe decree,
Death, still at hand, conducts us to the grave,
And humbles monarchs as he humbled thee.

2

When, lingering, to his end Alcander drew,
Officious friends besieg'd his lofty door,
Impatient they the dying man to view
And touch that hand they soon must touch no more.

* Text from the edition of 1786. [Ed.]

3

"Alas, he's gone!" the sad attendants cry,
Fled is the breath that never shall return—
"Alas! he's gone!" his tearful friends reply,
"Spread the dark crape, and round his pale corpse mourn.

4

"Ye that attend the pompous funeral, due,
"In sable vestments let your limbs be clad,
"For vulgar deaths a common sorrow shew,
"But costly griefs are for the wealthy dead.

5

"Prepare the blessings of the generous vine,
"Let bulls and oxen groan beneath the steel,
"Throughout the board let choicest dainties shine,
"To every guest a generous portion deal."—

6

A mighty crowd approach'd the mourning dome,
Some came to hear the sermon and the prayer,
Some came to shun Xantippe's voice at home,
And some with Bacchus to relieve their care.

7

A *Levite* came, and sigh'd among the rest,
A rusty band and tatter'd gown he wore,
His leaves he tumbled, and the house he blest,
And conn'd his future sermon o'er and o'er.

8

And oft a glance he cast towards the wine
That briskly sparkled in the glassy vase,
And often drank, and often wish'd to dine,
And red as Phoebus glow'd his sultry face.

9

Much did he chatter, and on various themes,
He publish'd news that came from foreign climes,

He told his jests, and told his last year's dreams,
And quoted dull stuff from lord Wilmot's rhymes.

10

And dunn'd the mourners for his parish dues
With face of brass, and scrutinizing eye,
And threaten'd law-suits if they dar'd refuse
To pay his honest earnings punctually.

11

An honest sire, who came in luckless hour
To hear the sermon and to see the dead,
Presuming on this consecrated hour,
Ventur'd to check the parson on that head.

12

Quoth he, "My priest, such conduct is not fit,
"For other speech this solemn hour demands:
"What if your parish owes its annual debt,
"Your parish ready to discharge it stands."

13

No more he said—for charg'd with wounds and pain,
The parson's staff like Jove's own lightning flew,
Which cleft his jaw-bone and his cheek in twain,
And from their sockets half his grinders drew.

14

Nor less deceas'd some moments lay the sire
Than if from heav'n the forked lightnings thrown
Had pierc'd him with their instantaneous fire,
And sent him smoking to the world unknown.

15

At last he mov'd, and, weltering in his gore,
Thus did the rueful, wounded victim say,
"Convey me hence—so bloody and so sore
"I cannot wait to hear the parson pray;

16

"And if I did, what pleasure could be mine—
"Can he allure me to the world of bliss—
"Can he present me at the heavenly shrine
"Who breaks my bones, and knocks me down in this?

17

"The scripture says—the text I well recall—
"*A Priest or Bishop must no striker be,*
"Then how can such a wicked priest but fall,
"Who at a funeral thus has murdered me?"—

18

Thus he—But now the sumptuous dinner came,
The *Levite* boldly seiz'd the nobler place,
Beside him sate the woe-struck widow'd dame,
Who help'd him drain the brimful china vase.

19

Which now renew'd, he drank that ocean too,
Like Polypheme, the boon Ulysses gave;
Another came, nor did another do,
For still another did the monster crave

20

With far-fetch'd dainties he regal'd his maw,
And prais'd the various meats that crown'd the board:
On tender capons did the glutton gnaw,
And well his platter with profusion stor'd.

21

But spoke no words of grace—I mark'd him well,
I fix'd my eye upon his brazen brow—
He look'd like Satan aiming to rebel,
Such pride and madness were his inmates now.

2

But not contented with this hectoring priest,
Sick of his nonsense, softly I withdrew,

And at a calmer table shar'd the feast
To sorrow sacred, and to friendship due,

23

Which now atchiev'd, the tolling bell remote
Summon'd the living and the dead to come,
And through the dying sea-breeze swell'd the note,
Dull on the ear, and lengthening through the gloom

24

The Bier was brought, the costly coffin laid,
And prayers were mutter'd in a doleful tone,
While the sad pall, above the body spread,
From many a tender breast drew many a groan.

25

The *Levite*, too, some tears of Bacchus shed—
Reeling before the long procession, he
Strode like a general at his army's head,
His gown in tatters, and his wig—ah me!

26

The words of faith in both hands he bore,
Prayers, cut and dry, by ancient prelates made,
Who, bigots while they liv'd, could do no more
Than leave them still by bigots to be said.

27

But he admir'd them all!—he read with joy
St. Athanasius in his thundering creed,
And curs'd the men whom Satan did employ
To make king Charles, that heav'n-born martyr, bleed.

28

At last they reach'd the spiry building high,
And soon they enter'd at the eastern gate—
The parson said his prayers most learnedly,
And mutter'd more than memory can relate.

29

Then through the temple's lengthy aisles they went,
Approaching still the pulpit's painted door,
From whence on Sundays, many a vow was sent,
And sermons plunder'd from some prelate's store.

30

Here, as of right, the priest prepar'd to rise,
And leave the corpse and gaping crowd below,
Like sultry Phoebus glar'd his flaming eyes,
Less fierce the stars of Greenland evenings glow.

31

Up to the pulpit strode he with an air,
And from the *Preacher* thus his text he read,
"More I esteem, and better is by far
"A dog existing than a lion dead.

32

"Go, eat thy dainties with a joyful heart,
"And quaff thy wine with undissembled glee,
"For he who did these heavenly gifts impart
"Accepts thy prayers, thy gifts, thy vows, and thee."

The SERMON.

33

THESE trutns, my friends, congenial to my soul,
Demand a faithful and attentive ear—
No longer for your 'parted friend condole,
No longer shed the tributary tear.

34

Curs'd be the sobs, these useless floods of woe
That vainly flow for the departed dead—

If doom'd to wander on the coasts below,
What are to him these seas of grief you shed?

35

If heaven in pleasure doth his hours employ—
If sighs and sorrows reach a place like this,
They blast his glories, and they damp his joy,
They make him wretched in the midst of bliss.

36

And can you yet—and here he smote his breast—
And can you yet bemoan that torpid mass
Which now for death, and desolation drest,
Prepares the deep gulph of the grave to pass.

37

You fondly mourn—I mourn Alcander too,
Alcander late the living, not the dead;
His casks I broach'd, his liquors once I drew,
And freely there on choicest dainties fed.

38

But vanish'd are they now!—no more he calls,
No more invites me to his plenteous board;
No more I caper at his splendid balls,
Or drain his cellars, with profusion stor'd.

39

Then why, my friends, for yonder senseless clay,
That ne'er again befriends me, should I mourn?
Yon' simple slaves that through the cane-lands stray
Are more to me than monarchs in the urn.

40

The joys of wine, immortal as my theme,
To days of bliss the aspiring soul invite;
Life, void of this, a punishment I deem,
A Greenland winter, without heat or light.

41

Count all the trees that crown Jamaica's hills,
Count all the stars that through the heavens you see,
Count every drop that the wide ocean fills;
Then count the pleasures Bacchus yields to me.

42

The aids of wine for toiling man were meant;
I prize the smiling *Caribbëan* bowl—
Enjoy those gifts that bounteous nature lent,
Death to thy cares, refreshing to the soul.

43

Here fixt to-day in plenty's smiling vales,
Just as the month revolves we laugh or groan,
September comes, seas swell with horrid gales,
And old *Port Royal's* fate may be our own.

44

A few short years, at best, will bound our span,
Wretched and *few*, the Hebrew exile said;
Live while you may, be jovial while you can,
Death as a debt to nature must be paid.

45

When nature fails, the man exists no more,
And death is nothing but an empty name,
Spleen's genuine offspring at the midnight hour,
The coward's tyrant, and the bad man's dream.

46

You ask me where these mighty hosts have fled,
That once existed on this changeful ball?—
If aught remains, when mortal man is dead,
Where, ere their birth they were, they now are all.*

* *Quaeris, quo jaceas post obitum loco?—*
  Quo non nata jacent."—Senec. Troas.

47

Like insects busy, in a summer's day,
We toil and squabble, to increase our pain,
Night comes at last, and, weary of the fray,
To dust and darkness all return again.

48

Then envy not, ye sages too precise,
The drop from life's gay tree, that damps our woe,
Noah himself, the wary and the wise,
A vineyard planted, and the vines did grow:

49

Of social soul was he—the grape he press'd,
And drank the juice oblivious to his care;
Sorrow he banish'd from his place of rest,
And sighs and sobbing had no entrance there.

50

Such bliss be ours through every changing scene;
The glowing face bespeaks the glowing heart;
If heaven be joy, wine is to heaven a-kin,
Since wine, on earth, can heavenly joys impart.

51

Mere glow-worms are we all, a moment shine;
I, like the rest, in giddy circles run,
And Grief shall say, when I this life resign,
"His glass is empty, and his frolics done!"

52

He said, and ceas'd—the funeral anthem then
From the deep choir and hoarse-ton'd organ came;
Such are the honours paid to wealthy men,
But who for Irus would attempt the same?

53

Now from the church returning, as they went,
Again they reach'd Alcander's painted hall,

Their sighs concluded, and their sorrows spent,
They to oblivion gave the *Funeral*.

54

The holy man, by bishops holy made,
Tun'd up to harmony his trembling strings,
To various songs in various notes he play'd,
And, as he plays, as gallantly he sings,

55

The widow'd dame, less pensive than before,
To sprightly tunes as sprightly did advance,
Her lost Alcander scarce remember'd more;
And thus the funeral ended in a dance.

[w. 1776]   1786

The
BEAUTIES OF SANTA CRUZ *

1776

Sweet orange grove, the fairest of the isle,
  In thy soft shade luxuriously reclined,
Where, round my fragrant bed, the flowrets smile,
  In sweet delusions I deceive my mind.

But Melancholy's glooms assail my breast,
  For potent nature reigns despotic there;—
A nation ruined, and a world oppressed,
  Might rob the boldest Stoic of a tear.

SICK of thy northern glooms, come, shepherd, seek
More equal climes, and a serener sky:
Why shouldst thou toil amid thy frozen ground,
Where half years' snows, a barren prospect, lie,

* Or St. Croix, a Danish island (in the American Archipelago),
commonly, tho' erroneously, included in the cluster of the Virgin
Islands; belonging to the crown of Denmark.

When thou mayst go where never frost was seen,
Or north-west winds with cutting fury blow,
Where never ice congealed the limpid stream,
Where never mountain tipt its head with snow?

Twice ten days prosperous gales thy barque shall bear
To isles that flourish in perpetual green,
Where richest herbage glads each fertile vale,
And ever verdant plants on every hill are seen.

Nor dread the dangers of the billowy deep,
Autumnal winds shall safely waft thee o'er;
Put off the timid heart, or, man unblest,
Ne'er shalt thou reach this gay enchanting shore.

Thus *Judah's* tribes beheld the promised land,
While *Jordan's* angry waters swelled between;
Thus trembling on the brink I see them stand,
Heav'n's type in view, the Canaanitish green.

Thus, some mean souls, in spite of age and care,
Are held so firmly to this earth below,
They never wish to cross fate's dusky main,
That parting them and happiness, doth flow.

Though Reason's voice might whisper to the soul
That nobler climes for man the heavens design—
Come, shepherd, haste—the northern breezes blow,
No more the slumbering winds thy barque confine.

Sweet orange grove, the fairest of the isle,
In thy soft shade luxuriously reclined,
Where, round my fragrant bed, the flowrets smile,
In sweet delusions I deceive my mind.

But Melancholy's glooms assail my breast,
For potent nature reigns despotic there;—
A nation ruined, and a world oppressed,
Might rob the boldest Stoic of a tear.

From the vast caverns of old Ocean's bed,
Fair SANTA CRUZ arising, laves her waist,
The threatening waters roar on every side,
For every side by ocean is embraced.

Sharp, craggy rocks repel the surging brine,
Whose caverned sides by restless billows wore,
Resemblance claim to that remoter isle
Where once the winds' proud lord the sceptre bore.

Betwixt old Cancer and the mid-way line,
In happiest climate lies this envied isle:
Trees bloom throughout the year, soft breezes blow,
And fragrant Flora wears a lasting smile.

Cool, woodland streams from shaded clifts descend,
The dripping rock no want of moisture knows,
Supplyed by springs that on the skies depend,
That fountain feeding as the current flows.

Such were the isles which happy *Flaccus* sung,
Where one tree blossoms while another bears,
Where spring forever gay, and ever young,
Walks her gay round through her unceasing years.

Such were the climes which youthful Eden saw
Ere crossing fates destroyed her golden reign—
Reflect upon thy loss, unhappy man,
And seek the vales of *Paradise* again.

No lowering skies are here—the neighbouring sun
Clear and unveiled, his brilliant journey goes,
Each morn emerging from the ambient main,
And sinking there, each evening, to repose.

In June's fair month the spangled traveller gains
The utmost limits of his northern way,
And blesses with his beams cold lands remote,
Sad Greenland's coast, and Hudson's frozen bay.

The shivering swains of those unhappy climes
Behold the side-way monarch through the trees,
Here glows his fiercer heat, his vertic beams,
Tempered with cooling gales and trade-wind breeze.

The native here, in golden plenty blest,
Bids from the soil the verdant harvests spring;
Feasts in the abundant dome, the joyous guest;
Time short,—life easy,—pleasure on the wing.

Here, fixt today in plenty's smiling vales,
Just as the year revolves, they laugh or groan;
September comes, seas swell with horrid gales,
And old Port-Royal's fate is found their own!

And, though so near heaven's blazing lamp doth run,
They court the beam that sheds the golden day,
And hence are called the children of the sun,
Who, without fainting, bear his downward ray.

No threatening tides upon their island rise,
Gay Cynthia scarce disturbs the ocean here,
No waves approach her orb, and she, as kind,
Attracts no ocean to her silver sphere.

The happy waters boast, of various kinds,
Unnumbered myriads of the scaly race,
Sportive they glide above the deluged sand,
Gay as their clime, in ocean's ample vase.

Some streaked with burnished gold, resplendent glare,
Some cleave the limpid deep, all silvered o'er,
Some, clad in living green, delight the eye,
Some red, some blue; of mingled colours more.

Here glides the spangled Dolphin through the deep,
The giant carcased whales at distance stray,
The huge green turtles wallow through the wave,
Well pleas'd alike with land or water, they.

The *Rainbow* cuts the deep, of varied green,
The well-fed *Grouper* lurks remote, below,
The swift *Bonetta* coasts the watery scene,
The diamond-coated *Angels* kindle as they go.

Delicious to the taste, salubrious food,
Which might some temperate studious sage allure
To curse the fare of his abstemious cell
And turn, for once, a cheerful epicure.

Unhurt mayest thou this luscious food enjoy,
To fulness feast upon the scaly kind;
These, well selected from a thousand more,
Delight the taste, and leave no bane behind.

Nor think *Hygeia* * is a stranger here—
To sensual souls the climate may fatal prove,
Anguish and death attend, and pain severe,
The midnight revel, and licentious love.

Full many a swain, in youth's serenest bloom,
Is borne untimely to this alien clay,
Constrained to slumber in a foreign tomb,
Far from his friends, his country far away.

Yet, if devoted to a sensual soul,
If fondly their own ruin they create,
These victims to the banquet and the bowl
Must blame their folly only, not their fate.

But thou, who first drew breath in northern air,
At early dawn ascend the sloping hills:
And oft, at noon, to lime tree shades repair,
Where some soft stream from neighbouring groves distills.

And with it mix the liquid of the lime.
The old-aged essence of the generous cane,

* The goddess of health, in the Grecian mythology.

And sweetest syrups of this liquorish clime,
And drink, to cool thy thirst, and drink again.

This happy beverage, joy-inspiring bowl,
Dispelling far the shades of mental night,
Beams bright ideas on the awakened soul,
And sorrow turns to pleasure and delight.

Sweet verdant isle! through thy dark woods I rove,
And learn the nature of each native tree,
The *fustick* hard, the poisonous manchineel,
Which for its fragrant apple pleaseth thee;

Alluring to the smell, fair to the eye,
But deadliest poison in the taste is found—
O shun the dangerous tree, nor touch, like *Eve*,
This interdicted fruit in Eden's ground.

The lowly *mangrove*, fond of watery soil,
The white-barked *gregory*, rising high in air,
The *mastic* in the woods you may descry,
Tamarind, and lofty bay-trees flourish there.

Sweet orange groves in lonely vallies rise
And drop their fruits, unnoticed and unknown,
And cooling acid limes in hedges grow,
The juicy lemons swell in shades their own.

Sweet, spungy plums on trees wide spreading hang,
Bell-apples here, suspended, shade the ground,
Plump *grenadilloes* and *güavas* grey,
With *melons* in each plain and vale abound.

The conic-form'd *cashew*, of juicy kind,
Which bears at once an apple and a nut;
Whose poisonous coat, indignant to the lip,
Doth in its cell a wholesome kernel shut.

The prince of fruits, whom some *jayama* call,
Anana some, the happy flavoured pine;
In which unite the tastes and juices all
Of apple, quince, peach, grape, and nectarine,

Grows to perfection here, and spreads his crest,
His diadem toward the parent sun;
His diadem, in fiery blossoms drest,
Stands armed with swords, from potent Nature won.

Yon' cotton shrubs with bursting knobs behold,
Their snow white locks these humbler groves array;
On slender trees the blushing coffee hangs,
Like thy fair cherry, and would tempt thy stay.

Safe from the winds, in deep retreats, they rise;
Their utmost summit may thy arm attain;
Taste the moist fruit, and from thy closing eyes
Sleep shall retire, with all his drowsy train.

The spicy berry, they *güava* call,
Swells in the mountains on a stripling tree;
These some admire, and value more than all,
My humble verse, besides, unfolds to thee.

The smooth white cedar, here, delights the eye,
The bay-tree, with its aromatic green,
The sea-side grapes, sweet natives of the sand,
And pulse, of various kinds, on trees are seen.

Here mingled vines, their downward shadows cast,
Here, clustered grapes from loaded boughs depend,
Their leaves no frosts, their fruits no cold winds blast,
But, reared by suns, to time alone they bend.

The plantane and banana flourish here,
Of hasty growth, and love to fix their root
Where some soft stream of ambling water flows,
To yield full moisture to their clustered fruit.

No other trees so vast a leaf can boast,
So broad, so long—through these, refreshed, I stray,
And though the noon-sun all his radiance shed,
These friendly leaves shall shade me all the way.

And tempt the cooling breeze to hasten there,
With its sweet odorous breath to charm the grove;
High shades and verdant seats, while underneath
A little stream by mossy banks doth rove,

Where once the Indian dames slept with their swains,
Or fondly kiss'd the moon-light eves away;—
The lovers fled, the tearful stream remains,
And only I console it with my lay.

Among the shades of yonder whispering grove
The green palmittoes mingle, tall and fair,
That ever murmur, and forever move,
Fanning with wavy bough the ambient air.

Pomegranates grace the wild, and sweet-sops there
Ready to fall, require thy helping hand,
Nor yet neglect the papaw or mamee,
Whose slighted trees with fruits unheeded stand.

Those shaddocks juicy shall thy taste delight,
And yon' high fruits, the noblest of the wood,
That cling in clusters to the mother tree,
The cocoa-nut; rich, milky, healthful food.

O grant me, gods, if yet condemned to stray,
At least to spend life's sober evening here,
To plant a grove where winds yon' sheltered bay,
And pluck these fruits, that frost nor winter fear.

Cassada shrubs abound—transplanted here
From every clime, exotic blossoms blow;
Here Asia plants her flowers, here Europe trees,
And hyperborean herbs, un-wintered, grow.

Here, a new herbage glads the generous steed,
Mules, goats, and sheep, enjoy these pastures fair,
And for thy hedges, Nature has decreed,
Guards of thy toils, the date and prickly pear.

But chief the glory of these Indian isles
Springs from the sweet, uncloying sugar-cane:
Hence comes the planter's wealth, hence commerce sends
Such floating piles, to traverse half the main.

Whoe'er thou art that leavest thy native shore
And shalt to fair West-India climates come,
Taste not the enchanting plant—to taste forbear,
If ever thou wouldst reach thy much loved home.

Ne'er through the isle permit thy feet to rove,
Or, if thou dost, let prudence lead the way,
Forbear to taste the virtues of the cane,
Forbear to taste what will complete your stay.

Whoever sips of this enchanting juice,
Delicious nectar, fit for Jove's own hall,
Returns no more from his lov'd Santa Cruz,
But quits his friends, his country, and his all.

And thinks no more of home—Ulysses so
Dragged off by force his sailors from that shore
Where *lotos* grew, and, had not strength prevailed,
They never would have sought their country more.

No annual toil inters this thrifty plant,
The stalk lopt off, the freshening showers prolong
To future years, unfading and secure,
The root is vigorous, and the juice so strong.

Unnumbered plants, besides, these climates yield,
And grass peculiar to the soil that bears:
Ten thousand varied herbs array the field,
This glads thy palate, that thy health repairs.

Along the shore a wondrous *flower* is seen,
Where rocky ponds receive the surging wave,
Some drest in yellow, some attired in green,
Beneath the water their gay branches lave.

This mystic plant, with its bewitching charms,
Too surely springs from some enchanted bower,
Fearful it is, and dreads impending harms,
And ANIMAL the natives call the flower.

From the smooth rock its little branches rise,
The object of thy view, and that alone,
Feast on its beauties with thy ravished eyes,
But aim to touch it, and—the flower is gone.

Nay, if thy shade but intercept the beam
That gilds their boughs beneath the briny lake,
Swift they retire, like a deluding dream,
And even a shadow for destruction take.

Warned by experience, hope not thou to gain
The magic plant thy curious hand invades;
Returning to the light, it mocks thy pain,
Deceives all grasp, and seeks its native shades!

On yonder blue-browed hill, fresh harvests rise,
Where the dark tribe from Afric's sun burnt plain,
Oft o'er the ocean turn their wishful eyes
To isles remote high looming o'er the main.

And view soft seats of ease and fancied rest,
Their native groves new painted on the eye,
Where no proud misers their gay hours molest,
No lordly despots pass, unsocial, by.

See, yonder slave that slowly bends this way,
With years, and pain, and ceaseless toil opprest,
Though no complaining words his woes betray,
The eye dejected proves the heart distrest.

Perhaps in chains he left his native shore,
Perhaps he left a helpless offspring there,
Perhaps a wife, that he must see no more,
Perhaps a father, who his love did share.

Cursed be the ship that brought him o'er the main,
And curs'd the men who from his country tore;
May she be stranded, ne'er to float again,
May they be shipwrecked on some hostile shore—

O gold accurst, of every ill the spring,
For thee compassion flies the darkened mind,
Reason's plain dictates no conviction bring,
And madness only sways all human kind.

O gold accurst! for thee we madly run,
With murderous hearts across the briny flood,
Seek foreign climes beneath a foreign sun,
And, there, exult to shed a brother's blood.

But thou, who ownest this sugar-bearing soil,
To whom no good the great FIRST CAUSE denies,
Let free-born hands attend thy sultry toil,
And fairer harvests to thy view shall rise,

The teeming earth will mightier stores disclose
Than ever struck thy longing eyes before,
And late content shall shed a soft repose,
Repose, so long a stranger at thy door.

Give me some clime, the favorite of the sky,
Where cruel slavery never sought to reign—
But shun the theme, sad muse, and tell me why
These abject trees lie scattered o'er the plain?

These isles, lest Nature should have proved too kind,
Or man have sought his happiest heaven below,
Are torn with mighty winds, fierce hurricanes,
Nature convulsed in every shape of woe.

Nor scorn yon' lonely vale of trees so reft:
There plantane groves late grew of liveliest green,
The orange flourished, and the lemon bore,
The genius of the isle dwelt there, unseen.

Wild were the skies, affrighted Nature groaned
As though approached her last decisive day.
Skies blazed around and bellowing winds had nigh
Dislodg'd these cliffs, and tore yon' hills away.

O'er the wild main, dejected and afraid,
The trembling pilot lashed his helm a-lee
Or swiftly scudding, asked thy potent aid,
Dear *Pilot of the Galilëan sea.*

Low hung the clouds, distended with the gale
The clouds, dark brooding, winged their circling flight,
Tremendous thunders joined the hurricane,
Daughter of chaos, and eternal night!

And how, alas! could these fair trees withstand
The wasteful madness of so fierce a blast,
That stormed along the plain, seized every grove,
And deluged with a sea this mournful waste.

That plantane grove, where oft I fondly strayed,
Thy darts, dread Phoebus, in those glooms to shun,
Is now no more a refuge or a shade,
Is now with rocks and deep sands over-run.

Those late proud domes of splendour, pomp, and ease
No longer strike the view, in grand attire;
But, torn by winds, flew piece-meal to the seas,
Nor left one nook to lodge the astonished squire.

But other groves the hand of Time shall raise,
Again shall Nature smile, serenely gay,
So soon each scene revives, why haste I leave
These green retreats, o'er the dark seas to stray.

For I must go where the mad pirate roves,
A stranger on the inhospitable main,
Lost to the scenes of Hudson's sweetest groves,
Cesarea's forests, and my native plain.

There endless waves deject the wearied eye,
And hostile winds incessant toil prepare;
But should loud bellowing storms all art defy,
The manly heart alone must conquer there.—

There wakes my fears, the guileful *Celenture*
Tempting the wanderer on the deep-sea main,
That paints gay groves upon the ocean floor,
Beckoning her victim to the faithless scene.

On these blue hills, to cull bright Fancy's flowers,
Might yet awhile the unwelcome work delay,
Might yet beguile the few remaining hours—
Ere to those waves I take my destined way.

Thy vales, *Bermuda*, and thy sea-girt groves
Can never like these southern forests please;
And, lashed by stormy waves, you court in vain
The northern shepherd to your cedar trees.

Not o'er those isles such equal planets rule.
All, but the cedar, dread the wintry blast;
Too well thy charms the banished *Waller* sung;
Too near the *pilot's star* thy doom is cast.

Far o'er the waste of yonder surgy field
My native climes in fancied prospect lie,
Now hid in shades, and now by clouds concealed,
And now by tempests ravished from my eye.

There, triumphs to enjoy, are, Britain, thine,
There, thy proud navy awes the pillaged shore;
Nor sees the day when nations shall combine
That pride to humble, and our rights restore.

Yet o'er the globe shouldst thou extend thy reign,
Here may thy conquering arms one grotto spare;
Here—though thy conquests vex—in spite of pain
I sip the enlivening glass, in spite of care.

What though we bend to a *tyrannic crown;*
Still Nature's charms in varied beauty shine—
What though we own the rude imperious *Dane,*
Gold is his sordid care, the Muses mine.

Winter, and winter's glooms are far removed,
Eternal spring with smiling summer joined:—
Absence, and death, and heart-corroding care,
Why should they cloud the sun-shine of the mind?

But, shepherd, haste, and leave behind thee far
Thy bloody plains, and iron glooms above;
Quit the cold northern star, and here enjoy,
Beneath the smiling skies, this land of love.

The drowsy pelican wings home his way,
The misty eve sits heavy on the sea,
And though yon' storm hangs brooding o'er the main,
Say, shall a moment's gloom discourage thee?

To-morrow's sun new paints the faded scene:
Though deep in ocean sink his western beams,
His spangled chariot shall ascend more clear,
More radiant from the drowsy land of dreams.

Of all the isles the neighbouring ocean bears,
None can with this their equal landscapes boast,
What could we do on *Saba's* cloudy height;
Or what could please on *'Statia's* barren coast?

Couldst thou content on rough *Tortola* stray,
Confest the fairest of the *Virgin* train;
Or couldst thou on these rocky summits play
Where high *St. John* stands frowning o'er the main?

Haste, shepherd, haste—Hesperian fruits for thee
And clustered grapes from mingled boughs depend—
What pleasure in thy forests can there be
That, leafless now, to every tempest bend?

To milder stars, and skies of clearer blue,
Sworn foe to tyrants, for a time repair:
And, till to mightier force proud Britain bends—
Despise her triumphs, and forget your care.

Soon shall the genius of the fertile soil
A new creation to thy view unfold—
Admire the works of Nature's magic hand,
But scorn that vulgar bait—the thirst for gold.—

Yet, if persuaded by no verse of mine,
You still admire your climes of frost and snow,
And pleased, prefer above these southern groves,
The darksome forests, that around you grow:

Still there remain—your native air enjoy,
Repell the TYRANT who thy peace invades:
While charmed, we trace the vales of SANTA CRUZ,
And paint with rapture, her inspiring shades.

[w. 1776]   1779

THE JEWISH LAMENTATION

at Euphrates.*

BY Babel's streams we sate and wept,
When Sion bade our sorrows flow;
Our harps on lofty willows slept
That near those distant waters grow:
The willows high, the waters clear,
Beheld our toils and sorrows there.

* In the 1786 edition this poem was entitled "Psalm CXXXVII
Versified." [Ed.]

The cruel foe, that captive led
Our nation from their native soil,
The tyrant foe, by whom we bled,
Required a song, as well as toil:
"Come, with a song your sorrows cheer,
"A song, that Sion loved to hear."

How shall we, cruel tyrant, raise
A song on such a distant shore?—
If I forget my Sion's praise,
May my right hand assume no more
To strike the silver sounding string,
And thence the slumbering music bring.

If I forget that happy home,
My perjured tongue, forbear to move!
My eyes, be closed in endless gloom—
My joy, my rapture, and my love!
No rival grief my mind can share,
For thou shalt reign unrivalled there.

Remember, Lord, that hated foe
(When conquered Sion drooped her head)
Who laughing at our deepest woe,
Thus to our tears and sorrows said,
"From its proud height degrade her wall,
"Destroy her towers—and ruin all."

Thou, Babel's offspring, hated race,
May some avenging monster seize,
And dash your venom in your face
For crimes and cruelties like these:
And, deaf to pity's melting moan,
With infant blood stain every stone.

1779

ON AMANDA'S SINGING BIRD:

A native of the Canary Islands,
    confined in a small cage.

"HAPPY in my native grove,
I from spray to spray did rove,
Fond of music, full of love.

Dressed as fine as bird could be,
Every thing that I did see,
Every thing was mirth to me.

There had I been, happy still,
With my mate to coo and bill
In the vale, or on the hill.

But the cruel tyrant, man,
(Tyrant since the world began)
Soon abridged my little span.

How shall I the wrong forget!
Over me he threw a net;
And I am his prisoner yet.

To this rough Bermudian shore
Ocean I was hurried o'er,
Ne'er to see my country more!

To a narrow cage confined
I, who once so gaily shined,
Sing to please the human kind.

Dear Amanda!—leave me free,
And my notes will sweeter be;
On your breast, or in the tree!

On your arm I would repose—
One—oh make me—of your beaus—
There I would relate my woes.

Now, all love, and full of play,
I so innocently gay,
Pine my little life away.

Thus to grieve and flutter here,
Thus to pine from year to year;
This is usage too severe.

From the chiefs who rule this isle,
I will never court a smile;
All, with them, is *prison style*.

But from your superior mind
Let me but my freedom find,
And I will be all resigned.

Then your kiss will hold me fast—
If but once by you embraced,
In your 'kerchief I will rest.—

Gentle shepherds of the plain,
Who so fondly hear my strain;
Help me to be free again.

'Tis a blessing to be free:—
Fair Amanda!—pity me,
Pity him who sings for thee.

But if, cruel, you deny
That your captive bird should fly,
Here detained so wrongfully,

Full of anguish, faint with woe,
I must, with my music, go
To the cypress groves below.

1782

CAPTAIN J. P. JONES'S INVITATION.

THOU, who on some dark mountain's brow
Hast toiled thy life away, till now,
And often from that rugged steep
Beheld the vast extended deep,
Come from thy forest, and, with me
Learn what it is to go to sea.

There endless plains the eye surveys
As far from land the vessel strays;
No longer hill nor dale is seen,
The realms of death intrude between,
But fear no ill; resolve, with me,
To share the dangers of the sea.

But look not there for verdant fields—
Far different prospects Neptune yields;
Blue seas shall only greet the eye,
Those seas encircled by the sky,
Immense and deep—come then with me
And view the wonders of the sea.

Yet sometimes groves and meadows gay
Delight the seamen on their way;
From the deep seas that round us swell,
With rocks, the surges to repel,
Some verdant isle, by waves embraced,
Swells, to adorn the watery waste,

Though now this vast expanse appear
With glassy surface, calm and clear:
Be not deceived—'tis but a show,
For many a corpse is laid below—
Even Britain's lads—*it cannot be*—
They were the *masters* of the sea!

Now combating upon the brine,
Where ships in flaming squadrons join,

At every blast the brave expire
'Midst clouds of smoke, and streams of fire;
But scorn all fear; advance with me—
'Tis but the custom of the sea.

Now we the peaceful wave divide,
On broken surges now we ride,
Now every eye dissolves with woe
As on some lee-ward coast we go—
Half lost, half buried in the main
Hope scarcely beams on life again.

Above us storms distract the sky,
Beneath us depths unfathom'd lie,
Too near we see, disheartening sight,
The realms of everlasting night,
A watery tomb of ocean-green
And only one frail plank between!

But winds must cease, and storms decay,
Not always lasts the gloomy day,
Again the skies are warm and clear,
Again soft zephyrs fan the air,
Again we find the long-lost shore,
The winds oppose our wish no more.

If thou hast courage to despise
The various changes of the skies,
To disregard the ocean's rage,
Unmoved when hostile ships engage—
Come from thy forest, and with me
Learn what it is to go to sea.

1786.

THE SEA VOYAGE *

FROM a gay island green and fair,
With gentle blasts of southern air,
    Across the deep we held our way,
Around our barque smooth waters played,

* Text from *United States Magazine*, Oct., 1779. [Ed.]

No envious clouds obscur'd the day,
Serene came on the evening shade.

Still farther to the north we drew,
And Porto Rico's mountains blue,
  Were just decaying on the eye,
When from the main arose the sun;
  Before his ray the shadows fly,
As we before the breezes run.

Now northward of the tropic pass'd,
The fickle skies grew black at last;
  The ruffian winds began to roar,
The sea obey'd their tyrant force,
  And we, alas! too far from shore,
Must now forsake our destin'd course.

The studding sails at last to hand,
The vent'rous captain gave command;
  But scarcely to the task went they
When a vast billow o'er us broke,
  And tore the sheets and tacks away,
Nor could the booms sustain the stroke.

Still vaster rose the angry main,
The winds through every shroud complain;
  The topsails we could spread no more,
Though doubly reef'd, the furious blast
  Away the fluttering canvas bore,
And vow'd destruction to the mast.

When now the northern storm was quell'd,
A calm ensued—but ocean swell'd
  Beyond the towering mountain's height,
Till from the south new winds arose;
  Our sails we spread at dead of night,
And fair, though fierce, the tempest blows.

When morning rose, the skies were clear
The gentle breezes warm and fair,
  Convey'd us o'er the wat'ry road;
A ship o'ertook us on the way,
  Her thousand sails were spread abroad,
And flutter'd in the face of day.

At length, through many a climate pass'd,
Caesaria's hills we saw at last,
  And reach'd the land of lovely dames;
My charming Caelia there I found,
  'Tis she my warmest friendship claims,
The fairest maid that treads the ground.

1779.

The VANITY OF EXISTENCE.

To Thyrsis

IN youth, gay scenes attract our eyes,
  And not suspecting their decay
Life's flowery fields before us rise,
  Regardless of its winter day.

But vain pursuits, and joys as vain,
  Convince us life is but a dream.
Death is to wake, to rise again
  To that true life you best esteem.

So nightly on some shallow tide,
  Oft have I seen a splendid show;
Reflected stars on either side,
And glittering moons were seen below.

But when the tide had ebbed away,
  The scene fantastic with it fled,
A bank of mud around me lay,
  And sea-weed on the river's bed.

1781

TO AN OLD MAN *

WHY, dotard, wouldst thou longer groan
  Beneath a weight of years and woe,
Thy youth is lost, thy pleasures flown,
  And age proclaims, " 'Tis time to go."

To willows sad and weeping yews
  With us a while, old man, repair,
Nor to the vault thy steps refuse,
  Thy constant home must soon be there.

To summer suns and winter moons
  Prepare to bid a long adieu,
Autumnal seasons shall return
  And spring shall bloom, but not for you.

Why so perplext with cares and toil
  To rest upon this darksome road;
'Tis but a thin, a thirsty soil,
  A barren and a bleak abode.

Constrained to dwell with pain and care,
  These dregs of life are bought too dear,
'Tis better far to die than bear
  The torments of life's closing year.

Subjected to perpetual ills
  A thousand deaths around us grow:
The frost the tender blossom kills,
  And roses wither as they blow.

Cold nipping winds thy fruits assail,
  The blasted apple seeks the ground,
The peaches fall, the cherries fail,
  The grape receives a mortal wound.

* Entitled "Plato, the Philosopher, to his friend Theon," in the
1786 edition. [Ed.]

The breeze that gently ought to blow,
　　Swells to a storm, and rends the main,
The sun that charmed the grass to grow
　　Turns hostile, and consumes the plain;

The mountains waste, the shores decay,
　　Once purling streams are dead and dry—
'Twas Nature's work—'tis nature's play,
　　And Nature says, that all must die.

Yon' flaming lamp, the source of light,
　　In chaos dark shall shroud his beam
And leave the world to mother Night,
　　A farce, a phantom, or a dream.

What now is young must soon be old,
　　Whate'er we love, we soon must leave
'Tis now too hot, 'tis now too cold—
　　To live, is nothing but to grieve.

How bright the morn her course begun,
　　No mists bedimmed the solar sphere—
The clouds arise—they shade the sun,
　　For nothing can be constant here.

Now hope the longing soul employs,
　　In expectation we are blest;
But soon the airy phantom flies,
　　For, lo! the treasure is possest.

Those monarchs proud that havoc spread,
　　(While pensive reason dropt a tear)
Those monarchs have to darkness fled
　　And ruin bounds their mad career.

The grandeur of this earthly round,
　　Where folly would forever stay,
Is but a name, is but a sound—
　　Mere emptiness and vanity.

Give me the stars, give me the skies,
  Give me the heaven's remotest sphere,
Above these gloomy scenes to rise
  Of desolation and despair.

Those native fires that warmed the mind,
  Now languid grown too dimly glow,
Joy has to grief the heart resigned
  And love itself is changed to woe.

The joys of wine are all you boast,
  These, for a moment, damp thy pain;
The gleam is o'er, the charm is lost—
  And darkness clouds the soul again.

Then seek no more for bliss below,
  Where real bliss can ne'er be found;
Aspire where sweeter blossoms blow
  And fairer flowers bedeck the ground.

Where plants of life the plains invest;
  And green eternal crowns the year,
The little god, that warms the breast,
  Is weary of his mansion here.

Like Phosphor, sent before the day,
  His height meridian to regain,
The dawn arrives—he must not stay
  To shiver on a frozen plain.

Life's journey past, for fate prepare,—
  'Tis but the freedom of the mind,
Jove made us mortal—his we are,
  To Jove, be all our cares resigned.

1782

STANZAS

Occasioned by the Ruins of a Country INN, unroofed and blown down in a storm.

WHERE now these mingled ruins lie
A Temple once to Bacchus rose,
Beneath whose roof, aspiring high,
Full many a guest forgot his woes:

No more this dome, by tempests torn,
Affords a social safe retreat;
But ravens here, with eye forlorn,
And clustering bats henceforth shall meet.

The Priestess of this ruin'd shrine,
Unable to survive the stroke,
Presents no more the ruddy wine,
Her glasses gone, her china broke.

The friendly Host, whose social hand
Accosted strangers at the door,
Has left at length his wonted stand,
And greets the weary guest no more.

Old creeping time, that brings decay,
Might yet have spar'd these mouldering walls,
Alike beneath whose potent sway
A *temple* or a *tavern* falls.

Is this the place where mirth and joy,
Coy nymphs and sprightly lads were found?
Alas! no more the nymphs are coy,
No more the flowing bowls go round.

Is this the place where festive song
Deceiv'd the wintry hours away?
No more the swains the tune prolong,
No more the maidens join the lay:

Is this the place where Chloe slept
In downy beds of blue and green?
Dame Nature here no vigils kept,
No cold, unfeeling guards were seen.

'Tis gone!—and Chloe tempts no more,
Deep, unrelenting silence reigns;
Of all that pleas'd, that charm'd before,
The tottering chimney scarce remains!

Ye tyrant winds, whose ruffian blast
From locks and hinges rent the door.
And all the roof to ruin cast,
The roof that sheltered us before,

Your wrath appeased, I pray be kind
If Mopsus should the dome renew;
That we again may quaff his wine,
Again collect our jovial crew.

1782

THE ARGONAUT;

or, Lost Adventurer

TRUE to his trade—the slave of fortune still—
In a sweet isle, where never winter reigns,
I found him at the foot of a tall hill,
Mending old sails, and chewing sugar canes:
Pale ivy round him grew, and mingled vines,
Plaintains, bananas ripe, and yellow pines.

And flowering night-shade, with its dismal green,
Ash-coloured iris, painted by the sun,
And fair-haired hyacinth was near him seen,
And China pinks by marygolds o'er-run:—
"But what (said he) have men that sail the seas,
"Ah, what have they to do with things like these!

"I did not wish to leave those shades, not I,
"Where Amoranda turns her spinning-wheel;
"Charmed with the shallow stream, that murmured by,
"I felt as blest as any swain could feel,
"Who, seeking nothing that the world admires,
"On one poor valley fixed his whole desires.

"With masts so trim, and sails as white as snow,
"The painted barque deceived me from the land,
"Pleased, on her sea-beat decks I wished to go,
"Mingling my labours with her hardy band;
"To reef the sail, to guide the foaming prow
"As far as winds can waft, or oceans flow.

"To combat with the waves who first essayed,
"Had these gay groves his lightsome heart beguiled,
"His heart, attracted by the charming shade,
"Had changed the deep sea for the woody wild;
"And slighted all the gain that Neptune yields
"For *Damon's* cottage, or *Palemon's* fields.

"His barque, the bearer of a feeble crew,
"How could he trust when none had been to prove her;
"Courage might sink when lands and shores withdrew,
"And feeble hearts a thousand deaths discover:
"But *Fortitude*, tho' woes and death await,
"Still views bright skies, and leaves the dark to fate.

"From monkey climes where limes and lemons grow,
"And the sweet orange swells her fruit so fair,
"To wintry worlds, with heavy heart, I go
"To face the cold glance of the northern bear,
"Where lonely waves, far distant from the sun,
"And gulphs, of mighty strength, their circuits run.

"But how disheartening is the wanderer's fate!
"When conquered by the loud tempestuous main,

"On him, no mourners in procession wait,
"Nor do the sisters of the harp complain.—
"On coral beds and deluged sands they sleep,
"Who sink in storms, and mingle with the deep.

"'Tis folly all—and who can truly tell
"What storms disturb the bosom of that main,
"What ravenous fish in those dark climates dwell
"That feast on men—then stay, my gentle swain!
"Bred in yon' happy shades, be happy there,
"And let these quiet groves claim all your care."

So spoke poor RALPH, and with a smooth sea gale
Fled from the magic of the enchanting shore,
But whether winds or waters did prevail
I saw the black ship ne'er returning more,
Though long I walked the margin of the main,
And long have looked—and still must look in vain!

1788

SCANDINAVIAN WAR SONG.*

> BALDERI *patris scamna*
> *Parata scio in aula:*
> *Bibemus Cerevisiam*
> *Ex concavis crateribus craniorum.*
> *Non gemit vir fortis contra mortem*
> *Magnifici in* ODINI *domibus, &c:*

Translation

BRAVE deeds atchieved, at death's approach I smile,
—In Balder's hall I see the table spread,
The enlivening ALE shall now reward my toil,
Quaffed from their sculls, that by my faulchion bled.

* Composed (with a great deal more) by one warrior chief of the Scandinavians, more that 800 years ago, a few hours before he expired.

Heroes no more at death's approach shall groan:
  In lofty ODIN's dome all sighs forbear—
Conscious of bloody deeds, my fearless soul
  Mounts to great ODIN's * hall, and revels there.

1782

THE

PROPHECY of King TAMMANY †

THE Indian chief who, fam'd of yore,
Saw Europe's sons adventuring here,
Look'd sorrowing to the crowded shore,
And sighing dropt a tear!
He saw them half his world explore,
He saw them draw the shining blade,
He saw their hostile ranks display'd,
And cannons blazing through that shade
Where only peace was known before.

"Ah, what unequal arms!" he cri'd,
"How art thou fallen, my country's pride,
"The rural, sylvan reign!
"Far from our pleasing shores to go
"To western rivers, winding slow,
"Is this the boon the gods bestow!
"What have we done, great patrons, say,
"That strangers seize our woods away,
"And drive us, naked, from our native plain.

"Rage and revenge inspire my soul,
"And passion burns without controul;
"Hence, strangers, to your native shore!
"Far from our Indian shades retire,
"Remove these *gods*, that vomit fire,
"And stain with blood these ravag'd glades no more.

---

* Odin (or Woden) one of the ancient Saxon deities: Balder was son of Odin.
  † Text from the edition of 1795. [Ed.]

"Invain I weep, invain I sigh,
"These strangers all our arms defy,
"As they advance our chieftains die!—
"What can their hosts oppose!
"The bow has lost its wonted spring,
"The arrow faulters on the wing,
"Nor carries ruin from the string
"To end their being and our woes.

"Yes, yes,—I see our nation bends;
"The gods no longer are our friends,
"But why these weak complaints and sighs?
"Are there not gardens in the west,
"Where all our far fam'd Sachems rest?—
"I'll go, an unexpected guest,
"And the dark horrors of the way despise.

"Even now the thundering peals draw nigh,—
"'Tis theirs to triumph, ours to die!
"But mark me, Christian, ere I go—
"Thou, too, shalt have thy share of woe,
"The time rolls on, not moving slow,
"When hostile squadrons for your blood shall come,
"And ravage all your shore!
"Your warriors and your children slay,
"And some in dismal dungeons lay,
"Or lead them captive, far away,
"To climes unknown, thro' seas untry'd before.

"When struggling long, at last with pain
"You break a cruel tyrant's chain,
"That never shall be join'd again,—
"When half your foes are homeward fled,
"And hosts on hosts in triumph led,
"And hundreds maim'd and thousands dead,
"A timid race shall then succeed,
"Shall slight the virtues of the firmer race,
"That brought your tyrant to disgrace,

"Shall give your honours to an odious train,
"Who shun'd all conflicts on the main
"And dar'd no battles on the bloody plain;
"Whose little souls sunk in the gloomy day
"When VIRTUE ONLY could support the fray;
"And sunshine friends kept off—or ran away."

So spoke the chief, and rais'd his funeral pyre—
Around him soon the crackling flames ascend;
He smil'd amid the fervours of the fire
To think his troubles were so near their end,
'Till the freed soul, her debt to Nature paid,
Rose from the ashes that her prison made,
And sought the world unknown, and dark oblivion's shade.

1782

THE DYING INDIAN:

Tomo-Chequi.

"ON yonder lake I spread the sail no more!
Vigour, and youth, and active days are past—
Relentless demons urge me to that shore
On whose black forests all the dead are cast:—
Ye solemn train, prepare the funeral song,
For I must go to shades below,
Where all is strange and all is new;
Companion to the airy throng!—
    What solitary streams,
    In dull and dreary dreams,
All melancholy, must I rove along!

To what strange lands must *Chequi* take his way!
Groves of the dead departed mortals trace:
No deer along those gloomy forests stray,
No huntsmen there take pleasure in the chace,
But all are empty unsubstantial shades,
That ramble through those visionary glades;
No spongy fruits from verdant trees depend,

But sickly orchards there
Do fruits as sickly bear,
And apples a consumptive visage shew,
And withered hangs the hurtle-berry blue.

Ah me! what mischiefs on the dead attend!
Wandering a stranger to the shores below,
Where shall I brook or real fountain find?
Lazy and sad deluding waters flow—
Such is the picture in my boding mind!
Fine tales, indeed, they tell
Of shades and purling rills,
Where our dead fathers dwell
Beyond the western hills,
But when did ghost return his state to shew;
Or who can promise half the tale is true?

I too must be a fleeting ghost!—no more—
None, none but shadows to those mansions go;
I leave my woods, I leave the Huron shore,
For emptier groves below!
Ye charming solitudes,
Ye tall ascending woods,
Ye glassy lakes and prattling streams,
Whose aspect still was sweet,
Whether the sun did greet,
Or the pale moon embraced you with her beams—
Adieu to all!
To all, that charmed me where I strayed,
The winding stream, the dark sequestered shade;
Adieu all triumphs here!
Adieu the mountain's lofty swell,
Adieu, thou little verdant hill,
And seas, and stars, and skies—farewell,
For some remoter sphere!

Perplexed with doubts, and tortured with despair,
Why so dejected at this hopeless sleep?
Nature at last these ruins may repair,

When fate's long dream is o'er, and she forgets to weep
Some real world once more may be assigned,
Some new born mansion for the immortal mind!
Farewell, sweet lake; farewell surrounding woods,
To other groves, through midnight glooms, I stray,
Beyond the mountains, and beyond the floods,
    Beyond the Huron bay!
Prepare the hollow tomb, and place me low,
My trusty bow and arrows by my side,
The cheerful bottle and the venison store;
For long the journey is that I must go,
Without a partner, and without a guide."
    He spoke, and bid the attending mourners weep,
Then closed his eyes, and sunk to endless sleep!

1784

THE HURRICANE *

HAPPY the man who, safe on shore,
Now trims, at home, his evening fire;
Unmoved, he hears the tempests roar,
That on the tufted groves expire:
Alas! on us they doubly fall,
Our feeble barque must bear them all.

Now to their haunts the birds retreat,
The squirrel seeks his hollow tree,
Wolves in their shaded caverns meet,
All, all are blest but wretched we—
Foredoomed a stranger to repose,
No rest the unsettled ocean knows.

While o'er the dark abyss we roam,
Perhaps, with last departing gleam,
We saw the sun descend in gloom,
No more to see his morning beam;
But buried low, by far too deep,
On coral beds, unpitied, sleep!

* Near the east end of Jamaica, July 30, 1784.

But what a strange, uncoasted strand
Is that, where fate permits no day—
No charts have we to mark that land,
No compass to direct that way—
What PILOT shall explore that realm,
What new COLUMBUS take the helm!

While death and darkness both surround,
And tempests rage with lawless power,
Of friendship's voice I hear no sound,
No comfort in this dreadful hour—
What friendship can in tempests be,
What comforts on this raging sea?

The barque, accustomed to obey,
No more the trembling pilots guide:
Alone she gropes her trackless way,
While mountains burst on either side—
Thus, skill and science both must fall;
And ruin is the lot of all.

1785

Written

AT PORT ROYAL

in the island of Jamaica—

September, 1784.

HERE, by the margin of the murmuring main,
Fond, her proud remnants I explore—in vain—
And lonely stray through these dejected lands,
Cheered by the noon-tide breeze on burning sands,
Where the dull *Spaniard*, owned these mangrove shades,
And ports defended by his Pallisades—*

* Pallisades a narrow strip of land about seven miles in length,
running nearly from north to south, and forming the harbours of
Port Royal and Kingston.—

Though lost to HIM, Port Royal claims a sigh,
Nor will the muse the humble gift deny.
  Of all the towns that graced *Jamaica's* isle
This *was* her glory, and her *proudest* pile,
Where *toils on toils* bade wealth's gay structures rise,
And *commerce* reared her *glory* to the skies:
ST. IAGO, seated on a distant plain,
Ne'er saw the tall ship entering from the main—
Unnoticed streams her *Cobra's* * margin lave,
Where yond' tall plantains cool her flowing wave,
And barren sands, or rock-surrounded hill
Confess its founder's *fears*—or want of skill.
  While o'er these wastes with wearied step we go
Past scenes of fate return, in all their woe,
Here *for their crimes (perhaps)* in ages fled,
Some vengeful fiend, familiar with the dead—
Through these sad shores, in angry triumph passed,
Stormed in the winds, and raged with every blast—
Here, † *opening gulphs* confessed the Almighty hand,
Here, the dark ocean rolled across the land:
Here, house and boats a moment tore away,
Here, mangled man with deadly aspect lay,
Whom fate refused to end their rakeish feast,
And time to call the sexton, or the priest!
  Where yond' tall barque, with all her ponderous load,
Commits her anchor to its dark abode,
Eight fathoms down,—where unseen waters flow
To stain the sulphur of the caves below;
There, midnight sounds torment the stranger's ear,
And *drums and fifes* play *drowsy concerts there*

* A small river falling into Kingston Bay, nearly opposite Port Royal—and which has its source in the hills beyond Spanish Town.

† Old Port-Royal contained more than 1500 buildings, and these for the most part large and elegant. This unfortunate town was for a long time reckoned the most considerable mart of trade in the West Indies. It was destroyed on the 17th of June, 1692, by an earthquake which in two minutes sunk the greater part of the buildings; in which disaster near 3000 people lost their lives.

Of ghosts all restless!—(cease they to complain—
More than a century should relieve their pain—).
Sad tunes of woe disturb the hours of sleep,
And *Fancy aids* the *fiddlers* of the deep;
Dull *superstition* hears the drowsy hum;
Smit with false terrors of THE WORLD TO COME.

What now, Port Royal! rests of all your pride?—
Lost are your glories which were spread so wide—
A *spit* of sand is thine,—by heaven's decree;
And wasting shores that scarce resist the sea:
Is this PORT ROYAL on *Jamaica's* coast,
The Spaniard's *envy*, and the Briton's boast?—
A shattered roof on every *hut* appears,
And mouldering *brick-work* wakes the stranger's fears!
—A church, with scarce a priest, we grieve to see,
Grass round its door, and *rust upon its key!*—
One only INN with tiresome search was found,
Where one sad negro dealt his beverage round:
His was the task to wait the impatient call;
He was our landlord, post-boy, pimp—and all—
His wary eyes on every side were cast,
(He saw the present—and revolved the *past*)
They here, now there, in quick succession stole,
Glanced at the *bar*, or watched the—*unsteady bowl*.

No sprightly lads, or handsome *Yankee* maids,
Rove in these wastes or wander in these shades—
No charmers here, with lively step, are seen
To court the shade, or wander on the green—
To other lands past time beheld them go;
And some are slumbering in the deep—we know—
A negro tribe, but ill their place supply,
With *bending back*, *short hair*, and vengeful eye—
That gloomy race lead up the evening dance,
Skip on the sands, or dart the *alluring* glance:
Sincere are they?—no—on your gold they doat—
And in one hour—for that would cut your throat.
All is deceit—half hell is in their song
And from the silent thought?—*You have done us wrong!*

A feeble rampart guards this luckless town,
Where banished Tories come to seek renown,
Where hungry slaves their little stores retail,
And *worn out veterans* watch the approaching sail.
  Here, scarce escaped the wild Tornado's rage
Why came I here to plan some future page?
To these dull scenes with curious view, who came
Should tell a story of some ancient fame—
Not worth the search!—What roofs are left to fall,
Guns, gales, and earthquakes will confound them all—
All will be lost!—though hosts their aid implore,
The Twelve Apostles * shall protect no more,
Nor guardian heroes save the impoverished plain,
No priest, shall paw-paw—and no church remain—
Nor this Palmetto yield her evening shade
Where the dark negro his dull music played, ;
He casts his view beyond the adjacent strand,
And looks, still grieving, to his native land:
Turns and returns from yonder murmuring shore,
And points to Gambia—he must see no more!
Where shall we go?—what Lethé can we find,
To drive the devil's ideas from the mind?—
No *buckram* hero can relieve the eye;
And *buckram* dresses shine—*most mournfully!*
  Ye mountains vast! whose base the heaven sustain:
Farewell, blue mountains, and fair Kingston's plain.
Though nature here almost herself transcends,
On this gay spot the dear attachment ends!—
  Who would be sad, to leave a sultry clime,
Where *true Columbian virtue* is a crime:
Where *parching sands* are driven by every blast,
And pearl to swine are by the muses cast—
Where *want*, and *death*, and *care*, and grief reside;
And boisterous gales impell the imperious tide.
  Ye stormy winds! awhile your wrath suspend—
Who leaves the land, a female and a friend;

* A strong commanding Battery in the hills opposite Port Royal.

Quits this bright isle for a dark sea, and sky—
Or even *Port-Royal* leaves—without a sigh!—

[w. 1784]   1788

THE SEASONS MORALIZED.

THEY, who to warmer regions run,
May bless the favour of the sun,
But seek in vain what charms us here,
Life's picture, varying with the year.

Spring, and her wanton train advance
Like *Youth* to lead the festive dance,
All, all her scenes are mirth and play,
And blushing blossoms own her sway.

The *Summer* next (those blossoms blown)
Brings on the fruits that spring had sown,
Thus men advance, impell'd by time,
And Nature triumphs in her prime.

Then *Autumn* crowns the beauteous year,
The groves a sicklier aspect wear;
And mournful she (*the lot of all*)
Matures her fruits, to make them fall.

Clad in the vestments of a tomb,
Old age is only *Winter's* gloom—
Winter, alas! shall spring restore,
But youth returns to man no more.

1785

On
THE VICISSITUDES OF THINGS

"THE constant lapse of rolling years
Awakes our hopes, provokes our fears
Of something yet unknown;
We saw the last year pass away,

But who, that lives can safely say,
The next shall be his own?"

So hundreds talk—and thousands more
Descant their moral doctrines o'er;
And when the preaching's done,
Each goes his various, wonted way,
To labour some, and some to play—
So goes the folly on.

How swift the vagrant seasons fly;
They're hardly born before they die,
Yet in their wild career,
Like atoms round the rapid wheel,
We seem the same, though changing still,
Mere reptiles of a year.

Some haste to seek a wealthy *bride*,
Some, rhymes to make on *one* that died;
And millions curse the day,
When first in Hymen's *silken* bands
The parson joined mistaken hands,
And bade the bride *obey*.

While sad Amelia vents her sighs,
In epitaphs and elegies,
For her departed *dear*,
Who would suppose the muffled bell,
And mourning gowns, were meant to tell,
Her grief will last—a year?

In folly's path how many meet—
What hosts will live to *lie* and *cheat*—
How many empty pates
May, in this wise, eventful year,
In native dignity appear
To manage RISING STATES!

How vain to sigh!—the wheel must on
And straws are to the whirlpool drawn,
With ships of gallant mien—
What has been once, may time restore;
What now exists, has been before—
Years only change the scene.

In endless circles all things move;
Below, about, far off, above,
This motion all attain—
If Folly's self should flit away,
She would return some New Year's day,
With millions in her train.

Sun, moon, and stars, are each a sphere,
The earth the same, (or very near,)
Sir Isaac has defined—
In circles each coin is cast,
And hence our cash departs so fast,
Cash—that no charm can bind.

From you to us—from us it rolls
To comfort other cloudy souls:—
If again we make it *square*,*
Perhaps the uneasy guest will stay
To cheer us in some wint'ry day,
And smooth the brow of care.

1785

TO SYLVIUS:

On the Folly of Writing Poetry.

———

OF all the fools that haunt our coast
The scribbling tribe I pity most:
Their's is a standing scene of woes,
And their's no prospect of repose.

* The old Continental.

Then, SYLVIUS, why this eager claim
To light your torch at Clio's flame?
To few she shews sincere regard,
And none, from her, should hope reward.

A garret high, dark dismal room,
Is still the pensive poet's doom:
Hopes raised to heaven must be their lot,
Yet bear the curse, to be forgot.

Hourly they deal with Grecian Jove,
And draw their bills on *banks* above:
Yet stand abashed, with all their fire,
When brought to face some country 'squire.

To mend the world, is still their aim:
The world, alas! remains the same,
And so must stand to every age,
Proof to the morals of the page!

The knave that keeps a tippling inn,
The red-nosed boy that deals out gin,
If aided by some paltry skill
May both be statesmen when they will.

The man that mends a beggar's shoes,
The quack that heals your negro's bruise,
The wretch that turns a cutler's stone,
Have wages they can call their own:

The head, that plods in trade's domains,
Gets something to reward its pains;
But *Wit*—that does the world beguile,
Takes for its pay—an empty smile!

Yet each presumes his works will rise,
And gain a name that never dies:
From earth, and cold oblivion freed,
Immortal, in the poet's creed!

Can Reason in that bosom reign
Which fondly feeds a hope so vain,
When every age that passes by
Beholds a crowd of poets die!

Poor Sappho's fate shall Milton know—
His scenes of grief and tales of woe
No honours, that all Europe gave,
No merit—shall from ruin save.—

To all that write and all that read
Fate shall, with hasty step, succeed!
Even SHAKESPEARE'S page, his mirth, his tears
May sink beneath this weight of years.

Old SPENSER'S doom shall, POPE, be thine
The music of each moving line
Scarce bribes an age or two to stay,
Admire your strain—then flit away.

The people of old *Chaucer's* times
Were once in raptures with his rhymes,
But Time—that over verse prevails,
To other ears tells other tales.

Why then so sad, dear rhyming friends—
One common fate on both attends,
The bards that sooth the statesman's ear,
And him—who finds no audience there.

Mere structures formed of common earth,
Not they from heaven derive their birth,
Or why through life, like vagrants, pass
To mingle with the mouldering mass?—

Of all the souls, from Jove that came
To animate this mortal frame,
Of all the myriads, on the wing,
How few can taste the Muse's spring!

Sejanus, of mercantile skill,
Without whose aid the world stands still,
And by whose wonder-working play
The sun goes round—(his flatterers say)

Sejanus has in house declared
"These States, as yet, can boast no bard,
And all the sing-song of our clime
Is merely nonsense, fringed with rhyme."

With such a bold, conceited air
When such assume the critic's chair,
Low in the dust is genius laid,
The muses with the man in trade.

Then, Sylvius, come—let you and I
On Neptune's aid, once more rely:
Perhaps the muse may still impart
Her balm to ease the aching heart.

Though cold might chill and storms dismay,
Yet *Zoilus* will be far away:
With us at least, depart and share
No garret—but resentment there.

1788

THE WILD HONEY SUCKLE.

Fair flower, that dost so comely grow,
Hid in this silent, dull retreat,
Untouched thy honied blossoms blow,
Unseen thy little branches greet:
    No roving foot shall crush thee here,
    No busy hand provoke a tear.

By Nature's self in white arrayed,
She bade thee shun the vulgar eye,
And planted here the guardian shade,

And sent soft waters murmuring by;
   Thus quietly thy summer goes,
   Thy days declining to repose.

Smit with those charms, that must decay,
I grieve to see your future doom;
They died—nor were those flowers more gay,
The flowers that did in Eden bloom;
   Unpitying frosts, and Autumn's power
   Shall leave no vestige of this flower.

From morning suns and evening dews
At first thy little being came:
If nothing once, you nothing lose,
For when you die you are the same;
   The space between, is but an hour,
   The frail duration of a flower.

1786

On
A BOOK

CALLED UNITARIAN THEOLOGY *

IN this choice work, with wisdom penned, we find
The noblest system to reform mankind,
Bold truths confirmed, that bigots have denied,
By most perverted, and which some deride.
   Here, truths divine in easy language flow,
Truths long concealed, that now all climes shall know:
Here, like the blaze of our material *sun*,
Enlightened *Reason* proves, that GOD IS ONE—
As that, concentered in itself, a sphere,
Illumes all Nature with its radiance here,
Bids towards itself all trees and plants aspire,
Awakes the winds, impels the seeds of fire,

* First entitled "On the Honourable Emanuel Swedenborg's Universal Theology." [Ed.]

And still subservient to the Almighty plan,
Warms into life the changeful race of man;
So—like that sun—in heaven's bright realms we trace
One POWER OF LOVE, that fills unbounded space,
Existing always by no borrowed aid,
Before all worlds—eternal, and not made—
To THAT indebted, stars and comets burn,
Owe their swift movements, and to THAT return!
Prime source of wisdom, all-contriving mind,
First spring of *Reason*, that this globe designed;
Parent of order, whose unwearied hand
Upholds the fabric that his wisdom planned,
And, its due course assigned to every sphere,
Revolves the seasons, and sustains the year!—
  Pure light of TRUTH! where'er thy splendours shine,
Thou art the image of the power divine;
Nought else, in life, that full resemblance bears,
No sun, that lights us through our circling years,
No stars, that through yon' charming azure stray,
No moon, that glads us with her evening ray,
No seas, that o'er their gloomy caverns flow,
No forms beyond us, and no shapes below!
  Then slight—ah slight not, this instructive page,
For the mean follies of a dreaming age:
Here to the truth, by REASON's aid aspire,
Nor some dull preacher of romance admire;
See ONE, SOLE GOD, in these convincing lines,
Beneath whose view perpetual day-light shines;
At whose command all worlds their circuits run,
And night, retiring, dies before the sun!
  Here, MAN *no more disgraced by Time appears,*
Lost in dull slumbers through ten thousand years:
Plunged in that gulph, whose dark unfathomed waves
Men of all ages to perdition gave;
An empty dream, or still more empty shade,
The substance vanished, and the form decayed;—
  Here Reason proves, that when this life decays,
Instant, new life in the warm bosom plays,

As that expiring, still its course repairs
Through endless ages, and unceasing years.
   Where parted souls with kindred spirits meet,
Wrapt to the bloom of beauty all complete;
In that celestial, vast, unclouded sphere,
Nought there exists but has its image here!
All there is MIND!—That INTELLECTUAL FLAME,
From whose vast stores all human genius came,
In which all Nature forms on REASON's plan—
FLOWS TO THIS ABJECT WORLD, AND BEAMS ON MAN!

1786

TO
ZOILUS,

[A severe Critic.] *

SIX sheets compos'd, struck off, and dry,
The work may please the world (thought I)—
If some impell'd by spleen or spite,
Refuse to read, then let them write:
I too, with them, shall have my turn,
And give advice—to tear or burn.

Now from the binder's, hurried home,
In neat array my leaves are come:
Alas, alas! is this my all?
The volume is so light and small,
That, aim to save it as I can,
'Twill fly before Myrtilla's fan.

Why did I no precautions use?
To curb these frolics of the Muse?
Ah! why did I invoke the nine
To aid these humble toils of mine—
That now forebode through every page
The witling's sneer, the critic's rage.

* Text from the edition of 1795. [Ed.]

Did I, for this, so often rise
Before the sun illum'd the skies,
And near by Hudson's mountain stream
Invoke the Muses' morning dream,
And scorn the winds that blew so cool!
I did—and I was more the fool.

Yet slender tho' the book, and small,
And harmless, take it all in all,
I see a monstrous wight appear,
A quill suspended from his ear;
Its fate depends on his decree,
And what he says, must sacred be!

A brute of such terrific mien
At wild *Sanduski* ne'er was seen,
And in the dark *Kentuckey* groves
No beast, like this, for plunder roves,
Nor dwells in Britain's lowering clime
A reptile, so severe on rhyme.

The monster comes, severe and slow,
His eyes with arrowy lightnings glow,
Takes up the book, surveys it o'er,
Exclaims, "damn'd stuff!"—but says no more:
The book is *damn'd* by his decree,
And what he says must gospel be!

But was there nothing to his taste?—
Was all my work a barren waste—
Was not one bright idea sown,
And not one image of my own?—
Its doom was just, if this be true:
But ZOILUS shall be sweated too.

Give me a cane of mighty length,
A staff proportion'd to my strength,
Like that, by whose destructive aid
The man of *Gath* his conquest made;

Like that, which once on *Etna's* shore
The shepherd of the mountain bore:

For wit traduc'd at such a rate
To other worlds I'll send him, straight,
Where all the past shall nothing seem,
Or just be imag'd like a dream;
Where new vexations are design'd,
No dull *quietus* for the mind!

Arm'd with a staff of such a size
Who would not smite this man of lies:
Here, scribbler, help me! seize that pen
With which he blasts all rhyming men:
His goose-quill must not with him go
To persecute the bards below.—

How vast a change an hour may bring!
How abject lies this snarling thing!
No longer wit to him shall bow,
To him the world is nothing now;
And all he writ, and all he read
Is, with himself, in silence laid!

Dead tho' he be—(not sent to rest)
No keen remorse torments my breast:
Yet, something in me seems to tell
I might have let him live, as well;—
'Twas his to snarl, and growl, and grin,
And life had, else, a burthen been.

1786

THE BERMUDA ISLANDS.

"BERMUDA, *walled with rocks, who does not know,*
That happy island, where huge lemons grow," &c.
Waller's Battle of the Summer Islands.

THESE islands fair with many a grove are crowned,
With cedars tall, gay hills, and verdant vales,

But dangerous rocks on every side is found,
Fatal to him who unsuspecting sails.

The gay Palmetto shades the adjacent wave:
Blue, ocean water near the lime-tree breaks!—
I leave the scene!—this stormy quarter leave,
And rove awhile by Harrington's sweet lake.

In every vale fair woodland nymphs are seen
In bloom of youth, to mourn some absent love,
Who, wandering far on Neptune's rude domain,
Heaves the fond sigh at every new remove.

From hill to hill I see Amanda stray,
Searching, with anxious view, the encircling main,
To espy the sail, so long, so far away,
Rise from the waves, and bless her sight again.

Now, on some rock, with loose, dishevelled hair,
Near dashing waves, the sorrowing beauty stands,
Hoping that each approaching barque may bear
Homeward the wandering youth from foreign lands.

Oh! may no gales such faithful loves destroy,
No hidden rock to Hymen fatal prove:
And thou, fond swain, thy nicest art employ
Once more on these sweet isles to meet your love.

　When verging to the height of *thirty-two*,
And east or west you guide the dashy prow;
Then fear by night the dangers of this shore,
Nature's wild garden, placed in sixty-four.*
Here many a merchant his lost freight bemoans,
And many a gallant ship has laid her bones.

                                        1788

* Lat. 32 deg. 20 min. N.—Long. 63.40 W.—and about 780 miles
East of the coast of South Carolina.

FLORIO TO AMANDA.

LAMP of the pilot's hope! the wanderer's dream,
Far glimmering o'er the wave, we saw thy beam:
Forced from your aid by cold December's gale
As near your isle we reefed the wearied sail:
From bar to bar, from cape to cape I roam,
From you still absent, still too far from home.—
What shall repay me for these nights of pain,
And weeks of absence on this restless main,
Where every dream recalls that charming shade,
Where once, AMANDA, once with you I strayed,
And fondly talked, and counted every tree,
And minutes, ages, when removed from thee.

What sad mistake this wandering fancy drew
To quit my native shores, the woods, and YOU,
When safely anchored on that winding stream,
Where you were all my care, and all my theme:
There, pensive, loitering, still from day to day,
The pilot wondered at such strange delay,
Musing, beheld the northern winds prevail,
Nor once surmised that LOVE detained the sail.

Blest be the man, who, fear beneath him cast,
From his firm decks first reared the tapering mast;
And catching life and motion from the breeze,
Stretched his broad canvas o'er a waste of seas;
And taught some swain, whom absence doomed to
    mourn
His distant fair one—taught a quick return:
He, homeward borne by favouring gales, might find
Remembrance welcome to his anxious mind,
And grateful vows, and generous thanks might pay
To Him, who filled the sail, and smoothed the way.

To me, indeed! the heavens less favouring prove:
Each day, returning, finds a new remove—
Sorrowing, I spread the sail, while slowly creeps
The weary vessel o'er a length of deeps;
Her northern course no favouring breeze befriends,

Hail, storm, and lightning, on her path attends:
Here, wintry suns their shrouded light restrain,
Stars dimly glow, and boding birds complain;
Here, boisterous gales the rapid GULPH controul,
Tremendous breakers near our Argo roll;
Here cloudy, sullen HATTERAS, restless, raves
Scorns all repose, and swells his weight of waves:
Here, drowned so late, sad cause of many a tear,
AMYNTOR floats upon his watery bier;
By bursting seas to horrid distance tossed,
Thou, PALINURUS, in these depths wert lost,
When, torn by waves, and conquered by the blast,
Art strove in vain, and ruin seized each mast.
   Now, while the winds their wonted aid deny,
For other ports, from day to day, we try;
Strive, all we can, to gain the unwilling shore,
Dream still of you—the faithful chart explore;
See other groves, in happier climates placed
Untouched their bloom, and not one flower defaced.
   Did Nature, there, a heaven of pleasure shew,
Could they be welcome, if not shared with you?—
Lost are my toils—my longing hopes are vain:
Yet, 'midst these ills, permit me to complain,
And half regret, that, finding fortune fail,
I left your cottage—to direct the sail:
Unmoved, amidst this elemental fray,
Let me, once more, the muses' art essay,
Once more—amidst these scenes of Nature's strife,
Catch at her forms and mould them into life;
By Fancy's aid, to unseen coasts repair,
And fondly dwell on absent beauty there.

[w. 1789]   1795

THE FAIR SOLITARY.

NO more these groves a glad remembrance claim
Where grief consumes a half deluded dame,

Whom to these isles a modern Theseus bore,*
And basely left, frail virtue to deplore;—

In foreign climes detained from all she loved,
By friends neglected, long by Fortune proved,
While sad and solemn passed the unwelcome day
What charms had life for her, to tempt her stay?

Deceived in all; for *meanness* could deceive,
Expecting still, and still condemned to grieve,
She scarcely saw—to different hearts allied
That her dear *Florio* ne'er pursued a bride!

Are griefs, like thine, to *Florio's* bosom known?—
Must these, alas! be ceaseless in your own?
Life is a dream!—its varying shades I see;
But this cold wanderer hardly dreams of thee—

The bloom of health, which bade all hearts adore,
To your pale cheek what physic shall restore?
Vain are those drugs that art and love prepares,
No art redeems the waste of sighs and tears!

1795

AMANDA IN A CONSUMPTION.

SMIT by the glance of your bright eyes
When I, Amanda, fondly gaze,
Strange feelings in my bosom rise
And passion all my reason sways:
Worlds I would banish from my view,
And quit the gods—to talk with you.

The smile that decks your fading cheek,
To me a heavy heart declares;
When you are silent I would speak

* Alluding to Theseus, when he left Ariadne in a desert Island in the Mediterranean Archipelago. See Ovid's *Epistolae Heroidum*, or, Epistoles of the Heroines of Greece.

But cowardice alarms my fears:
All must be sense that you do prize,
All that I say—be grave and wise.

When wandering in the evening shade
I shared her pain, and calmed her grief,
A thousand tender things I said,
But all I said gave no relief:
When from her hair I dried the dew,
She sighed, and said—I am not for you!

When drooping, dull, and almost dead
With fevers brought from sultry climes,
She would not wrap my fainting head;
But recommended me some rhymes
On patience and on fortitude,
And other things—less understood.

When, aiming to engage her heart
With verses from the muses' stock;
She sighed, regardless of the art,
And counted seconds by the clock;
"And thus, (she said) "will verse decay,
"And thus the muse will pass away!"

When languishing upon her bed
In willow shades, remote from towns,
We came; and while Priscilla read
Of chrystal skies and golden crowns:
She bade us at a distance stand,
And leaned her head upon her hand.

So, drooping hangs the fading rose,
When summer sends the beating shower:
So, to the grave Amanda goes,
Her whole duration—but an hour!
Who shall controul the sad decree,
Or what, fair girl, recover thee?

Such virtue in that spirit dwells—
Such fortitude amidst such pain!—
And, now, with pride my bosom swells,
To think I have not lived in vain.
For, slighting all the sages knew,
I learn philosophy from you.

1787

ELEGIAC LINES.

WITH life enamoured, but in death resigned,
To seats congenial flew the unspotted mind:
Attending spirits hailed her to that shore
Where this world's winter chills the soul no more.
Learn hence, to live resigned;—and when you die
No fears will seize you, when that hour is nigh.

Transferred to heaven, Amanda has no share
In the dull business of this world of care.
Her blaze of beauty, even in death admired,
A moment kindled, but as soon expired.
Sweet as the favourite offspring of the May
Serenely mild, not criminally gay:

Adorned with all that nature could impart
To please the fancy and to gain the heart;
Heaven ne'er above more innocence possessed,
Nor earth the form of a diviner guest:
A mind all virtue!—flames descended here
From some bright seraph of some nobler sphere;
Yet, not her virtues, opening into bloom,
Nor all her sweetness saved her from the tomb,
From prospects darkened, and the purpose crossed,
Misfortune's winter,—and a lover lost;
Nor such resemblance to the forms above,
The heart of goodness, and the soul of love!
Ye thoughtless fair!—her early death bemoan,
Sense, virtue, *beauty, to oblivion* gone.

1788

MAY TO APRIL.

WITHOUT your showers, I breed no flowers,
  Each field a barren waste appears;
If you don't weep, my blossoms sleep,
  They take such pleasures in your tears.

As your decay made room for *May*,
  So I must part with all that's mine:
My balmy breeze, my blooming trees
  To torrid suns their sweets resign!

O'er *April* dead, my shades I spread:
  To her I owe my dress so gay—
Of daughters three, it falls on me
  To close our triumphs on one day:

Thus, to repose, all Nature goes;
  Month after month must find its doom:
Time on the wing, May ends the Spring,
  And Summer dances on her tomb!

1787

TO AN AUTHOR.

YOUR leaves bound up compact and fair,
In neat array at length prepare,
To pass their hour on learning's stage,
To meet the surly critic's rage;
The statesman's slight, the smatterer's sneer—
Were these, indeed, your only fear,
You might be tranquil and resigned:
What most should touch your fluttering mind;
Is that, few critics will be found
To sift your works, and deal the wound.

Thus, when one fleeting year is past
On some bye-shelf *your* book is cast—

Another comes, with *something new*,
And drives you fairly out of view:
With some to praise, *but more to blame*,
The mind returns to—whence it came;
And some alive, who *scarce could read*
Will publish satires on the dead.

Thrice happy Dryden,* who could meet
Some rival bard in every street!
When all were bent on writing well
It was some credit to excel:—

Thrice happy Dryden, who could find
A *Milbourne* for his sport designed—
And *Pope*, who saw the harmless rage
Of *Dennis* bursting o'er his page
Might justly spurn the *critic's aim*,
Who only helped to swell his fame.

On these bleak climes by Fortune thrown,
Where rigid *Reason* reigns alone,
Where lovely *Fancy* has no sway,
Nor magic forms about us play—
Nor nature takes her summer hue
Tell me, what has the muse to do?—

An age employed in edging steel
Can no poetic raptures feel;
No solitude's attracting power,
No leisure of the noon day hour,
No shaded stream, no quiet grove
Can this fantastic century move;

The muse of love in no request—
Go—try your fortune with the rest,
One of the nine you should engage,
To meet the follies of the age:—

* See Johnson's lives of the English Poets.

On *one*, we fear, your choice must fall—
The least engaging of them all—
Her visage stern—an angry style—
A clouded brow—malicious smile—
A mind on *murdered victims* placed—
She, only she, can please the taste!

1788

TO
MISFORTUNE.*

DIRE Goddess of the haggard brow,
Misfortune! at that shrine I bow
Where forms uncouth pourtray thee still,
A leaky ship, a doctor's bill:

A poem damn'd, a beggar's prayer,
The critic's growl, the pedant's sneer,
The urgent dun, the law severe,
A smoky house, rejected love,
And friends that all but friendly prove.

Foe to the pride of scheming man
Whose frown controuls the wisest plan,
To your decree we still submit
Our views of gain, our works of wit.

Untaught by you the feeble mind
A dull repose, indeed, might find:
But life, unvext by such controul,
Can breed no vigour in the soul.

The calm that smooths the summer seas
May suit the man of sloth and ease:
But skies that fret and storms that rave
Are the best schools to make us brave.

* Text from the edition of 1795. [Ed.]

On *Heckla's* heights who hopes to see
The blooming grove, the orange tree
Awhile on hope may fondly lean
'Till sad experience blots the scene.

If Nature acts on Reason's plan,
And Reason be the guide of man;
Why should he paint fine prospects there,
Then sigh, to find them disappear?

For ruin'd states or trade perplext
'Tis almost folly to be vext:
The world at last will have its way
And we its torrent must obey.

On other shores a happier guest
The mind must fix her heaven of rest,
Where better men and better climes
Shall soothe the cares of future times.

1787

THE INDIAN BURYING GROUND.

IN spite of all the learned have said,
I still my old opinion keep;
The *posture*, that *we* give the dead,
Points out the soul's eternal sleep.

Not so the ancients of these lands—
The Indian, when from life released,
Again is seated with his friends,
And shares again the joyous feast.*

His imaged birds, and painted bowl,
And venison, for a journey dressed.

* The North American Indians bury their dead in a sitting posture;
decorating the corpse with wampum, the images of birds, quadru-
peds, &c: And (if that of a warrior) with bows, arrows, tomhawks
and other military weapons.

Bespeak the nature of the soul,
ACTIVITY, that knows no rest.

His bow, for action ready bent,
And arrows, with a head of stone,
Can only mean that life is spent,
And not the old ideas gone.

Thou, stranger, that shalt come this way,
No fraud upon the dead commit—
Observe the swelling turf, and say
They do not *lie*, but here they *sit*.

Here still a lofty rock remains,
On which the curious eye may trace
(Now wasted, half, by wearing rains)
The fancies of a ruder race.

Here still an aged elm aspires,
Beneath whose far-projecting shade
(And which the shepherd still admires)
The children of the forest played!

There oft a restless Indian queen
(Pale *Shebah*, with her braided hair)
And many a barbarous form is seen
To chide the man that lingers there.

By midnight moons, o'er moistening dews,
In habit for the chase arrayed,
The hunter still the deer pursues,
The hunter and the deer, a shade!

And long shall timorous fancy see
The painted chief, and pointed spear,
And Reason's self shall bow the knee
To shadows and delusions here.

1788

THE INDIAN STUDENT:
or, FORCE OF NATURE.

FROM Susquehanna's farthest springs
Where savage tribes pursue their game,
(His blanket tied with yellow strings,)
A shepherd of the forest came.

Not long before, a wandering priest
Expressed his wish, with visage sad—
"Ah, why (he cried) in Satan's waste,
"Ah, why detain so fine a lad?

"In white-man's land there stands a town
"Where learning may be purchased low—
"Exchange his blanket for a gown,
"And let the lad to college go."—

From long debate the council rose,
And viewing *Shalum's* tricks with joy
To *Cambridge Hall*, o'er wastes of snows,
They sent the copper-coloured boy.

One generous chief a bow supplied,
This gave a shaft, and that a skin;
The feathers, in vermillion dyed,
Himself did from a turkey win: ·

Thus dressed so gay, he took his way
O'er barren hills, alone, alone!
His guide a star, he wandered far,
His pillow every night a stone.

At last he came, with foot so lame,
Where learned men talk heathen Greek,
And Hebrew lore is gabbled o'er,
To please the Muses,—twice a week.

Awhile he writ, awhile he read,
Awhile he conned their grammar rules—
(An Indian savage so well bred
Great credit promised to the schools.)

Some thought he would in *law* excel,
Some said in *physic* he would shine;
And one that knew him, passing well,
Beheld, in him, a sound Divine.

But those of more discerning eye
Even then could other prospects show,
And saw him lay his *Virgil* by
To wander with his dearer *bow*.

The tedious hours of study spent,
The heavy-moulded lecture done,
He to the woods a hunting went,
Through lonely wastes he walked, he run.

No mystic wonders fired his mind;
He sought to gain no learned degree,
But only sense enough to find
The squirrel in the hollow tree.

The shady bank, the purling stream,
The woody wild his heart possessed,
The dewy lawn, his morning dream
In fancy's gayest colours dressed.

"And why (he cried) did I forsake
"My native wood for gloomy walls;
"The silver stream, the limpid lake
"For musty books and college halls.

"A little could my wants supply—
"Can wealth and honour give me more;
"Or, will the sylvan god deny
"The humble treat he gave before?

"Let seraphs gain the bright abode,
"And heaven's sublimest mansions see—
"I only bow to NATURE'S GOD—
"The land of shades will do for me.

"These dreadful secrets of the sky
"Alarm my soul with chilling fear—
"Do planets in their orbits fly,
"And is the earth, indeed, a sphere?

"Let planets still their *course* pursue,
"And comets to the CENTRE run—
"In HIM my faithful friend I view,
"The image of my God—the SUN.

"Where Nature's ancient forests grow,
"And mingled laurel never fades,
"My heart is fixed;—and I must go
"To die among my native shades."

He spoke, and to the western springs,
(His gown discharged, his money spent,
His blanket tied with yellow strings,)
The shepherd of the forest went.

                                        1788

MAN OF NINETY.

"TO yonder boughs that spread so wide,
 Beneath whose shade soft waters glide,
Once more I take the well known way;
With feeble step and tottering knee
I sigh to reach my WHITE OAK tree,
Where rosy health was wont to play.

If to the shades, consuming slow,
The shadow of myself, I go,
When I am gone, wilt thou remain!—
From dust you rose, and grew like me;

I man became, and you a tree,
Both natives of one grassy plain.

How much alike; yet not the same!—
You could no kind protector claim;
Alone you stood, to chance resigned:
When winter came, with blustering sky,
You feared its blasts—and so did I,
And for warm suns in secret pined.

When vernal suns began to glow
You felt returning vigour flow;
Which once a year new leaves supplied;
Like you, fine days I wished to see,
And May was a sweet month to me,
But when November came—I sighed!

If through your bark some ruffian arm
A mark impressed, you took the alarm,
And tears awhile I saw descend;
Till Nature's kind maternal aid
A plaister on your bruises laid,
And bade your trickling sorrows end.

Like you, I feared the lightning's stroke,
Whose flame dissolves the strength of oak,
And ends at once this mortal dream;—
You saw, with grief, the soil decay
That from your roots was torn away;
You sighed—and cursed the stream.

With borrowed earth, and busy spade,
Around your roots new life I laid,
While joy revived in every vein;
(The care of man shall life impart)—
Though *Nature* owns the aid of art,
No art, immortal, makes their reign.

How much alike our fortune—say—
Yet, why must I so soon decay

When thou hast scarcely reached thy prime—
Erect and tall, you joyous stand;
The staff of age has found my hand,
That guides me to the grave of time.

Could I, fair tree, like you, resign,
And banish all those fears of mine,
Grey hairs would be no cause of grief;
Your blossoms die, but you remain,
Your fruit lies scattered o'er the plain—
Learn wisdom from the falling leaf.

As you survive, by heaven's decree,
Let withered flowers be thrown on me
Sad compensation for my doom,
While winter greens and withering pines,
And cedars dark, and barren vines,
Point out the lonely tomb.

The enlivening sun, that burns so bright,
Ne'er had a noon without a night,
So LIFE and DEATH agree;
The joys of man by years are broke"—
'Twas thus the man of ninety spoke,
    Then rose, and left his tree.

1788

ALCINA'S ENCHANTED ISLAND.*

IN these fair fields unfading flowers abound,
Here purple roses cloathe the enchanted ground;
Here, to the sun expand the lillies pale
Fann'd by the sweet breath of the western gale:

Here, fearless hares through dark recesses stray,
And troops of leverets take the woodland way,

* Text from the 1795 edition, where it is entitled—in the table of contents—a "translation." Freneau's note on the poem reads, "From the Italian of Ariosto." [Ed.]

Here stately stags, with branching horns, appear,
And rove unsought for, unassail'd by fear:

Unknown the snare, the huntsman's fatal dart
That wings the death of torture to the heart,
In social bands they trace the sylvan reign,
Chew the rich cud, or graze along the plain.

In these gay shades the nimble deer delight,
While herds of goats ascend the rocky height,
Browse on the shrubs that shade the vale below,
And crop the plants, that there profusely grow.

1788

HORACE, LIB. I. ODE 15.

Nereus prophesies the destruction of Troy.

AS 'cross the deep to Priam's shore
The Trojan prince bright Helen bore,
Old *Nereus* hushed each noisy breeze
And calmed the tumults of the seas.

Then, musing on the traitor's doom,
Thus he foretold the woes to come;
"Ah why remove, mistaken swain,
"The prize that Greece shall seize again!

"With omens sad, you sail along;
"And Europe shall resent the wrong,
"Conspire to seize your bride away,
"And Priam's town in ashes lay.

"Alas! what toils and deaths combined!
"What hosts of man and horses joined!—
"Bold Pallas now prepares her shield,
"And arms her chariot for the field.

"Can *you* with heavenly forms engage,
"A goddess kindling into rage;
"*Who* ne'er have dared a mortal foe
"And wars, alone, of Venus, know.

"In vain you dress your flowing hair,
"And songs, to aid the harp, prepare;
"The harp, that sung to female ears,
"Shall fail when *Mars* and *Greece* appears.

"In vain will you bewail your bride,
"And meanly in her chamber hide,
"In hopes to shun, when lingering there,
"The massy dart, and *Cretan* spear.

"In vain will you, with quickening pace,
"Avoid fierce Ajax in the chace;
"For late those locks, that please the eye,
"In dust and death must scattered lie.

"Do you not see *Ulysses*, too,
"The sage that brings your nation low:
"And *Nestor* from the land of *Pyle*—
"Chiefs skilled in arms and martial toil.

"Dost thou not see bold *Teucer* here,
"And *him*—no tardy charioteer;
"Who both pursue with eager force,
"And both controul the thundering horse.

"Thou, to thy grief, shalt *Merion* know,
"And *Tydeus' son* shall prove thy foe,
"Who wastes your realms with sword and fire;
"*Tydides*, greater than his sire.

"Like timorous deer, prepared to fly
"When hungry wolves are passing by,
"No more the herbs their steps detain,
"They quit their pastures, and the plain:

"So you from his triumphant arms
"Will fly, with all your female charms;
"Can deeds, like these, your valour prove,
"Was this your promise to your love?

"*Achilles'* wrath shall but delay
"Your ruin to a later day—
"The Trojan matrons then may mourn,
"And Troy by Grecian vengeance burn."

1788

PALEMON TO LAVINIA.

(*Written 1788*)

"TORN from your arms by rude relentless hands,
No tears recall our lost Alcander home,
Who, far removed by fierce piratic bands,
Finds in a foreign soil * an early tomb:

Well may you grieve!—his race so early done,
No years he reached, to urge some task sublime;—
No conquests made, no brilliant action won,
No verse to bear him through the gulph of time.

Amidst these shades and heart depressing glooms,
What comfort shall we give—what can we say;
In her distress shall we discourse on tombs,
Or tell *Lavinia*, 'tis a cloudy day?

The pensive priest accosts her with a sigh:
With movement slow, in sable robes he came—
But why so sad, philosopher, ah, why,
Since from the tomb alone all bliss we claim?

By pining care and wakeful sorrow worn,
While silent griefs her downcast heart engage,
She saw me go, and saw me thrice return
To pen my musings on some vacant page.

To learning's store, to Galen's science bred,
I saw *Orestes* rove through all the plain:
His pensive step no friendly genius led
To find one plant that might relieve your pain!

* Algiers, the piratical city on the coast of Barbary.

Say, do I wake?—or are your woes a dream!
Depart, dread vision!—waft me far away:
Seek me no more by this sky painted stream
That glides, unconscious, to the Indian bay.

Alcander!—ah!—what tears for thee must flow—
What doom awaits the wretch that tortured thee!
May never flower in his cursed garden blow,
May never fruit enrich his hated tree:

May that fine spark, which Nature lent to man,
Reason, be thou extinguished in his brain;
Sudden his doom, contracted be his span,
Ne'er to exist, or spring from dust again.

May no kind genius save his step from harms:
Where'er he sails, may tempests rend the sea;
May never maiden yield to him her charms,
Nor prattling infant hang upon his knee!

Retire, retire, forget the inhuman shore:
Dark is the sun, when woes like these dismay;
Resign your groves, and view with joy no more
The fragrant orange, and the floweret gay."

[w. 1788]   1795

TO LYDIA.*

> "*Tu procul a patria, ah dura! inculta deserta,*
> *Me sine, sola videbis* . . . .
>
> Virg. ECLOG.

THUS, safe arrived, she greets the strand,
And leaves her pilot for the land;
But LYDIA, why to the deserts roam,
And thus forsake your floating home!

* Miss Lydia Morriss, a young quaker lady, on her landing from
the sloop Industry at Savannah, in Georgia, December 30*th*. 1806.

To what fond care shall I resign
The bosom, that must ne'er be mine:
With lips, that glow beyond all art,
Oh! how shall I consent to part!—

Long may you live, secure from woes,
Late dying, meet a calm repose,
And flowers, that in profusion grow,
Bloom round your steps, where'er you go.

On you all eyes delight to gaze,
All tongues are lavish in your praise;
With you no beauty can compare,
Nor GEORGIA boast one flower so fair.

Could I, fair girl, transmit this page,
A present, to some future age,
You should through every poem shine,
You, be adored in every line:

From JERSEY coasts too loath to sail,
Sighing, she left her native vale;
Borne on a stream that met the main,
Homeward she looked, and looked again.

The gales that blew from off the land
Most wantonly her bosom fanned,
And, while around that heaven they strove,
Each whispering zephyr owned his love.

As o'er the seas, with you I strayed,
The hostile winds our course delayed,
But, proud to waft a charge so fair,
To me were kind—and held you there.

I could not grieve, when you complained
That adverse gales our barque detained
Where foaming seas to mountains grow,
From gulphs of death, concealed below.

When travelling o'er that lonely wave
To me your feverish hand you gave,
And sighing, bade me tell you, true,
What lands again would rise to view!

When night came on, with blustering gale,
You feared the tempest would prevail,
And anxious asked, if I was sure
That on those depths we sailed secure?

Delighted with a face so fair,
I half forgot my weight of care,
The dangerous shoal, that seaward runs,
Encircled moons, and shrouded suns.

With timorous heart and tearful eyes,
You saw the deep Atlantic rise,
Saw wintry clouds their storms prepare,
And wept, to find no safety there.

Throughout the long December's night,
(While still your lamp was burning bright)
To dawn of day from evening's close
My pensive girl found no repose.

Then now, at length arrived from sea,
Consent, fair nymph, to stay with me—
The barque—still faithful to her freight,
Shall still on your direction wait.

Such charms as your's all hearts engage!
Sweet subject of my glowing page,
Consent, before my Argo roves
To sun-burnt isles and savage groves.

When sultry suns around us glare,
Your poet, still, with fondest care,
To cast a shade, some folds will spread
Of his coarse topsails o'er your head.

When round the barque the billowy wave
And howling winds, tempestuous, rave,
By caution ruled, the helm shall guide
Safely, that Argo o'er the tide.

Whene'er some female fears prevail,
At your request we'll reef the sail,
Disarm the gales that rudely blow,
And bring the loftiest canvas low.

When rising to harass the main
Old Boreas drives his blustering train,
Still shall they see, as they pursue,
Each tender care employed for you.

To all your questions—every sigh!
I still will make a kind reply;
Give all you ask, each whim allow,
And change my style to *thee* and *thou*.

If verse can life to beauty give,
For ages I can make you live;
Beyond the stars, triumphant, rise,
While Cynthia's tomb neglected lies:

Upon that face of mortal clay
I will such lively colours lay,
That years to come shall join to seek
All beauty from your modest cheek.

Then, Lydia, why our bark forsake;
The road to western deserts take?
That lip—on which hung half my bliss,
Some savage, now, will bend to kiss;

Some rustic soon, with fierce attack,
May force his arms about that neck;
And you, perhaps, will weeping come
To seek—in vain—your floating home!

1788

TO CYNTHIA.

THROUGH Jersey groves, a wandering stream
That still its wonted music keeps,
Inspires no more my evening dream,
Where Cynthia, in retirement, sleeps.

Sweet murmuring stream! how blest art thou
To kiss the bank where she resides,
Where Nature decks the beechen bough
That trembles o'er your shallow tides.

The cypress-tree on *Hermit's height*,
Where Love his soft addresses paid
By Luna's pale reflected light—
No longer charms me to its shade!

To me, alas! so far removed,
What raptures, once, that scenery gave,
Ere wandering yet from all I loved,
I sought a deeper, drearier wave.

Your absent charms my thoughts employ:
I sigh to think how sweet you sung,
And half adore the painted toy
That near my careless heart you hung.

Now, fettered fast in icy fields,
In vain we loose the sleeping sail;
The frozen wave no longer yields,
And useless blows the favouring gale.

Yet, still in hopes of vernal showers,
And breezes, moist with morning dew,
I pass the lingering, lazy hours,
Reflecting on the spring—and you.

1789

AMANDA'S COMPLAINT.

"IN shades we live, in shades we die,
Cool zephyrs breathe for our repose;
In shallow streams we love to play,
But, cruel you, that praise deny
Which you might give, and nothing lose,
And then pursue your destined way.

Ungrateful man! when anchoring here,
On shore you came to beg relief;
I shewed you where the fig trees grow,
And wandering with you, free from fear,
To hear the story of your grief
I pointed where the cisterns are,
And would have shewn, if streams did flow!

The MEN that spurned your ragged crew,
So long exposed to Neptune's rage—
I told them what your sufferings were:
Told them that landsmen never knew
The trade that hastens frozen age,
The life that brings the brow of care.

A lamb, the loveliest of the flock,
To your disheartened crew I gave,
Life to sustain on yonder deep—
Sighing, I cast one sorrowing look
When on the margin of the main
You slew the loveliest of my sheep.

Along your native northern shores,
From cape to cape, where'er you stray,
Of all the nymphs that catch the eye,
They scarce can be excelled by our's—
Not in more fragrant shades they play;—
The summer suns come not so nigh.

Confess your fault, mistaken swain,
And own, at least, our equal charms—
Have you no flowers of ruddy hue,
That please your fancy on the plain?—
Would you not guard those flowers from harm,
If NATURE'S SELF each picture drew!

Vain are your sighs—in vain your tears,
Your barque must still at anchor lay,
And you remain a slave to care;
A thousand doubts, a thousand fears,
'Till what you said, you shall unsay,
Bermudian damsels are not fair!

1790

HATTERAS.*

IN fathoms five the anchor gone;
While here we furl the sail,
No longer vainly labouring on
Against the western gale:
While here thy bare and barren cliffs,
O HATTERAS, I survey,
And shallow grounds and broken reefs—
What shall console my stay!

The dangerous shoal, that breaks the wave
In columns to the sky;
The tempests black, that hourly rave,
Portend all danger nigh:
Sad are my dreams on ocean's verge!
The Atlantic round me flows,
Upon whose ancient angry surge
No traveller finds repose!

The PILOT comes!—from yonder sands
He shoves his barque, so frail,
And hurrying on, with busy hands,
Employs both oar and sail.

* Text from the edition of 1795. [Ed.]

Beneath this rude unsettled sky
Condemn'd to pass his years,
No other shores delight his eye,
No foe alarms his fears.

In depths of woods his hut he builds,
Devoted to repose,
And, blooming, in the barren wilds
His little garden grows:
His wedded nymph, of sallow hue,
No mingled colours grace—
For her he toils—to her is true,
The captive of her face.

Kind Nature here, to make him blest,
No quiet harbour plann'd;
And poverty—his constant guest,
Restrains the pirate band:
His hopes are all in yonder flock,
Or some few hives of bees,
Except, when bound for OCRACOCK,*
Some gliding barque he sees:

His Catharine then he quits with grief,
And spreads his tottering sails,
While, waving high her handkerchief,
Her commodore she hails:
She grieves, and fears to see no more
The sail that now forsakes,
From HATTERAS' sands to banks of CORE
Such tedious journies takes!

Fond nymph! your sighs are heav'd in vain;
Restrain those idle fears:

* All vessels from the northward that pass within Hatteras Shoals,
bound for Newbern and other places on Palmico Sound, commonly
in favourable weather take a Hatteras pilot to conduct them over the
dangerous bar of *Ocracock*, eleven leagues north southwest of the cape.

Can you—that should relieve his pain—
Thus kill him with your tears!
Can absence, thus, beget regard,
Or does it only seem?
He comes to meet a wandering bard
That steers for ASHLEY's stream.

Though disappointed in his views,
Not joyless will we part;
Nor shall the god of mirth refuse
The BALSAM OF THE HEART:
No niggard key shall lock up JOY—
I'll give him half my store
Will he but half his skill employ
To guard us from your shore.

Should eastern gales once more awake,
No safety will be here:—
Alack! I see the billows break,
Wild tempests hovering near:
Before the bellowing seas begin
Their conflict with the land,
Go, pilot, go—your Catharine join,
That waits on yonder sand.

1789

St. CATHARINE's.*

HE that would wish to rove a while
In forests green and gay,
From Charleston bar to Catharine's isle
Might sigh to find the way!
What scenes on every side appear,
What pleasure strikes the mind,
From Folly's train, thus wandering far,
To leave the world behind.

* An island on the sea-coast of Georgia. [Text from the edition of 1795.—Ed.]

The music óf these savage groves
In simple accents swells,
And freely, here, their sylvan loves
The feather'd nation tells;
The panting deer through mingled shades
Of oaks forever green
The vegetable world invades,
That skirts the watery scene.

Thou sailor, now exploring far
The broad Atlantic wave,
Crowd all your canvas, gallant tar,
Since Neptune never gave
On barren seas so fine a view
As here allures the eye,
Gay, verdant scenes that Nature drew
In colours from the sky.

Ye western winds! awhile delay
To swell the expecting sail—
Who would not here, a hermit, stay
In yonder fragrant vale,
Could he engage what few can find,
That coy, unwilling guest
(All avarice banish'd from the mind)
CONTENTMENT, in the breast!

[w. 1789]   1792

NEVERSINK.*

THESE Hills, the pride of all the coast,
To mighty distance seen,
With aspect bold and rugged brow,
That shade the neighbouring main:
These heights, for solitude design'd,
This rude, resounding shore—

* Text from the edition of 1795. [Ed.]

These vales impervious to the wind,
Tall oaks, that to the tempest bend,
Half Druid, I adore.

From distant lands, a thousand sails
Your hazy summits greet—
You saw the angry Briton come,
You saw him, last, retreat!
With towering crest, you first appear
The news of land to tell;
To him that comes, fresh joys impart,
To him that goes, a heavy heart,
The lover's long farewell.

'Tis your's to see the sailor bold,
Of persevering mind,
To see him rove in search of care,
And leave true bliss behind;
To see him spread his flowing sails
To trace a tiresome road,
By wintry seas and tempests chac'd
To see him o'er the ocean haste,
A comfortless abode!

Your thousand springs of waters blue
What luxury to sip,
As from the mountain's breast they flow
To moisten Flora's lip!
In vast retirements herd the deer,
Where forests round them rise,
Dark groves, their tops in aether lost,
That, haunted still by Huddy's ghost,
The trembling rustic flies.

Proud heights! with pain so often seen,
(With joy beheld once more)
On your firm base I take my stand,
Tenacious of the shore:—

Let those who pant for wealth or fame
Pursue the watery road;—
Soft sleep and ease, blest days and nights,
And health, attend these favourite heights,
Retirement's blest abode!

1791

The
WANDERER *

AS Southward bound to Indian isles
O'er lonely seas he held his way,
A songster of the feather'd kind
Approach'd, with golden plumage gay:

By sympathetic feelings led
And grieving for her sad mischance,
Thus Thyrsis to the wanderer said,
As circling in her airy dance.

" Sad pilgrim on a watery waste,
What cruel tempest has compell'd
To leave so far your native grove,
To perish on this liquid field!

Not such a dismal swelling scene
(Dread Neptune's wild unsocial sea)
But crystal brooks and groves of green,
Dear rambling bird, were made for thee.

Ah, why amid some flowery mead
Did you not stay, where late you play'd:
Not thus forsake the cypress grove
That lent its kind protecting shade.

In vain you spread your weary wings
To shun the hideous gulph below;

* Text from the edition of 1795. [Ed.]

Our barque can be your only hope—
But *man* you justly deem your foe.

Now hovering near, you stoop to lodge
Where yonder lofty canvas swells—
Again take wing—refuse our aid,
And rather trust the ruffian gales.

But Nature tires! your toils are vain—
Could you on stronger pinions rise
Than eagles have—for days to come
All you could see are seas and skies.

Again she comes, again she lights,
And casts a pensive look below—
Weak wanderer, trust the traitor, MAN,
And take the help that we bestow."

Down to his side, with circling flight,
She flew, and perch'd, and linger'd there;
But, worn with wandering, droop'd her wing,
And life resign'd in empty air.

1790

ON THE SLEEP OF PLANTS.

WHEN suns are set, and stars in view,
Not only *man* to slumber yields;
But Nature grants this blessing too,
To yonder *plants*, in yonder fields.

The Summer heats and lengthening days
(To them the same as toil and care)
Thrice welcome make the evening breeze,
That kindly does their strength repair.

At early dawn each plant survey,
And see, revived by Nature's hand,
With youthful vigour, fresh and gay,
Their blossoms blow, their leaves expand.

Yon' garden plant, with weeds o'er-run,
Not void of *thought*, perceives its hour,
And, watchful of the parting sun,
Throughout the night conceals her flower.

Like us, the slave of cold and heat,
She too enjoys her little span—
With *Reason*, only less complete
Than *that* which makes the boast of *man*.

Thus, moulded from one common clay,
A varied life adorns the plain;
By Nature subject to decay,
BY NATURE MEANT TO BLOOM AGAIN.

1790

STANZAS,

Occasioned by Lord Bellamont's, Lady Hay's, and
Other Skeletons, being dug up in Fort George
(N. Y.), 1790.

TO sleep in peace when life is fled,
Where shall our mouldering bones be laid—
What care can shun—(I ask with tears)
The shovels of succeeding years!

Some have maintained, when life is gone,
This frame no longer is our own:
Hence doctors to our tombs repair,
And seize death's slumbering victims there.

Alas! what griefs must MAN endure!
Not even in FORTS he rests secure:—
Time dims the splendours of a crown,
And brings the loftiest rampart down.

The breath, once gone, no art recalls!
Away we haste to vaulted walls:

Some future whim inverts the plain,
And stars behold our bones again.

Those teeth, dear girls—so much your care—
(With which no ivory can compare)
Like *these* (that once were lady Hay's)
May serve the belles of future days.

Then take advice from yonder scull;
And, when the flames of life grow dull,
Leave not a TOOTH in either jaw,
Since dentists steal—and fear no law.

He, that would court a sound repose,
To barren hills and deserts goes:
Where busy hands admit no sun,
Where he may doze, 'till all is done.

Yet there, even there tho' slyly laid,
'Tis folly to defy the spade:
Posterity invades the hill,
And plants our relics where she will.

But O! forbear the rising sigh!
All care is past with them that die:
Jove gave, when they to fate resigned,
An opiate of the strongest kind:

Death is a sleep, that has no dreams:
In which all time a moment seems—
And skeletons perceive no pain
Till Nature bids them wake again.

1790

The
ORATOR OF THE WOODS.

EACH traveller asks, with fond surprize,
Why *Thyrsis* wastes the fleeting year
Where gloomy forests round him rise,

And only rustics come to hear—
His taste is odd (they seem to say)
Such talents in so poor a way!

To those that courts and titles please
How dismal is his lot;
Beyond the hills, beneath some trees,
To live—and be forgot—
In dull retreats, where Nature binds
Her mass of clay to vulgar minds.

While you lament his barren trade,
Tell me—in yonder vale
Why grows that flower beneath the shade,
So feeble and so pale!—
Why was she not in sun-shine placed
To blush and please your men of taste?

In lonely wilds, those flowers so fair
No curious step allure;
And *chance*, not choice, has placed them there,
(Still charming, tho' obscure)
Where, heedless of such sweets so nigh,
The lazy hind goes loitering by.

1790

THE BERGEN PLANTER.

ATTACHED to lands that ne'er deceived his hopes,
This rustic sees the seasons come and go,
His autumn's toils returned in summer's crops,
While limpid streams, to cool his herbage, flow;
And, if some cares intrude upon his mind,
They are such cares as heaven for man designed.

He to no pompous dome comes, cap in hand,
Where new-made 'squires affect the courtly smile:
Nor where Pomposo, 'midst his foreign band

Extols the sway of kings, in swelling style,
With tongue that babbled when it should have hushed,
A head that never thought—a face that never blushed.

He on no party hangs his hopes or fears,
Nor seeks the vote that baseness must procure;
No stall-fed *Mammon*, for his gold, reveres,
No splendid offers from his chests allure.
While showers descend, and suns their beams display,
The same to him, if Congress go or stay.

He at no levees watches for a glance,
(Slave to disgusting, distant forms and modes)
Heeds not the herd of Bufo's midnight dance,
Dullman's mean rhymes, or Sawny's birth-day odes:
Follies, like these, he deems beneath his care,
And TITLES leaves for simpletons to wear.

Where wandering brooks from mountain sources roll,
He seeks at noon the waters of the shade,
Drinks deep, and fears no poison in the bowl
That Nature for her happiest children made:
And from whose clear and gently-passing wave
All drink alike—the master and the slave.

The scheming statesman shuns his homely door,
Who, on the miseries of his country fed,
Ne'er glanced his eye from that base pilfered store,
To view the sword, suspended by a thread—
Nor that "hand-writing," graved upon the wall,
That tells him—but in vain—"the sword must fall."

He ne'er was made a holiday machine,
Wheeled here and there by 'squires in livery clad,
Nor dreads the sons of legislation keen,
Hard-hearted laws, and penalties most sad—
In humble hope his little fields were sown,
A trifle, in your eye—but all his own.

1790

TOBACCO.

(Supposed to be written by a Young Beginner.)

THIS *Indian weed*, that once did grow
On fair *Virginia's* fertile plain,
From whence it came—again may go,
To please some happier swain:
Of all the plants that Nature yields
This, least beloved, shall shun my fields.

In evil hour I first essayed
To chew this vile forbidden leaf,
When, half ashamed, and half afraid,
I touched, and tasted—to my grief:
Ah me! the more I was forbid,
The more I wished to take a *quid*.

But when I smoaked, in thought profound,
And raised the spiral circle high,
My heart grew sick, my head turned round—
And what can all this mean, (said I)—
Tobacco surely was designed
To poison, and destroy mankind.

Unhappy they, whom choice, or fate
Inclines to prize this bitter weed;
Perpetual source of female hate;
On which no beast—but man will feed;
That sinks my heart, and turns my head,
And sends me, reeling, home to bed!

1790

THE BANISHED MAN.*

SINCE man may every region claim,
And Nature is, in most, the same,
And *we* a part of her wide plan,
Tell me, what makes THE BANISH'D MAN.

* Professor Pattee notes that this poem was "Published in the
Daily Advertiser, September 1, 1790, with the introduction: "A little

The favourite spot, that gave us birth,
We fondly call our mother earth;
And hence our vain distinctions grow,
And man to man becomes a foe.

That friendship to all nations due,
And taught by reason to pursue,
That love, which should the world combine,
To *country*, why do we confine!

The Grecian sage * (old stories say)
When question'd where his country lay,
Inspired by heaven, made no reply,
But rais'd his finger to the sky.

No region has, on earth, been known
But some, of choice, have made their own:—
Your tears are not from Reason's source
If *choice* assumes the path of *force*.

"Alas! (you cry) that is not all:
" My former friendships I recall,
" My house, my farm, my days, my nights,
" Scenes vanish'd now, and past delights."—

Distance for *absence* you mistake—
Here, days and nights their circuits make:
Here, Nature walks her beauteous round,
And friendship may—perhaps—be found.

If times grow dark, or wealth retires,
Let Reason check your proud desires:
Virtue the humblest garb can wear,
And loss of wealth is loss of care.

before Lord Bolingbroke was banished into France, he wrote an essay
upon Exile.—Some of his thoughts on that occasion are expressed
in the following Stanzas." [Ed.]
    * Anaxagoras.

Thus half unwilling, half resign'd,
Desponding, why, the generous mind?—
Think right,—nor be the hour delayed
That flies the sun to seek the shade.

Though injured, exiled, or alone,
Nobly presume the world your own,
Convinced that, since the world began,
Time, only, makes *The Banish'd Man.*

1790

LINES,

Occasioned by a Law passed by the Corporation of
New-York, early in 1790, for cutting down the trees
in the streets of that city, previous to June 10,
following.

THE CITIZEN'S SOLILOQUY.

A MAN that owned some trees in town,
(And much averse to cut them down)
Finding the *Law* was full and plain,
No trees should in the streets remain,
One evening seated at his door,
Thus gravely talked the matter o'er:

"The fatal DAY, dear trees, draws nigh,
When you must, like your betters, die,
Must die!—and every leaf will fade
That many a season lent its shade,
To drive from hence the summer heat,
And make my porch a favourite seat.

"Thrice happy age, when all was new,
And trees untouched, unenvied grew,
When yet regardless of the axe,
They feared no law, and paid no tax!

The shepherd then at ease was laid,
Or walked beneath their cooling shade;
From slender twigs a garland wove,
Or traced his god within the grove;
Alas! those times are now forgot,
An iron age is all our lot:
Men are not now what once they were,
To hoard up gold is all their care:
The busy tribe old Plutus calls
To pebbled streets and painted walls;
Trees now to grow, is held a crime,
And THESE must perish in their prime!

"The trees that once our fathers reared,
And even the plundering Briton spared,
When shivering here full oft he stood,
Or kept his bed for want of wood—
These trees, whose gently bending boughs
Have witnessed many a lover's vows,
When half afraid, and half in jest,
With Nature busy in his breast,
With many a sigh, he did not feign,
Beneath these boughs he told his pain,
Or coaxing here his nymph by night,
Forsook the parlour and the light,
In talking love, his greatest bliss
To squeeze her hand or steal a kiss—
These trees that thus have lent their shade,
And many a happy couple made,
These old companions, thus endeared,
Who never tattled what they heard,
Must these, indeed, be killed so soon—
Be murdered by the tenth of June!

" But if my harmless trees must fall,
A fortune that awaits us all,
(All, all must yield to Nature's stroke,
And now a man, and now an oak)

Are *those* that round the churches grow
In this decree included too?
Must these, like common trees, be bled?
Is it a crime to shade the dead?
Review the *law*, I pray, at least,
And have some mercy on the priest
Who every Sunday sweats in black
To make us steer the skyward track:
The church has lost enough, God knows,
Plundered alike by friends and foes—
I hate such mean attempts as these—
Come—let the parson keep his trees!

" Yet things, perhaps, are not so bad—
Perhaps, a *respite* may be had:
The vilest rogues that cut our throats,
Or knaves that counterfeit our *notes*,
When, by the judge their sentence passed,
The gallows proves their doom at last,
Swindlers and pests of every kind,
For weeks and months a *respite* find;
And shall such nuisances as they,
Who make all honest men their prey—
Shall they for months avoid their doom,
And you, my trees, in all your bloom,
Who never injured small or great,
Be murdered at so short a date!

" Ye men of law, the occasion seize,
And name a counsel for the trees—
Arrest of judgment, sirs, I pray;
Excuse them till some future day:
These trees that such a nuisance are,
Next NEW YEAR we can better spare,
To warm our shins, or boil the pot—
The LAW, *by then* will be forgot."

[w. 1790]   1792

LINES,

By H. Salem, on his Return from Calcutta.

YOUR men of the land, from the king to JACK KETCH,
All join in supposing the sailor a wretch,
That his life is a round of vexation and woe,
With always too much or too little to do:
In the dead of the night, when other men sleep,
He, starboard and larboard, his watches must keep;
Imprisoned by Neptune, he lives like a dog,
And to know where he is, must depend on a LOG,
Must fret in a calm, and be sad in a storm;
In winter much trouble to keep himself warm:
Through the heat of the summer pursuing his trade,
No trees, but his topmasts, to yield him a shade:
Then, add to the list of the mariner's evils,
The water corrupted, the bread full of weevils,
Salt junk to be eat, be it better or worse,
And, often bull beef of an Irishman's horse:
Whosoever is free, he must still be a slave,
(Despotic is always the rule on the wave;)
Not relished on water, your lords of the main
Abhor the republican doctrines of PAINE,
And each, like the despot of Prussia, may say
That his crew has no right, but the right to obey.
    Such things say the lubbers, and sigh when they've said 'em,
But things are not so bad as their fancies persuade 'em:
There ne'er was a task but afforded some ease,
Nor a calling in life, but had something to please.
If the sea has its storms, it has also its calms,
A time to sing songs and a time to sing psalms.—
Yes—give me a vessel well timbered and sound,
Her bottom good plank, and in rigging well-found,
If her spars are but staunch, and her oakham swelled tight,
From tempests and storms I'll extract some delight—
At sea I would rather have Neptune my jailor,
Than a lubber on shore, that despises a sailor.
Do they ask me what pleasure I find on the sea?—

Why, absence from land is a pleasure to me:
A hamper of porter, and plenty of grog,
A friend, when too sleepy, to give me a jog,
A coop that will always some poultry afford,
Some bottles of gin, and no parson on board,
A crew that is brisk when it happens to blow,
One compass on deck and another below,
A girl, with more sense than the girl at the head,
To read me a novel, or make up my bed—
The man that has these, has a treasure in store
That millions possess not, who live upon shore:
But if it should happen that commerce grew dull,
Or Neptune, ill-humoured, should batter our hull,
Should damage my cargo, or heave me aground,
Or pay me with farthings instead of a pound:
Should I always be left in the rear of the race,
And this be forever—forever the case;
Why then, if the honest plain truth I may tell,
I would clew up my topsails, and bid him farewell.

1791

MODERN DEVOTION.

(By H. Salem.)

TO church I went, with good intent,
To hear *Sangrado* preach and pray;
But objects there, black, brown, and fair,
Turned eyes and heart a different way.

Miss Patty's fan, miss Molly's man,
With powdered hair and dimple cheek;
Miss Bridget's eyes, that once made prize
Of *Fopling* with his hair so sleek:

Embroidered gowns, and play-house tunes
Estranged all hearts from heaven too wide:
I felt most odd, this house of God
Should all be flutter, pomp, and pride.

Now, pray be wise, no prayers will rise
To heaven—where hearts are not sincere.
No church was made for Cupid's trade;
Then why these arts of ogling here?

Since time draws nigh, when you and I,
At church must claim the sexton's care!—
Leave pride at home, when'er you come
To pay to heaven your offerings, *there!*

1791

THE PARTING GLASS.

(Written at an Inn)

(By Hezekiah Salem.)

THE man that joins in life's career
And hopes to find some comfort here;
To rise above this earthly mass,
The only way's to drink his GLASS.

But, still, on this uncertain stage,
Where hopes and fears the soul engage;
And while, amid the joyous band,
Unheeded flows the measured sand,
Forget not as the moments pass,
That TIME *shall bring the parting glass!*

In spite of all the mirth I've heard,
This is the glass I always feared;
The glass that would the rest destroy,
The farewell cup, the close of joy!

With YOU whom Reason taught to *think*,
I could, for ages, sit and drink:
But with the fool, the sot, the ass,
I haste to take the parting glass.

The luckless wight, that still delays
His draught of joys to future days,
Delays too long—for then, alas!
Old age steps up, and—breaks the glass!

The nymph, who boasts no borrowed charms,
Whose sprightly wit my fancy warms;
What tho' she tends this country inn,
And mixes wine, and deals out *gin?*
With such a kind, obliging lass
I sigh, to take the parting glass.

With him, who always talks of gain,
(Dull Momus, of the plodding train)—
The wretch, who thrives by others' woes,
And carries grief where'er he goes:—
With people of this knavish class
The first is still my parting glass.

With those that drink before they dine—
With him that apes the grunting swine,
Who fills his page with low abuse,
And strives to act the gabbling goose
Turned out by fate to feed on grass—
Boy, give me quick, the parting glass.

The man, whose friendship is sincere,
Who knows no guilt, and feels no fear:—
It would require a heart of brass
With him to take the parting glass!

With him, who quaffs his pot of ale;
Who holds to all an even scale;
Who hates a knave, in each disguise,
And fears him not—whate'er his size—
With him, well pleased my days to pass,
May heaven forbid the PARTING GLASS!

1790

THE DISH OF TEA.

Let some in beer place their delight,
O'er bottled porter waste the night,
   Or sip the rosy wine:
A dish of TEA more pleases me,
Yields softer joys, provokes less noise,
   And breeds no base design.

From China's groves, this present brought,
Enlivens every power of thought,
   Riggs many a ship for sea:
Old maids it warms, young widows charms;
And ladies' men, not one in ten
   But courts them for their TEA.

When throbbing pains assail my head,
And dullness o'er my brain is spread,
   (The muse no longer kind)
A single sip dispels the hyp:
To chace the gloom, fresh spirits come,
   The flood-tide of the mind.

When worn with toil, or vext with care,
Let *Susan* but this draught prepare,
   And I forget my pain.
This magic bowl revives the soul;
With gentlest sway, bids care be gay;
   Nor mounts, to cloud the brain.—

If learned men the truth would speak
They prize it far beyond their GREEK,
   More fond attention pay;
No HEBREW root so well can suit;
More quickly taught, less dearly bought,
   Yet *studied* twice a day.

This leaf, from distant regions sprung,
Puts life into the female tongue,
   And aids the cause of love.
Such power has TEA o'er bond and free;
Which *priests* admire, delights the *'squire*,
   And *Galen's* sons approve.

1792

STANZAS

TO THE MEMORY OF TWO YOUNG PERSONS (TWIN BROTH-
ERS), ROBERT SEVIER AND WILLIAM SEVIER, WHO WERE
KILLED BY THE SAVAGES ON CUMBERLAND RIVER, IN
NORTH-CAROLINA, IN ATTEMPTING TO ASSIST A NEW
SETTLER, WHO WAS THEN PASSING THE RIVER WITH A
NUMEROUS FAMILY.

IN the same hour two lovely youths were born,
   Nature, with care, had moulded either clay:
In the same hour, from this world's limits torn,
   The murderous Indian seized their lives away.

Distress to aid, impelled each generous breast;
   With nervous arm they braved the adverse tide,
In friendship's cause encountered death's embrace,
   Blameless they lived, in honour's path they died.

But ah! what art shall dry a father's tears!
   Who shall relieve, or what beguile his pain!
Clouds shade his sun, and griefs advance with years—
   Nature gave joys, to take those joys again.

Thou, that shall come to these sequestered streams,
   When times to come their story shall relate;
Let the fond heart, that native worth esteems,
   Revere their virtues, and bemoan their fate.

1792

ELEGY

On the Death of a Blacksmith.

WITH the nerves of a Samson, this son of the sledge,
By the anvil his livelihood got;
With the skill of old Vulcan could temper an edge;
And struck—while his iron was hot.

By *forging* he lived, yet never was tried,
Or condemned by the laws of the land;
But still it is certain, and can't be denied,
He often was *burnt in the hand*.

With the sons of St. Crispin no kindred he claimed,
With the *last* he had nothing to do;
He handled no awl, and yet in his time
Made many an excellent *shoe*.

He blew up no coals of sedition, but still
His bellows was always in blast;
And we will acknowledge (deny it who will)
That one *Vice*, and but *one*, he possessed.

No actor was he, or concerned with the stage,
No audience, to awe him, appeared;
Yet oft in his shop (like a crowd in a rage)
The voice of a *hissing* was heard.

Tho' *steeling* was certainly part of his cares,
In thieving he never was found;
And, tho' he was constantly *beating on bars*,
No vessel he e'er ran aground.

Alas and alack! and what more can I say
Of Vulcan's unfortunate son?—
The priest and the sexton have borne him away,
And the sound of his hammer is done.

1793

TO SYLVIUS,

On his Preparing to Leave the Town

CAN love of fame the gentle muse inspire
Where he that hoards the most has all the praise;
Where avarice, and her tribe, each bosom fire,
All heap the enormous store for rainy days;
Proving by such perpetual round of toil
That man was born to grovel on the soil?

Expect not, in these times of rude renown
That verse, like your's, will have the chance to please:
No taste for plaintive elegy is known,
Nor lyric ode—none care for things like these—
Gold, only gold, this niggard age delights,
That honours none but *money-catching* wights.

Sink not beneath the mean abusive strain
Of puny wits, dull sycophants in song,
Who, post, or place, or one poor smile to gain,
Besiege Mambrino's door, and round him throng
Like insects creeping to the morning sun
To enjoy his heat—themselves possessing none.

All must applaud your choice, to quit a stage
Where knaves and fools in every scene abound;
Where modest worth no patron can engage—
But boisterous folly walks her noisy round;
Some narrow-hearted demi-god adores,
And Fortune's path with servile step explores.

1795

The DRUNKARD'S APOLOGY *

" You blame the blushes on my nose,
" And yet admire the blushing rose;
" On CELIA's cheek the bloom you prize,
" And yet, on mine, that bloom despise.

* Text from the edition of 1795. [Ed.]

" The world of spirits you admire,
" To which all holy men aspire:
" Yet, me with curses you requite,
" Because in *spirits* I delight.

" Whene'er I fall, and crack my crown,
" You blame me much for *falling down*—
" Yet to some *god*, that you adore,
" You, too, fall prostrate on the floor.

" You call me fool, for drinking hard;
" And yet old HUDSON you regard,
" Who fills his jug from yonder bay,
" And drinks his guts-full, every day! "—

1795

To a
DECEASED DOG. *

IF all the world mourns for the loss of a friend,
And even in stanzas their virtues commend,
Why, SANCHO, shouldst thou by the green turf be prest,
And not have a stanza along with the rest?

The miser, that ne'er gave a farthing away,
Xantippe, that scolded throughout the long day,
The drunken young Quixote, that died in his prime,
In their graves never fail to be flatter'd with rhyme.

There is an old adage our poets have read,
That "nothing but good should be spoke of the dead:"
Hence, the prophet and the sexton alike we defy,
When we write of the DEAD—they allow us to lie.

But I, my dear DOG, will a poem compose
That shall break half the hearts of the belles and the beaus;

* Text from the edition of 1795. [Ed.]

To the view of each reader your VIRTUES shall shine
In verses, that HANNAH will fancy divine.

The Stoics, of old, were forbid to complain
At losses and crosses, vexation and pain;
When the day I recall, that depriv'd me of you,
I find, my dear Sancho, I'm not of their crew.

How oft in the year shall I visit your grave
Amid the long forest, that darkens the wave!
How often lament, when the day's at the close,
That a mile from the church is your place of repose!

Ah here (I will say) is the path where he run;
And there stands the tree where a squirrel he won;
And here, in this spot where the willow trees grow,
He dragg'd out a rabbit that lurk'd in the snow.

If absent, awhile, on the ocean I stray'd,
I still had in view to revisit this shade—
But alas! you consider'd the prospect as vain,
Or how could you die, 'till I saw you again?

A country there is—'tis in vain to deny—
Where monkies and puppies are sent when they die,
But you—and old Minos shall grant you a pass,
Must rank with the dogs of the gentleman class.

The boatman of STYX shall a passage prepare,
And the *Dog*, at the portal, shall welcome you there;
With the cynics of hell you shall walk a grave pace,
Where "Doctors with dogs" is no more a disgrace.

On the bark of this beech-tree, that shadows your bones,
With tears, I inscribe these poetical groans:
If a *tombstone of wood* serves a soldier, 'tis clear
This tree may preserve all your fame—for a year.

For the squirrel you tree'd, and the duck from the lake,
These stanzas are all the return I can make:
But these, unaffected, my friendship will shew,
And the world will allow—that I give you your due.

1795

JACK STRAW:

or the

FOREST BEAU.*

WHEN first to feel Love's fire JACK STRAW begins
He combs his hair, and cocks his hat with pins,
Views in some stream, his face, with fond regard,
Plucks from his upper lip the bristly beard,
With soap and sand his homely visage scowers
(Rough from the joint attack of sun and showers)
The sheepskin breeches stretch'd upon his thighs,—
Next on his back the homespun coat he tries;
Round his broad breast he wraps the jerkin blue,
And sews a spacious soal on either shoe.
Thus, all prepar'd, the fond adoring swain
Cuts from his groves of pine a ponderous cane;
In thought a beau, a savage to the eye,
Forth, from his mighty bosom, heaves the sigh;
Tobacco is the present for his fair,
This he admires, and this best pleases her—
The bargain struck—few cares his bosom move
How to maintain, or how to lodge his love;
Close at his hand the piny forest grows,
Thence for his hut a slender frame he hews,
With art, (not copied from *Palladio's* rules,)
A hammer and an axe, his only tools,
By Nature taught, a hasty hut he forms
Safe in the woods, to shelter from the storms;—
There sees the summer pass and winter come,
Nor envies Britain's king his loftier home.

1795

* Text from the edition of 1795. [Ed.]

EPISTLE

to a

Student of Dead Languages.*

I PITY him, who, at no small expense,
Has studied sound instead of sense:
He, proud some antique gibberish to attain;
Of Hebrew, Greek, or Latin, vain,
Devours the husk, and leaves the grain.

In *his own language* HOMER writ and read,
Not spent his life in poring on the *dead:*
Why then your native language not pursue
In which all ancient sense (that's worth review)
Glows in translation, fresh and new?

He better plans, who *things*, not *words*, attends,
And turns his studious hours to active ends;
Who ART through every secret maze explores,
Invents, contrives—and Nature's hidden stores
From mirrours, to their object true,
Presents to man's obstructed view,
That dimly meets the light, and faintly soars:—

His strong capacious mind
By fetters unconfin'd
Of Latin lore and heathen Greek,
Takes Science in its way,
Pursues the kindling ray
'Till Reason's morn shall on him break!

1795

HERMIT'S VALLEY.

WITH eastern winds, and flowing sail
To these sequestered haunts we came,
Where verdant trees and chrystal streams

* Text from the edition of 1795. [Ed.]

Adorn the sloping, winding vale;
Where, from the breezy grove we claim,
Our heaven on earth—poetic dreams.

These simple scenes have pleasures more
Than all the busy town can show—
More pleasure here Philanthus took,
And more he prized this lonely shore,
His pen, his pencil, and his book,
Than all the groves Madeira bore:

Here still is seen a hermit's cell,
Who, fond the haunts of men to fly,
Enjoyed his heaven beneath this shade:
In mouldering caves so blest to dwell,
He sought not from the flowers that die,
A verdure, that would never fade.

To crowded courts and would-be kings,
Where *fawning knaves* are most caressed,
Who would, though oft' invited, go—
When here so many charming things
By Nature to perfection dressed,
To please the man of fancy, grow?

The native of this happy spot
No cares of vain ambition haunt:
Pleased with the partner of his nest,
Life flows—and when the dream is out,
The earth, which once supplied each want,
Receives him—fainting—to her breast.

1795

TO A NIGHT-FLY,

Approaching a Candle.*

ATTRACTED by the taper's rays,
How carelessly you come to gaze
On what absorbs you in its blaze!

* Text from the edition of 1815. [Ed.]

O Fly! I bid you have a care:
You do not heed the danger near;
This light, to you a blazing star.

Already you have scorch'd your wings:
What courage, or what folly brings
You, hovering near such blazing things?

Ah me! you touch this little sun—
One circuit more and all is done!—
Now to the furnace you are gone!—

Thus folly with ambition join'd,
Attracts the insects of mankind,
And sways the superficial mind:

Thus, power has charms which all admire,
But dangerous is that central fire—
If you are wise in time retire.—

1797

THE INDIAN CONVERT.

AN Indian, who lived at *Muskingum*, remote,
Was teazed by a parson to join his dear flock,
To throw off his blanket and put on a coat,
And of grace and religion to lay in a stock.

The Indian long slighted an offer so fair,
Preferring to preaching his fishing and fowling;
A *sermon* to him was a heart full of care,
And singing but little superior to howling.

At last by persuasion and constant harassing
Our Indian was brought to consent to be *good;*
He saw that the malice of *Satan* was pressing,
And the *means* to repel him not yet understood.

Of heaven, one day, when the parson was speaking,
And painting the beautiful things of the place,
The *convert*, who something substantial was seeking,
Rose up, and confessed he had doubts in the case.—

Said he, *Master Minister*, this place that you talk of,
Of things for the stomach, pray what has it got;
Has it liquors in plenty?—if so I'll soon walk off
And put myself down in the heavenly spot.

You fool (said the preacher) no liquors are there!
The place I'm describing is most like our meeting,
Good people, all singing, with preaching and prayer;
They live upon these without eating or drinking.

But the doors are all locked against folks that are wicked:
And you, I am fearful, will never get there:—
A life of REPENTANCE must purchase the ticket,
And few of you, Indians, can buy it, I fear.

Farewell (said the Indian) I'm none of your mess;
On victuals, so airy, I faintish should feel,
I cannot consent to be lodged in a place
Where's there's nothing to eat and but little to steal.

1797

On
ARRIVING IN SOUTH CAROLINA, 1798. *

A HAPPY gale presents, once more,
The gay and ever verdant shore,
Which every pleasure will restore
   To those who come again:
You, Carolina, from the seas
Emerging, claim all power to please,
Emerge with elegance and ease
   From Neptune's briny main.

* Text from the edition of 1815. [Ed.]

To find in you a happier home,
Retirement for the days to come,
From northern coasts you saw me roam,
　　By flattering fancy moved:
I came, and in your fragrant woods,
Your magic isles and gay abodes,
In rural haunts and passing floods
　　Review'd the scenes I loved,

When sailing oft, from year to year
And leaving all I counted dear,
I found the happy country here
　　Where manly hearts abound;
Where friendship's kind extended hand,
All social, leads a generous band;
Where heroes, who redeem'd the land
　　Still live to be renown'd:

Who live to fill the trump of fame,
Or, dying, left the honor'd name
Which *Athens* had been proud to claim
　　From her historian's page. . . .
These with invading thousands strove,
These bade the foe their prowess prove,
And from their old dominions drove
　　The tyrants of the age.

Long, long may every good be thine,
Sweet country, named from *Caroline,*
Once seen in Britain's court to shine
　　The fairest of the fair:
Still may the wanderer find a home
Where'er thy varied forests bloom,
And peace and pleasure with him come
　　To take their station here.

Here *Ashley,* with his brother stream,
By *Charleston* gliding, all, may claim,

That ever graced a poet's dream
 Or sooth'd a statesman's cares;
She, seated near her forests blue,
Which winter's rigor never knew,
With half an ocean in her view
 Her shining turrets rears.

Here stately oaks of living green
Along the extended coast are seen,
That rise beneath a heaven serene,
 Unfading through the year. . . .
In groves the tall Palmetto grows,
In shades inviting to repose,
The fairest, loveliest, scenes disclose. . . .
 All nature charms us here.

Dark wilds are thine, the yellow field,
And rivers by no frost congeal'd,
And, Ceres, all that you can yield
 To deck the festive board;
The snow white fleece, from pods that grows,
And every seed that Flora sows—
The orange and the fig-tree shows
 A paradise restored.

There rural love to bless the swains
In the bright eye of beauty reigns,
And brings a heaven upon the plains
 From some dear Emma's charms;
Some Laura fair who haunts the mead,
Some Helen, whom the graces lead,
Whose charms the charms of her exceed
 That set the world in arms.

And distant from the sullen roar
Of ocean, bursting on the shore,
A region rises, valued more
 Than all the shores possess:

There lofty hills their range display,
Placed in a climate ever gay,
From wars and commerce far away,
    Sweet nature's wilderness.

There all that art has taught to bloom,
The streams that from the mountain foam,
And thine, Eutaw, that distant roam,
    Impart supreme delight:
The prospect to the western glade,
The ancient forest, undecay'd—
All these the wildest scenes have made
    That ever awed the sight.

There *Congaree* his torrent pours,
Saluda, through the forest roars,
And black *Catawba* laves his shores
    With waters from afar,
Till mingled with the proud *Santee*,
Their strength, united, finds the sea,
Through many a plain, by many a tree,
    Then rush across the bar.

But, where all nature's fancies join,
Were but a single acre mine,
Blest with the cypress and the pine,
    I would request no more;
And leaving all that once could please,
The northern groves and stormy seas—
I would not change such scenes as these
    For all that men adore.

1815

LINES WRITTEN AT SEA.

NO pleasure on earth can afford such delights,
As the heavenly view of these tropical nights:
The glow of the stars, and the breeze of the sea,
Are heaven—if heaven on ocean can be.—

The star of old Cancer is right overhead,
And the sun in the water has travelled to bed;
He is gone, as some say, to recline at his ease,
And not, like ourselves, to be pestered with fleas.

What pity that here is no insular spot,
Where quarrels, and murder, and malice are not:
Where a stranger might land, to recruit his worn crew,
Replenish the casks, and the water renew.

On this Empire of waves, this expanse of the main,
In the track we are sailing, no island is seen:
The glow of the stars, and the breath of the wind
Are lost!—for they bring not the scent of the land!

Huge porpoises swim, where there should be an isle,
Where an Eden might bloom, or a Cyprus might smile—
From PALMA,* thus far, with a tedious delay,
Salt water and aether is all we survey!

Like an artist that's busy in melting his *lead*,
At random it falls, and is carelessly spread,
So Nature, though wisely this globe she has planned,
Left the surface to chance—to be sea, or be land.

1809

THE NAUTICAL RENDEZVOUS.†

Written at a house in Guadaloupe, in 1800, where they were Collecting recruits for a privateer

THE ship preparing for the main
Enlists a wild, but gallant train,
Who in a moving jail would roam
Digusted with the *world at home*.

* The most north-westerly of the Canary Islands.
† Text from the 1815 edition. [Ed.]

They quit the fields and quit the trees
To seek their bread on stormy seas;
Perhaps to see the land no more,
Or see, but not enjoy the shore.

There must be some as this world goes
Who every joy and pleasure lose,
And round the world at random stray
To gain their bread the shortest way.

They hate the ax, they hate the hoe
And execrate the rural plough,
The mossy bank, the sylvan shade
Where once they wrought, where once they play'd:

Prefer a boisterous, mad career,
A broken leg, and wounds severe,
To all the joys that can be found
On mountain top or furrow'd ground.

A hammock holds them when they sleep;
A tomb, when dying, in the deep,
A crowded deck, a cann of beer
These sons of Amphitrite prefer
To all the verdure of the fields
Or all a quiet pillow yields.

There must be such a nervous race,
Who venture all, and no disgrace;
Who will support through every blast,
The shatter'd ship, the falling mast—
Who will support through every sea
The sacred cause of liberty,
And every foe to ruin drag
Who aims to strike the gallic flag.

[w. 1800]   1815

A

BACCHANALIAN DIALOGUE.*

Written 1803.

ARRIVED at Madeira, the island of vines,
    Where mountains and vallies abound,
Where the sun the wild juice of the cluster refines,
    To gladden the magical ground:

As pensive I stray'd in her elegant shade,
    Now halting and now on the move,
Old Bacchus I met, with a crown on his head,
    In the darkest recess of a grove.

I met him with awe, but no symptom of fear
    As I roved by his mountains and springs,
When he said with a sneer, " how dare you come here,
    You hater of despots and kings?—

Do you know that a prince, and a regent renown'd
    Presides in this island of wine?
Whose fame on the earth has encircled it round
    And spreads from the pole to the line?

Haste away with your barque: on the foam of the main
    To Charleston I bid you repair:
There drink your Jamaica, that maddens the brain;
    You shall have no Madeira—I swear."

" Dear Bacchus," (I answered) for Bacchus it was
    That spoke in this menacing tone:
I knew by the smirk and the flush on his face
    It was Bacchus, and Bacchus alone—

" Dear Bacchus, (I answered) ah, why so severe?—
    Since your nectar abundantly flows,
Allow me one cargo—without it I fear
    Some people will soon come to blows:

* Text from the edition of 1815. [Ed.]

I left them in wrangles, disorder, and strife,
   Political feuds were so high,
I was sick of their quarrels, and sick of my life,
   And almost requested to die."

The deity smiling, replied, " I relent:—
   For the sake of your coming so far,
Here, taste of my choicest—go, tell them repent,
   And cease their political war.

With the cargo I send, you may say, I intend
   To hush them to peace and repose;
With this present of mine, on the wings of the wind
   You shall travel, and tell them, here goes

A health to old Bacchus! who sends them the best
   Of the nectar his island affords,
The soul of the feast and the joy of the guest,
   Too good for your monarchs and lords.

No rivals have I in this insular waste,
   Alone will I govern the isle
With a king at my feet, and a court to my taste,
   And all in the popular style.

But a spirit there is in the order of things,
   To me it is perfectly plain,
That will strike at the scepters of despots and kings,
   And only king Bacchus remain."

[w. 1803]   1815

OCTOBER'S ADDRESS:*

October came the thirtieth day:
And thus I heard October say;

" THE lengthening nights and shortening days
   Have brought the year towards a close,

* Text from the 1815 edition. [Ed.]

The oak a leafless bough displays
  And all is hastening to repose;
    To make the most of what remains
    Is now to take the greater pains.

" An orange hue the grove assumes,
  The indian-summer-days appear;
When that deceitful summer comes
  Be sure to hail the winter near:
    If autumn wears a mourning coat
    Be sure, to keep the mind afloat.

" The flowers have dropt, their blooms are gone,
  The herbage is no longer green;
The birds are to their haunts withdrawn,
  The leaves are scatter'd through the plain;
    The sun approaches Capricorn,
    And man and creature looks forlorn.

" Amidst a scene of such a cast,
  The driving sleet, or falling snow,
The sullen cloud, the northern blast,
  What have you left for comfort now,
    When all is dead, or seems to die
    That cheer'd the heart or charm'd the eye?

" To meet the scene, and it arrives,
  (A scene that will in time retire)
Enjoy the *pine*—while that remains
  You need not want the winter fire.
    It rose unask'd for, from the plain,
    And when consumed, will rise, again.

"Enjoy the glass, enjoy the board,
  Nor discontent will fate betray,
Enjoy what reason will afford,
  Nor disregard what females say;
    Their chat will pass away the time,
    When out of cash or out of rhyme.

"The cottage warm and cheerful heart
  Will cheat the stormy winter night,
Will bid the glooms of care depart
  And to December give delight."—
    Thus spoke October—rather gay,
    Then seized his staff, and walk'd away.

1815

To

A CATY–DID.[1] *

In a branch of a willow hid
Sings the evening Caty-did:
From the lofty locust bough
Feeding on a drop of dew,
In her suit of green array'd
Hear her singing in the shade
    Caty-did, Caty-did, Caty-did!

While upon a leaf you tread,
Or repose your little head,
On your sheet of shadows laid,
All the day you nothing said:
Half the night your cheery tongue
Revell'd out its little song,
    Nothing else but Caty-did.

From your lodgings on the leaf
Did you utter joy or grief—?
Did you only mean to say,
I have had my summer's day,
And am passing, soon, away
To the grave of Caty-did;—
    Poor, unhappy Caty-did!

[1] Text from the edition of 1815.

* A well-known insect, when full grown, about two inches in length, and of the exact color of a green leaf. It is of the genius cicada, or grasshopper kind, inhabiting the green foliage of trees and singing such a song as *Caty-did* in the evening, towards autumn.

But you would have utter'd more
Had you known of nature's power—
From the world when you retreat,
And a leaf's your winding sheet,
Long before your spirit fled,
Who can tell but nature said,
Live again, my Caty-did!
Live, and chatter Caty-did.

Tell me, what did Caty do?
Did she mean to trouble you?—
Why was Caty not forbid
To trouble little Caty-did?—
Wrong, indeed at you to fling,
Hurting no one while you sing
Caty-did! Caty-did! Caty-did!

Why continue to complain?
Caty tells me, she again
Will not give you plague or pain:—
Caty says you may be hid
Caty will not go to bed
While you sing us Caty-did.
Caty-did! Caty-did! Caty-did!

But, while singing, you forgot
To tell us what did Caty *not:*
Caty-did not think of cold,
Flocks retiring to the fold,
Winter, with his wrinkles old,
Winter, that yourself foretold
When you gave us Caty-did.

Stay securely in your nest;
Caty now, will do her best,
All she can, to make you blest;
But, you want no human aid—
Nature, when she form'd you, said,

"Independent you are made,
My dear little Caty-did:
Soon yourself must disappear
With the verdure of the year,"—
And to go, we know not where,
    With your song of Caty-did.

1815

On Passing
BY AN OLD CHURCHYARD.*

PENSIVE, on this turf I cast my eye,
And almost feel inclined to muse and sigh:
Such tokens of mortality so nigh.

But hold,—who knows if these who soundly sleep,
Would not, alive, have made some orphan weep,
Or plunged some slumbering victim in the deep.

There may be here, who once were virtue's foes,
A curse through life, the cause of many woes,
Who wrong'd the widow, and disturb'd repose.

There may be here, who with malicious aim
Did all they could to wound another's fame,
Steal character, and filch away good name.

Perhaps yond' solitary turf invests
Some who, when living, were the social pests,
Patrons of ribands, titles, crowns and crests.

Can we on such a kindred tear bestow?
They, who, in life, were every just man's foe,
A plague to all about them!—oh, no, no.

What though sepultured with the funeral whine;
Why, sorrowing on such tombs should we recline,
Where truth, perhaps, has hardly penn'd a line.

* Text from the edition of 1815. [Ed.]

—Yet, what if here some honest man is laid
Whom nature of her best materials made,
Who all respect to sacred honor paid.

Gentle, humane, benevolent and just,
(Though now forgot and mingled with the dust,
There may be such, and such there are we trust.)

Yes—for the sake of that one honest man
We would on knaves themselves bestow a tear,
Think nature form'd them on some crooked plan,
And say *peace rest on all that slumber here.*

1815

ON A HONEY BEE,

Drinking from a Glass of Wine, and Drowned Therein.

(By Hezekiah Salem.)

Thou, born to sip the lake or spring,
Or quaff the waters of the stream,
Why hither come on vagrant wing?—
Does Bacchus tempting seem—
Did he, for you, this glass prepare?—
Will I admit you to a share?

Did storms harass or foes perplex,
Did wasps or king-birds bring dismay—
Did wars distress, or labours vex,
Or did you miss your way?—
A better seat you could not take
Than on the margin of this lake.

Welcome!—I hail you to my glass:
All welcome, here, you find;
Here, let the cloud of trouble pass,
Here, be all care resigned.—
This fluid never fails to please,
And drown the griefs of men or bees.

What forced you here, we cannot know,
And you can scarcely tell—
But cheery we would have you go
And bid a fond farewell:
On lighter wings we bid you fly,
Your dart will now all foes defy.

Yet take not, oh! too deep a drink,
And in this ocean die;
Here bigger bees than you might sink,
Even bees full six feet high.
Like Pharaoh, then, you would be said
To perish in a sea of red.

Do as you please, your will is mine;
Enjoy it without fear—
And your grave will be this glass of wine,
Your epitaph—a tear—
Go, take your seat in Charon's boat,
We'll tell the hive, you died afloat.

1809

REFLECTIONS

on the

Constitution, or Frame of Nature.

From what high source of being came
This system, Nature's aweful frame;
This sun, that motion gives to all,
The planets, and this earthly ball:

This sun, who life and heat conveys,
And comforts with his cheering rays;
This image of the God, whose beam
Enlivens like the GREAT SUPREME,

We see, with most exact design,
The WORLD revolve, the planets shine,

The nicest order all things meet,
A structure in ITSELF complete.

Beyond our proper solar sphere
Unnumbered orbs again appear,
Which, sunk into the depths of space,
Unvarying keep their destined place.

Great Frame! what wonders we survey,
In part alone, from day to day!
And hence the reasoning, human soul
Infers an author of the whole:

A power, that every blessing gives,
Who through eternal ages lives,
All space inhabits, space his throne,
Spreads through all worlds, confin'd to none;

Infers, through skies, o'er seas, o'er lands
A power throughout the whole commands;
In all extent its dwelling place,
Whose mansion is unbounded space.

Where ends this world, or when began
This spheric point displayed to man?—
No limit has the work divine,
Nor owns a circumscribing line.

Beyond what mind or thought conceives,
Our efforts it in darkness leaves;
Existing in the eternal scheme,
Vast, undivided, and supreme.

Here beauty, order, power behold
Exact, all perfect, uncontrouled;
All in its proper place arranged,
Immortal, endless, and unchanged.

Its powers, still active, never rest,
From motions, by THAT GOD impressed,
Who life through all creation spread,
Nor left the meanest atom dead.

1809

SCIENCE,

Favourable to Virtue.

THIS mind, in this uncertain state,
Is anxious to investigate
All knowledge through creation sown,
And would no atom leave unknown.

So warm, so ardent in research,
To wisdom's *source* she fain would march;
And find by study, toil, and care
The secrets of all nature *there*.

Vain wish, to fathom all we see,
For nature is all mystery;
The mind, though perch'd on eagle's wings,
With pain surmounts the scum of things.

Her knowledge on the surface floats,
Of things supreme she dreams or dotes;
Fluttering awhile, she soon descends,
And all in disappointment ends.

And yet this proud, this strong desire,
Such ardent longings to aspire,
Prove that this weakness in the mind
For some wise purpose was designed.

From efforts and attempts, like these,
Virtue is gained by slow degrees;
And science, which from truth she draws,
Stands firm on Reason and her cause.

However small, its use we find
To tame and civilize mankind,
To throw the brutal instinct by,
To honour Reason, ere we die.

The lovely philanthropic scheme
(Great image of the power supreme,)
On growth of science must depend;
With this all human duties end.

1809

The
BROOK OF THE VALLEY.*

THE world has wrangled half an age,
And we again in war engage,
While this sweet, sequester'd rill
Murmurs through the valley still.

All pacific as you seem:
Such a gay elysian stream;—
Were you always thus at rest
How the valley would be blest.

But, if always thus at rest;
This would not be for the best:
In one summer you would die
And leave the valley parch'd and dry.

Tell me, where your waters go,
Purling as they downward flow?
Stagnant, now, and now a fall?—
To the gulph that swallows all.

Flowing, peaceful, from your urn
Are your waters to return?—
Though the same you may appear,
You're not the same we saw last year.

* Text from 1815 edition. [Ed.]

Not a drop of that remains—
Gone to visit other plains,
Gone, to stray through other woods,
Gone, to join the ocean floods!

Yes—they may return once more
To visit scenes they knew before;—
Yonder sun, to cheer the vale
From the ocean can exhale

Vapors, that your waste supply,
Turn'd to rain from yonder sky;
Moisture, vapors, to revive
And keep your margin all alive.

But, with all your quiet flow,
Do you not some quarrels know!
Lately, angry, how you ran!
All at war—and much like man.

When the shower of waters fell,
How you raged, and what a swell!
All your banks you overflow'd,
Scarcely knew your own abode!

How you battled with the rock.
Gave my willow such a shock
As to menace, by its fall,
Underwood and bushes, all:

Now you are again at peace:
Time will come when that will cease;
Such the human passions are;
—You again will war declare.

Emblem, thou, of restless man;
What a sketch of nature's plan!
Now at peace, and now at war,
Now you murmur, now you roar;

Muddy now, and limpid next,
Now with icy shackles vext—
What a likeness here we find!
What a picture of mankind!

1815

Lines

on the

ESTABLISHMENT OF THE NEW THEATRE

and the management of the house being placed
in the hands of Mr. Cooper.—*

Quid Sophocles, et Thespis, et Aeschylus utile ferrent
Tentavit quoque, rem si digne vertere posset.—Hor.

THIS noble pile, superbly great
In *Athens*, might have graced her state,
And rivals all that London claims
From brilliant scenes, and boasted names.

Whate'er the tragic muse affords
Will *here* be told in glowing words:
From magic scenes to charm the eyes
All nature's pictures will arise.

And she, who charms the sprightly throng,
The goddess of the comic song
The muse of laughter, and of jest
Will bring amusement with the rest.

And COOPER, here, who leads the train
Of sorrow, pleasure, pity, pain,
A Roscius, of superior powers,
The modern Garrick now is ours.

He will display on nature's stage
(Or nature copied from her page)

* Text from the edition of 1815. [Ed.]

The force of all that Shakespeare writ,
All Otway's grief and Congreve's wit.

With him a chosen band agree
To make the stage what it should be,
The serious moral to impart,
To cheer the mind and mend the heart.

The manners of the age t'improve,
To enforce the power of virtuous love,
Chaste morals in the soul t'implant
Which most admire, and many want.

On such a plan, theatric shows
Do honor to the thespian muse,
Impart a polish to the mind;
Instruct and civilize mankind.

Ye sages who in morals deal,
But all the pleasing side conceal,
From hence confess that morals may
As surely take the brilliant way.

With such an object in our view
Let Thespis all her art pursue,
When autumn brings the lengthening nights
And reason to her feast invites.—

1815

BELIEF AND UNBELIEF:

Humbly recommended to the serious consideration of creed makers.*

WHAT some believe, and would enforce
Without reluctance or remorse,
Perhaps another may decry,
Or call a fraud, or deem a lie.

* Text from the edition of 1815. [Ed.]

Must he for that be doom'd to bleed,
And fall a martyr to some creed,
By hypocrites or tyrants framed,
By reason damn'd, by truth disclaim'd?

On mere belief no merit rests,
As unbelief no guilt attests:
Belief, if not absurd and blind,
Is but conviction of the mind,

Nor can conviction bind the heart
Till evidence has done its part:
And, when that evidence is clear,
Belief is just, and truth is near.

In evidence, belief is found;
Without it, none are fairly bound
To yield assent, or homage pay
To what confederate worlds might say.

They who extort belief from man
Should, in the out-set of their plan,
Exhibit, like the mid-day sun
An evidence denied by none.

From this great point, o'erlook'd or miss'd,
Still unbelievers will exist;
And just their plea; for how absurd
For evidence, to take *your word!*

Not to believe, I therefore hold
The right of man, all uncontrol'd
By all the powers of human wit,
What kings have done, or sages writ;

Not criminal in any view,
Nor—man!—to be avenged by you,
Till evidence of strongest kind
Constrains assent, and clears the mind.

1815

On the
UNIVERSALITY AND OTHER ATTRIBUTES
of the
GOD OF NATURE.*

ALL that we see, about, abroad,
What is it all, but nature's God?
In meaner works discover'd here
No less than in the starry sphere.

In seas, on earth, this God is seen;
All that exist, upon him lean;
He lives in all, and never stray'd
A moment from the works he made:

His system fix'd on general laws
Bespeaks a wise creating cause;
Impartially he rules mankind
And all that on this globe we find.

Unchanged in all that seems to change,
Unbounded space is his great range;
To one vast purpose always true,
No time, with him, is old or new.

In all the attributes divine
Unlimited perfectings shine;
In these enwrapt, in these complete,
All virtues in that centre meet.

This power who doth all powers transcend,
To all intelligence a friend,
Exists, the *greatest and the best* †
Throughout all worlds, to make them blest.

* Text from the edition of 1815. [Ed.]
† —— Jupiter, optimus, maximus.—Cicero.

All that he did he first approved
He all things into *being* loved;
O'er all he made he still presides,
For them in life, or death provides.

1815

On the
UNIFORMITY AND PERFECTION
of
NATURE.*

ON one fix'd point all nature moves,
Nor deviates from the track she loves;
Her system, drawn from reason's source,
She scorns to change her wonted course.

Could she descend from that great plan
To work unusual things for man,
To suit the insect of an hour—
This would betray a want of power,

Unsettled in its first design
And erring, when it did combine
The parts that form the vast machine,
The figures sketch'd on nature's scene.

Perfections of the great first cause
Submit to no contracted laws,
But all-sufficient, all-supreme,
Include no trivial views in them.

Who looks through nature with an eye
That would the scheme of heaven descry,
Observes her constant, still the same,
In all her laws, through all her frame.

* Text from the edition of 1815. [Ed.]

No imperfection can be found
In all that is, above, around,—
All, nature made, in reason's sight
Is order all, and *all is right*.

1815

ON THE
RELIGION OF NATURE.*

THE power, that gives with liberal hand
    The blessings man enjoys, while here,
And scatters through a smiling land
    Abundant products of the year;
        That power of nature, ever bless'd,
        Bestow'd religion with the rest.

Born with ourselves, her early sway
    Inclines the tender mind to take
The path of right, fair virtue's way
    Its own felicity to make.
        This universally extends
        And leads to no mysterious ends.

Religion, such as nature taught,
    With all divine perfection suits;
Had all mankind this system sought
    Sophists would cease their vain disputes,
        And from this source would nations know
        All that can make their heaven below.

This deals not curses on mankind,
    Or dooms them to perpetual grief,
If from its aid no joys they find,
    It damns them not for unbelief;
        Upon a more exalted plan
        Creatress nature dealt with man—

* Text from the edition of 1815. [Ed.]

Joy to the day, when all agree
  On such grand systems to proceed,
From fraud, design, and error free,
  And which to truth and goodness lead:
    Then persecution will retreat
    And man's religion be complete.

1815